Teach Yourself VISUALLY™

PowerPoint® 2010

Visual

by William Wood

Wiley Publishing, Inc.

Teach Yourself Visually™ PowerPoint® 2010

Published by
Wiley Publishing, Inc.
10475 Crosspoint Boulevard
Indianapolis, IN 46256

www.wiley.com

Published simultaneously in Canada

Library of Congress Control Number: 2010926832

ISBN: 978-0-470-57766-0

Manufactured in the United States of America

10 9 8 7 6 5 4 3 2 1

Trademark Acknowledgments

Disclaimer

In order to get this information to you in a timely manner, this book was based on a pre-release version of Microsoft Office 2010. There may be some minor changes between the screenshots in this book and what you see on your desktop. As always, Microsoft has the final word on how programs look and function; if you have any questions or see any discrepancies, consult the online help for further information about the software.

Contact Us

For general information on our other products and services please contact our Customer Care Department within the U.S. at 877-762-2974, outside the U.S. at 317-572-3993 or fax 317-572-4002.

For technical support please visit www.wiley.com/techsupport.

Wiley Publishing, Inc.

Sales

Contact Wiley
at (877) 762-2974 or
fax (317) 572-4002.

Credits

Acquisitions Editor
Aaron Black

Project Editor
Jade L. Williams

Technical Editor
Lee Musick

Copy Editor
Lauren Kennedy

Editorial Director
Robyn Siesky

Editorial Manager
Cricket Krengel

Business Manager
Amy Knies

Senior Marketing Manager
Sandy Smith

Vice President and Executive Group Publisher
Richard Swadley

Vice President and Executive Publisher
Barry Pruett

Project Coordinator
Katherine Crocker

Graphics and Production Specialists
Andrea Hornberger

Quality Control Technician
Lauren Mandelbaum

Proofreading
Melissa D. Buddendeck

Indexing
BIM Indexing & Proofreading Services

Screen Artist
Jill A. Proll
Ronald Terry

Illustrators
Ronda David-Burroughs
Cheryl Grubbs
Mark Pinto

About the Author

William (Bill) Wood is a consultant who teaches and writes programs in the Microsoft Office Suite and VBA programming. As a part time writer, he has written several self-published classroom workbooks about Microsoft Access and Excel. He has a formal education as a Biomedical Engineer, in which he worked for many years, and is currently attending graduate classes at Milwaukee School of Engineering in the field of Medical Informatics. Bill also works as a volunteer member of the National Ski Patrol.

Author's Acknowledgments

Thank you to the entire Wiley team for helping me complete my first published book. Special thanks to Jody Lefevere who invited me to write a book for Wiley, Jeff Parker who introduced me to Jody and encouraged me, Jade Williams for helping me learn the TYV style, and Aaron Black for guiding me through the entire process. Their friendly demeanor made this project a pleasant experience. Thank you to John Traxler MD, MBA, MSMI for providing several PowerPoint presentations that I used in this book. I send gratitude to Stephanie Richter, who took time from her busy schedule to help me write my proposal to Wiley. I also appreciate the encouragement given to me by Nancy Haberichter, Donna Castle, Anna Maria Kowalik, Steve and Kathryn Graves, and Kathleen Ard. Finally, thanks to Carol Wood, just because she's mom.

How to Use This Book

Who This Book Is For

This book is for the reader who has never used this particular technology or software application. It is also for readers who want to expand their knowledge.

The Conventions in This Book

❶ Steps

This book uses a step-by-step format to guide you easily through each task. Numbered steps are actions you must do; bulleted steps clarify a point, step, or optional feature; and indented steps give you the result.

❷ Notes

Notes give additional information — special conditions that may occur during an operation, a situation that you want to avoid, or a cross reference to a related area of the book.

❸ Icons and Buttons

Icons and buttons show you exactly what you need to click to perform a step.

❹ Tips

Tips offer additional information, including warnings and shortcuts.

❺ Bold

Bold type shows command names, options, and text or numbers you must type.

❻ Italics

Italic type introduces and defines a new term.

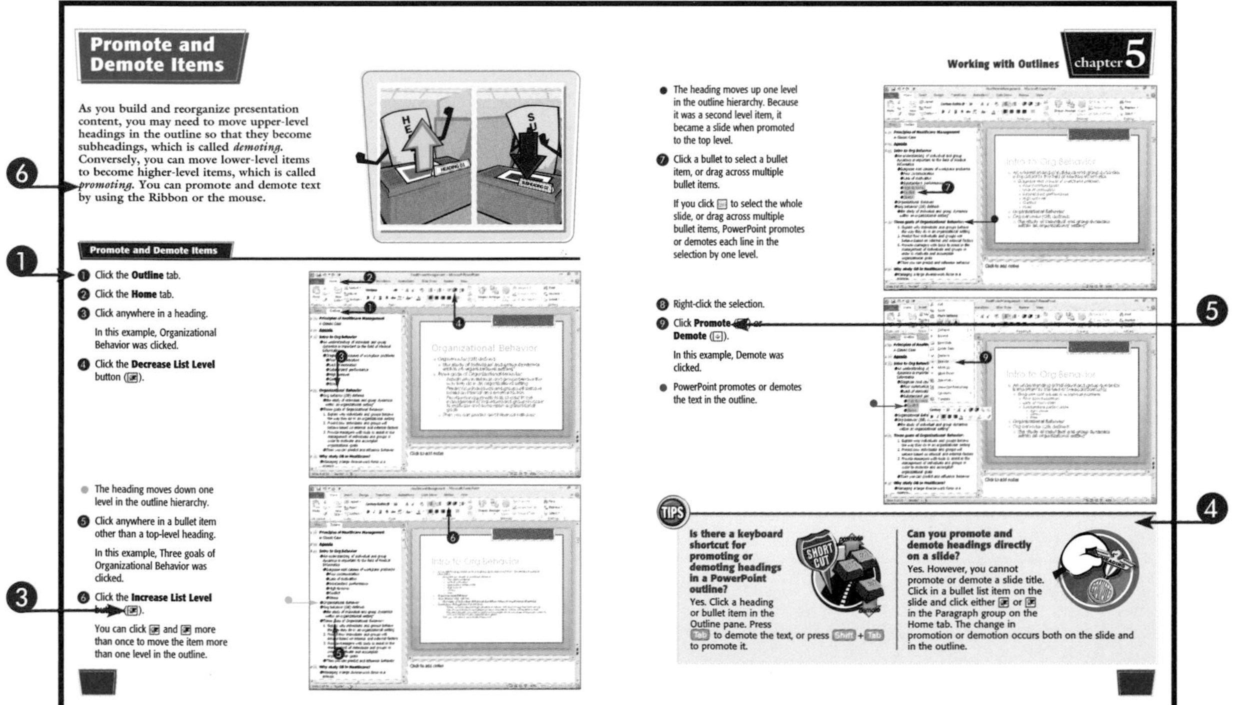

Promote and Demote Items

Working with Outlines chapter 5

As you build and reorganize presentation content, you may need to move upper-level headings in the outline so that they become subheadings, which is called *demoting*. Conversely, you can move lower-level items to become higher-level items, which is called *promoting*. You can promote and demote text by using the Ribbon or the mouse.

Promote and Demote Items

1. Click the **Outline** tab.
2. Click the **Home** tab.
3. Click anywhere in a heading.

   In this example, Organizational Behavior was clicked.
4. Click the **Decrease List Level** button.

- The heading moves down one level in the outline hierarchy.

5. Click anywhere in a bullet item other than a top-level heading.

   In this example, Three goals of Organizational Behavior was clicked.
6. Click the **Increase List Level** button.

   You can click and more than once to move the item more than one level in the outline.

- The heading moves up one level in the outline hierarchy. Because it was a second level item, it became a slide when promoted to the top level.

7. Click a bullet to select a bullet item, or drag across multiple bullet items.

   If you click to select the whole slide, or drag across multiple bullet items, PowerPoint promotes or demotes each line in the selection by one level.
8. Right-click the selection.
9. Click **Promote** or **Demote**.

   In this example, Demote was clicked.

- PowerPoint promotes or demotes the text in the outline.

TIPS

Is there a keyboard shortcut for promoting or demoting headings in a PowerPoint outline?
Yes. Click a heading or bullet item in the Outline pane. Press Tab to demote the text, or press Shift + Tab to promote it.

Can you promote and demote headings directly on a slide?
Yes. However, you cannot promote or demote a slide title. Click in a bullet list item on the slide and click either or in the Paragraph group on the Home tab. The change in promotion or demotion occurs both on the slide and in the outline.

Table of Contents

Getting Started with PowerPoint Basics

chapter 2

Changing PowerPoint Options

Beginning with Presentation Fundamentals

chapter 4

Writing and Formatting Presentation Text

Table of Contents

chapter 5 Working with Outlines

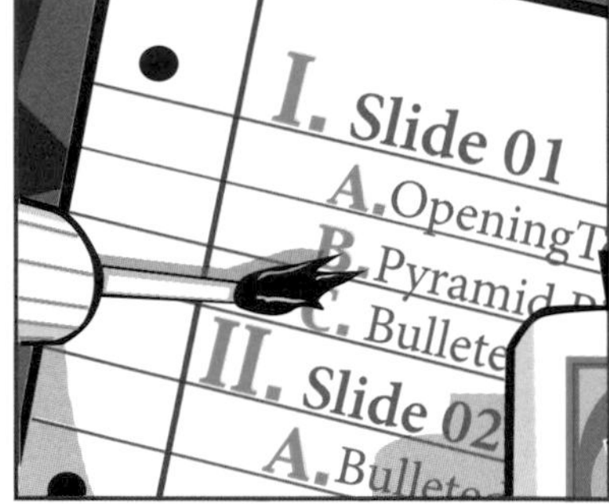

chapter 6 Working with Layouts and Placeholders

Using Themes

Table of Contents

chapter 8 Using Masters

chapter 9 Adding Graphics and Drawings

chapter 10 Organizing Slides

Table of Contents

Adding Action to Slides

chapter 12

Including Media Enhancements

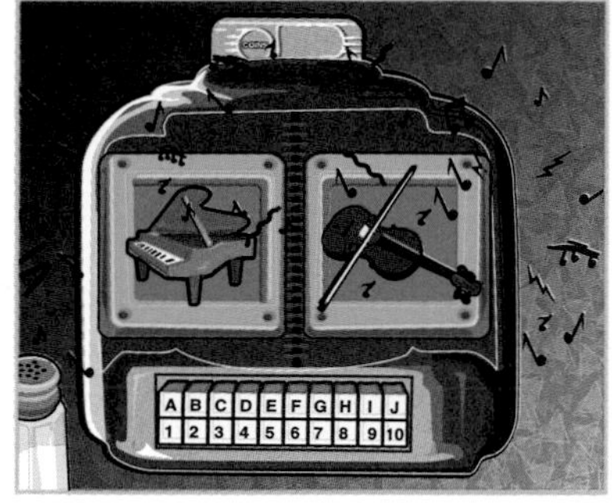

chapter 13 Finishing, Setting Up, and Running a Slide Show

Table of Contents

Printing Presentations

chapter 15

Publishing Presentations

chapter 16 Finalizing and Making a Presentation

CHAPTER 1

Getting Started with PowerPoint Basics

Discover PowerPoint basics such as starting a presentation and navigating through PowerPoint. In this chapter, you learn the various elements of the PowerPoint screen, and how to get help when you need it.

Introducing PowerPoint

The PowerPoint program provides various views and tools you can use to build a presentation that includes words, graphics, and media. PowerPoint enables you to accomplish the following tasks to design and build a presentation.

Build an Outline

You can use the Outline tab to type the text for your presentation. On the Outline tab, an icon represents each slide, and each slide contains a slide title next to the icon. Many slides contain second level text that represents slide bullet points. These bullets convey the main points you want to make about each topic.

Choose a Slide Design and Layout

The *slide design* applies preset design elements such as colors, background graphics, and text styles to a slide. The *slide layout* you apply to a slide determines what set of information the slide includes. For example, a Title and Content layout includes a placeholder for a title, plus a placeholder that holds a bulleted list or graphic element. A Title Slide layout has title and subtitle placeholders.

Add Content

You can add content such as text, charts, and pictures to the slide itself in the Slide pane of Normal view. You also can insert text boxes that enable you to add slide text that does not appear in the presentation outline.

Work with Masters

Masters enable you to add content that you want to appear in a particular location on every (or almost every) slide. This saves you from having to add repetitive content, such as your company logo, to each slide. For example, you can set up the master so an identical footer appears on every slide.

Format Text

After you enter the text for your presentation, you can format that text in various ways. You can change the font, increase the font size, and apply bold or italics to the text. Note that you can modify each individual text selection or apply text styles globally using masters.

Organize Slides

After creating several slides, you may need to reorganize them to create the proper sequence for your presentation. You can reorder slides in the Slide Sorter view. This view shows slide thumbnails that you can move, delete, duplicate, or hide. You can also accomplish these actions on the Slides tab of Normal view.

Set Up Your Show

You can add narrations, animations, and transitions to your slides. You can record a *narration* that plays when you give your presentation; use *animations* to move an element on-screen, such as a graphic flying onto the screen; and use a *transition* to control how a new slide appears on-screen; for example, the slide can wipe in from the corner of the screen.

Run a Slide Show

After you add the content, choose the slide design and layout, and add special effects, you are ready to run your slide show. A set of tools that appears on-screen during the slide show helps you control your presentation and even enables you to make annotations on your slides as you present them.

Start and Exit PowerPoint

You can start PowerPoint from the Windows Start menu. When you open PowerPoint, a blank presentation appears automatically. The blank presentation is ready for you to add your presentation contents.

Start and Exit PowerPoint

1. Click **Start** (▣).
2. Click **All Programs**.
3. Click **Microsoft Office**.
4. Click **Microsoft PowerPoint 2010**.

Note: *If you purchased PowerPoint as a stand-alone product, simply click* ***All Programs****, and then click* ***Microsoft PowerPoint 2010****.*

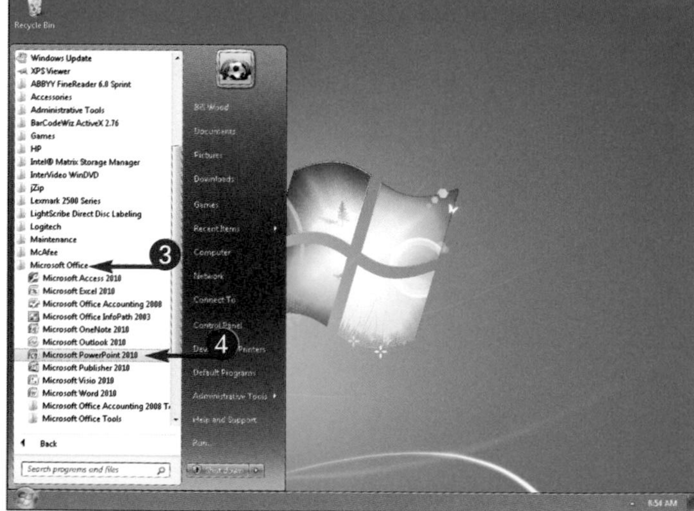

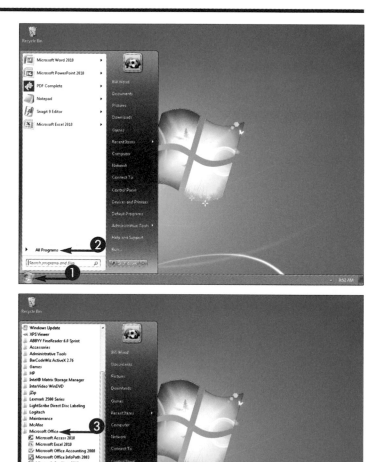

A new PowerPoint presentation appears with a blank slide.

5 To exit PowerPoint, click the **File** tab.

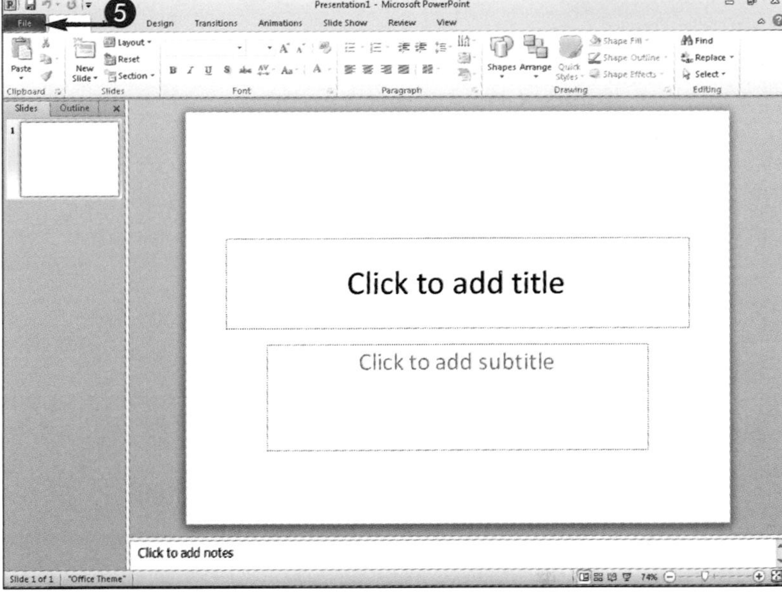

6 Click **Exit**.

The program closes and the Windows desktop reappears.

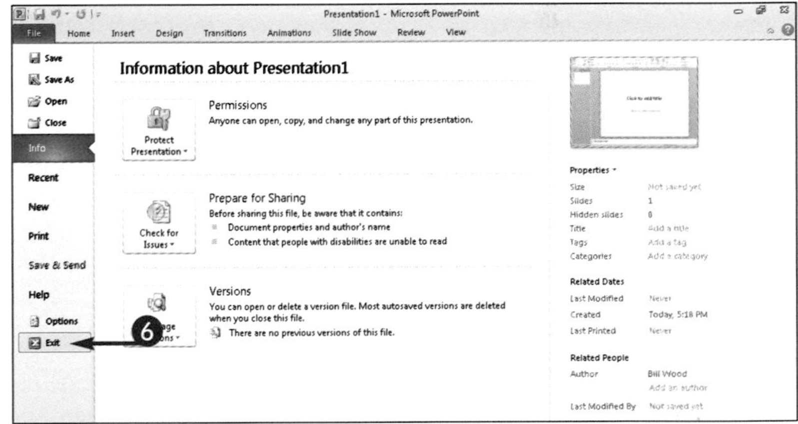

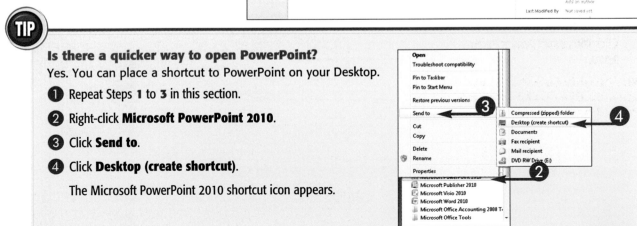

TIP

Is there a quicker way to open PowerPoint?

Yes. You can place a shortcut to PowerPoint on your Desktop.

1 Repeat Steps **1** to **3** in this section.

2 Right-click **Microsoft PowerPoint 2010**.

3 Click **Send to**.

4 Click **Desktop (create shortcut)**.

The Microsoft PowerPoint 2010 shortcut icon appears.

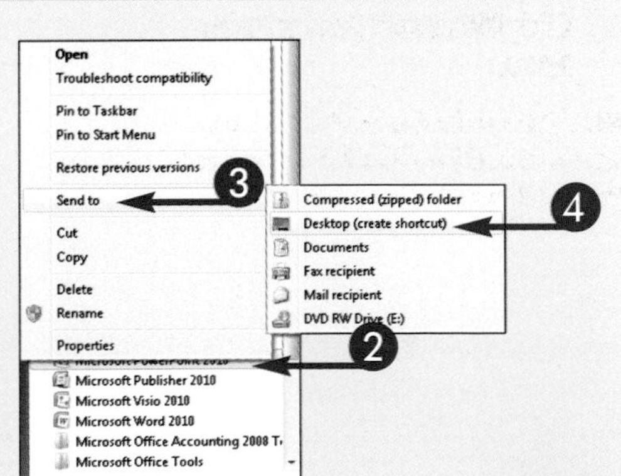

Explore the Normal View

PowerPoint offers several views you can display to work on different aspects of your presentation. You will most commonly work in Normal view, where you can create, position, and format objects on each slide. In Normal view, you can also enter presentation text in the Outline tab or add speaker's notes for each slide.

Slides Tab

The Slides tab contains thumbnails of each slide — they are numbered by the order that they appear in the slide show. You can drag the thumbnails to change the order of slides.

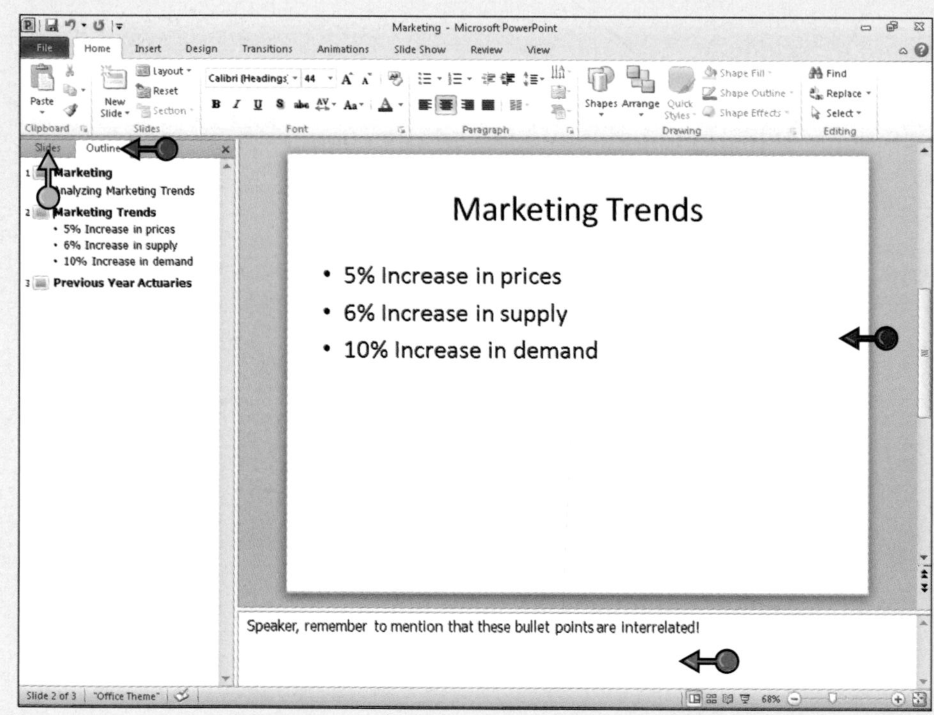

Slide Pane

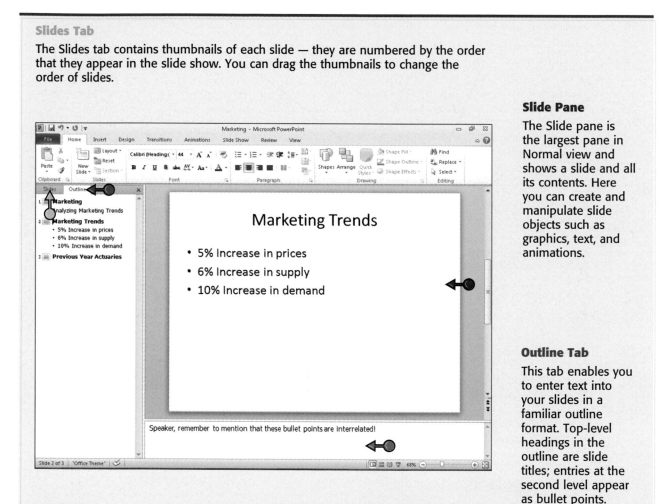

The Slide pane is the largest pane in Normal view and shows a slide and all its contents. Here you can create and manipulate slide objects such as graphics, text, and animations.

Outline Tab

This tab enables you to enter text into your slides in a familiar outline format. Top-level headings in the outline are slide titles; entries at the second level appear as bullet points.

Notes Pane

The Notes pane appears below the Slide pane. You can enter speaker notes associated with each individual slide into this pane. You can refer to these notes while presenting a slide show.

Navigate PowerPoint Views

In addition to Normal view, you can use Slide Sorter view to organize slides, Notes Page view to create detailed speaker notes, and Slide Show view or Reading view to display your presentation.

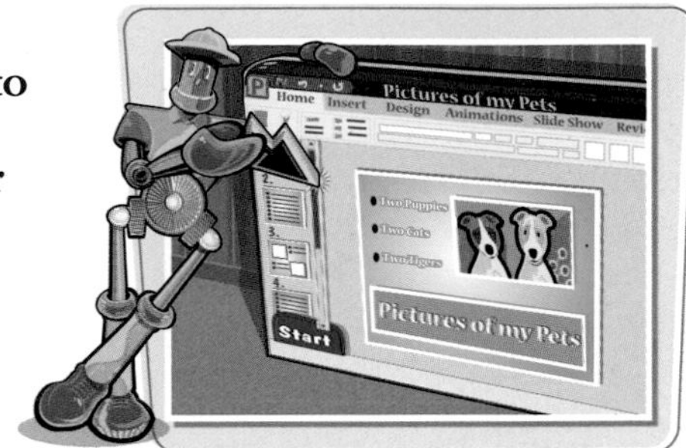

Navigation Buttons

Change views by clicking one of these status bar buttons: Normal (▣), Slide Sorter (▦), Slide Show (▣), or Reading View (▣). You can also click icons on the View tab of the Ribbon to switch views, including Notes Page view.

Slide Sorter View

Click Slide Sorter (▦) for the best view to reorder slides, delete slides, or duplicate slides. In the Slide Sorter view, you can drag a slide to move it. If you double-click a slide, PowerPoint changes to Normal view and displays that slide in the Slide pane.

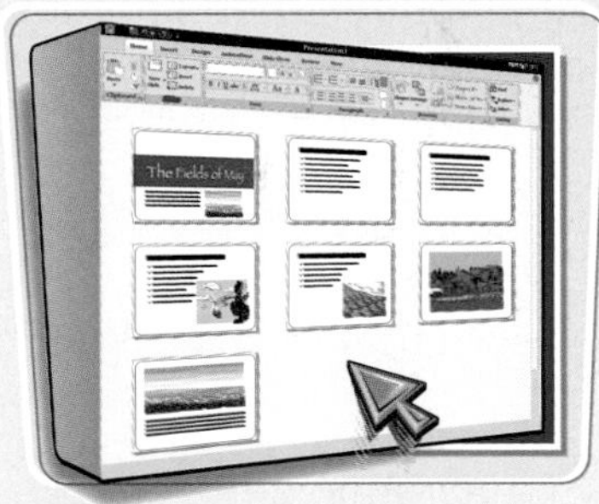

Reading View

Click Slide Show (▣) to present your show. Slides appear one at a time at full screen size. The Reading View (▣) is very similar to the Slide Show view, but gives you navigation flexibility. To exit either view, press Esc.

Notes Page View

Display each slide and the associated speaker notes as a full page. You can move objects and type notes on the page. From the View tab, click Notes Page to work with this view.

Work with Ribbon Groups, Commands, and Galleries

You can find all the commands that you need to design and present your slide show on the Ribbon. Related commands are displayed on the Ribbon tabs. Commands are further arranged into groups with the group names shown at the bottom of the tab. Some command buttons include down arrows that display menus or galleries of commands when you click them.

Work with Ribbon Groups, Commands, and Galleries

1. Click any tab on the Ribbon.

   In this example, Insert was clicked.

- The commands for the particular tab you clicked appear on the Ribbon.

2. Click the button or check box for any command.

   In this example, Clip Art Pane was clicked.

- The Clip Art task pane appears at the right. Use the task pane to finish executing the command, in this case, inserting clip art.

3. Click the down arrow (▾) next to any button to display a gallery.

   In this example, Layout was clicked.

***Note:** Clicking any button with a ▾ displays a menu or gallery.*

4. Click the desired choice from the gallery that appears.

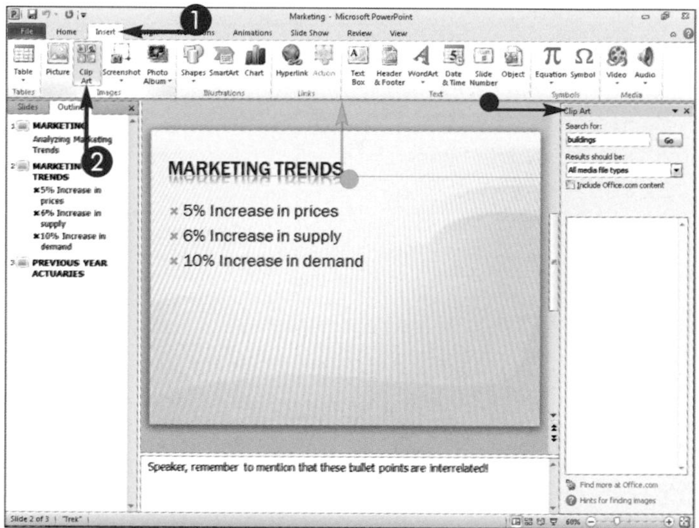

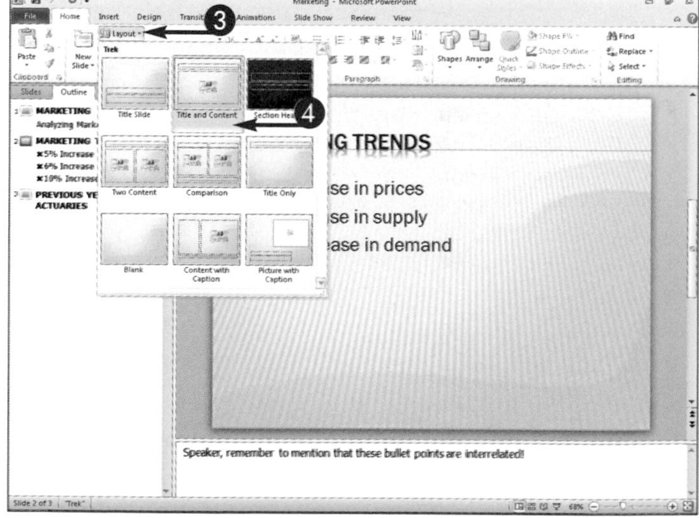

❺ Click the **Dialog Box Launcher** (⧉).

Note: *Any group with a Dialog Box Launcher (⧉) displays a dialog box when you click it.*

In this example, the Font dialog box appears.

❻ Click **OK** to accept any selections you have made in the dialog box.

The presentation reflects any changes you made.

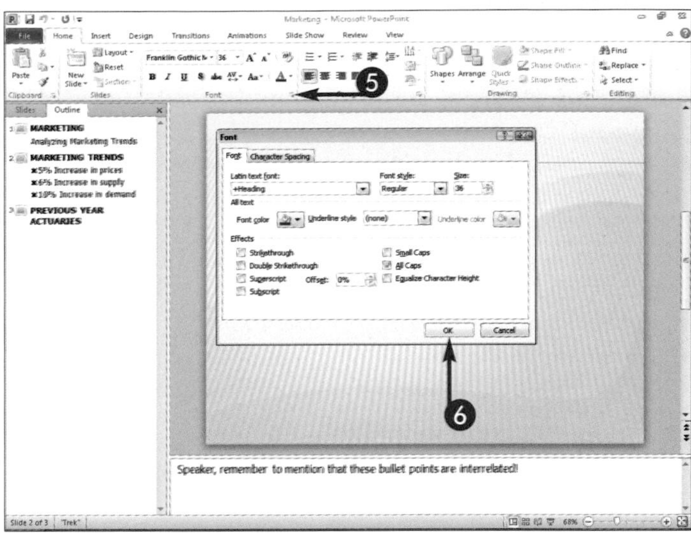

● For some Ribbon commands, such as those on a contextual tab, you must first select an object on the slide before choosing a command.

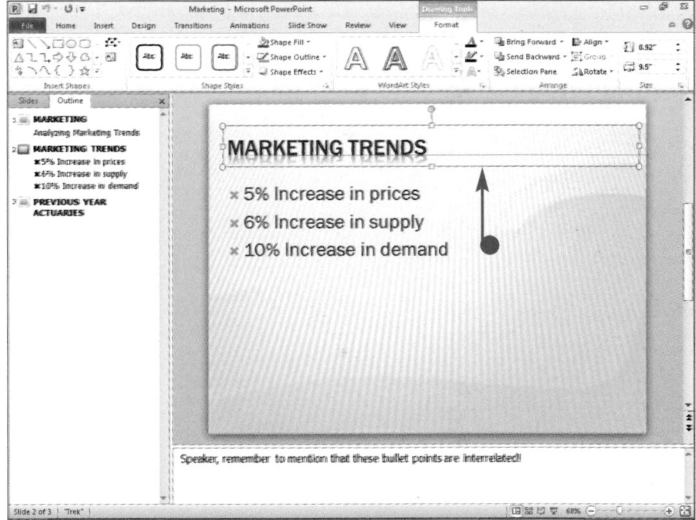

TIPS

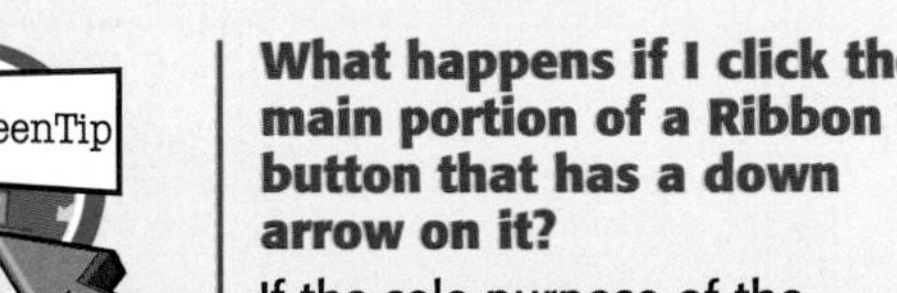

How do I learn what a particular Ribbon button does?

Position the mouse pointer (↖) over the button and a ScreenTip describing the button appears. You see an enhanced ScreenTip that lists the button name, any available shortcut key, and a brief description of the button. By default, ScreenTip features are enabled, but can be turned off in the PowerPoint Options dialog box (described in Chapter 2).

What happens if I click the main portion of a Ribbon button that has a down arrow on it?

If the sole purpose of the button is to open a gallery or menu, PowerPoint does that. If the main part of the button executes a command, either PowerPoint applies that command using the settings you last used or the most commonly used settings for that command.

Hide the Ribbon Commands

The Ribbon at the top of the PowerPoint application window is wide. You do not need to see the Ribbon commands at all times. You can hide the Ribbon commands, and then access them quickly when you need them. This enables you to see more of the slide that you are designing.

Hide the Ribbon Commands

❶ Click the **Minimize the Ribbon** button (⌃).

The Ribbon commands disappear from the top of the window, but the tabs remain visible.

Note: *You can also press* Ctrl *+* F1 *to hide the Ribbon.*

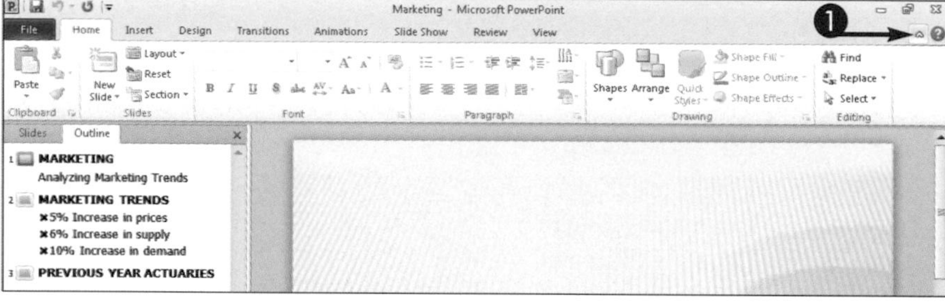

❷ Click a **Ribbon** tab.

- To display the Ribbon continuously again, click ⌄.

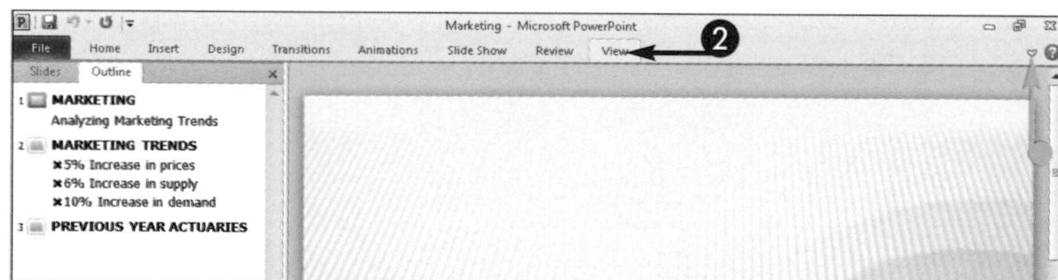

The Ribbon commands temporarily reappear, allowing you to click a command button.

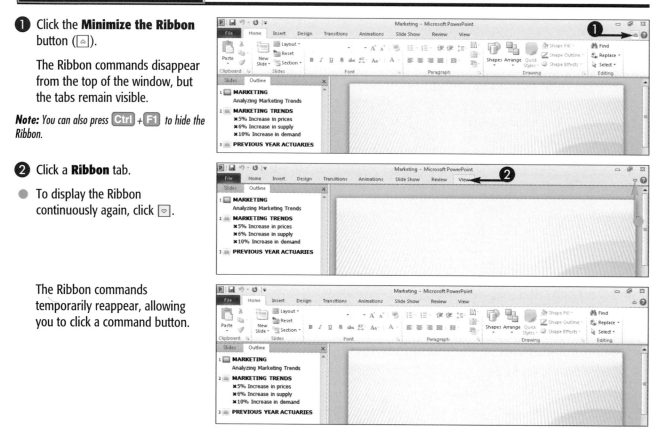

Find and Use KeyTips

You may be more comfortable using your keyboard instead of your mouse. This may be particularly true if you use a notebook computer with a finicky touchpad. You can use the KeyTips feature to employ keyboard shortcuts to select and execute Ribbon commands.

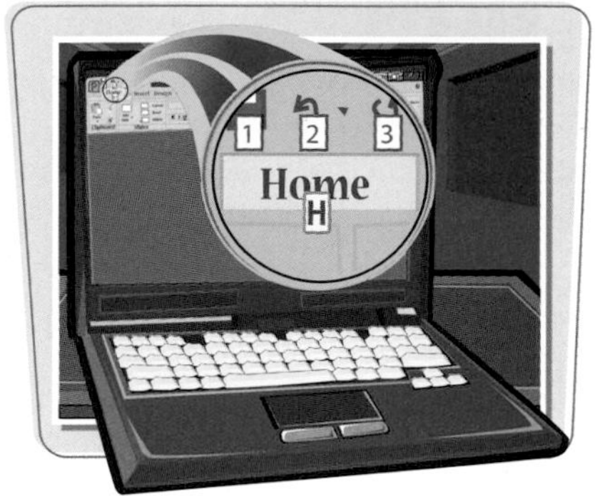

Find and Use KeyTips

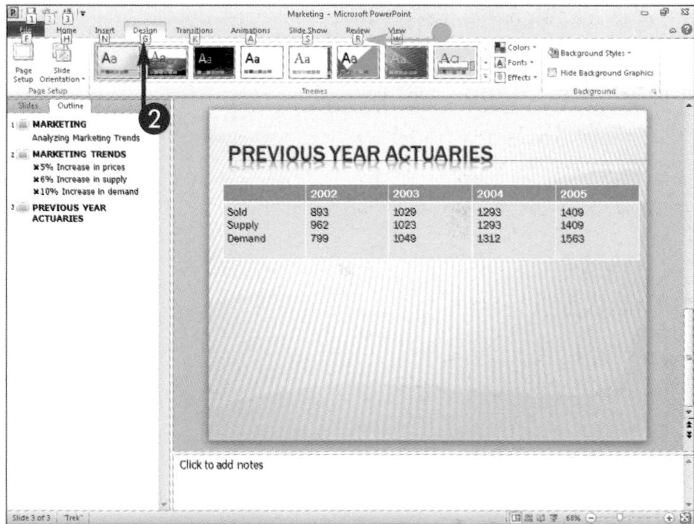

1. Press Alt.

- The KeyTips (shortcut keys) for the Ribbon tabs and Quick Access Toolbar appear in boxes beside the tabs and toolbar choices.

2. Press the shortcut key for the tab you want to use.

   In this example, G was pressed to display the Design tab.

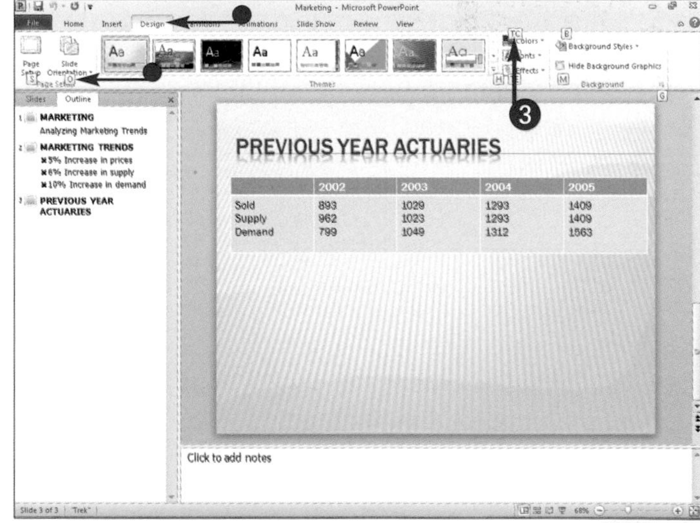

- The tab appears with KeyTips displayed for the commands.

***Note:** To hide the tab KeyTips, press Esc. To hide all KeyTips, press Esc twice.*

3. Press the shortcut key for the command you want to execute.

   In this example, press T + C to display the Colors gallery.

   The command executes, or a menu, gallery, or dialog box appears so you can finish choosing commands.

Using the Quick Access Toolbar

The Quick Access Toolbar appears above the File tab at the top of the PowerPoint application window. You can click buttons on the Quick Access Toolbar to execute the most commonly used commands quickly.

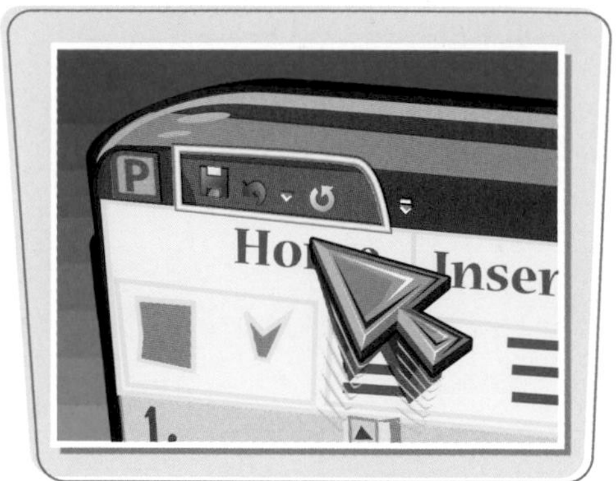

Using the Quick Access Toolbar

❶ Click the desired button on the Quick Access Toolbar.

PowerPoint executes the command.

***Note:** Use any menu or dialog box that appears to finish executing the command.*

- If you click the ▾ beside the Undo button (↶), a menu appears with a list of actions to undo.

❷ Click the **Quick Access Toolbar** ▾ to access the menu.

- Note the check mark (☑) appearing next to commands on the Quick Access Toolbar.
- Click **More Commands** to see all available commands.

❸ Click one of the commands from the menu list.

In this example, Open was clicked.

- The selected command appears as an icon on the Quick Access Toolbar and a ☑ appears next to it in the menu.

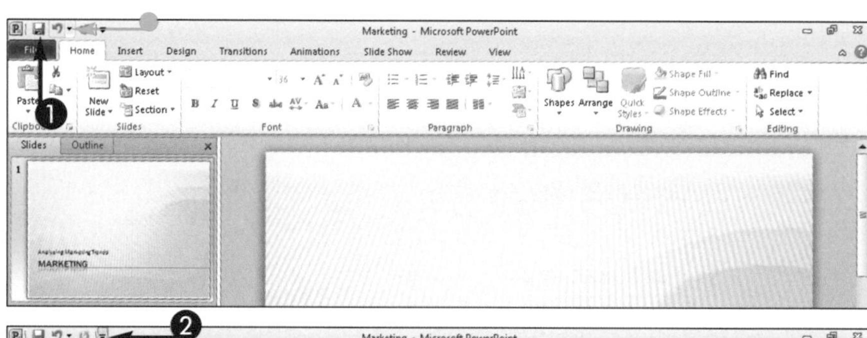

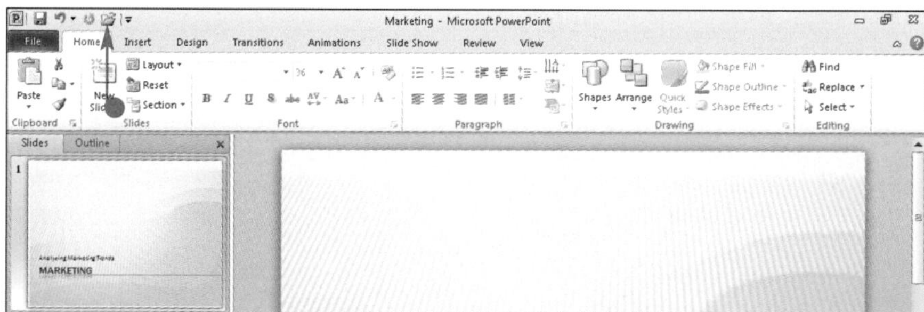

Resize the Notes Pane

You can enter speaker notes into the Notes pane. This area appears under the Slide pane in Normal view. You can show this area on your computer screen during a presentation. You can resize the Notes pane to make it easier to enter and read the notes.

Resize the Notes Pane

1. Position the mouse pointer (↖) over the pane divider until the mouse splitter pointer (÷) appears.
2. Click and drag downward until the pane disappears.

   The Notes pane disappears and the slide automatically fills the additional space in the Slide pane.

   If you click and drag upward, the Notes pane enlarges.

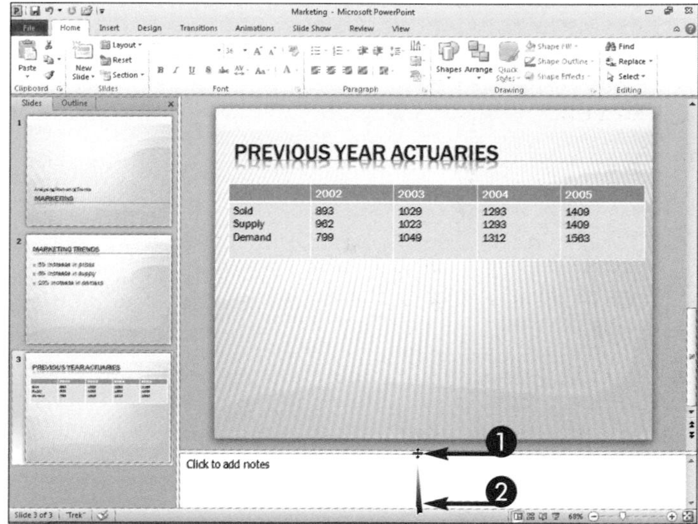

3. Click the **View** tab.
4. Click **Normal**.

- The Notes pane reappears.

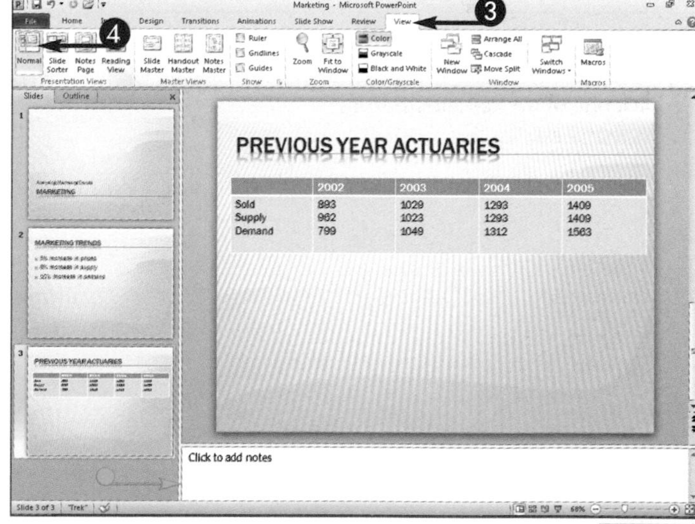

Microsoft Office PowerPoint Help provides help from Microsoft Office Online or Help files installed on your computer if you have no Internet connection. You can find answers to your questions by browsing a Table of Contents or by searching using keywords.

Using Help

1. Click the **Help** button (⍰).

   The PowerPoint Help window appears.

2. Click a main topic.

   In this example, Format slides or presentations was clicked.

***Note:** In some cases, after you click the main topic, a list of subcategories appears. Select the desired subcategory, and then continue to Step* **3**.

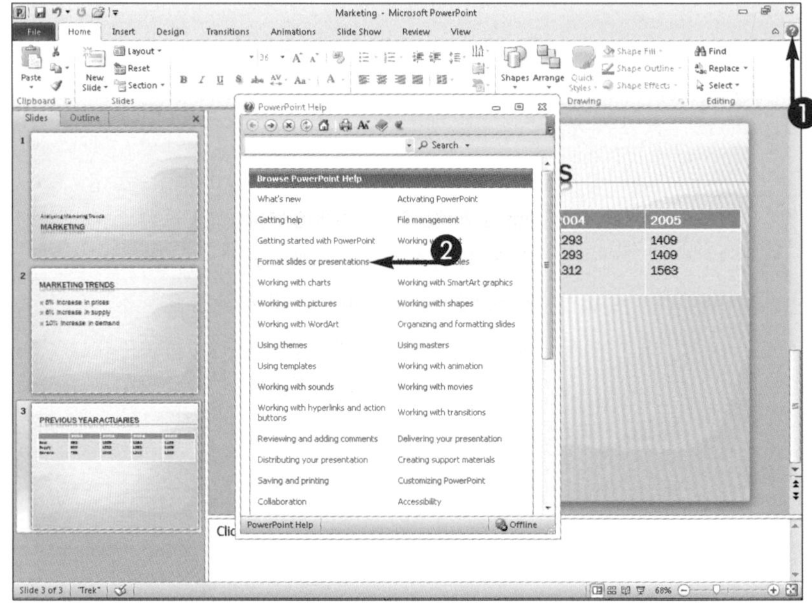

A window with a list of detail topics appears.

3. Click a detail topic.

   In this example, Create a photo album was clicked.

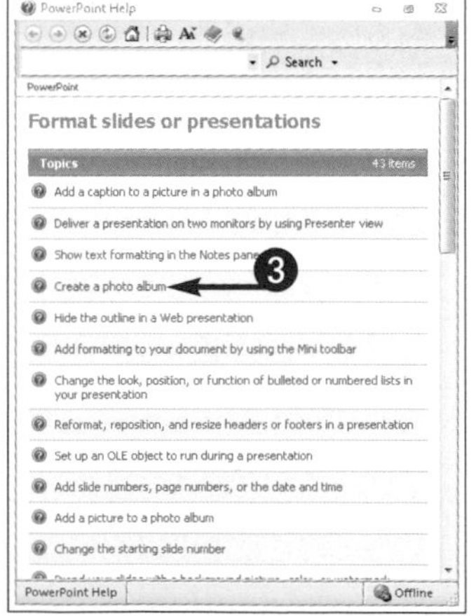

The detail topic help appears.

- You can drag the scroll bar downward as needed to read more of the information.

4 Click the **Back** button (⊛).

- The previous help information reappears.

***Note:** After you click ⊛, the Forward button (⊛) becomes active. Click these buttons to browse Help.*

5 Type a word or phrase.

In this example, Insert text was typed.

6 Click **Search**.

- The search results appear.

You can display a topic and browse using Steps **3** and **4**.

7 Click the **Close** button (⊠) to close the Help window when you finish using Help.

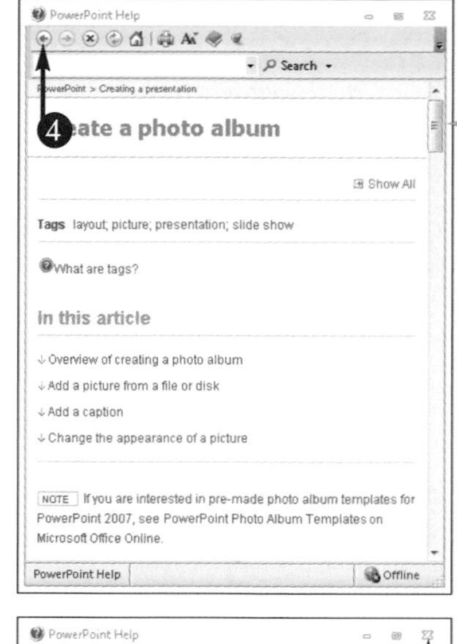

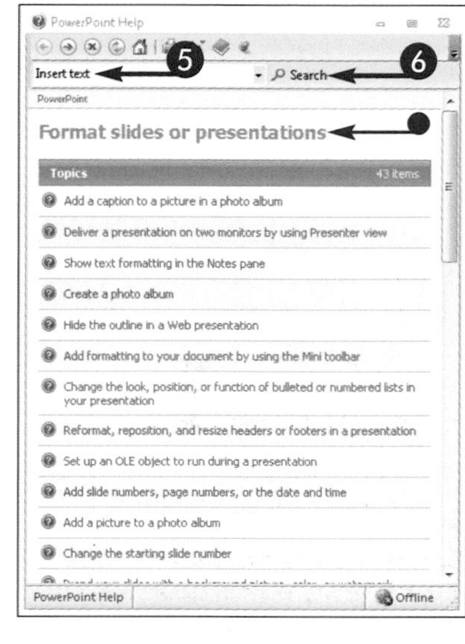

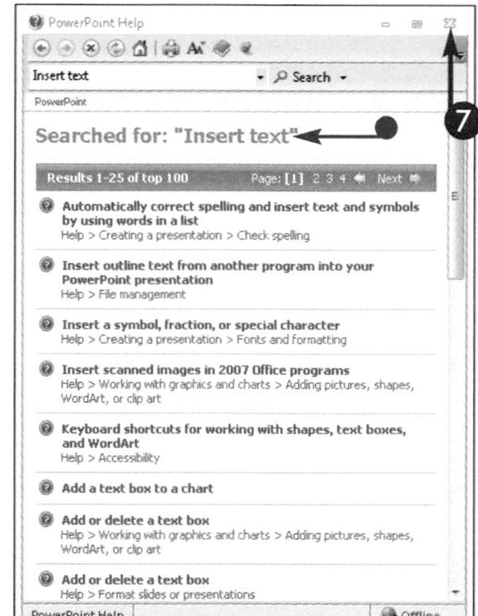

Can I keep the Table of Contents visible while I am using Help?

Yes. Follow these steps:

1 Click the **Show Table of Contents** button (⊡)

2 Click a main topic to display a list of its topics.

3 Click a topic to display the help for that topic.

- The Help information appears in the right-hand pane and the Table of Contents remains visible.

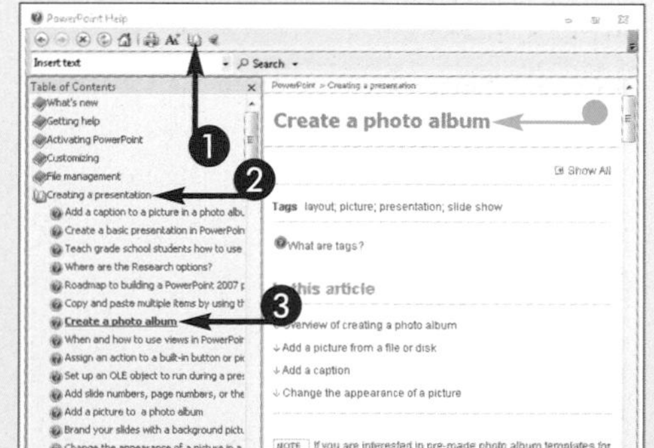

Changing PowerPoint Options

PowerPoint is a powerful tool that becomes even more powerful when you customize the way you want it to perform. You can adjust various settings to personalize PowerPoint, so you can use it in the most efficient and effective way.

Introducing PowerPoint Options

PowerPoint provides a wide variety of options and settings that enable you to customize how it performs. Related options and settings are grouped on tabs in the PowerPoint Options dialog box, and then further grouped into categories. You can change these options and settings to control the behavior of certain features in PowerPoint, and optimize less-noticeable things, such as the default save location.

General Options

In General Options, you can enable or disable Mini toolbars and Live Preview. A Mini toolbar gives you quick access to formatting commands when you select text. Live Preview shows how a feature affects your slide when you hover over a choice in a gallery. You can also enable or disable ScreenTips, and change the user name.

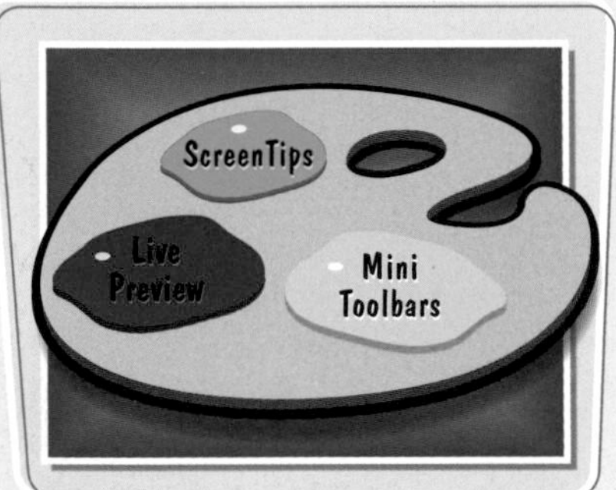

Proofing Options

The Proofing tab affects the way that Microsoft Office checks for spelling and grammar errors in PowerPoint. Changes to these settings affect the settings in the other Microsoft Office programs, too. You can add words to the dictionary and customize Microsoft's powerful AutoCorrect tool.

Save Options

You can adjust the way PowerPoint saves presentations with the Save options. This tab controls the default file location for saving documents, and allows you to choose the default file format. You can disable AutoRecovery or adjust how often AutoRecovery automatically saves documents.

Language Options

The Language tab allows you to choose the language used for the Ribbon, tabs, ScreenTips, and Help. You can include additional editing languages, which affect dictionaries, grammar checking, and sorting. This is useful if you use languages other than English in your presentations.

Advanced Options

Advanced options allow you to customize settings for printing, some editing, and slide show features. You can change some settings, such as certain print options, for individual documents. Cut and paste options and display options are also found here.

Ribbon and Quick Access Toolbar Options

Though you can add a limited number of commands to the Quick Access Toolbar from the toolbar, you can add any command to it from the Quick Access Toolbar tab. Not only can you add commands to the Ribbon, but you can also add tabs and rename existing groups and tabs.

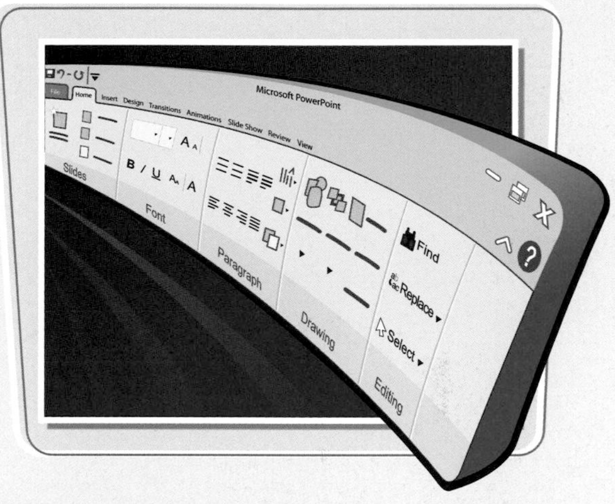

Add-ins

Add-ins are small chunks of programming that enhance the functionality of PowerPoint. Add-ins can be developed specifically for PowerPoint, or can be COM add-ins that enable you to use the functionality of another program in PowerPoint, such as a PDF writer or screen-capture program.

Trust Center

In the Trust Center, you can read the Microsoft privacy statements and learn about security. Malicious programs can be attached to documents in various ways. You can customize settings to control the behavior of safeguards used against these threats.

Modify General Options

PowerPoint provides a wide variety of options that enable you to customize how it works. Features such as Live Preview are found in General options. You can also change the user name, which PowerPoint logs into the properties of each presentation to identify who creates it. You can change these common options in the General tab of the PowerPoint Options dialog box.

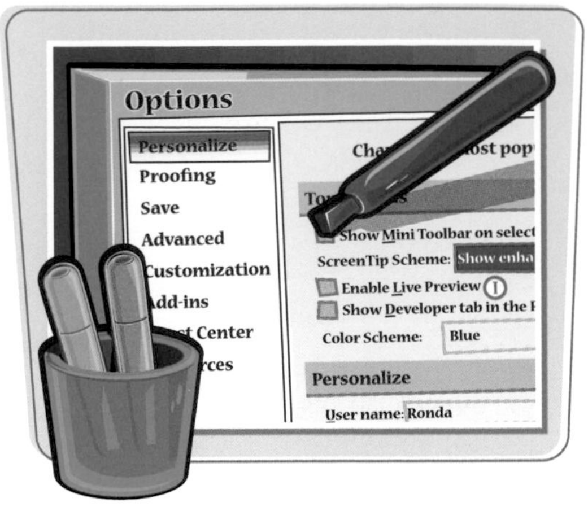

Modify General Options

1. Click the **File** tab.
2. Click **Options**.

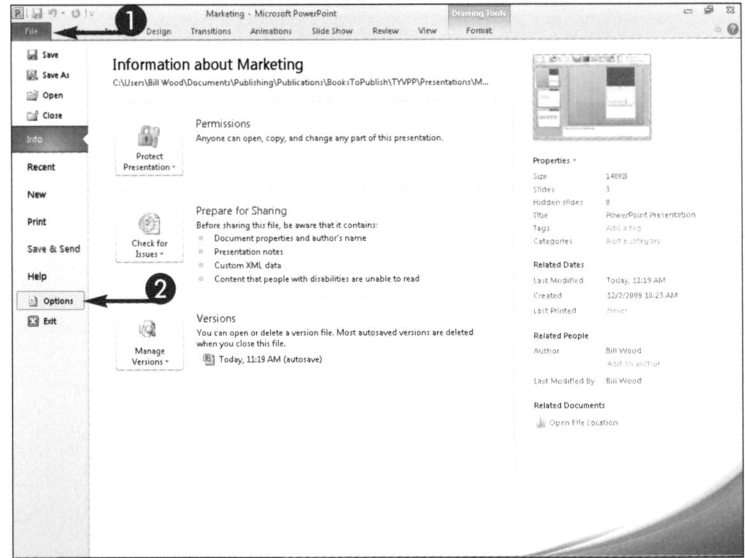

The PowerPoint Options dialog box appears.

3. Click **General**.
4. Click to enable (☑) or disable (☐) options under the User Interface options heading.

- You can click to disable the **Show Mini Toolbar on selection** option (☑ changes to ☐).
- You can click to disable the **Enable Live Preview** option (☑ changes to ☐).

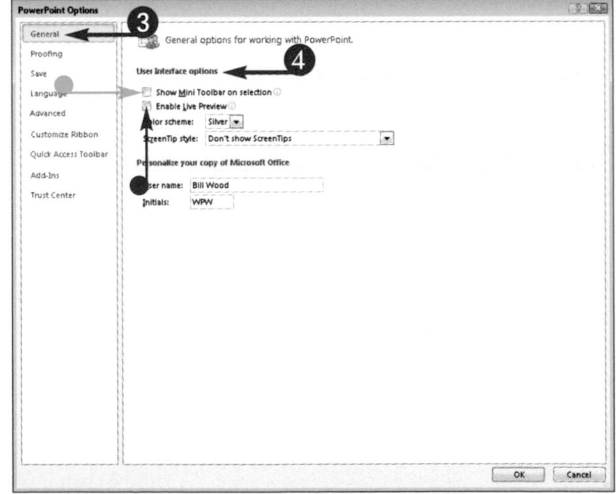

- You can position your mouse pointer (⇖) over the **Information** icon (ⓘ) to see a brief description of an option.
- You can click the **Color scheme** down arrow (▾) and select a scheme for the PowerPoint window.
- You can click the **ScreenTip style** ▾ and select a style to display when you position your ⇖ over a Ribbon command.

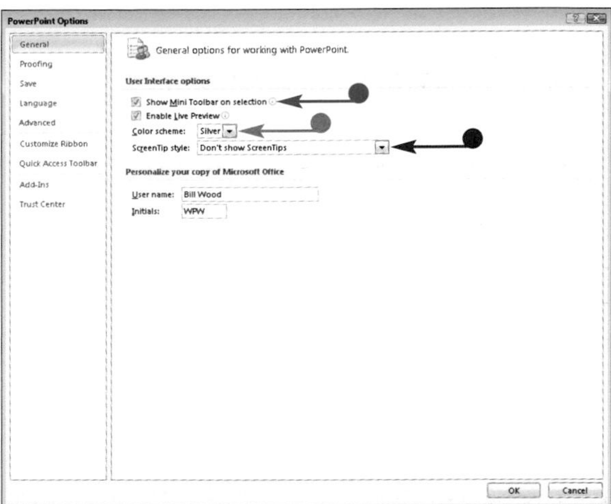

5. Type your name in the User name text box.

   In this example, Bill Wood was typed into the text box.

6. Type your initials in the Initials text box.

   In this example, WPW was typed into the text box.

7. Click **OK**.

   PowerPoint applies your new settings and closes the PowerPoint Options dialog box.

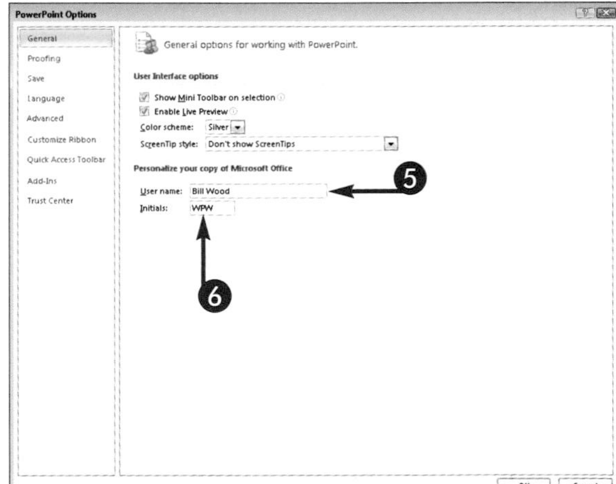

What is the Mini toolbar?

The Mini toolbar is a floating, contextual formatting toolbar that appears when you make a selection on a slide. Either it appears automatically, or it appears when you use the submenu. The Mini toolbar contains the most commonly used formatting commands for the object you select. You can right-click an object to display the Mini toolbar. The Mini toolbar appears automatically if you click and drag across text in a placeholder.

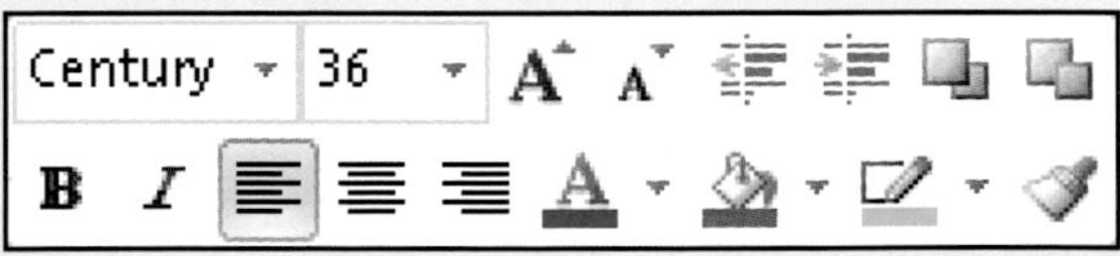

Change Spelling Options

The powerful spell-checker in Microsoft Office automatically and continually checks spelling in PowerPoint as you type. The spell-checker indentifies possible misspellings by underlining them with a red, wavy line. You can use this tool to perfect the text in your presentation, or disable it. You can always use the spell-checker manually. You can customize how the spell-checker indentifies possible misspellings in the PowerPoint Options dialog box.

Change Spelling Options

1. Click the **File** tab.
2. Click **Options**.

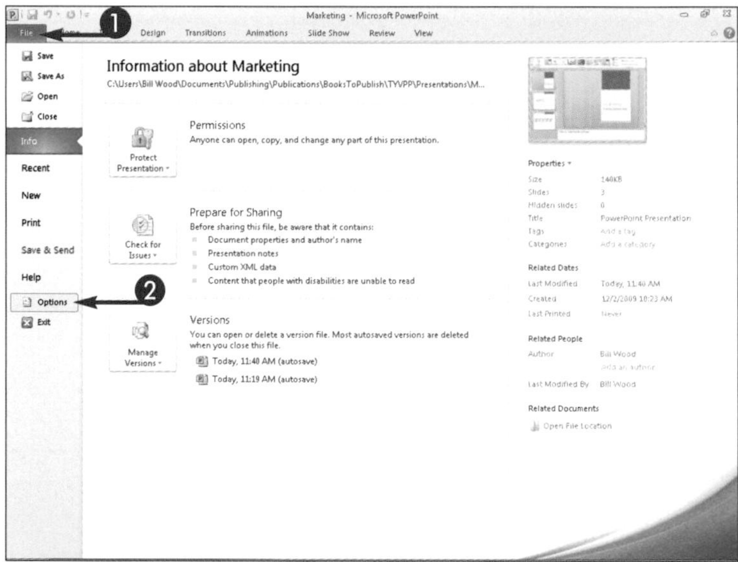

The PowerPoint Options dialog box appears.

3. Click **Proofing**.
4. Click to enable (☑) or disable (☐) options that determine how spell-checker flags certain errors, such as repeated words or words that contain numbers.

Note: *Changes made here affect the spell-checker in other Microsoft Office programs.*

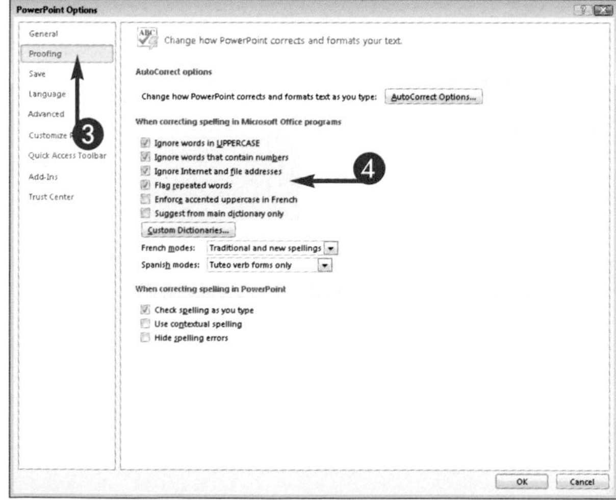

- PowerPoint automatically creates a custom dictionary (CUSTOM.DIC) when you add words during a spelling check. If you want to review, change, or add words in your custom dictionary, click **Custom Dictionaries**, select **CUSTOM.DIC** from the list, and then click **Edit Word List**.

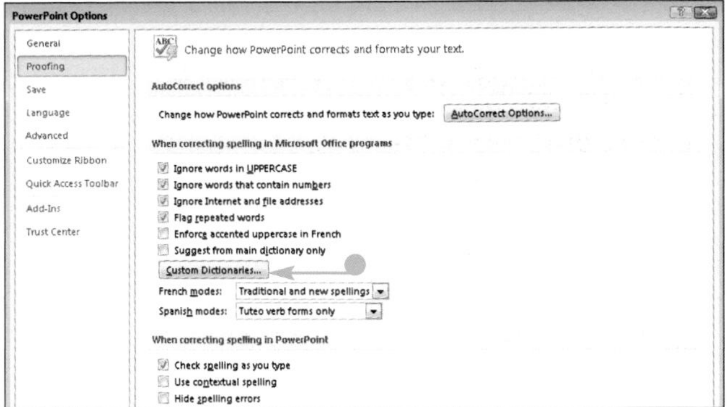

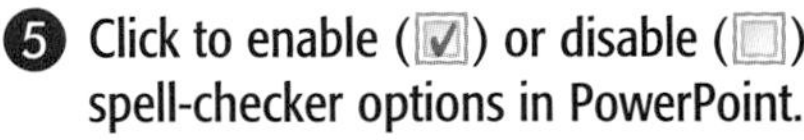

5. Click to enable (☑) or disable (☐) spell-checker options in PowerPoint.

- If you disable the Check spelling as you type option, the spell-checker will not automatically check spelling as you type. You must manually run the spell-checker with a Ribbon command.

6. Click **OK**.

   PowerPoint applies your new settings and closes the PowerPoint Options dialog box.

TIP

Can I stop PowerPoint from flagging proper and product names as misspelled?

Yes. You can add those words to the custom dictionary by following these steps:

1. Follow Steps **1** to **3** in this section.
2. Click the **Custom Dictionaries** button to open the Custom Dictionaries dialog box.
3. Click **Edit Word List** to open the CUSTOM.DIC dialog box.
4. Type each individual word in the Word(s) text box.
5. Click **Add**.
6. Click **OK** in each of the three open dialog boxes.

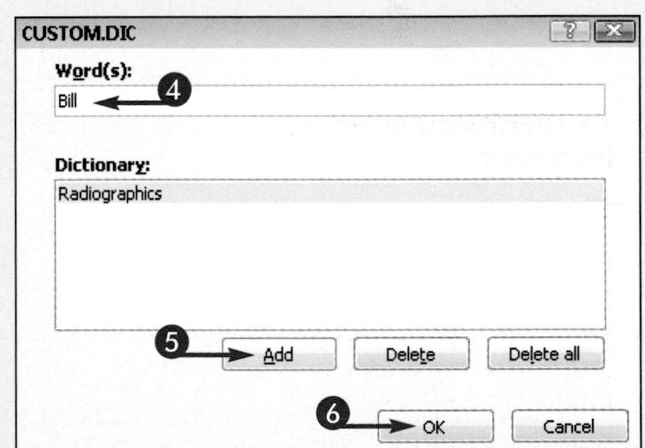

Change AutoCorrect Settings

The AutoCorrect feature automatically corrects common typing and spelling errors while you type. You can add words to a list of common misspellings, empowering AutoCorrect to automatically correct words that you routinely misspell. For example, you can tell it to change "actoin" to the word "action" automatically. You can also delete corrections that already exist on the list, such as changing (c) to ©.

Change AutoCorrect Settings

❶ Click the **File** tab.

❷ Click **Options**.

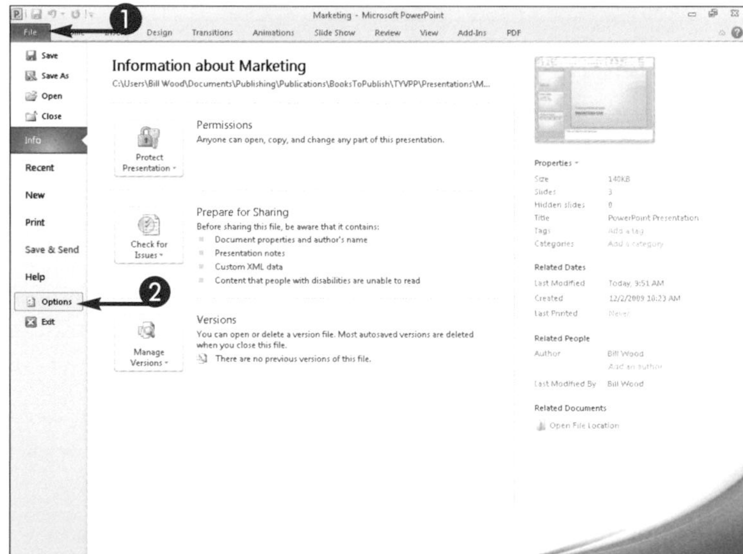

The PowerPoint Options dialog box appears.

❸ Click **Proofing**.

❹ Click **AutoCorrect Options**.

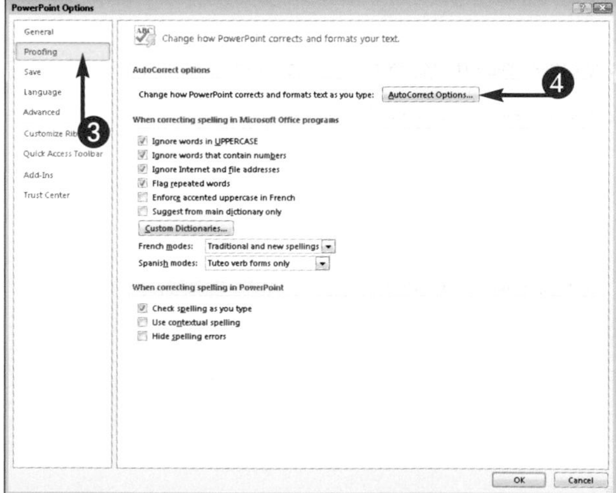

The AutoCorrect dialog box appears.

5. Click the **AutoCorrect** tab.
6. Click to enable (☑) or disable (☐) any of the standard AutoCorrect options.

- Click the **Exceptions** button to make exceptions to capitalizations, such as not automatically capitalizing after abbreviations.
- To disable the misspelling correction feature, click the **Replace text as you type** option (☑ changes to ☐).

7. To add a word to the list of commonly misspelled words, type the misspelled word in the Replace text box.
8. Type the correct spelling of the word in the With text box.
9. Click **Add**.
10. To delete an automatic correction, find it on the list and click it.
11. Click **Delete**.
12. Click **OK** for each of the two open dialog boxes.

PowerPoint applies your new settings.

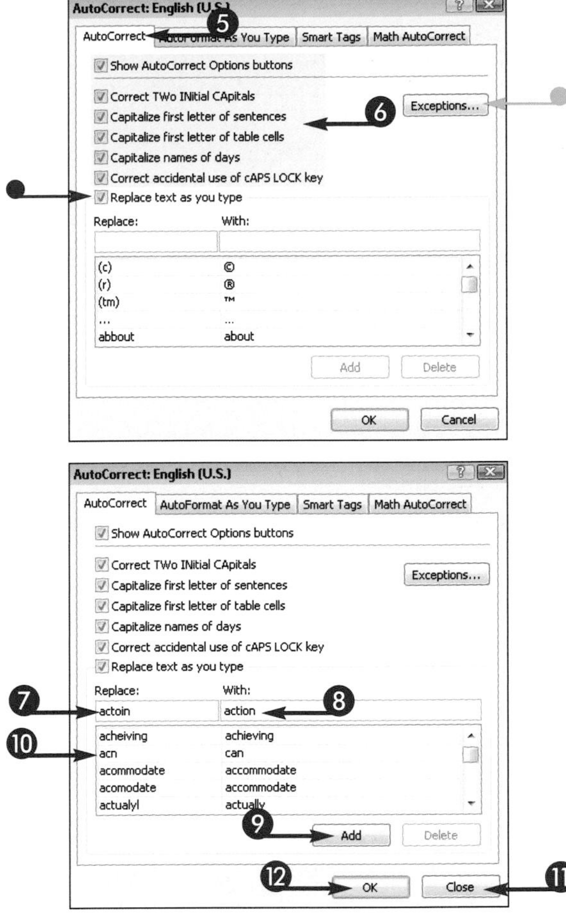

How can I prevent AutoCorrect from changing my acronym "acn" to the word "can" without deleting the setting from AutoCorrect?

You can click the **Undo** icon (↶) in the Quick Access Toolbar, or you can follow these steps:

1. Click the word that AutoCorrect changed.
2. Position the mouse (↖) over the blue autocorrect rectangle (▬).
3. Click the **AutoCorrect Option** icon (⚡▾).
4. Click **Change back to "Acn"**.

- Clicking **Stop Automatically Correcting "acn"** disables AutoCorrect from correcting acn throughout Microsoft Office.

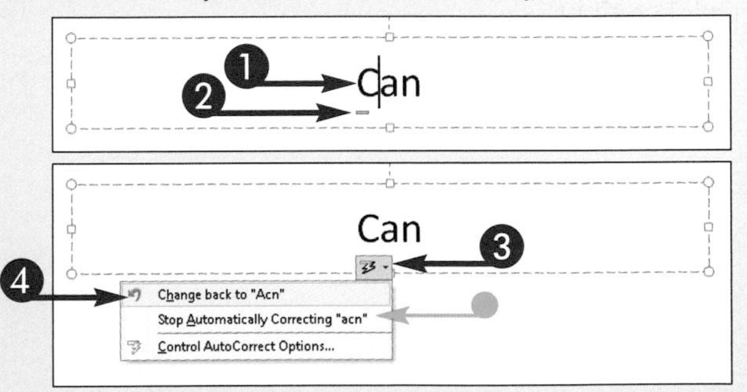

Change AutoFormat Settings

AutoCorrect has a feature called AutoFormat, which speeds up certain formatting that is cumbersome to perform. Examples include changing 1/2 to ½, replacing ordinals (1st) with superscript (1st), and changing Internet paths to hyperlinks (www.test.com). It also automates bulleted lists, and automatically fits text to placeholders. You can customize these settings to suit your particular needs to streamline your work.

Change AutoFormat Settings

❶ Click the **File** tab.

❷ Click **Options**.

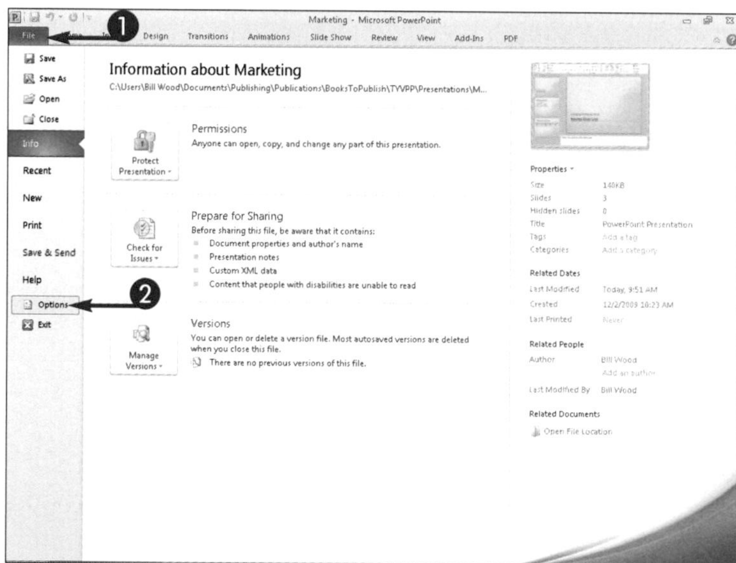

The PowerPoint Options dialog box appears.

❸ Click **Proofing**.

❹ Click **AutoCorrect Options**.

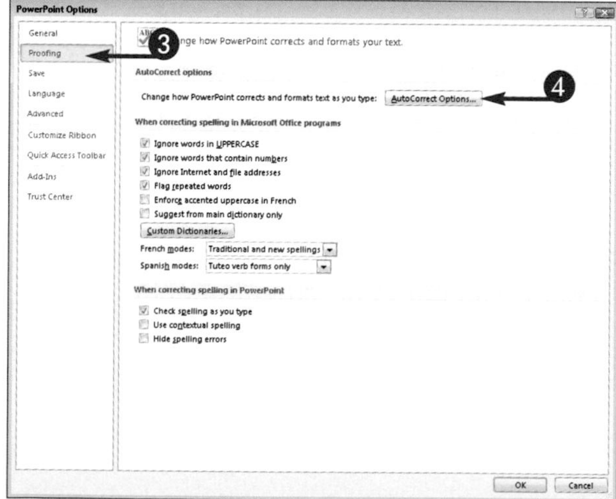

The AutoCorrect dialog box appears.

5. Click the **AutoFormat As You Type** tab.

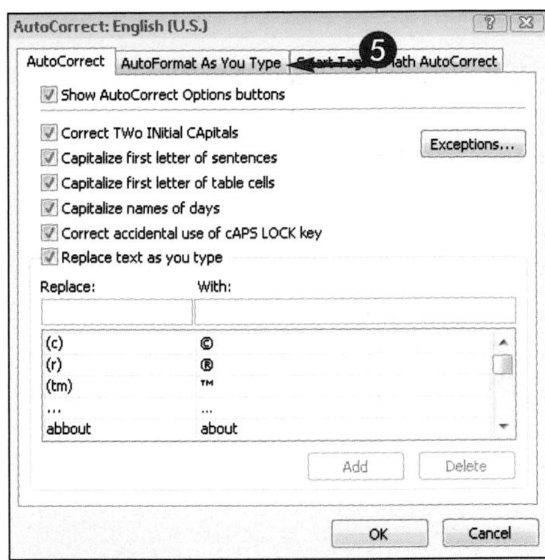

6. Click to enable (☑) or disable (☐) any of the options under Replace as you type.

7. Click to enable (☑) or disable (☐) any of the options under Apply as you type.

8. Click **OK** for each of the two open dialog boxes.

PowerPoint applies your new settings and closes both the AutoCorrect and PowerPoint Options dialog boxes.

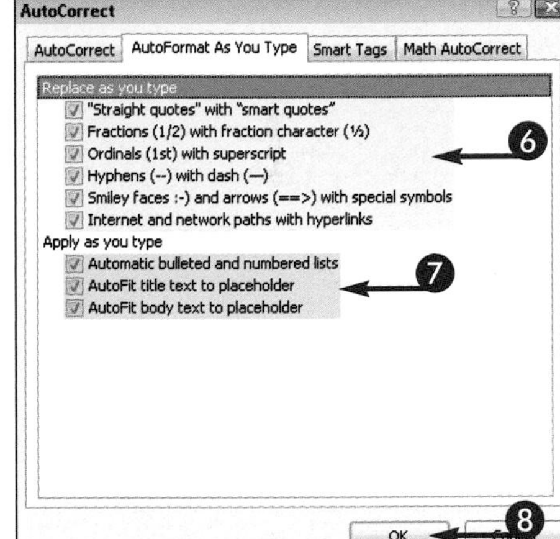

Why does PowerPoint change words I type in all caps to lowercase?

AutoCorrect has a setting that corrects the accidental use of the Caps Lock key. To disable this option

1. Follow Steps **1** to **4** in this section.
2. Click the **Correct accidental use of cAPS LOCK key** option (☑ changes to ☐).
3. Click **OK** to close each of the open dialog boxes.

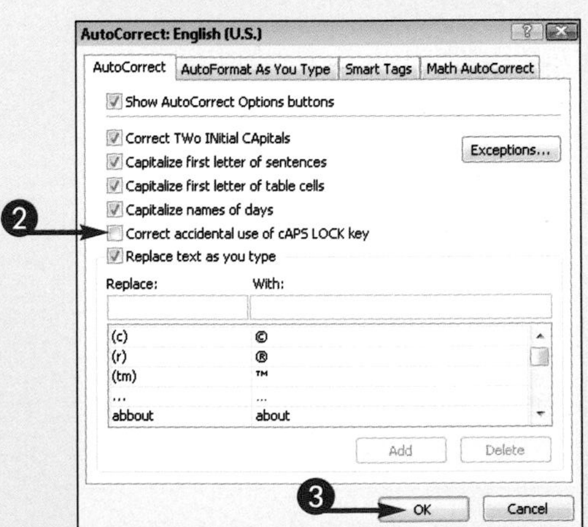

Customize Save Options

By default, PowerPoint saves a presentation in the PowerPoint 2010 format in your user Document folder, for example, `c:\Users\Your Name\My Documents\`. You can change these settings to save to the PowerPoint 2003 format, for example, if you share your presentations with colleagues who use an older PowerPoint version. You can also embed fonts in the saved presentation to preserve its look on any computer.

Customize Save Options

1. Click the **File** tab.
2. Click **Options**.

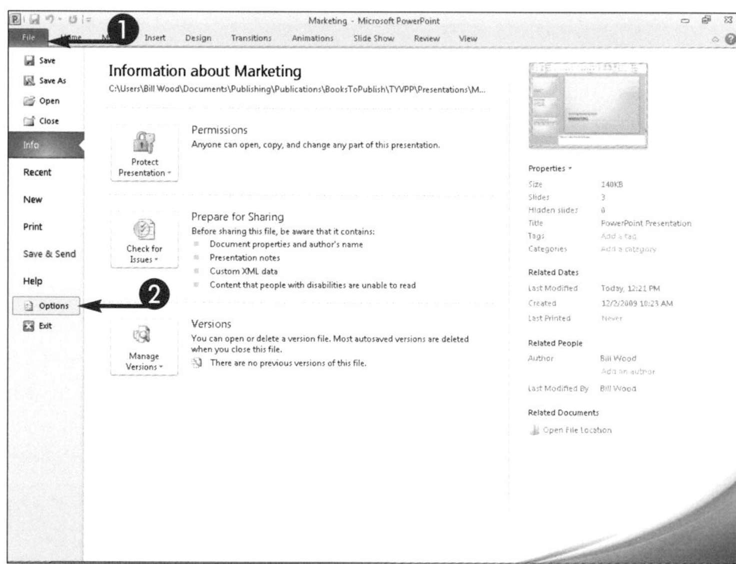

The PowerPoint Options dialog box appears.

3. Click **Save**.
4. Click the **Save files in this format** ▾ and select a file format.

Note: *The file type for PowerPoint 2010 is PowerPoint Presentation, or PowerPoint Macro-Enabled Presentation for presentations that contain macros.*

The next time you save a new file, the file type you specify here will appear as the file type in the Save As dialog box. To save a different file type, simply choose a different file type in the Save As dialog box during the save.

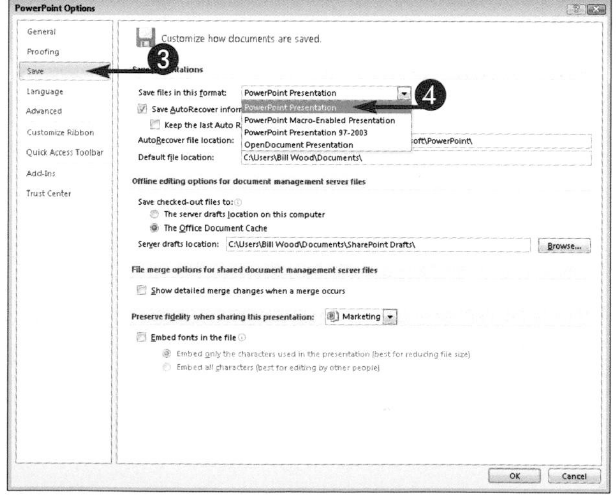

5. Click to enable (☑) or disable (☐) options under the Save presentations heading.

- If desired, click the **spinner** (⬍) to change the number of minutes between AutoRecover saves.
- Deselect the **Save AutoRecover Information** option to disable the automatic saving feature.
- AutoRecovery files are discarded when you close PowerPoint. Click this option to retain the last file if you close without saving the file.
- To change the default save location, type a new default file location.

6. Click the **Embed fonts in the file** option (☐ changes to ☑).

   PowerPoint now saves fonts in the presentation file so that the presentation does not appear differently when viewed on a system lacking the fonts used in it.

- You can further specify whether to embed all characters or only those in use.

7. Click **OK**.

   PowerPoint applies your new settings and closes the PowerPoint Options dialog box.

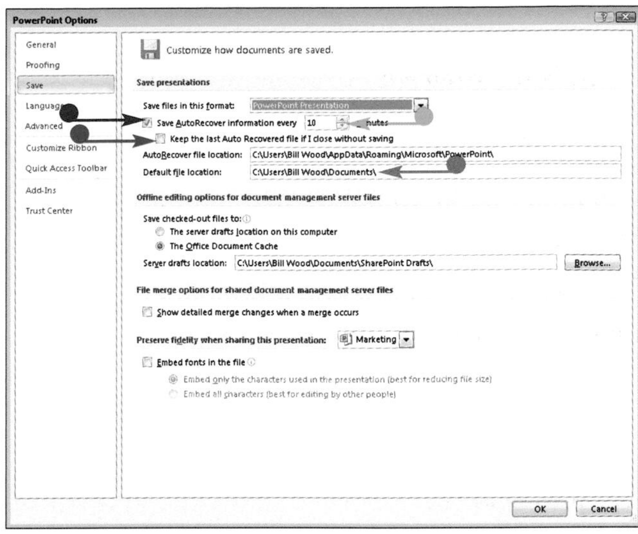

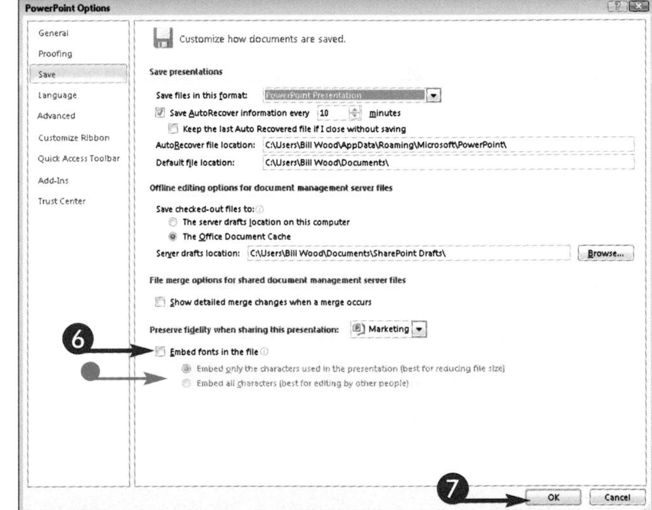

What are the pros and cons of having the AutoRecover feature make frequent saves?

AutoRecover automatically saves your work at regular intervals. If your system crashes, it makes the most recently auto-saved copy of your file available to you the next time you open PowerPoint. However, your system pauses during the save. You can disable AutoRecovery if you do not want to be inconvenienced with this pause.

Why would I want to embed fonts in a presentation?

Some fonts are not available to every computer. If you view your presentation on a computer missing the fonts you used to design it, PowerPoint replaces the fonts with standard fonts from that computer, which may throw off the presentation design. Embedding fonts ensures they remain with the presentation and are available on any computer.

Modify View and Slide Show Options

You can change which elements display in the various PowerPoint views. You also can select which view PowerPoint uses by default, such as Normal view or Slide Sorter view. You also can control whether the toolbar appears during the slide show. These choices ensure that your preferred tools are on-screen when you need them.

Modify View and Slide Show Options

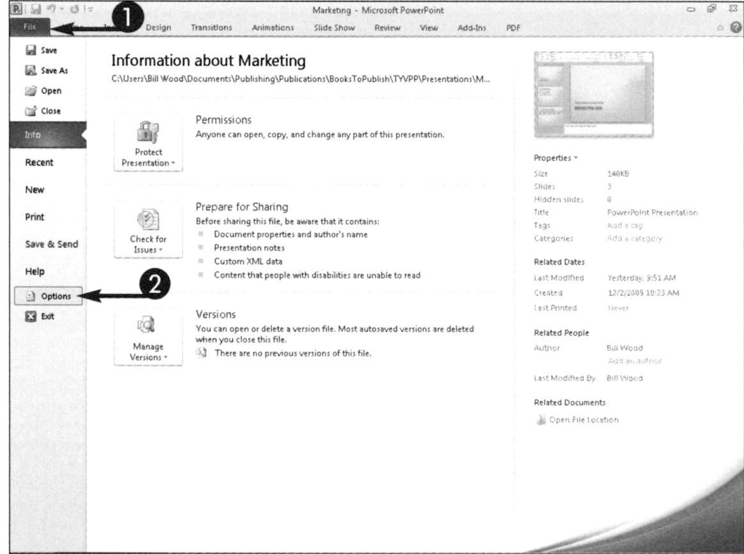

❶ Click the **File** tab.

❷ Click **Options**.

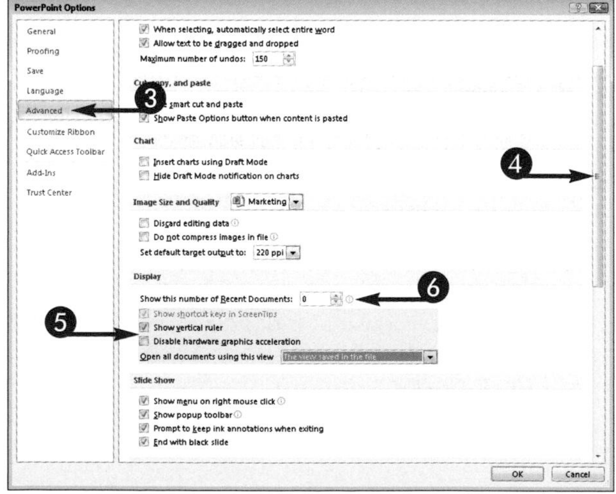

The PowerPoint Options dialog box appears.

❸ Click **Advanced**.

❹ Click and drag the scroll bar to locate the Display and Slide Show headings.

❺ Click to enable (☑) or disable (☐) options under the Display heading.

❻ Click ⬍ to change the number of files displayed in the Recent list on the File tab.

- You can position your mouse over the ⓘ to see a brief description of an option.

7. Click the **Open all documents using this view** ▾ and select a viewing choice.

   PowerPoint uses the specified view when opening presentations.

8. Click to enable (☑) or disable (☐) options affecting behavior during a slide show.

- Determines whether you can use the shortcut menu.
- Controls the toolbar that faintly appears at the bottom left of slides.
- Determines if you can save annotations you made on the slides upon exiting the slide show.
- Determines whether the slide show ends with a blank, black slide.

9. Click **OK**.

   PowerPoint applies your new settings and closes the PowerPoint Options dialog box.

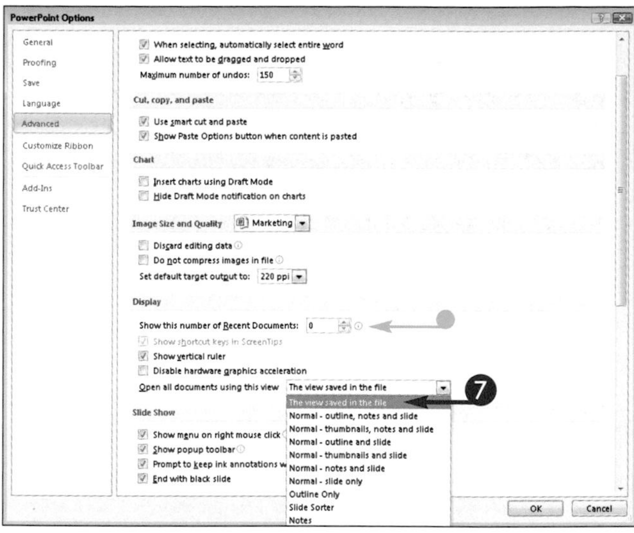

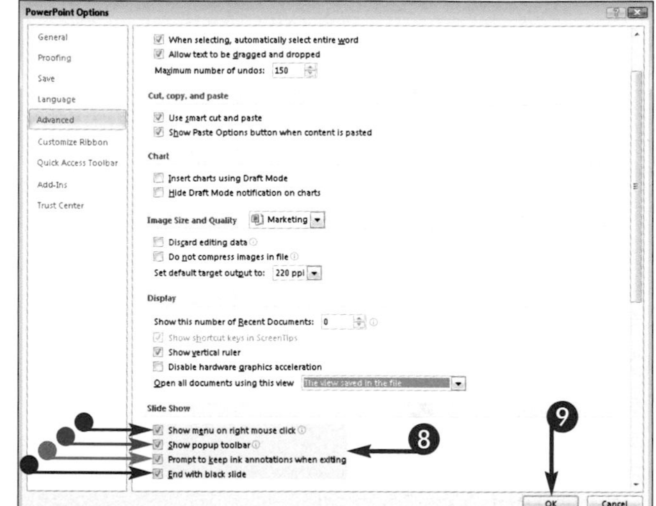

What is the benefit of opening the presentation in Outline only view?

If you start viewing the outline alone, you can concentrate on building the text for the presentation. This can be particularly helpful when you need a clean slate on which to organize your thoughts. It also can help you navigate the contents of a lengthy presentation more quickly.

Can I save annotations if I disable the Prompt me to keep ink annotations when exiting option?

Check spelling, and try and make sure final version is saved.

No. You can only save annotations by using the dialog box that prompts you to save them at the end of the slide show. When that option is disabled in the Advanced section of the PowerPoint Options dialog box, you cannot save annotations.

Change Editing Settings

You can change how certain editing tools work. For example, you can modify how the cutting and pasting, text selection, and Undo features perform. You can also control the use of features such as the Paste Options button. This button appears when you paste a cut or copied object or text. Click it to see commands for working with the pasted selection.

Change Editing Settings

1. Click the **File** tab.
2. Click **Options**.

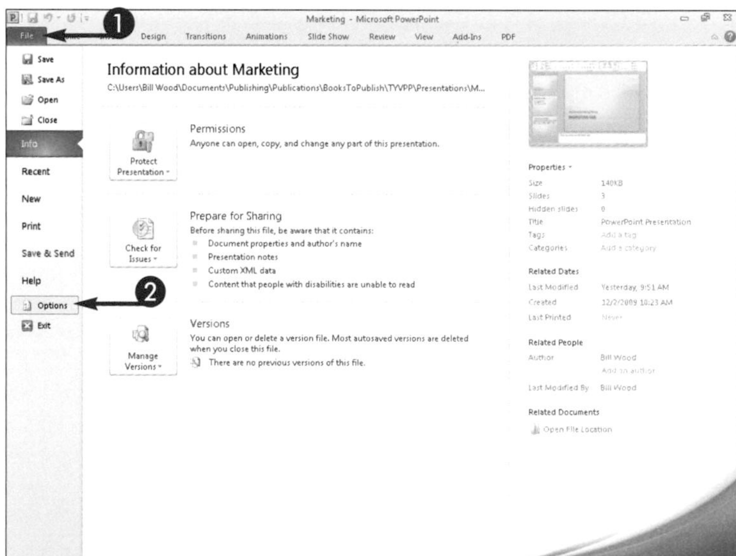

The PowerPoint Options dialog box appears.

3. Click **Advanced**.
4. Click to enable (☑) or disable (☐) options under the Editing options heading.

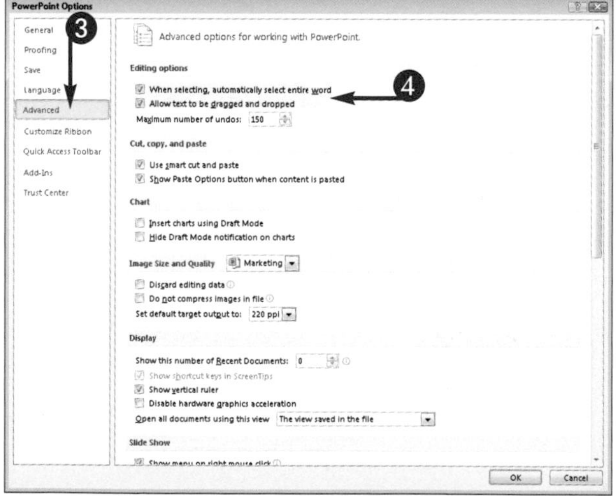

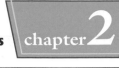

5. Click ⬍ to change the number of undo edits you can perform with ↶ from the Quick Access Toolbar.

   This feature consumes considerable system memory, so if PowerPoint's performance is slow, consider lowering this number.

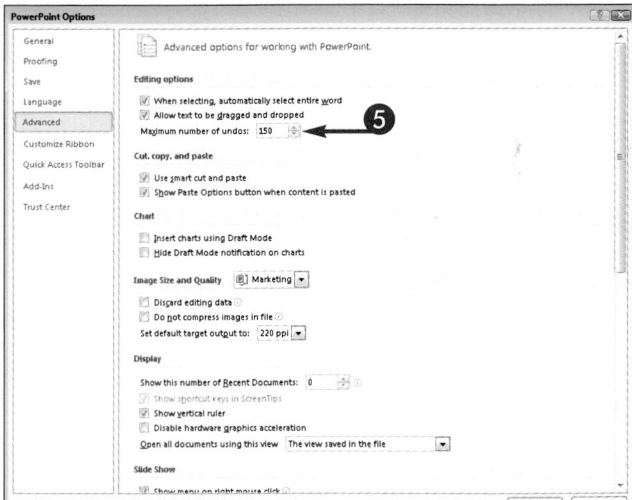

6. Click to enable (☑) or disable (☐) options under the Cut, copy, and paste heading.

- Smart cut and paste is a feature where PowerPoint adds missing spacing around pasted text or objects.
- Click to disable the **Paste Options** button ((Ctrl)) that appears when you perform a copy and paste operation (☑ changes to ☐).

7. Click **OK**.

   PowerPoint applies your new settings and closes the PowerPoint Options dialog box.

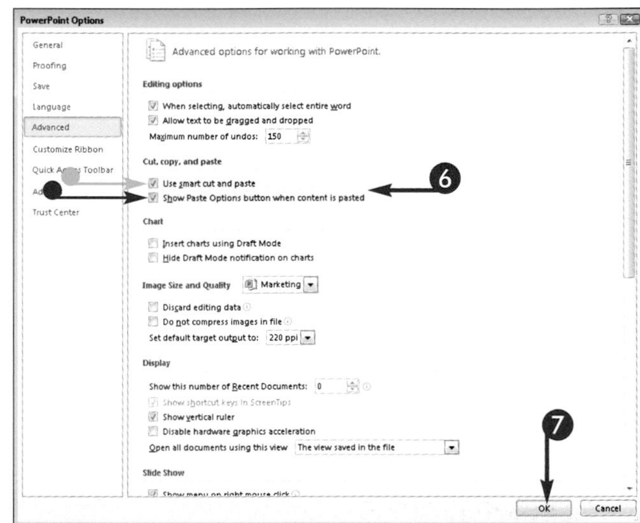

What is the difference between the Paste Options button and smart cut and paste?

The Paste Options button ((Ctrl)) appears below a pasted object and offers formatting options. Smart cut and paste helps to eliminate errors when you paste. If no spacing is selected around copied text, it bumps up against other text when pasted. Smart cut and paste inserts missing spaces while pasting.

What number should I use for maximum number of undos?

The default undo value is 20 and that is probably about right. If you need to undo more than 20 actions, it might be faster to reconstruct a slide from scratch. Alternatively, if you have not yet saved the unwanted changes, just close the file without saving the unwanted changes, and then open it again.

Work with Print Options

The PowerPoint Options dialog box offers several print options, making it easy to control presentation printing. For example, you can modify the way your printer handles fonts and the resolution of inserted graphics. You also can specify that a particular presentation always be printed with a particular printer and settings, saving you the trouble of choosing those settings every time you print that particular file.

Work with Print Options

1. Click the **File** tab.
2. Click **Options**.

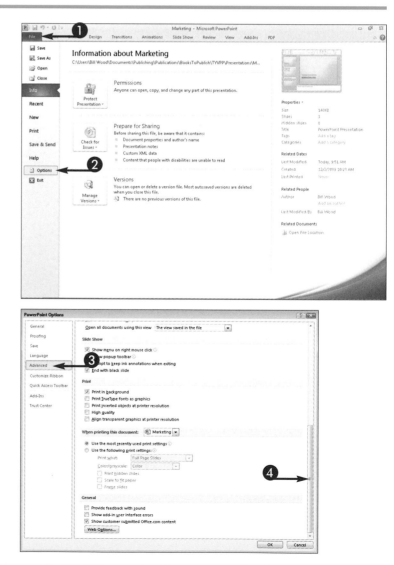

The PowerPoint Options dialog box appears.

3. Click **Advanced**.
4. Click and drag the scrollbar to the bottom of the PowerPoint Options dialog box.

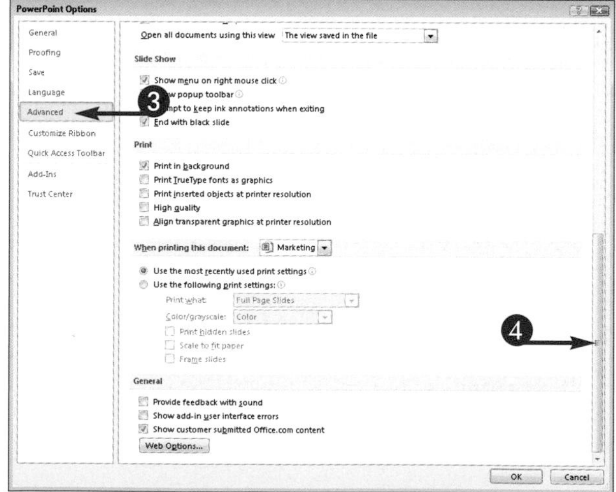

5. Click to enable (☑) or disable (☐) options under the Print heading.

- Print in background enables you to work in PowerPoint while printing.
- Print TrueType fonts as graphics prevents distortion of fonts.
- Print inserted objects at printer resolution uses printer resolution settings for printing to assure quality printing of graphics.
- High quality increases the resolution of graphics, but can slow printing.

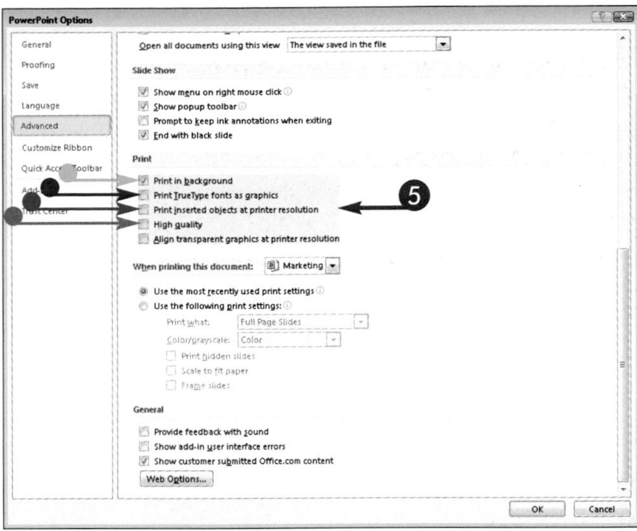

6. Click the **When printing this document** ▾ and select a presentation file.

7. Click the **Use the following print settings** option (◎ changes to ◉).

   The related settings become available.

8. Click to select your preferred print settings.

9. Click **OK**.

   PowerPoint applies your new settings and closes the PowerPoint Options dialog box.

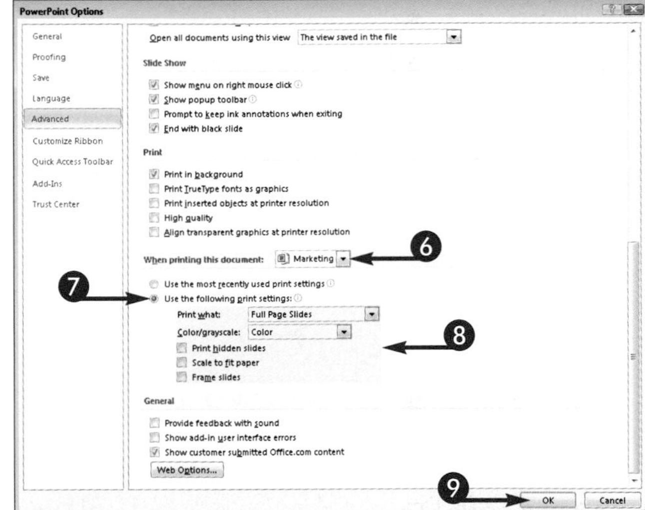

TIPS

How can I change print settings for a document not on the When printing this document drop-down list?

Only open documents appear on this list. Click **Cancel** to close the PowerPoint Options dialog box, open the presentation file, and then reopen the PowerPoint Options dialog box to change print settings for that presentation.

My printer prints slowly. Any suggestions about how to fix this?

You can try a couple of things. Enabling the Print in background option can slow down your printer, so disable the feature by selecting its check box (☑ changes to ☐). In addition, if you enabled Print inserted objects at printer resolution, it may slow printing because it may need to change the resolution of the graphics.

Customize the Quick Access Toolbar

The Quick Access Toolbar appears above the Ribbon in the upper-left corner of PowerPoint. You may also move it below the Ribbon. This toolbar offers buttons for the most frequently used commands, providing even easier access than the Ribbon. You can add buttons to the Quick Access Toolbar to give yourself quick access to the commands you use the most.

Customize the Quick Access Toolbar

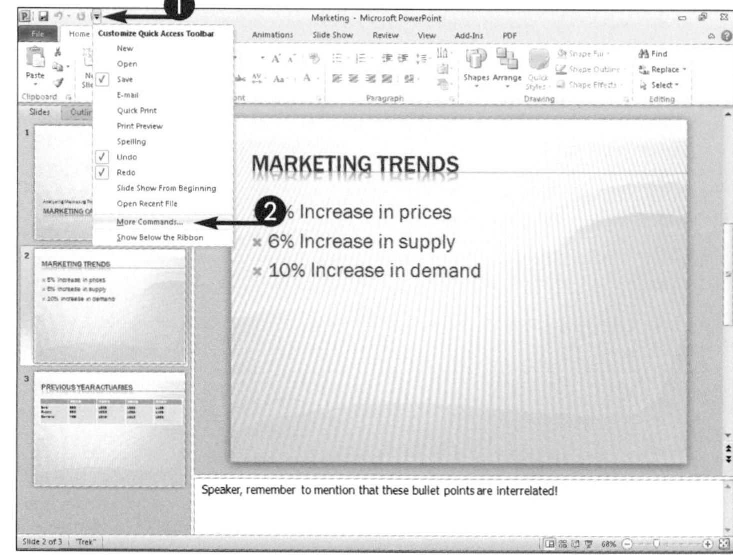

1. Click the **Quick Access Toolbar** down arrow (▾).
2. Click **More Commands**.

The PowerPoint Options dialog box appears, with Quick Access Toolbar displayed.

3. Click ▾ and select the category or tab that holds the command button you want to add to the Quick Access Toolbar.
4. Find your desired command on the list and click it.

In this example, Copy was clicked.

- To add a command only to the toolbar of a particular presentation, select that presentation from the Customize Quick Access Toolbar drop-down list, which only lists presentations that are open.

5. Click **Add**.

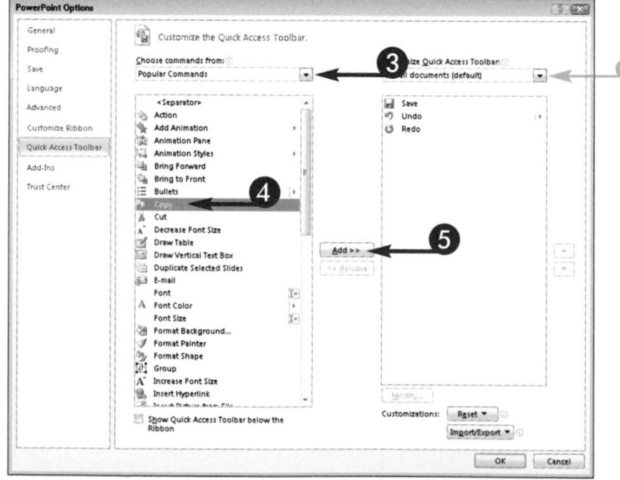

- The command appears on the list of commands on the Quick Access Toolbar.
- Click **Move Up** (▲) or **Move Down** (▼) to change a command's position.
- Click **Remove** to remove a command from the toolbar.

6 Click **OK**.

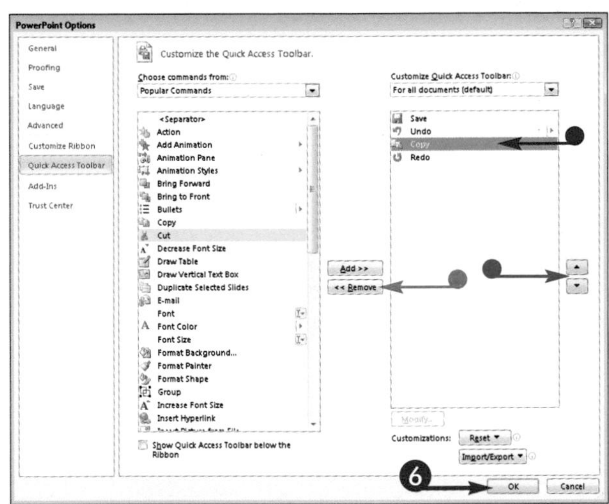

- The PowerPoint Options dialog box closes, and the Quick Access Toolbar reflects the changes you made.

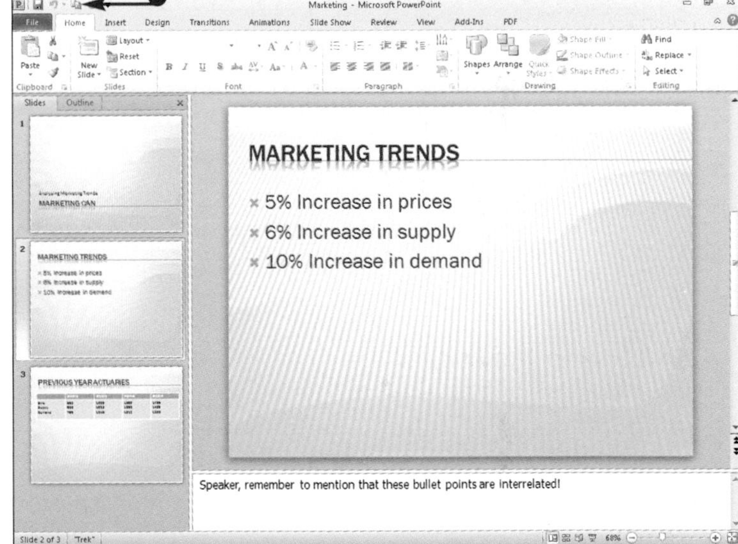

TIP

How do I change the Quick Access Toolbar to look as it did when I first installed PowerPoint?

Follow these steps to reset the Quick Access Toolbar:

1. Follow Steps **1** and **2** in this section.
2. In the PowerPoint Options dialog box, click the **Reset** button.
3. Click **Reset all customizations**.
4. Click **OK**.

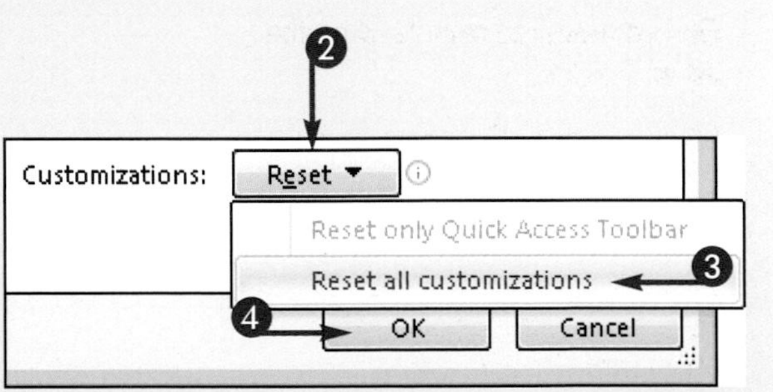

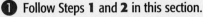

Customize the Ribbon

New to PowerPoint 2010 is the ability to customize the Ribbon. You can add tabs, groups, and commands to the Ribbon to add proficiency to the way you handle tasks and features. You cannot only add commands and groups to your own tabs, but also to existing tabs. You can also rename existing tabs and groups to names of your liking.

Customize the Ribbon

Tour the Ribbon Tab Outline

1. Click the **File** tab.
2. Click **Options**.

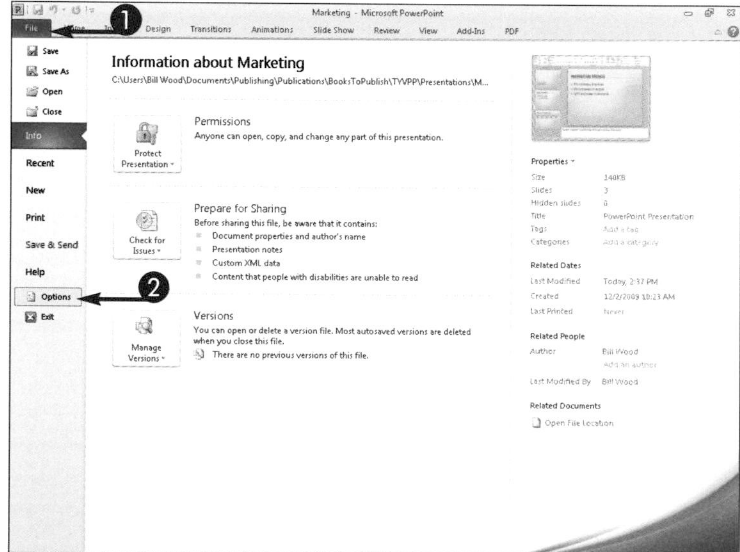

The PowerPoint Options dialog box appears.

3. Click **Customize Ribbon**.
4. Click the **Options plus sign** (⊞) to expand a level (⊞ changes to ⊟, which is used to collapse a level).

- The first level of names on the list is Ribbon tabs.
- The second level of names on the list is Ribbon groups.
- The third level of names is Ribbon commands.
- The fourth level of names is commands for Ribbon commands that have menus or galleries.

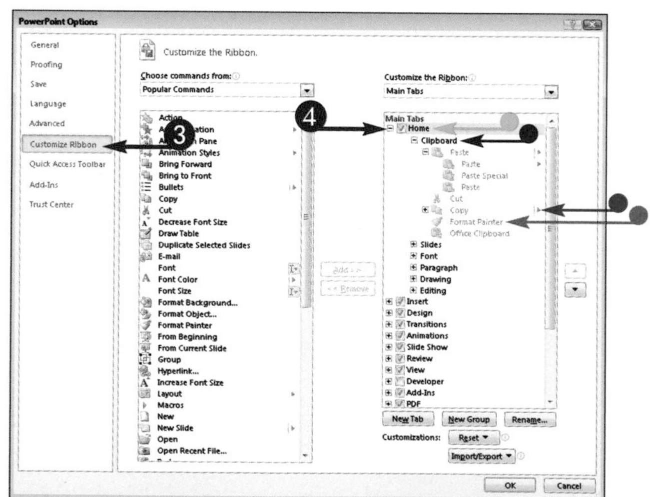

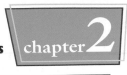

Add a Custom Tab to the Ribbon

1. Click ☑ to disable a tab and remove it from the Ribbon (☑ changes to ☐).
2. Click ⊟ to collapse the Home tab (⊟ changes to ⊞).
3. Click a tab name from the list — your custom tab will be inserted below it.

   In this example, Home was clicked.
4. Click **New Tab**.

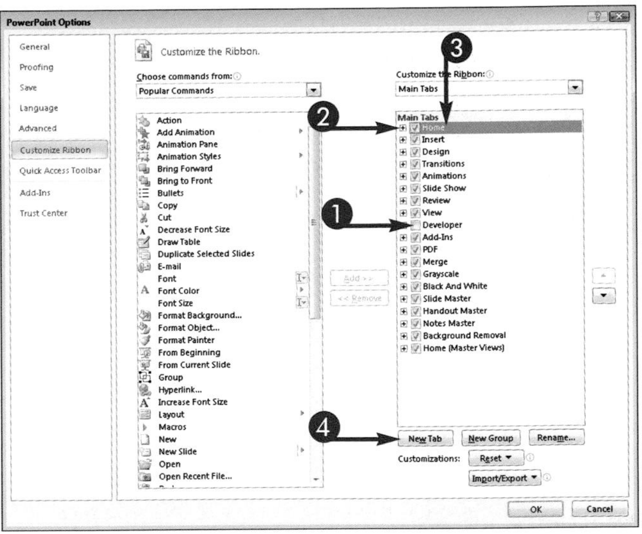

- A new tab level appears with one new group.

5. Click **New Tab (Custom)**.

- You can use the **Move Up arrow** (▲) and the **Move Down arrow** (▼) to change the position of the tab.
- You can remove a custom tab by clicking **Remove**.

6. Click **Rename**.

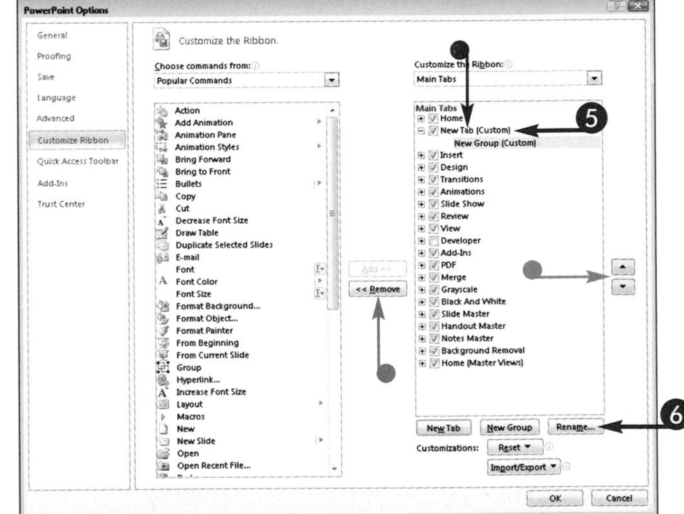

TIP

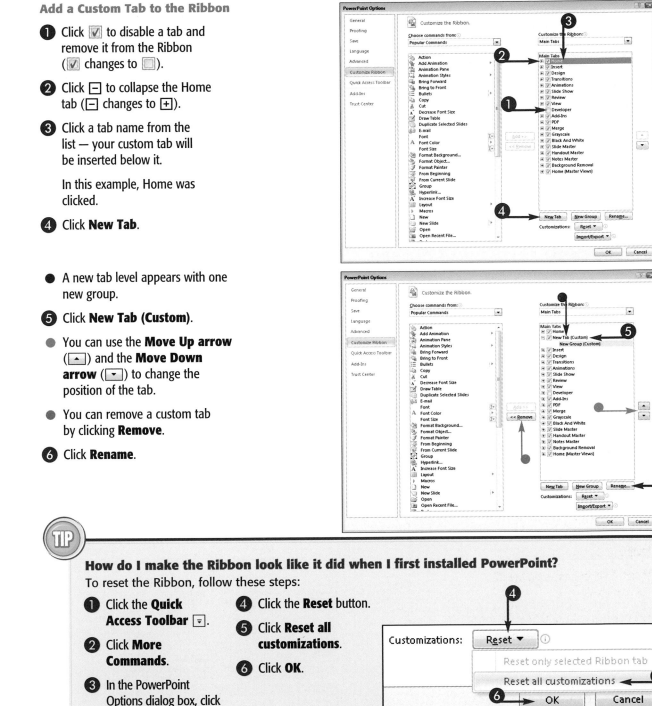

How do I make the Ribbon look like it did when I first installed PowerPoint?

To reset the Ribbon, follow these steps:

1. Click the **Quick Access Toolbar** ▾.
2. Click **More Commands**.
3. In the PowerPoint Options dialog box, click **Customize Ribbon**.
4. Click the **Reset** button.
5. Click **Reset all customizations**.
6. Click **OK**.

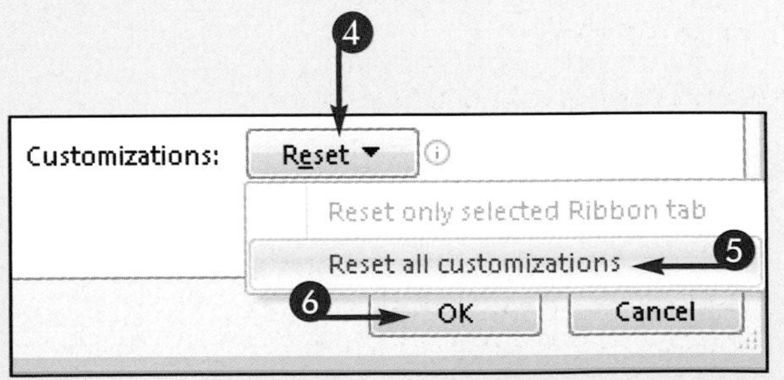

Customize the Ribbon *(continued)*

How people use Ribbon commands varies based upon how they use PowerPoint. Usually PowerPoint users have a group of commands that they frequently use. You can group commonly used commands on a custom tab to make it easier than ever to design your presentation.

Customize the Ribbon *(continued)*

The Rename dialog box appears.

7 Type a name.

8 Click **OK**.

The tab name changes to MyTab.

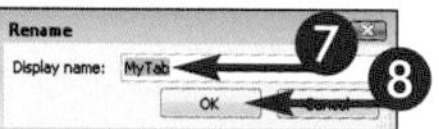

Add a Group

1 Click ⊞ to expand the Insert tab (⊞ changes to ⊟).

2 Click a group name from the list — your custom tab will be inserted below it.

3 Click **New Group**.

A new group level appears.

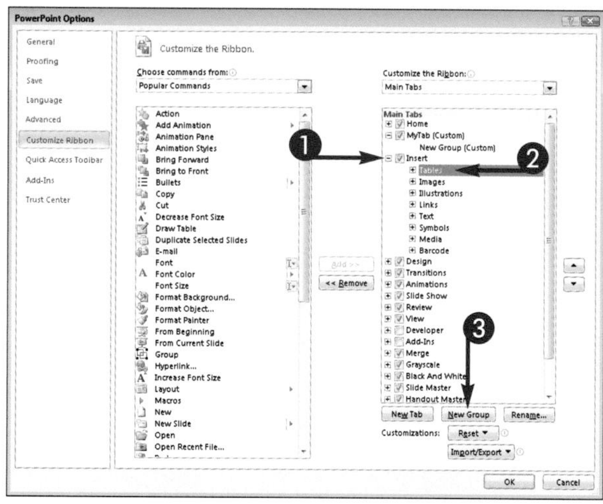

Add a Command

1 Click **New Group (Custom)**.

2 Click a command from the list.

In this example, Bring Forward was clicked.

3 Click **Add**.

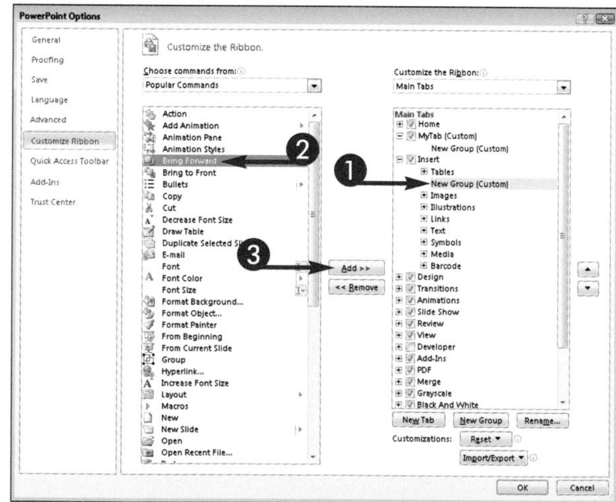

Repeat this process for any commands you want in any group, including existing groups.

- Your commands are added to New Group (Custom).

4 Click **OK**.

The PowerPoint Options dialog box closes, and the Ribbon reflects the changes you made.

- MyTab was added to the Ribbon.
- The group, New Group, was added with the selected commands.

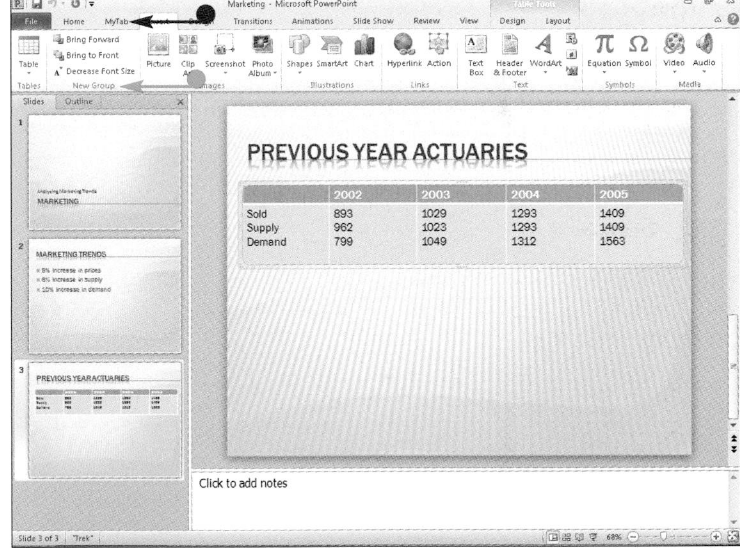

TIPS

Why do some of the commands that I added to my custom group not work?

Some commands require you to select an object or text before they are enabled for you to use. Select an object or text, and then try using the commands.

I cannot find the command I want in the selected category. Is there another place to look?

Yes, there is a category for all commands. After displaying the choices for customizing the Ribbon, click the Choose commands from ▾ and then click **All Commands**. If the command is currently available, it will appear in the list. Keep in mind that PowerPoint 2010 removed some commands available in previous versions.

CHAPTER

3

Beginning with Presentation Fundamentals

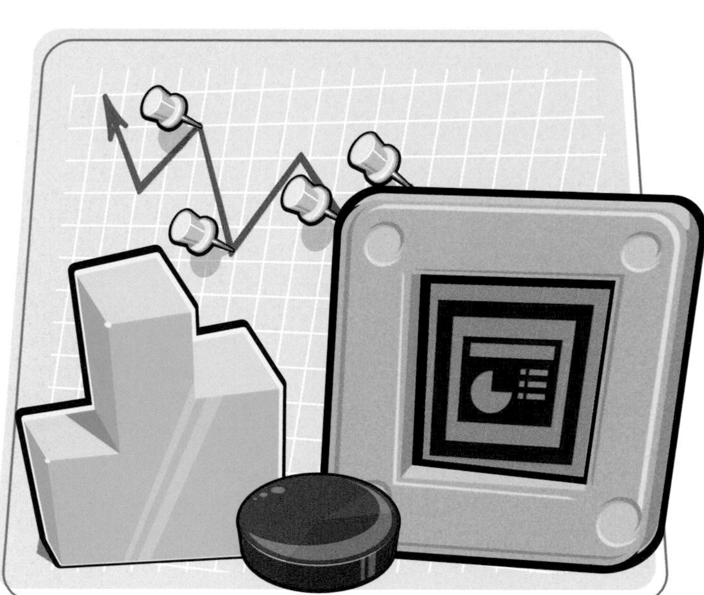

Each presentation you build will exist in its own separate PowerPoint file. This chapter begins by showing you how to create a new presentation file. After you create a presentation file and save it, you will work with that file. This chapter shows you how to open and manage your presentation files.

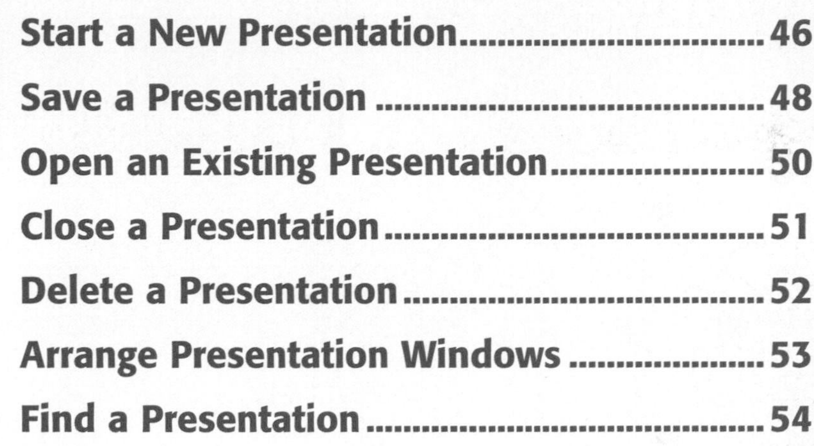

Start a New Presentation

Starting PowerPoint creates a new blank presentation file. After PowerPoint starts up, there are a few ways to create a new presentation, including making a blank presentation or using a template.

Some templates are installed on your hard disk, but even more are offered online. Your system needs to have a live Internet connection to download online templates.

Start a New Presentation

1. Click the **File** tab.
2. Click **New**.

   The Available Templates and Themes page appears.

- You can choose a blank template, with a particular theme.
- Some templates are on your hard drive as sample templates.
- You can search for templates by typing a key word or phrase in the **Search** box.

3. Click a category under **Office.com Templates**.

   In this example, Presentations was clicked.

- PowerPoint finds your category online and displays the contents.

4. Click a category.

   In this example, Academic was clicked.

- Click the **Back** button (◉) to go back to the Available Templates and Themes page.

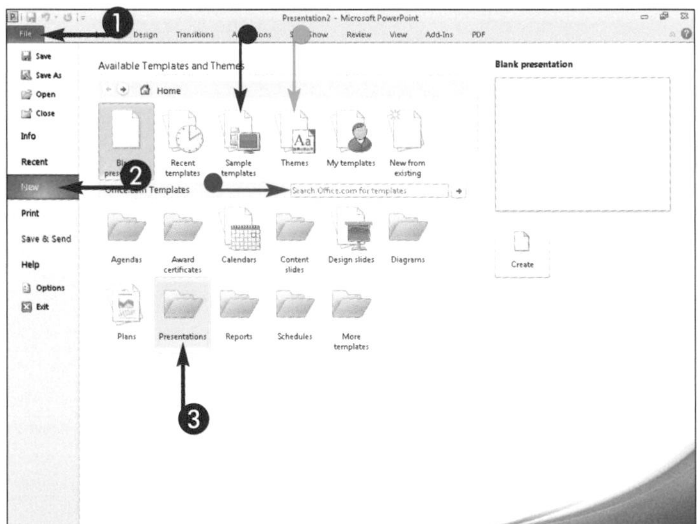

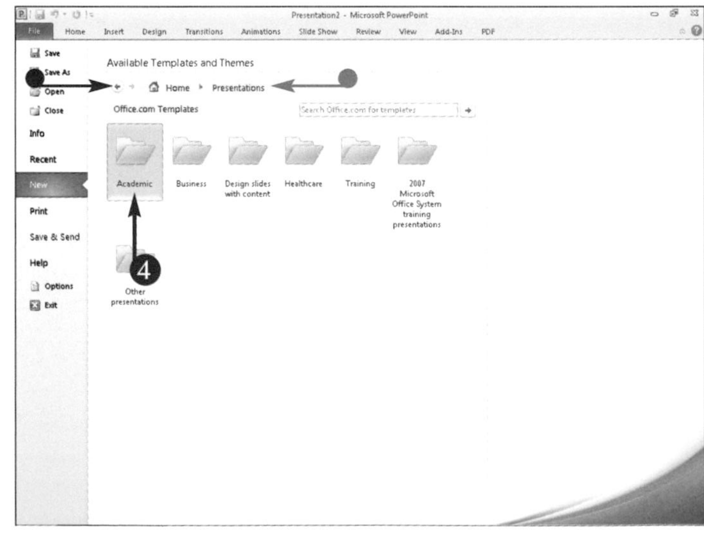

- PowerPoint displays the contents of the folder.

5 Click your presentation template choice.

In this example, Classroom expectations presentation was clicked.

6 Click **Download**.

PowerPoint creates a presentation from the template.

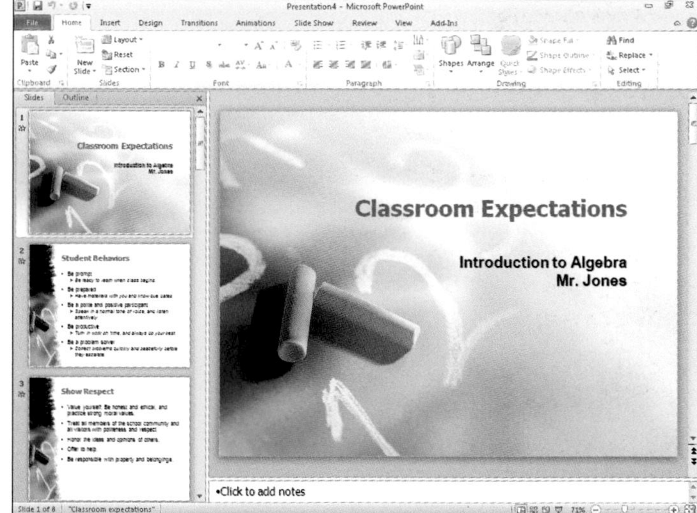

TIPS

Is there another way to create a blank presentation?

Click the **File** tab and then click **New**. The default choice is Blank presentation. Click **Create.**

Are there templates installed on my computer?

Yes, if you did a standard installation of PowerPoint. Click the **File** tab, and then click **New**. Click **Sample templates** to see a list of templates. Click one of them, and then click **Create**.

Save a Presentation

After you create a presentation and have added text or other content, you should save the presentation to ensure you are able to use it later. Saving a PowerPoint file works much like saving any other Office program file: You need to specify the location in which to save the file and give the file a name.

Save a Presentation

❶ Click the **File** tab.

❷ Click **Save As**.

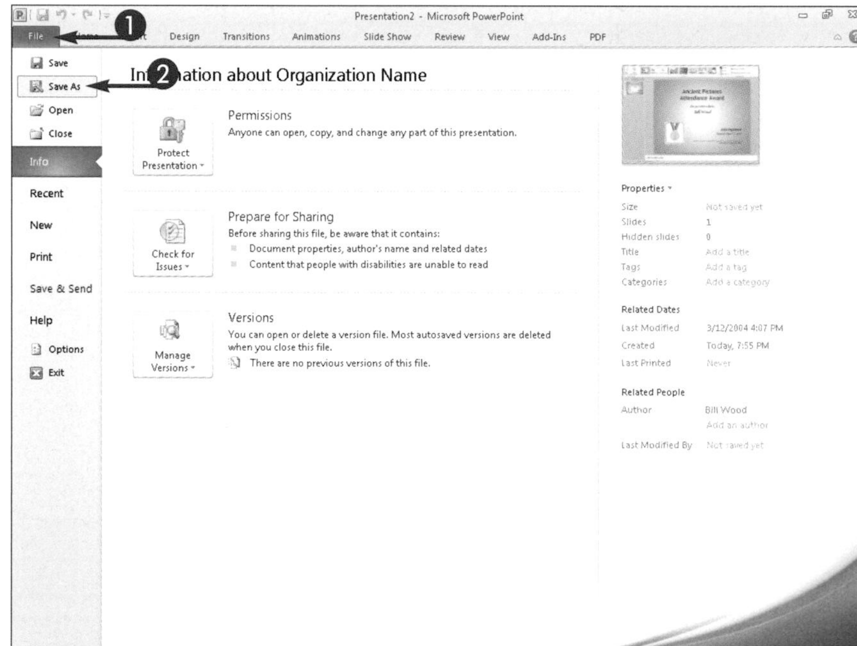

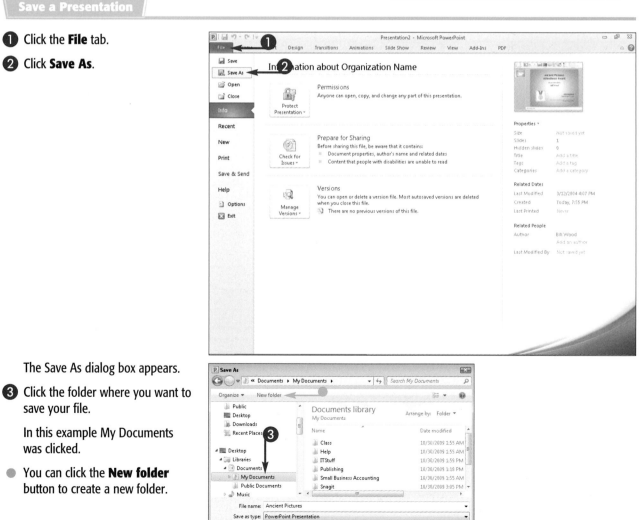

The Save As dialog box appears.

❸ Click the folder where you want to save your file.

In this example My Documents was clicked.

● You can click the **New folder** button to create a new folder.

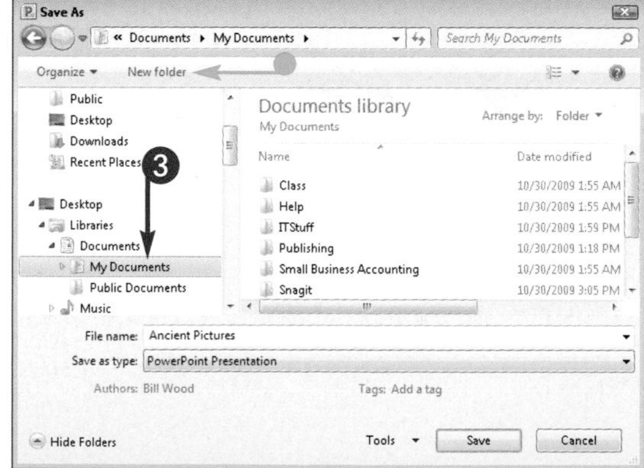

4. Click the **File name** text box to select it and then type a filename.

   In this example, Certificate was typed.

5. Click the **Save as Type** (▾) to change the file type to one other than the default.

***Note:** If you choose a format other than the default PowerPoint format, you may see a prompt about an issue such as version compatibility. Respond to the prompt to continue saving.*

6. Click **Save**.

   The presentation is saved and the Save As dialog box closes.

- The new filename appears in the title bar.

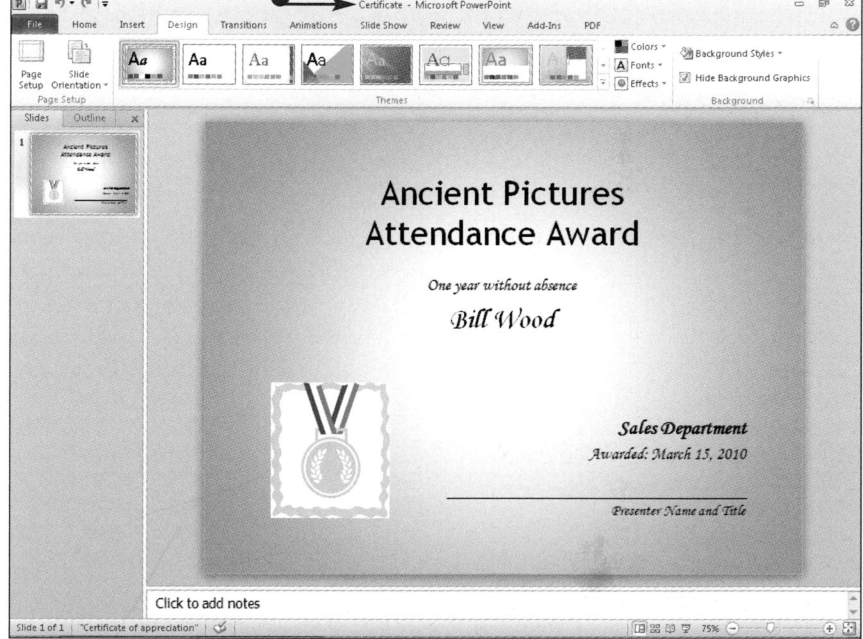

TIPS

I save presentations in a specific folder all the time. Is there a quick way to locate that folder in the Save As dialog box?

Yes. You can change the default file location in the PowerPoint Options dialog box to your favorite folder location. When you perform a save, that folder will be the default folder that appears in the Save As dialog box. See Chapter 2 for details.

Must I always use the Save As dialog box?

No. To save changes to a presentation you previously saved, press Ctrl + S. You can also click the **Save** icon (💾) on the Quick Access Toolbar. To save a copy of the current presentation under a new name, click the **File** tab, click **Save As**, and specify a new filename and save location.

Open an Existing Presentation

After you save and close a presentation, you must locate it and reopen it the next time you want to use it.

If you used a presentation recently, the quickest way to open it is in the list of recently used files on the File tab.

Open an Existing Presentation

1. Click the **File** tab.
2. Click **Recent**.

   ● If your presentation is on the Recent Presentations list, click it and the presentation opens.

3. If your presentation is not on the Recent Presentations list, Click **Open**.

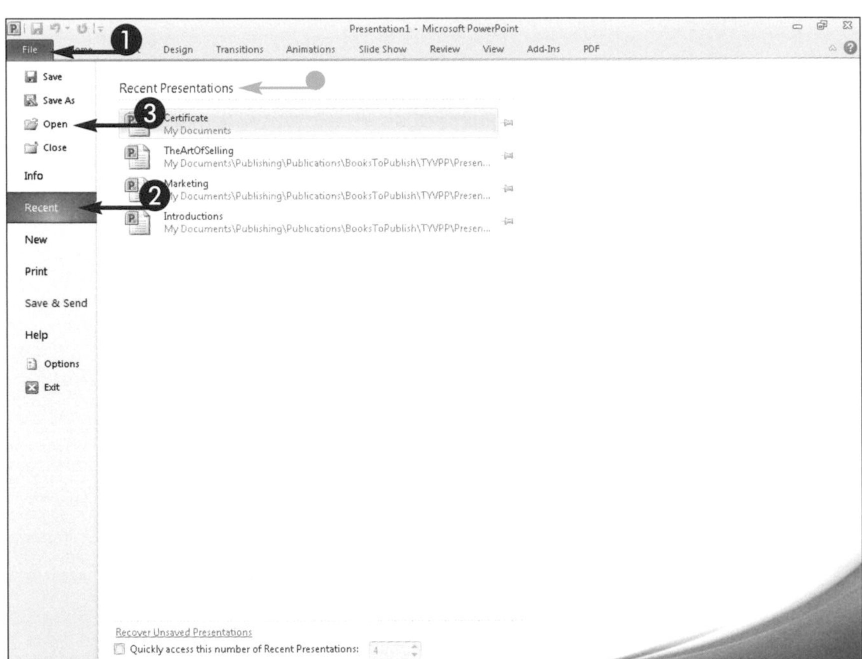

The Open dialog box appears.

4. Click the folder that holds the presentation file you want to open.
5. Click the filename.

   In this example, Certificate was clicked.

6. Click **Open**.

   PowerPoint opens the file.

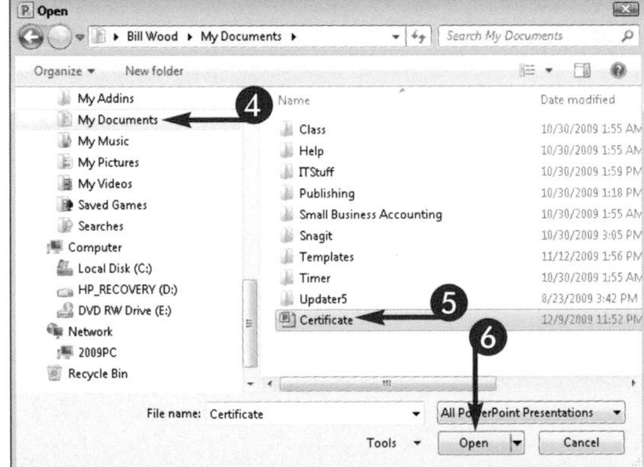

Close a Presentation

When you finish working with a presentation, you can close the file. Doing so leaves PowerPoint open so you can work with other presentations.

When you close an unsaved file or one with unsaved changes, PowerPoint prompts you to save the presentation before closing it. For more on saving a presentation, see the section "Save a Presentation."

Close a Presentation

1. Click the **File** tab.
2. Click **Close**.

A message may appear asking if you want to save changes.

3. Click **Save**.

- If you do not want to save the changes to your presentation, click **Don't Save**.

The file closes, but PowerPoint remains open.

Note: *You also can close a presentation by pressing Alt + F4, but this method also closes PowerPoint.*

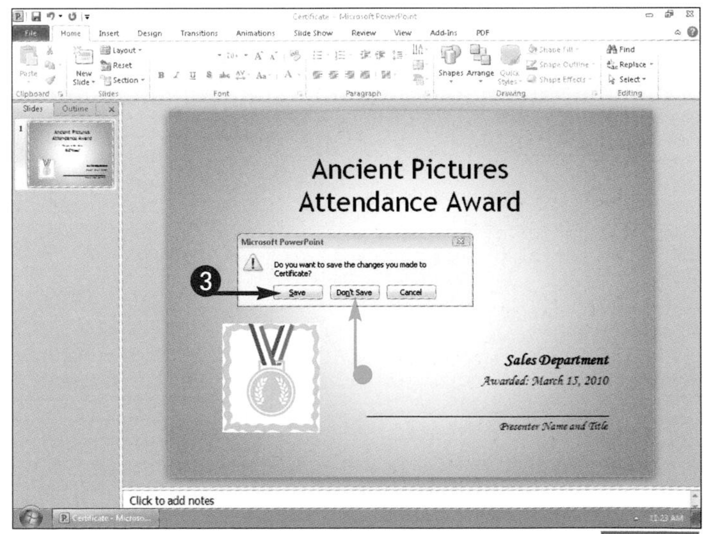

Delete a Presentation

If a presentation file has out-of-date information or is an unneeded backup copy, you may decide to delete the presentation file. You can delete files to free up space on your hard drive.

If you think that you may need the presentation again, copy the presentation file to a CD or other backup medium before deleting the file from your computer.

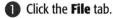

Delete a Presentation

1. Click the **File** tab.
2. Click **Open**.

The Open dialog box appears.

3. Right-click the folder that holds the file you want to delete.

   In this example, MyFile was right-clicked.

   The submenu appears.

4. Click **Delete**.

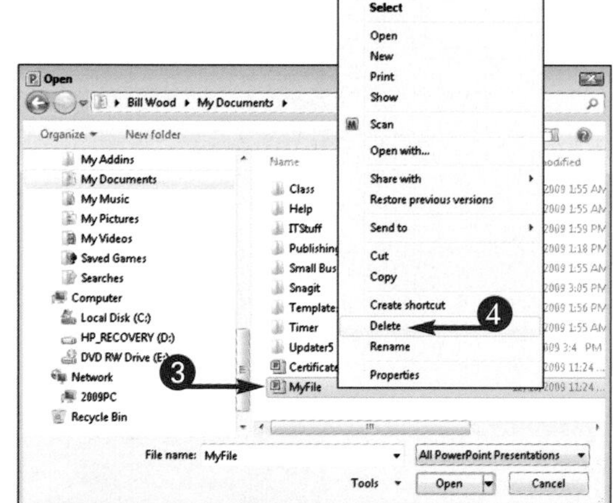

The Delete File dialog box appears.

5. Click **Yes**.

   PowerPoint deletes the file.

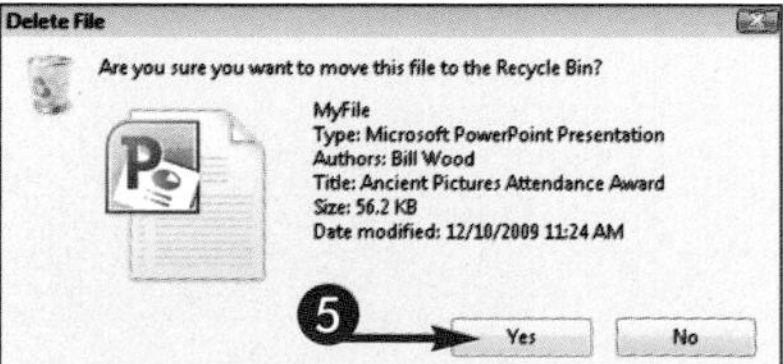

Note: *You also can browse file folders from Windows and delete any file.*

Arrange Presentation Windows

You can open multiple presentations on-screen at once; for example, when you want to compare their contents. You can arrange the open presentation files by using commands on the View tab.

Limit the number of open presentations to three or fewer. Otherwise, you cannot see enough of each presentation to make this feature useful.

Arrange Presentation Windows

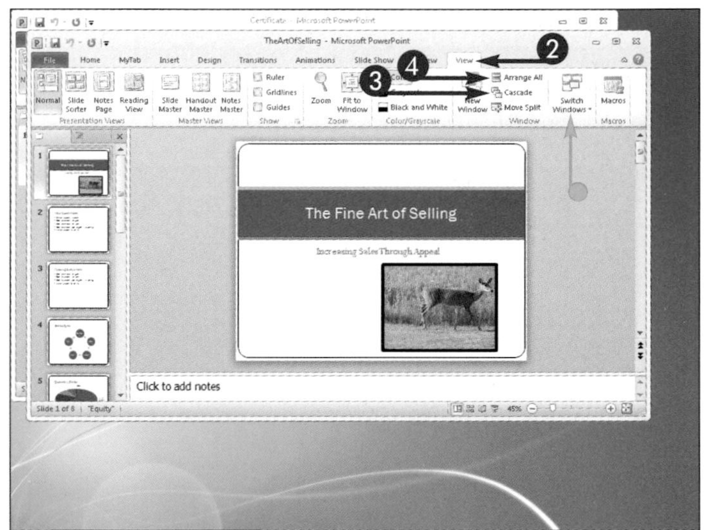

1. Open two or more presentations.
2. Click the **View** tab.
3. Click **Cascade**.

   The presentation windows move so they overlap.

- Click **Switch Windows** and then click a presentation in the menu to make a presentation active.

4. Click **Arrange All**.

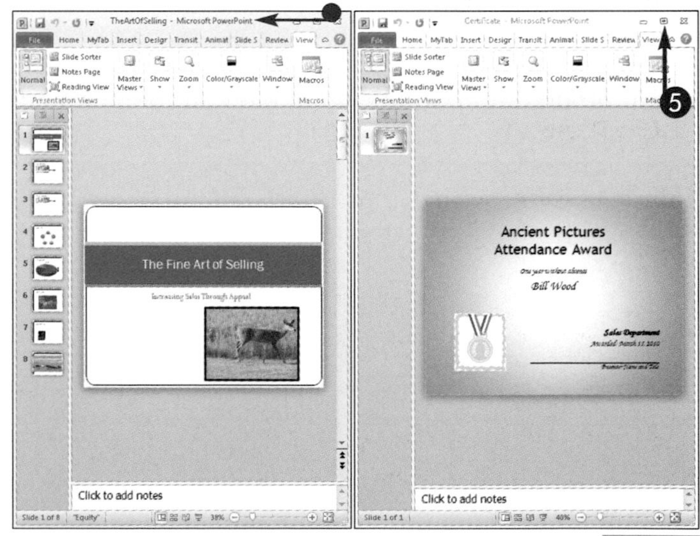

The presentation windows appear side by side.

- You can drag a window's title bar to move the window.

5. Click the **Maximize** button (▣) on one of the windows.

   The window appears full screen again.

Find a Presentation

Sometimes you want to open a file but you forget what you named it or you forget which folder contains it. You can use the Search feature to locate the file.

You also can use the Search feature on the Windows Start menu to locate a file.

Find a Presentation

Use the Open Dialog Box

❶ Click the **File** tab.

❷ Click **Open**.

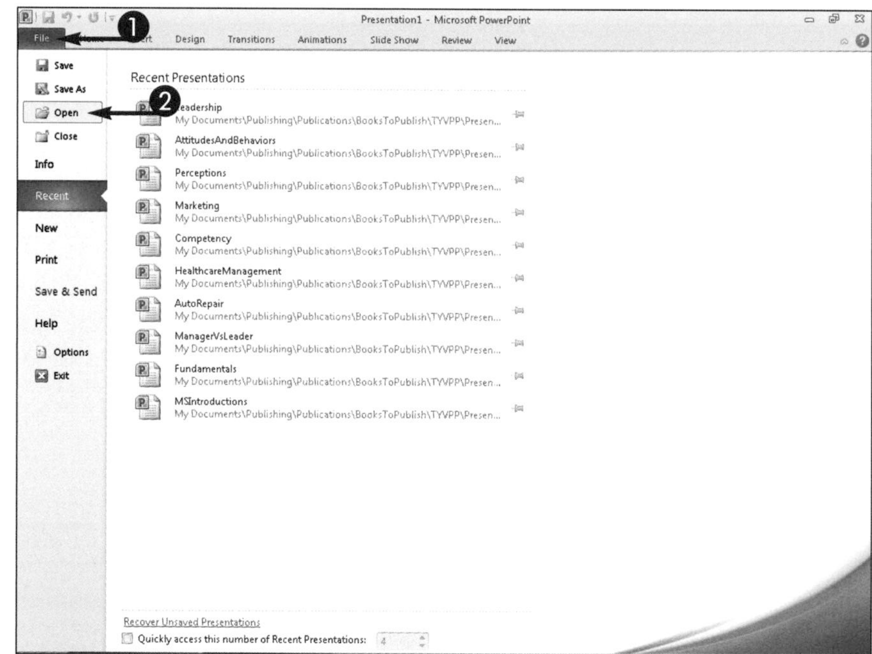

The Open dialog box appears.

❸ Click the parent folder that you think may hold the file, even if you think it is in a subfolder.

❹ Type all or part of the presentation filename in the Search Documents text box.

In this example Certi was typed.

As you type, the Open dialog box shows potentially matching files.

❺ After you finish typing the Search entry, click a matching file or shortcut icon.

❻ Click **Open**.

The file opens.

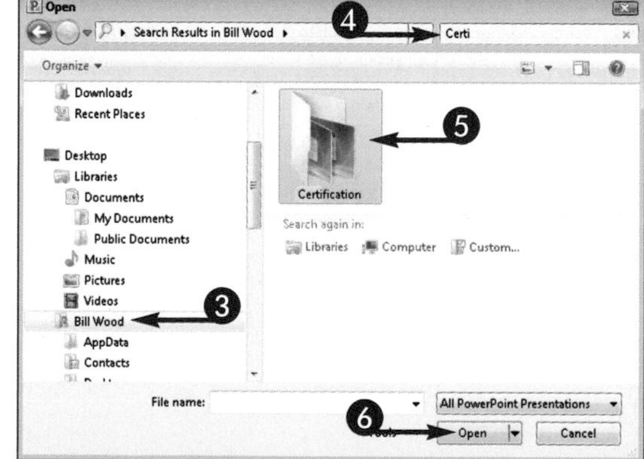

Use the Windows Start Menu

1. Click **Start** (![start button]).

Note: *These steps cover Windows 7 and Vista, not earlier Windows versions.*

2. Type all or part of the presentation filename in the Search text box.

   In this example, Certi was typed.

   Windows searches and lists files that match your search criteria.

3. Click the name of the file you want to open.

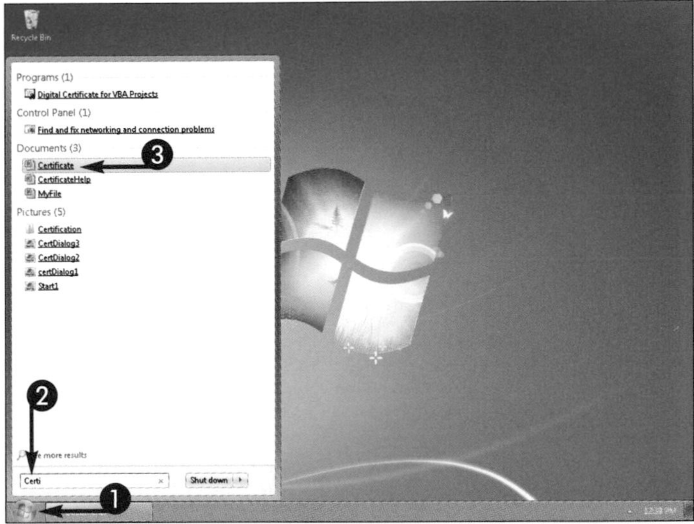

Windows launches PowerPoint, if needed, and opens the presentation file.

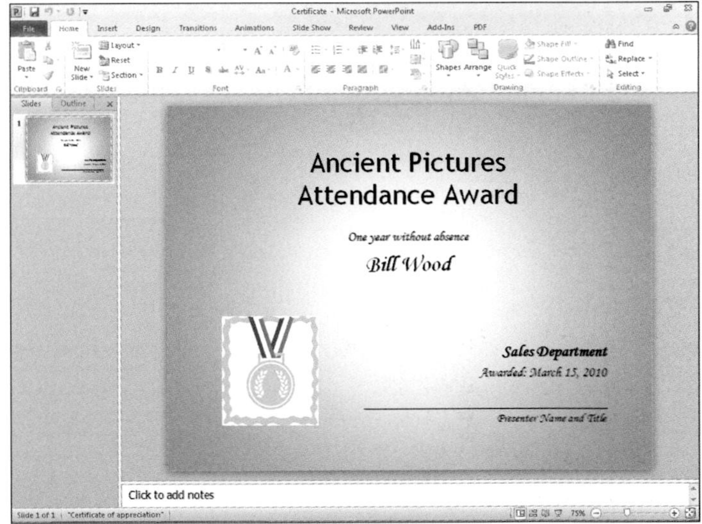

TIPS

I remember the file type of the presentation and the last date I saved it, but nothing else. Any tips on how to find it?

Start the search in the Open dialog box and type the file information you do have. The Search Documents text box becomes a drop-down list, giving you three choices under Add a search filter. Click **Authors**, **Type** (file type), or **Date modified** to search by that information.

While searching from the Start menu, is there a way to check the detailed properties of a file returned by a search without opening the file?

Yes. Right-click the file in the search results and click **Properties**. The Properties dialog box appears. In the Properties dialog box, you can view a variety of information about your file.

Writing and Formatting Presentation Text

Words form the basis of any presentation, so taking the time to format text can pay off in many ways. Nice formatting makes text easier to read and helps make your slides more attractive and polished.

Understanding Presentation Structure

You use PowerPoint to build a presentation slide by slide. Those slides, whether shown as a slide show or printed, make up your presentation. Different types of slides (*slide layouts*) serve different functions in your presentation. The slide layout controls which objects a slide contains and the placement of those objects on the slide. Learn more about layouts in Chapter 6.

Title Slide

The Title slide typically appears first and includes the presentation title or topic, and a subtitle. The subtitle might be the presenter's name or the name of the presenting company, or it might be the date and location of the presentation. There is usually just one title slide in a presentation.

Title and Content Slide

A Title and Content slide is perhaps the most frequently used slide layout. It includes a title plus a placeholder where you can add one of several types of content: a bulleted list, table, chart, clip art, picture, SmartArt graphic (diagram), or media clip (sound or video).

Other Slide Content

PowerPoint provides other slide layouts for your convenience: Two Content, Comparison, Content with Caption, Picture with Caption, and Blank. Each layout includes placeholders to position your information. Choose the layout that best presents your concepts and the associated data or graphics.

Organizational Slide

You may need to divide a presentation into logical sections. Section breaks allow your audience to ask questions or for the group to take a break. You can easily change the slide theme of each section. You can place a slide at the beginning of each section using the Section Header or Title Only layout.

Explore Text Formatting Options

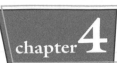

You can use various text formatting tools in PowerPoint to change the appearance of selected text. The Font and Paragraph groups on the Home tab of the Ribbon provide most of the tools you need, or you can make formatting changes in the Font or Paragraph dialog boxes.

Change the Font

When you type text on a slide, it is formatted with a font that is determined by the presentation theme you apply. The font (lettering type) gives a certain look and feel to your presentation, such as one that is formal or informal. You can change the font for selected text or for all text in a title or bulleted list.

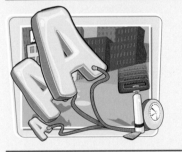

Resize Text

Properly sizing presentation text makes the text more readable and attractive. You can modify the text size to reflect the environment where you make the presentation. Smaller text may be readable for a presentation viewed on a kiosk, but larger text may be needed to ensure clarity in a lecture hall.

Change Text Color

You can use text color for both design and practical purposes. The slide text color should be attractive to the eye. Most important, the text color should provide good contrast against the background of your slides so your audience can easily read the text. You can also use color on text for emphasis.

Add Attributes

You can apply attributes such as bold, italic, shadow, emboss, and underline to slide text. Because attributes add emphasis, you should use them sparingly throughout your presentation; for example, to call the viewer's attention to an important word or phrase.

Add a Slide

When you open a new presentation, PowerPoint creates a blank title slide. To build your presentation, you can add as many slides as you like.

Determine the number of slides in your presentation based on how many topics you want to cover and the time you have available to cover them. Each slide should cover or detail a new topic.

Add a Slide

1. With a presentation open (either blank or existing), click the **Home** tab.
2. Click the **New Slide** button ▾.
3. Click the desired slide layout from the gallery.

A new blank slide with the specified layout appears.

***Note:** Clicking the top half of the New Slide button inserts a slide with the Title and Content layout (after the selected slide), or the same layout as the current slide.*

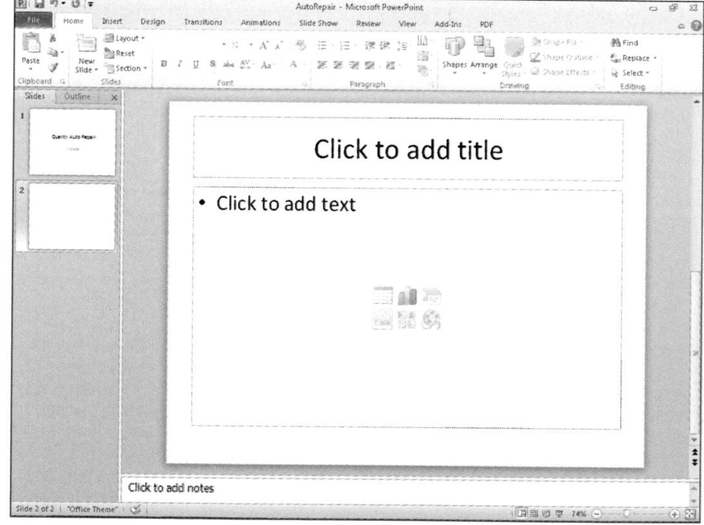

Delete a Slide in Normal View

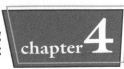

As you build your presentation, you may decide you do not need a particular slide. In this case, you can simply delete that slide.

It is common to use an existing presentation as the basis for other presentations. In that situation, you may need to delete several slides that are irrelevant or out of date.

Delete a Slide in Normal View

1. Click the **View** tab.
2. Click **Normal**.

Note: For more on Normal view, see Chapter 1.

3. Right-click the slide you want to delete.

   The submenu appears.

4. Click **Delete Slide**.

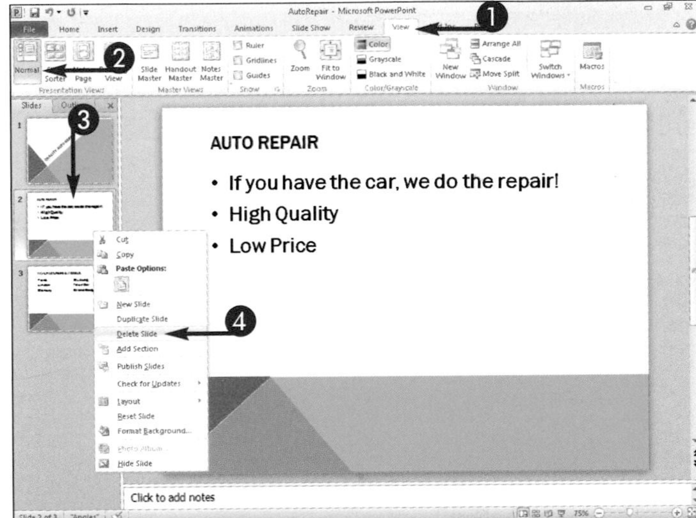

- PowerPoint deletes the slide.

Note: You can also click the slide, and then press Delete.

- Click **Undo** ( ) on the Quick Access Toolbar if you decide you need the slide and want it back in the presentation.

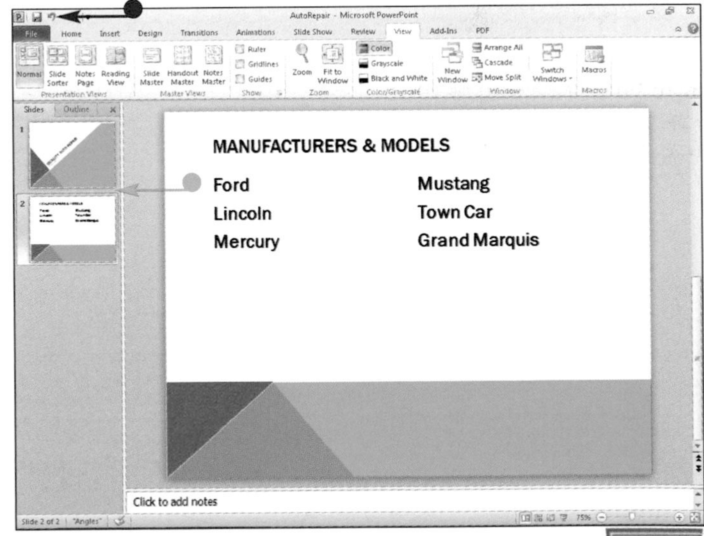

Navigate Slides

Often there will be many slides in your presentation. PowerPoint provides different ways to navigate the slides so that you can choose one that is most efficient for what you are doing. You can use the scroll bar buttons in Normal view, click to select a slide using the Slides tab of the Navigator, or click slide thumbnails in other views.

Navigate Slides

Navigate Using the Scroll Bar

1. Click and drag the scroll bar to scroll through slides.
2. Click **Next Slide** (⯯) to display the next slide.
3. Click **Previous Slide** (⯭) to display the previous slide.

Navigate Using the Slides Tab

1. Click the **Slides** tab.
2. Click and drag the scroll box on the scroll bar to scroll through the slides.
3. Click a slide thumbnail.

The selected slide appears in the Slide pane.

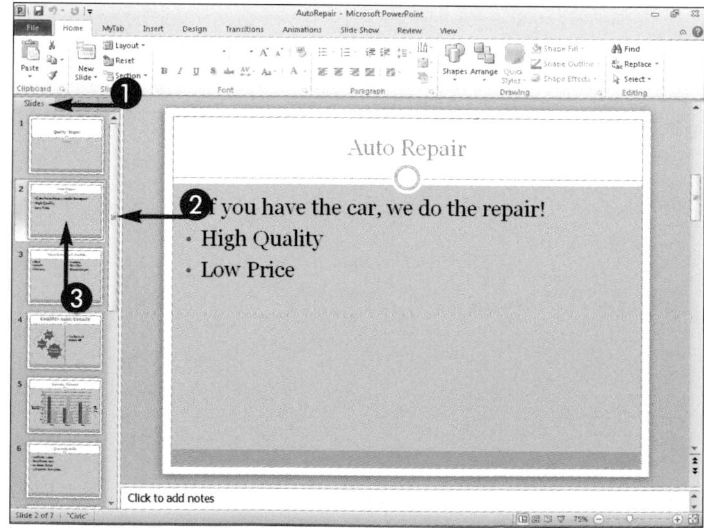

Navigate Using the Outline tab

1. Click the **Outline** tab.
2. Click and drag the scroll box on the scroll bar to scroll through the slides.
3. Click a slide icon.

   The selected slide appears in the Slide pane.

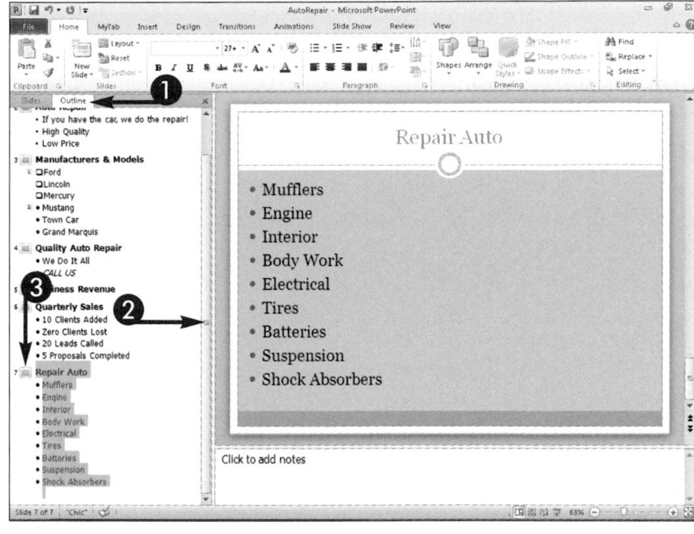

Navigate in the Slide Sorter View

1. Click the **View** tab.
2. Click **Slide Sorter**.

   The Slide Sorter view appears.
3. Click and drag the scroll box on the scroll bar to scroll through the slides.
4. Click a slide.

   The slide is selected.

***Note:** Double-click a slide to view it in Normal view.*

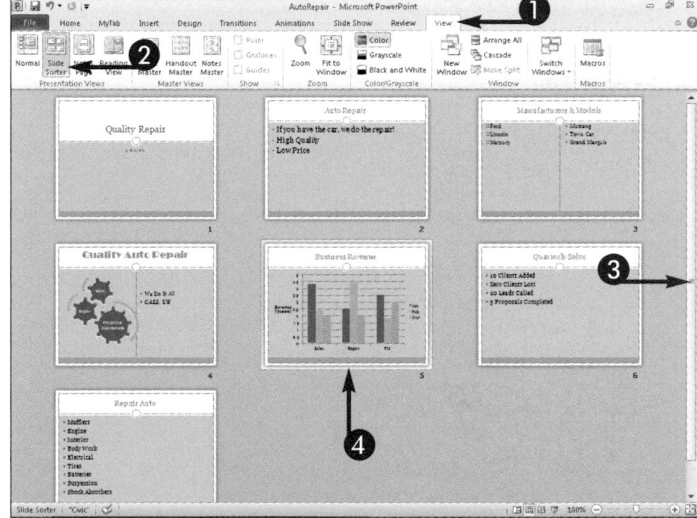

Why are there no scroll bars in the Slides or Outline tabs?

If PowerPoint can display the slides in your presentation without scrolling down or up, it does not display a scroll bar.

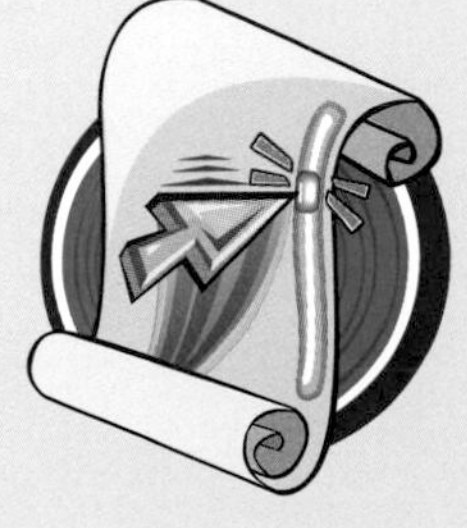

Is there a way to see more slides in Slide Sorter view so I can more easily find the one I want to view?

Yes. You can click and drag the **Zoom** slider or click the **Zoom Out** (−) or **Zoom In** (+) buttons at each end of the slider. Select a lower zoom percentage to display more slides at a time.

Type and Edit Text on a Slide

You can type text into a placeholder on a slide so you can convey information to the presentation audience through the written word. There are three types of placeholders that can hold text: title, content (bulleted list), and subtitle. You simply click the placeholder and then start typing. You also can go back and edit text you have already typed.

Type and Edit Text on a Slide

Enter Title or Subtitle Text

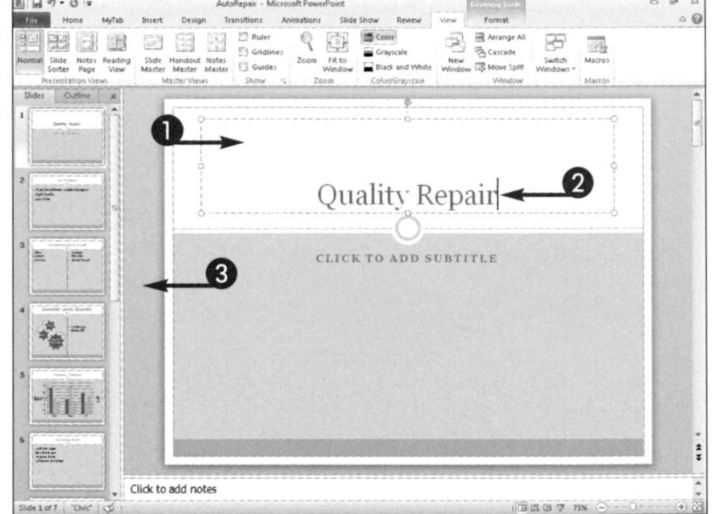

1. With a PowerPoint presentation open in Normal view, click any title or subtitle placeholder.

   The insertion point appears in the placeholder.

2. Type your text.

   In this example, Quality Repair was typed.

3. Click outside the placeholder.

   The text is added.

Enter Bulleted Text

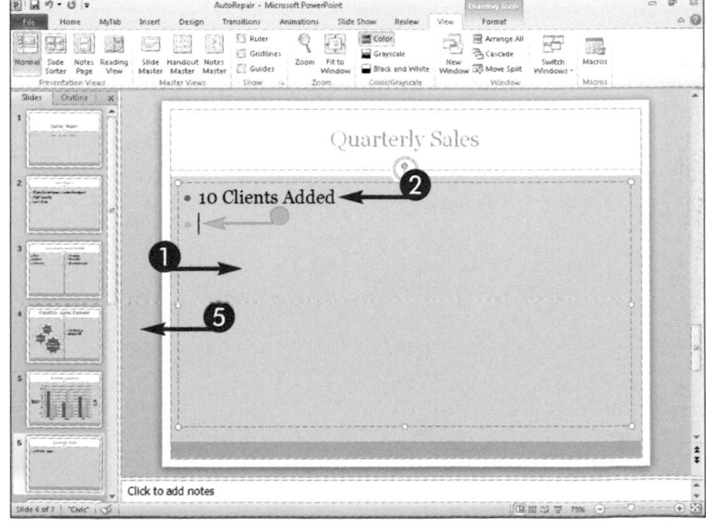

1. Click a content placeholder.
2. Type your text.
3. Press Enter.

- The insertion point moves to the next line.

4. Repeat Steps **2** and **3** for all bullet points for that slide.
5. Click outside the placeholder.

   The text is added.

Edit Text

1. Click anywhere within a title, subtitle, or text placeholder.
2. Click the existing text where you want to change it.

   The insertion point appears where you clicked. Press Backspace to delete text to the left, or press Delete to delete text to the right of the insertion point.
3. Press Backspace.

   In this example, 0 was deleted.

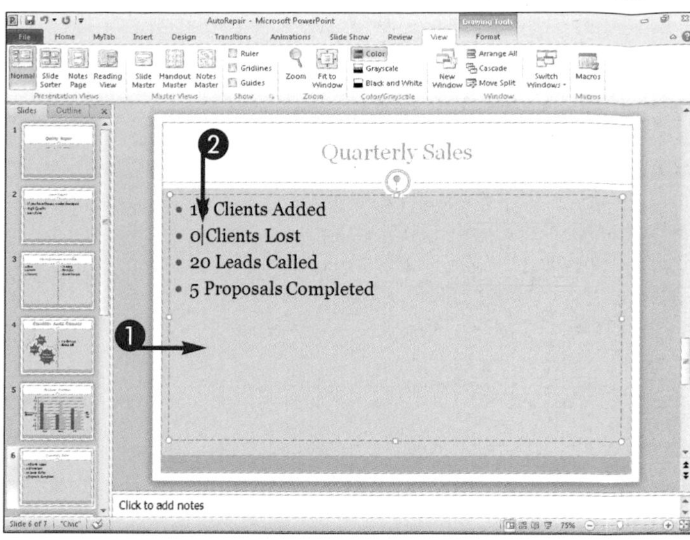

4. Type any text you want to add.

   In this example, Zero was typed.
5. Click and drag over one or more words.
6. Press Delete.

   PowerPoint deletes the selected text.

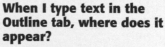

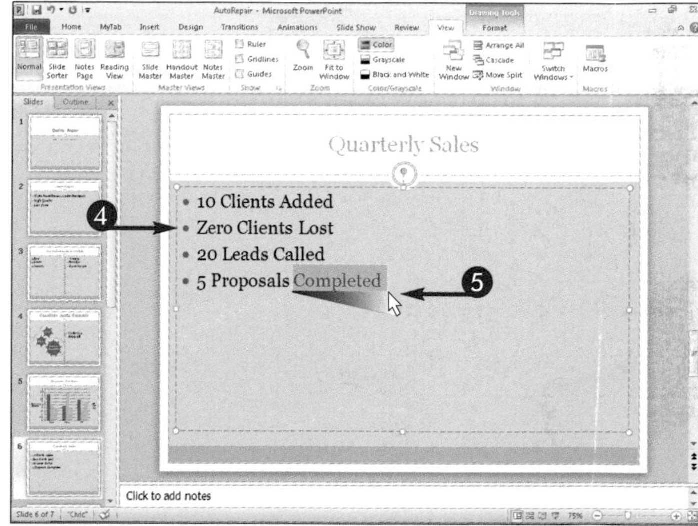

Why does my placeholder say "Click to add text"? Will this appear if I print or run my presentation?

That is simply an instruction to let you know that this placeholder currently has no text entered in it. The words and the placeholder neither print nor appear when you present the slide show.

When I type text in the Outline tab, where does it appear?

Text that you type in the Outline tab appears on the currently displayed slide. The top-level heading in a slide corresponds to the title placeholder on the slide. Second-level entries become the bullet items in the text placeholder.

Format Text Color and Style

Color adds flair to any presentation. You can use text color to make your text more readable and more attractive. You can select colors from a standard palette or work with custom colors. You can use text styles such as bold or shadow to add emphasis.

Format Text Color and Style

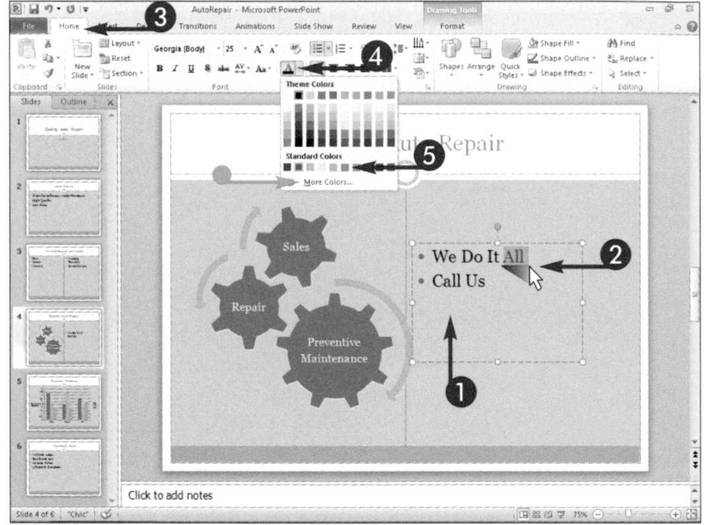

1. Click a placeholder to select it.
2. Click and drag over one or more words.
3. Click the **Home** tab.
4. Click ▾ on the **Font Color** button (A ▾).

   A color palette appears.
5. Select a color from the palette.

- For a custom color, click **More Colors**.

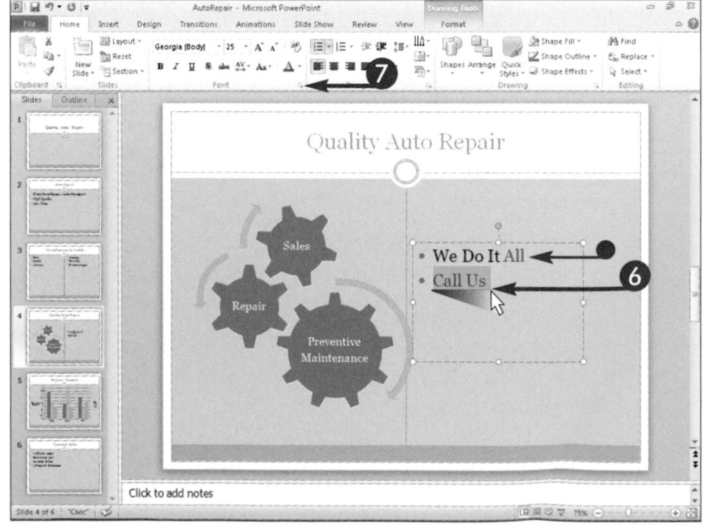

- The text you selected changes to the color you selected.

6. Click and drag over one or more other words.
7. Click the **Dialog Box Launcher** (⧉) on the **Font** group.

The Font dialog box appears.

8. Click the **Font style** ▼.
9. Click a style from the list.

   In this example, Bold Italic was clicked.

10. Click an effect to apply to your text (☐ changes to ☑).

    In this example, All Caps was clicked.

11. Click **OK**.

- The text is changed to the style that you selected.

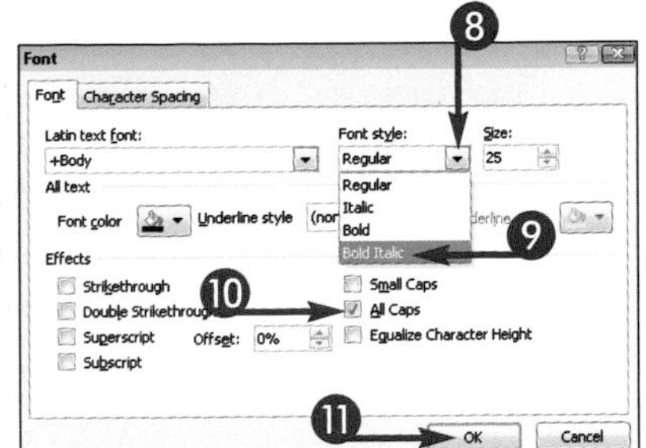

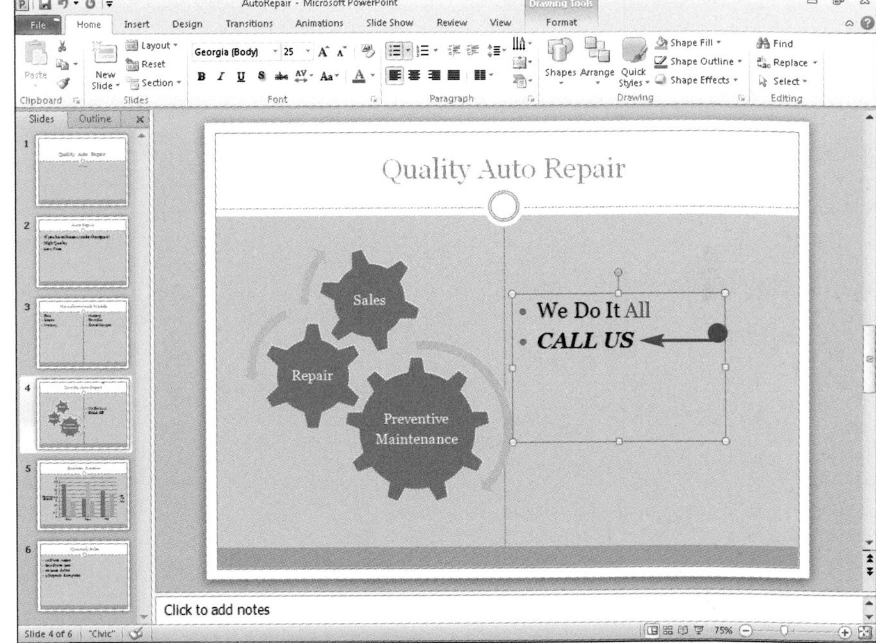

TIPS

What is the difference between applying formats with the Home tab buttons or the Font dialog box?

The Font dialog box enables you to apply several formats at one time from a central location. There are also some specialized attributes in the Font dialog box, such as superscript and subscript, which you do not see in the Font group on the Home tab.

What are superscript and subscript?

These formats either raise (superscript) or lower (subscript) the selected text a set distance from the regular text. Superscript and subscript are often used for footnote or scientific notation, such as 4^2 representing 4 to the second power, or f_x to represent a function of x.

Format Text Font and Size

The font you choose for text portrays a certain look or feel. Some fonts are playful; others more formal. Fonts are divided into four main types: serif, with cross strokes on the letter ends; sans serif, with no cross strokes; script, which looks handwritten; and decorative. Font size is important because your audience should be able to read all the text in your presentation.

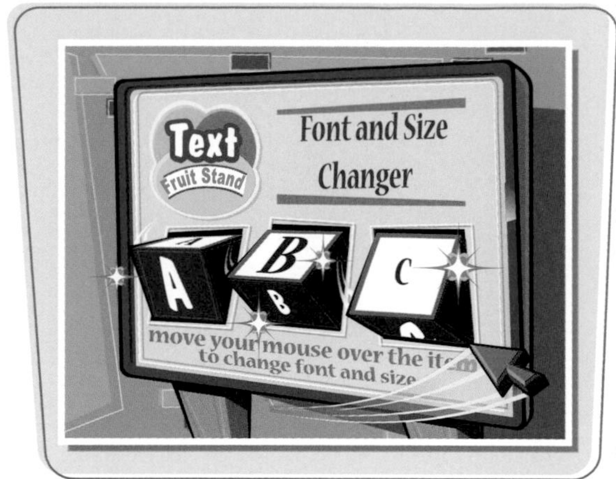

Format Text Font and Size

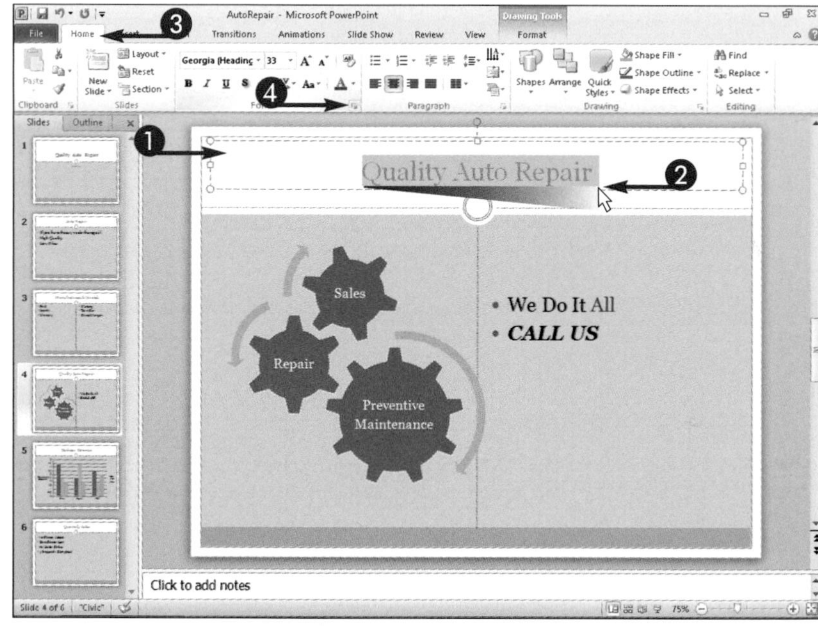

1. Click a placeholder to select it.
2. Click and drag over one or more words.
3. Click the **Home** tab.
4. Click the **Font** group ⧉.

The Font dialog box appears.

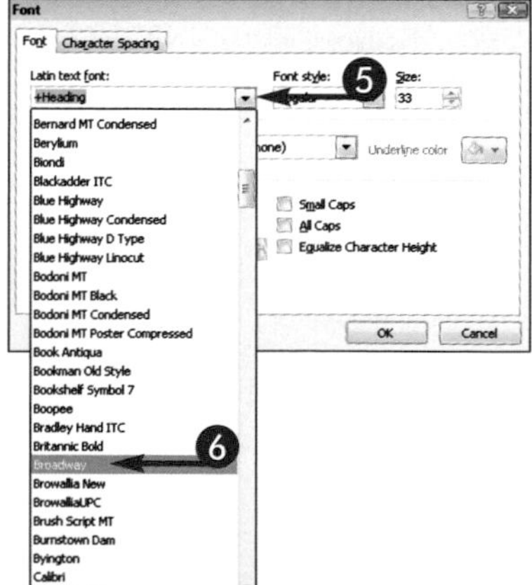

5. Click the **Latin text font** ▾.
6. Click the desired font.

In this example, Broadway was clicked.

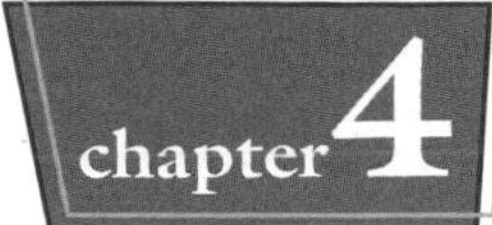

7. Double-click the number in the Size text box and type a new font size.

   In this example, 44 was typed.

- You can also click the spinner beside the Size text box to increase or decrease the font size.

8. Click **OK**.

- PowerPoint applies the new formatting to the text.

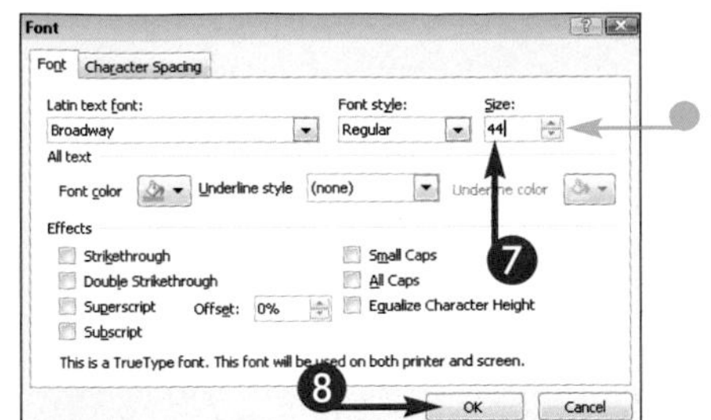

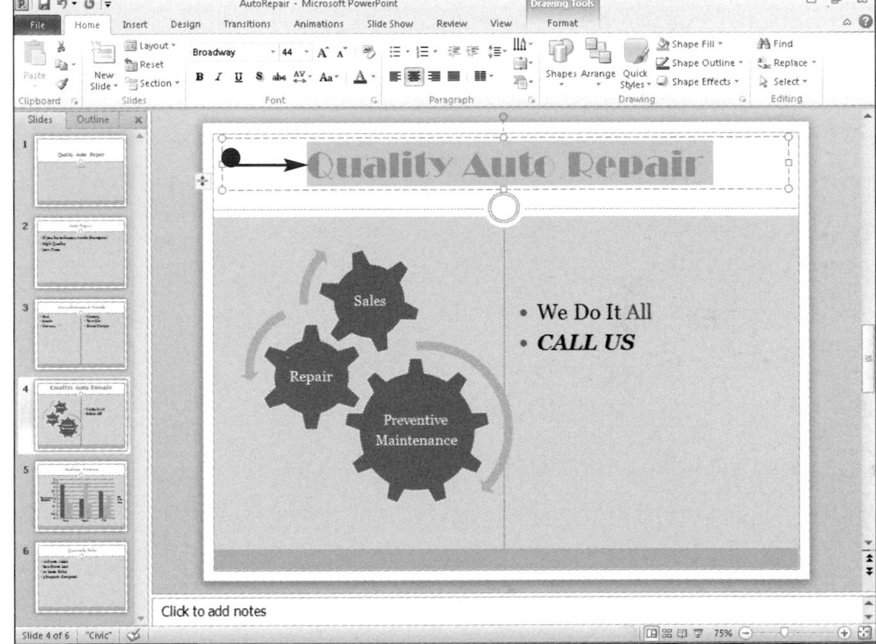

On the Home tab, in the font drop-down list in the Font group, why are TT symbols next to the fonts in the font list?

TT stands for TrueType. This is a WYSIWYG (What You See Is What You Get) font technology. This means that the font you see on the screen accurately reflects the appearance of your font on a printed page.

Are there limitations on how large or small text can be?

You can type whatever font size you like, with the lower limit being 1 and no practical upper limit. But remember to keep the text readable for the viewer. A very small text size is almost always difficult to see and read; a huge text size may make text merely a design element.

Cut, Copy, and Paste Text

When you edit your presentation, you can move text from one slide to another by using the Cut, Copy, and Paste features. Cut removes text from its original location. Copy duplicates the text, leaving the original in place. Paste places either cut or copied text into another location. You can also copy, cut, and paste objects like placeholders.

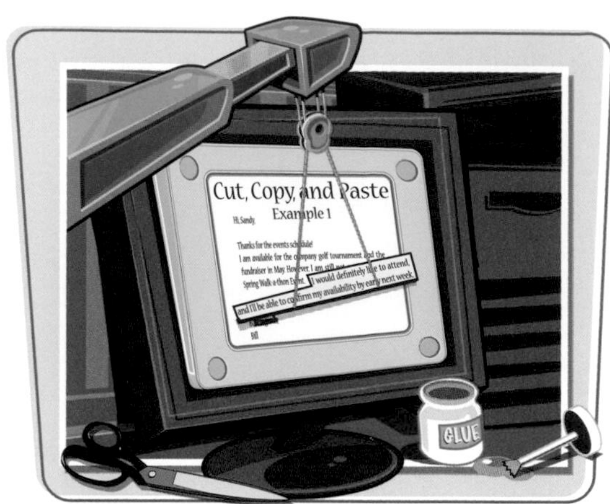

Cut, Copy, and Paste Text

Cut and Copy Text

1. Click the **Home** tab.
2. Click [icon] on the **Clipboard** group.

   The Clipboard task pane appears.
3. Click a text placeholder to select it.
4. Click and drag to select text.

   In this case, Auto was selected.
5. Click the **Cut** button ([icon]).

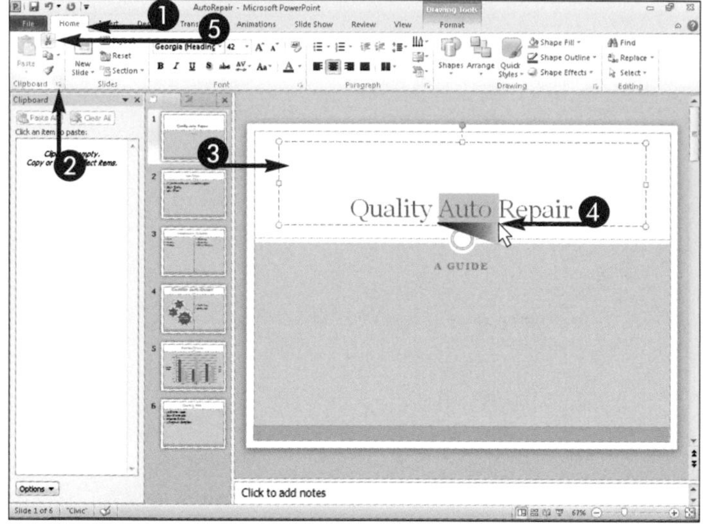

- The selected text is removed and placed on the Windows Clipboard.

6. Click and drag to select different text.

   In this case, Repair was selected.
7. Click the **Copy** button([icon]).

- The selected text is copied to the Clipboard.

Note: *If you do not open the Clipboard, it will hold only your most recent copy or cut text.*

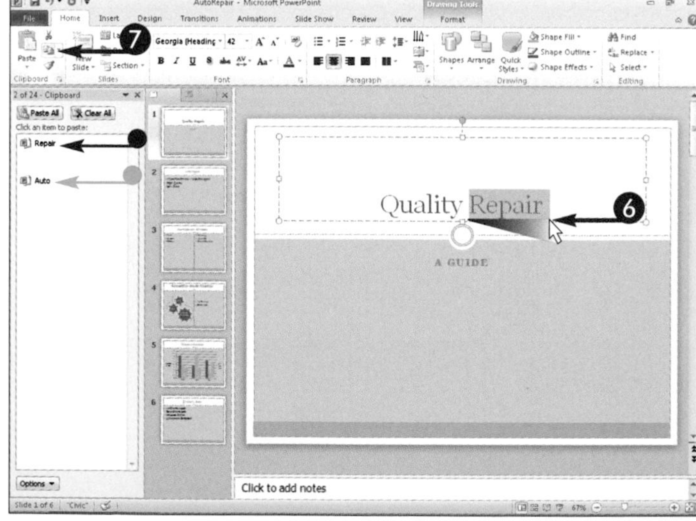

Paste Text

1. Select the slide where you want to paste the text.

Note: *See the section "Navigate Slides" to locate the destination slide.*

2. Click the destination placeholder.

   If the placeholder contains text, click within the text to position the insertion point where you want to paste the text.

- The insertion point appears in the placeholder.

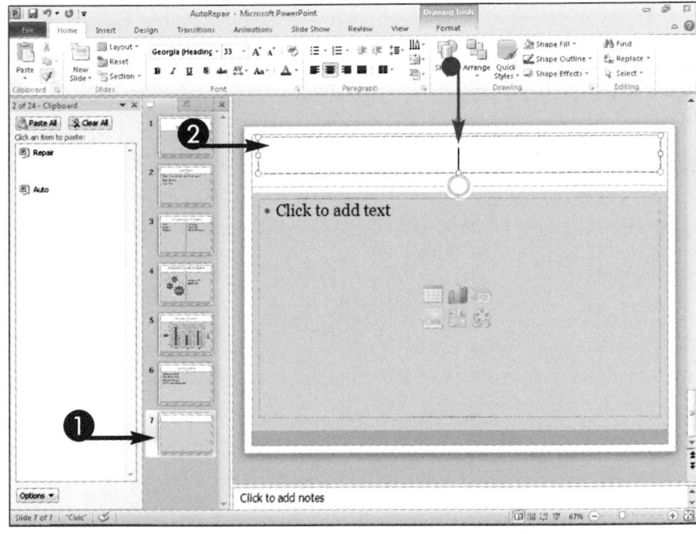

3. Click the **Home** tab, if needed.
4. To paste the most recently copied text, click **Paste**.

- The most recently cut or copied text, in this case Repair, is pasted into the placeholder.

5. To paste any other previously copied text, click it in the Clipboard.

   In this example, Auto was clicked.

- The cut or copied text is pasted into the placeholder.

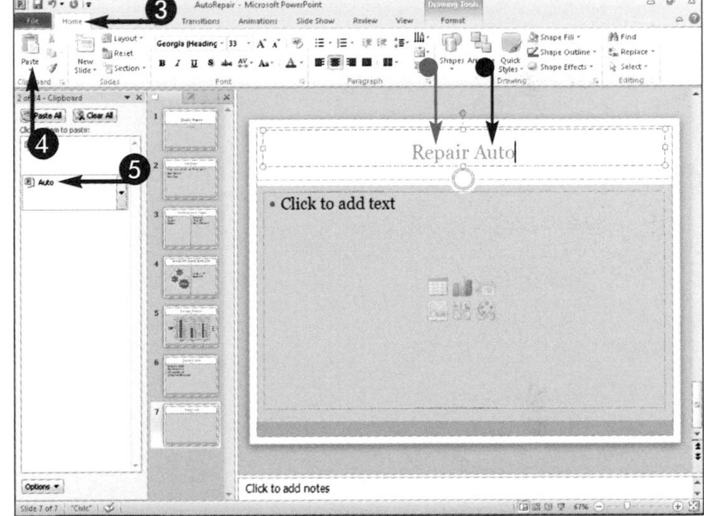

Can I easily paste copied text into several slides?

Yes. After you copy the text, but before you perform a different operation, you can paste as many times as you want by clicking **Paste** or pressing Ctrl + V. After you perform a different operation, you must click an item from the Clipboard to paste it.

Can I retrieve cut text if I change my mind?

Yes. You can click the **Undo** icon (↶) on the Quick Access Toolbar to undo the cut. If you performed more actions than your Undo feature is set to hold, it is lost and you must retype it.

Format Bulleted Lists

Bulleted lists are the heart of any presentation. Bulleted lists summarize key points the presenter wants to make. You can format bulleted lists with different styles of bullets. In a presentation for a gardening business, for example, you can format bullets as a flower or tree. You can use check marks as bullets in a list of points for a project.

Format Bulleted Lists

Apply a Standard Bullet Style

1. Click a placeholder containing a bulleted list.

Note: *If you place the insertion point within the text, PowerPoint changes the bullet for that line only. To change all bullets, click the placeholder border to select the entire placeholder.*

2. Click the **Home** tab.
3. Click ▾ on the **Bullets** button (☰▾).
4. Click a bullet style from the gallery.

- Click **Bullets and Numbering** for more options.

- The bullets change to the new style.

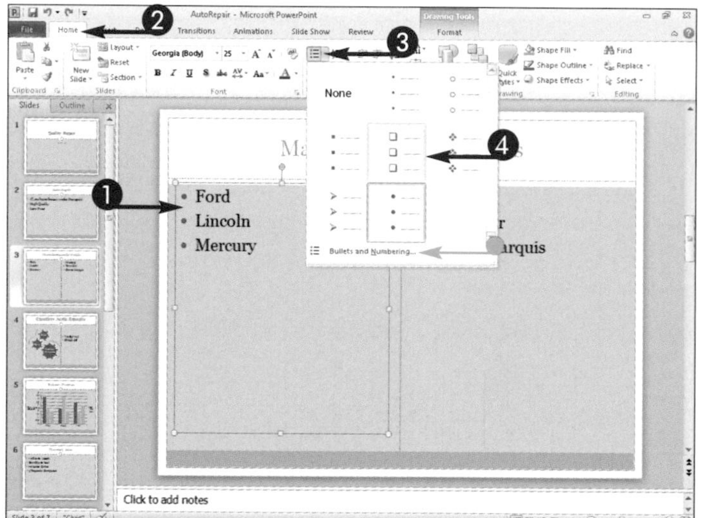

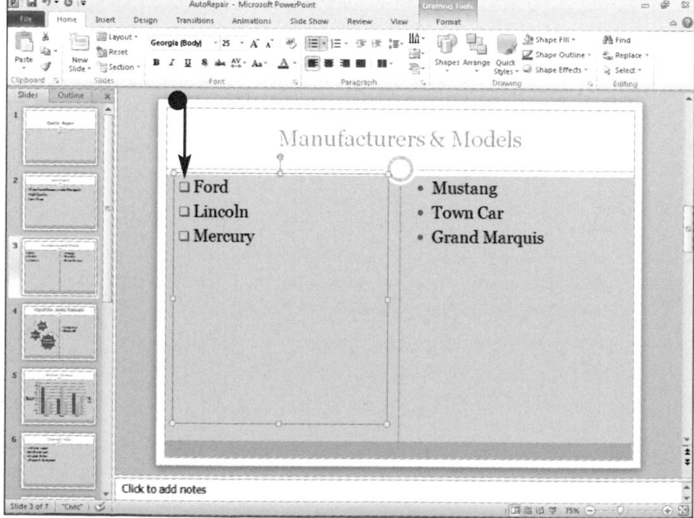

Apply a Custom Bullet Style

1. Click a placeholder containing a bulleted list.
2. Click the **Home** tab.
3. Click the **Bullets** button ▾.
4. Click **Bullets and Numbering** at the bottom of the gallery.

   The Bullets and Numbering dialog box appears.
5. Click **Customize**.

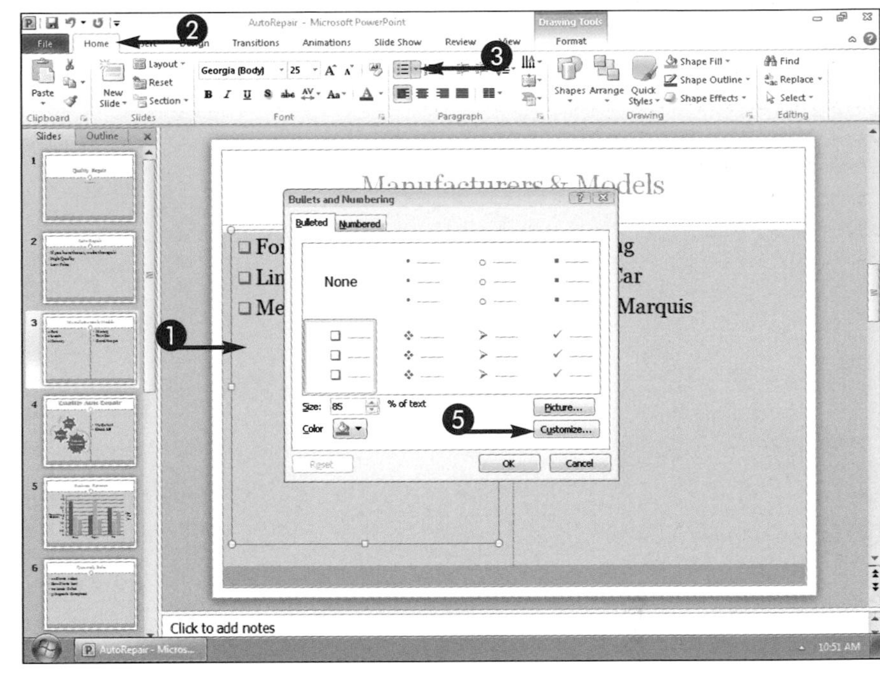

The Symbol dialog box appears.

6. Click the **Font** ▾ and select a font from the drop-down list.
7. Click the symbol you want to use as bullets.
8. Click **OK** to close the Symbol dialog box.
9. Click **OK** to close the Bullets and Numbering dialog box.

   The new bullet style appears in the list in the placeholder.

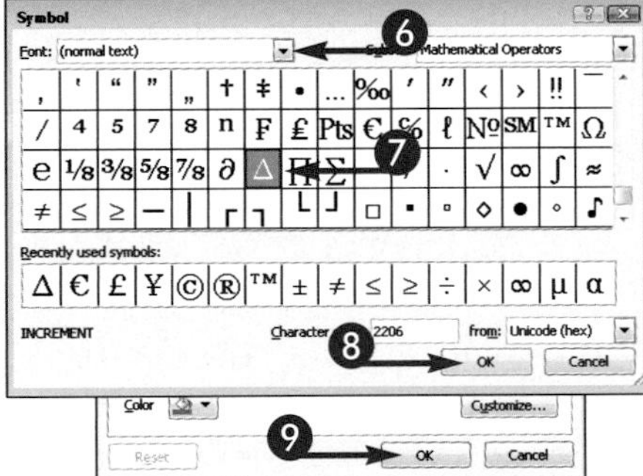

TIPS

How can I make the bullets larger?

The Bullets and Numbering dialog box includes a Size setting. This setting is expressed in percentage of the text size. If you increase the text size, the bullet size increases proportionally. Double-click in the **Size** text box and type the size you want, and then click **OK** to apply the sizing.

Can I apply a new bullet style to every bullet in the presentation without having to change it on each and every slide?

Yes. You can use the Master Slide feature to make formatting changes that apply to every slide in the presentation. Chapter 8 covers master slides in detail.

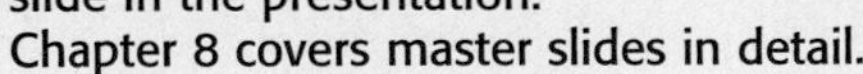

Using the Spelling Feature

You should check the contents of your presentation for spelling accuracy. Not all of us are spelling bee winners. Luckily, PowerPoint offers a spelling check feature to make spelling accuracy simple. You can check the spelling of all words throughout the presentation so it is as professional as possible.

Using the Spelling Feature

❶ Click the **Review** tab.

❷ Click **Spelling**.

Note: *You can also press* F7 *to start the spelling check.*

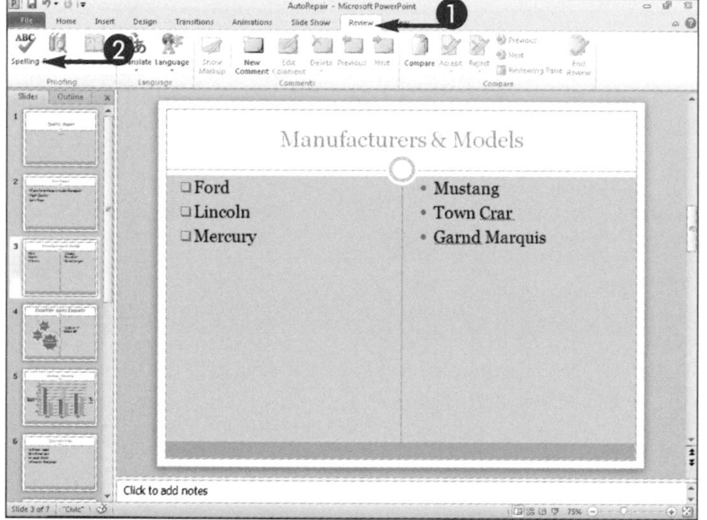

- The Spelling dialog box appears, displaying the first questionable word and suggested spellings.

❸ Click an option to perform a task.

- Click **Ignore** to leave the spelling as is.
- Click **Ignore All** to leave all instances of this spelling as they are.
- Click a suggestion from the Suggestions list, or type the correct spelling in the Change to text box.
- Click **Change** to replace the misspelling.
- Click **Change All** to replace all instances of the misspelled word.

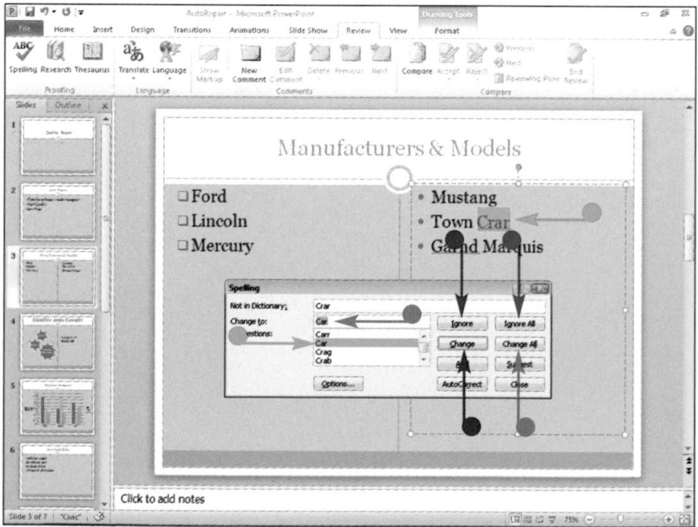

- The spelling check proceeds to the next questionable word.

4. Repeat Step **3** until the spell check is complete.

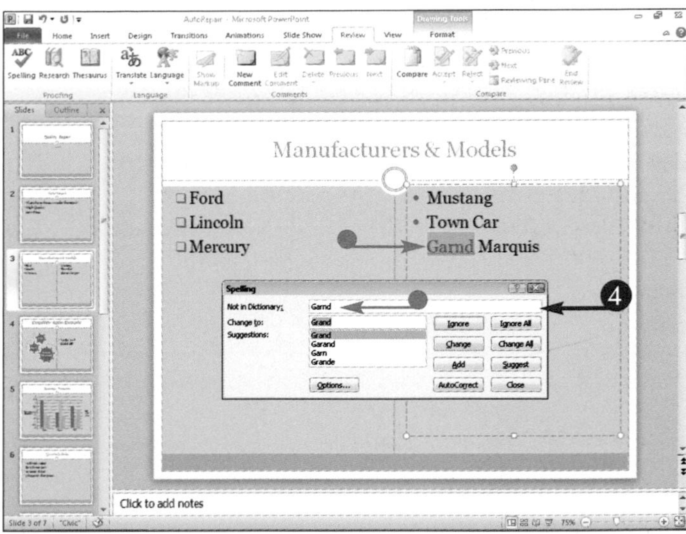

A dialog box appears notifying you when the spelling check is complete.

5. Click **OK**.

   The Spelling dialog box closes.

Note: *If PowerPoint options are set to check spelling as you type, red wavy lines may appear under possibly misspelled words as you type. You can right-click the word and then click an option in the shortcut menu that appears.*

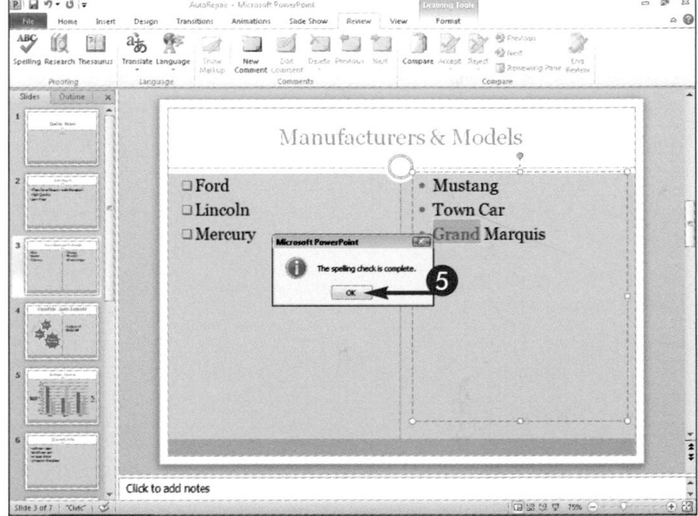

Is it possible to check spelling for just one specific word?

Yes. Select the word before running the spelling check. The spelling check starts with the word you select. After taking the appropriate action, simply click the **Close** button (☒) in the Spelling dialog box.

Is there a way to get PowerPoint to stop flagging a particular word as misspelled?

In the Spelling dialog box, click **Add**. This adds the word to your custom dictionary, so it recognizes it as a legitimate spelling in the future. Your custom dictionary affects all Microsoft programs though, so the word you add will be viewed as a legitimate spelling in all Microsoft programs.

Using the Research Feature

As you type text in a presentation, you may need to check definitions or facts. If your computer has an Internet connection, you can use the Research feature to search reference books and research sites for relevant information on your topic.

Using the Research Feature

1. Click the **Review** tab.
2. Click and drag across the text you want to research.
3. Click **Research**.

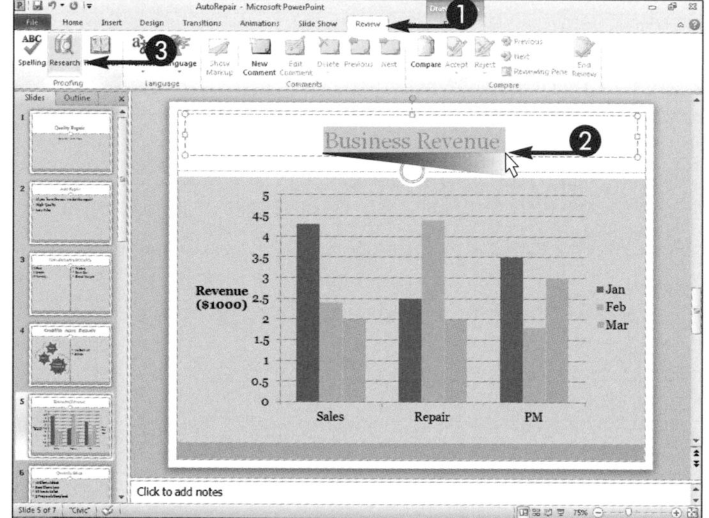

The Research task pane appears with the selected text in the Search for text box.

4. Click the **Search** button (▣ changes to ▣).

   You can click ▣ to cancel the search.

- The search results appear.
- If you want to change the search topic, type it in the Search for text box and click ▣.

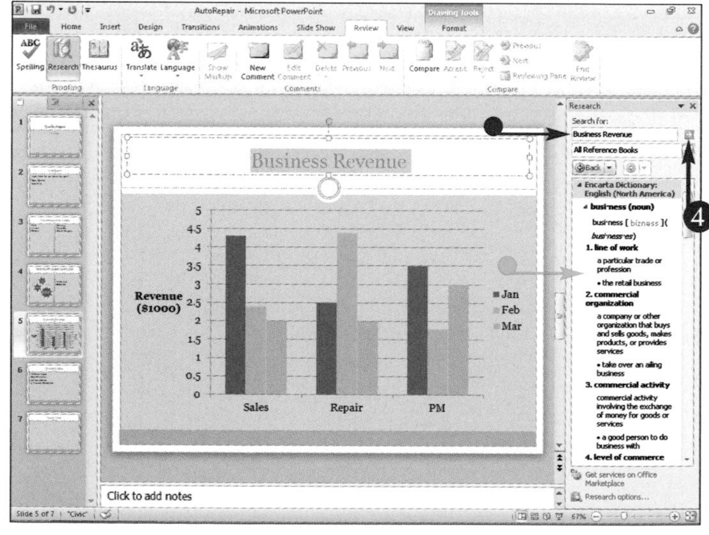

5 Click the **Search for** ▾ to change where the Research feature looks for information.

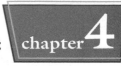

6 Click to select a research site from the drop-down list.

In this example, Bing was clicked.

PowerPoint changes the search results reflecting your change.

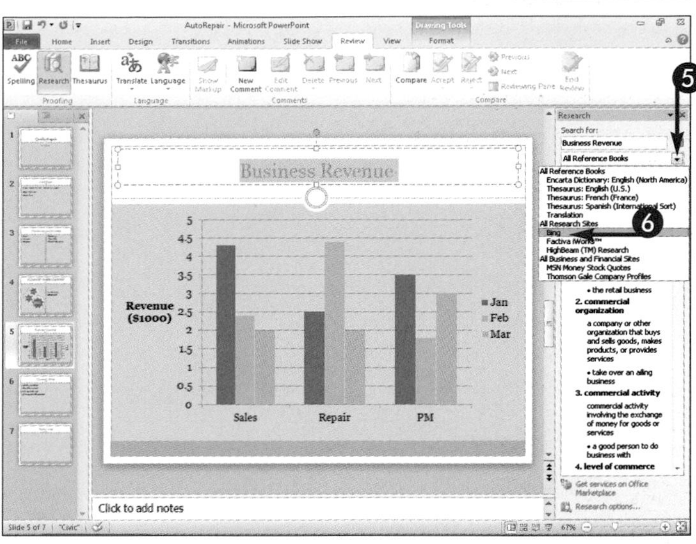

- Click ▷ to expand a listing (▷ changes to ◢).
- Click ◢ to collapse a listing (◢ changes to ▷).
- Click **Next** to see the next listings.

7 Click a link.

Additional information appears or a Web site opens, depending on the type of link.

8 Click ☒ to close the Research feature.

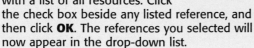

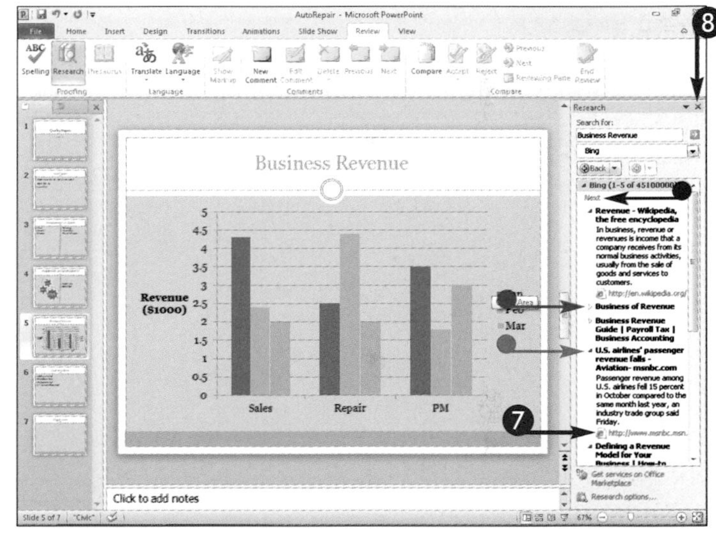

Can I specify which research sites PowerPoint will check?

Yes. With the Research task pane displayed, click the **Research options** link at the bottom. A dialog box appears with a list of all resources. Click the check box beside any listed reference, and then click **OK**. The references you selected will now appear in the drop-down list.

I followed a link but what was there was of no interest. Is there a way to go back to the original item that was displayed?

Yes. Click the button for the presentation file on the Windows task bar to switch from your browser back to PowerPoint, where you can choose another topic in the Research task pane. Working within PowerPoint, you also can click the **Back** button (Back ▾) in the Research task pane.

CHAPTER 5

Working with Outlines

The Outline tab provides the easiest and most convenient place to enter presentation text. The Outline tab helps you organize your thoughts into a simple outline hierarchy so that you can focus on idea flow in your presentation. It is a great place to make changes to text, too.

Hide and Redisplay the Outline Tab

The Outline tab appears next to the Slides tab in the left pane of Normal view. You can use the Outline tab to build a text outline, which automatically adds slides to your presentation. When you finish working with text, you can close the pane to work on the slide design. You can later redisplay Normal view, which shows the pane with the Outline tab again.

Hide and Redisplay the Outline Tab

Hide the Outline Tab

1. Click the **Close** button (☒) on the pane with the Outline tab.

   PowerPoint hides the pane with the Outline tab.

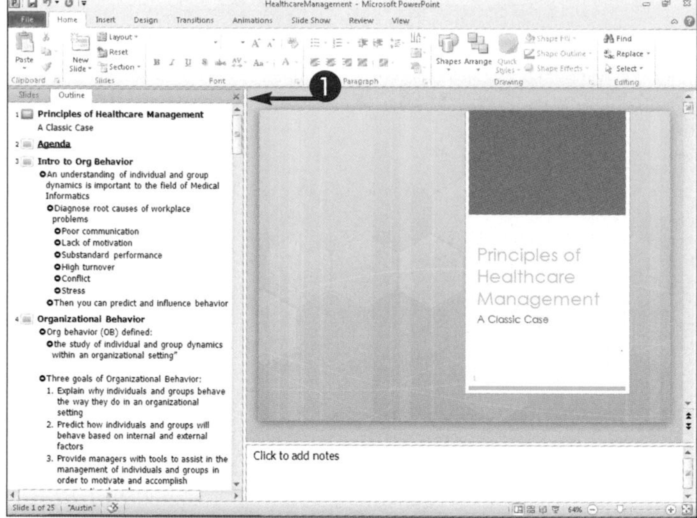

Redisplay the Outline Tab

1. Click the **View** tab on the Ribbon.
2. Click **Normal**.

   The pane with the Outline tab appears.

3. Click the **Outline** tab in the pane.

   The Outline tab appears.

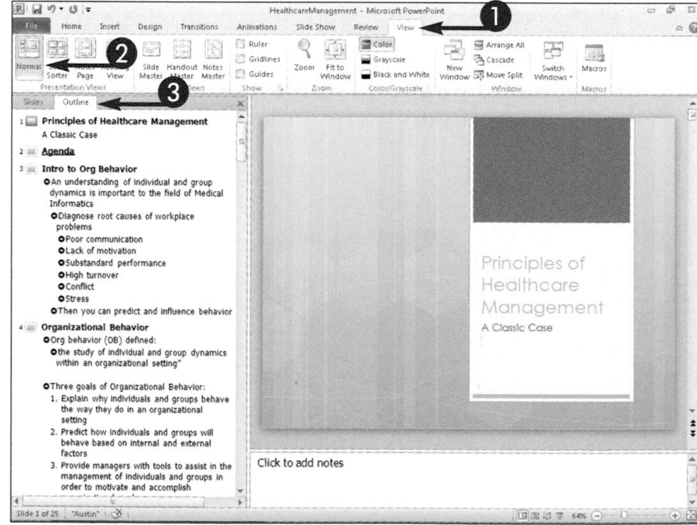

Understanding How Outline and Slide Content Relate

You can enter presentation text in the Outline tab or directly on a slide in the Slide pane in Normal view. You can work more effectively when you understand how the contents of the outline and each slide placeholder relate.

One Heading, One Slide

Every top-level heading (a heading at level one in the outline) is the title of a slide. When you type text in a title placeholder on a slide, it appears as a level one heading in the outline. When you type a level one heading in the outline, it appears in the title placeholder on the slide.

Bullet to Bullet

The second level of headings in an outline becomes the bullets in the content placeholder on the corresponding slide. If you have more than one level of bullets in the outline, there will be multiple levels of bullets on the slide, and vice versa.

Where Graphics Live

Graphics never appear in the outline. You place graphics on slides and you see them in the Slide pane. You can insert graphics either in a content placeholder, in a header or footer, or in any available location on the slide.

Special Text

Special text elements include headers, footers, text boxes, and in some cases, WordArt. As for graphics, some have text elements. Graphics text elements that appear on a slide or a master do not appear as part of the outline.

Enter Presentation Content in an Outline

Build the text for a new presentation in moments on the Outline tab. Type text using keyboard shortcuts to demote (move to a lower level) and promote (move to a higher level) headings. The first slide entered automatically becomes the presentation's Title slide. Additional slides use another slide layout automatically, although you can change the layout later.

Enter Presentation Content in an Outline

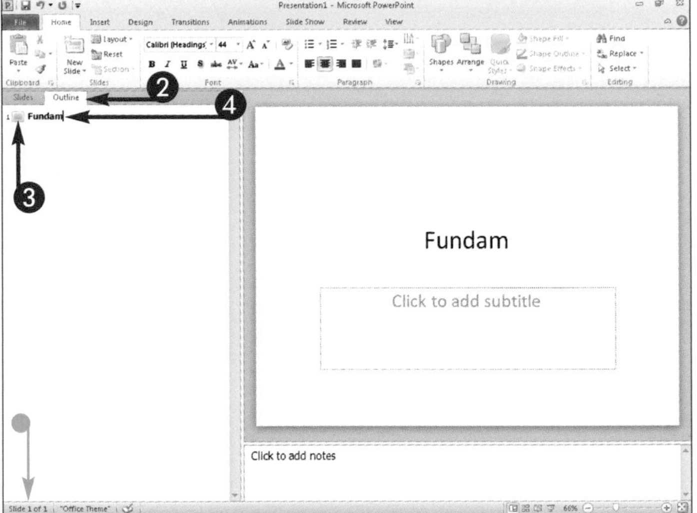

1. Open a new, blank presentation file.

   The blank presentation appears in Normal view.

- Note Slide 1 of 1.

2. Click the **Outline** tab.
3. Click beside the first slide icon.
4. Type a line of text — the text appears on the slide as you type.

   In this example, the user has started to type Fundamentals.

5. Press Enter.

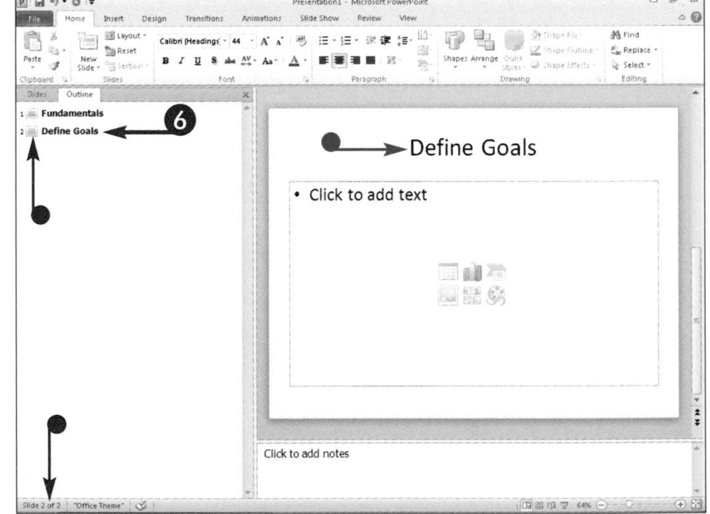

- A second blank slide and slide icon appear. Note Slide 2 of 2.

6. Type a second line of text — the text appears on the slide as you type.

   In this example, Define Goals was typed.

- The text becomes the title of the second slide.

7. Press Enter.
8. Press Tab.

- The insertion point moves to the next line and right, becoming the first bullet on the second slide.

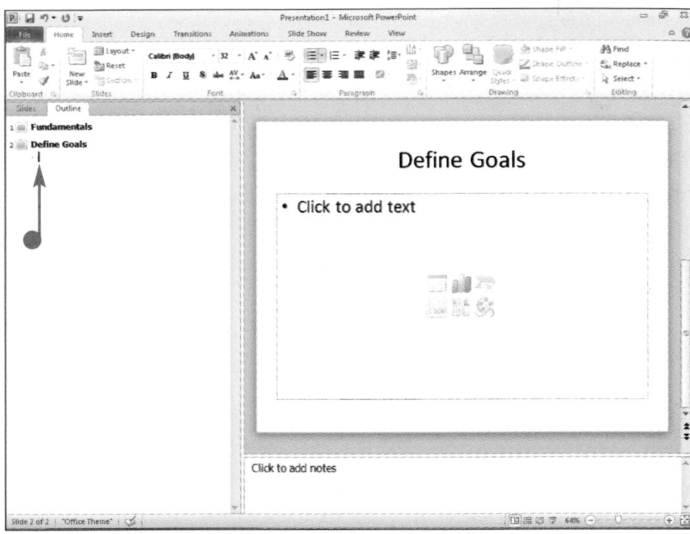

9. Type text for the first bullet item.

   In this example, Convey Ideas was typed.

10. Press Enter.

    The insertion point moves to the next line.

11. Repeat Steps **9** and **10** to add bullet items as needed.
12. To start a new slide, press Shift + Tab.

- The insertion point moves left to become the title for the new slide.

  You can continue adding slides and bulleted lists using Tab and Shift + Tab to create bulleted lists and new slides as needed.

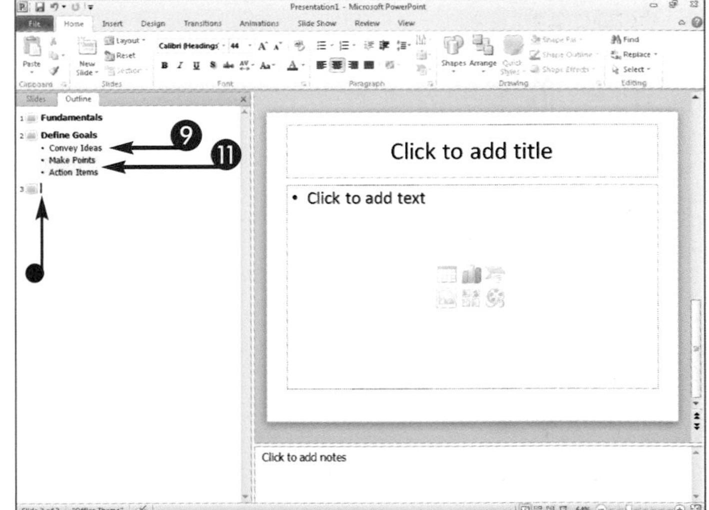

Is there a way to enlarge the Outline tab to view my outline text?

Yes. Simply click the mouse pointer (↖) over the splitter bar at the right edge of the pane and drag the bar to the right. To reduce the size of the left pane again, drag to the left. If you drag too far, the pane disappears. To get it back, click the **View** tab and then click **Normal** on the Ribbon.

Can I print just the presentation outline?

Yes. Doing so can be handy if you want to proofread the presentation text alone or use the outline while delivering the presentation. See Chapter 14 to learn how to print the outline. No graphics or text box contents appear in the printed outline. You can copy and paste an outline into Word to save it as a text document.

Move Slides in an Outline

As with the content of other types of documents, presentation content evolves. You may review your presentation and decide on a more logical flow for the information. When that happens, you can rearrange the slides and other elements in your presentation by dragging and dropping them in the Outline tab.

Move Slides in an Outline

1. Click the **Outline** tab.
2. In the Outline tab, click the **Slide** icon ( ) for the slide you want to move.

- The and all the slide text are selected in the Outline tab.

3. Click and drag the up or down until the horizontal line representing its outline position reaches the desired position.

Note: *You can also move, cut, copy, and paste text in the Outline tab.*

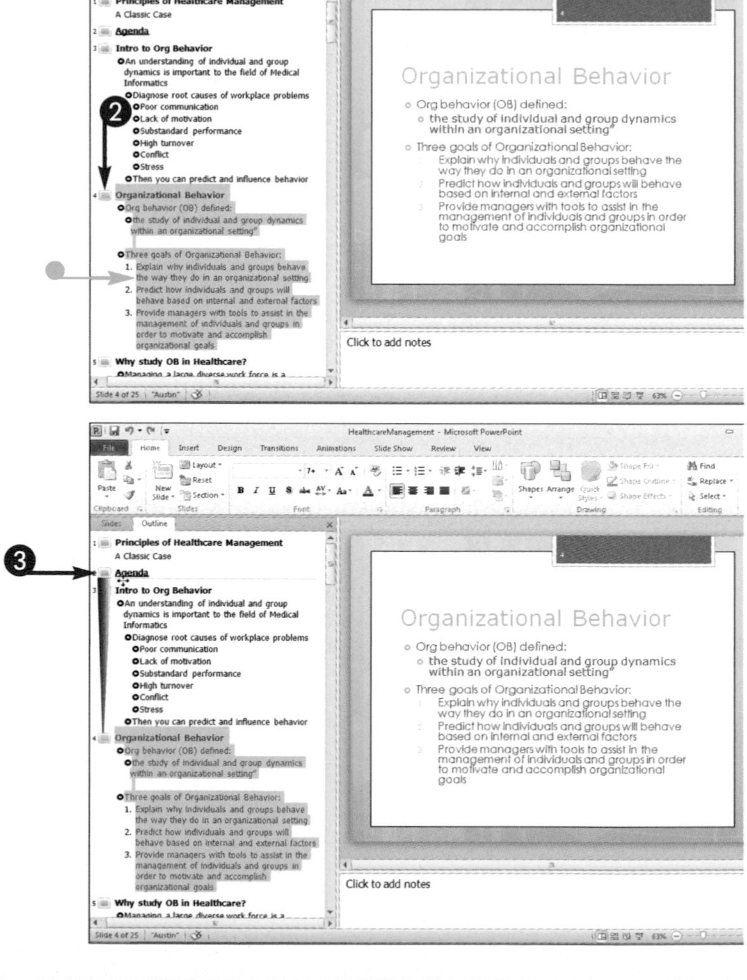

- When you release the mouse button, the slide contents moves to where you dragged it.

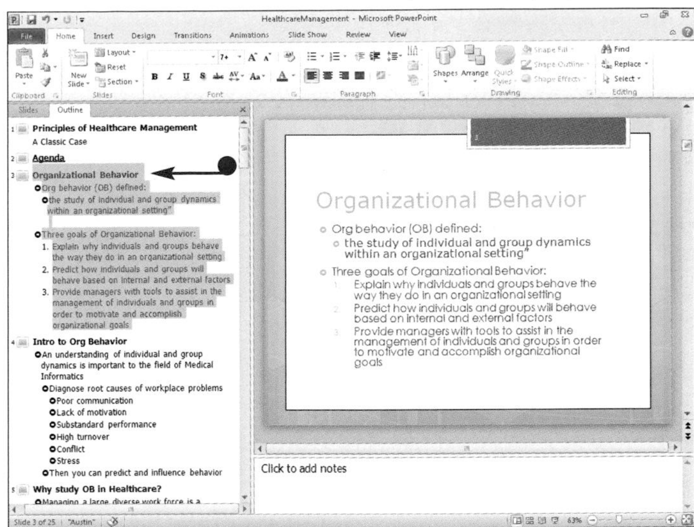

4. Click the bullet of a bullet item.
   - The bullet text is selected.
5. Drag the bullet item up or down to a new location in the bulleted list.

   When you release the mouse button, the bullet item moves to where you dragged it.

Note: *You can use this method to move a bullet item from one slide to another.*

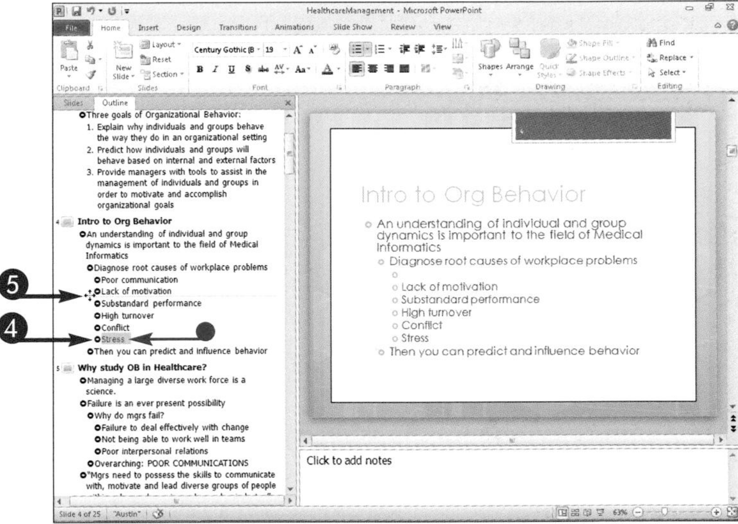

Are there button commands for moving a selection in the Outline tab?

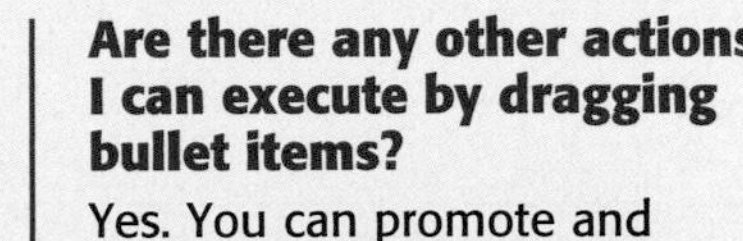

Yes. You can add Move Up and Move Down buttons to the Quick Access Toolbar. See Chapter 2 to learn how to customize the Quick Access Toolbar.

Are there any other actions I can execute by dragging bullet items?

Yes. You can promote and demote bullet items in the outline. Select the bullet text by clicking the bullet. Drag the bullet left or right until the vertical line representing its outline position reaches the desired outline level. Release the click and the bullet item moves.

Promote and Demote Items

As you build and reorganize presentation content, you may need to move upper-level headings in the outline so that they become subheadings, which is called *demoting*. Conversely, you can move lower-level items to become higher-level items, which is called *promoting*. You can promote and demote text by using the Ribbon or the mouse.

Promote and Demote Items

1. Click the **Outline** tab.
2. Click the **Home** tab.
3. Click anywhere in a heading.

   In this example, Organizational Behavior was clicked.

4. Click the **Decrease List Level** button (⇤).

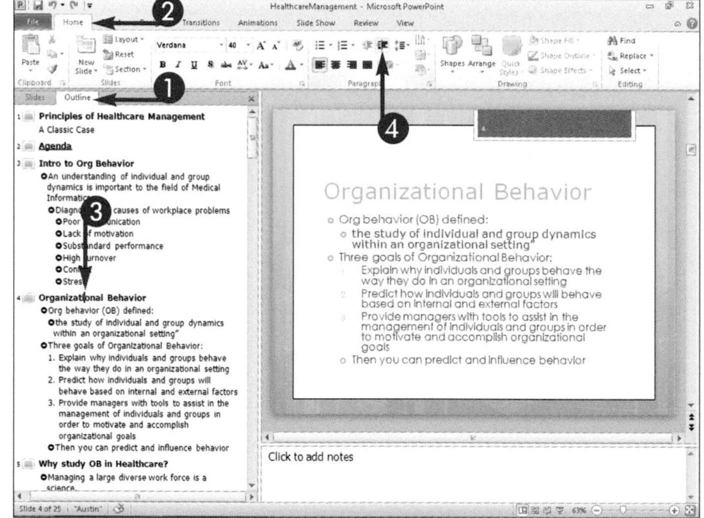

- The heading moves down one level in the outline hierarchy.

5. Click anywhere in a bullet item other than a top-level heading.

   In this example, Three goals of Organizational Behavior was clicked.

6. Click the **Increase List Level** button (⇥).

   You can click ⇤ and ⇥ more than once to move the item more than one level in the outline.

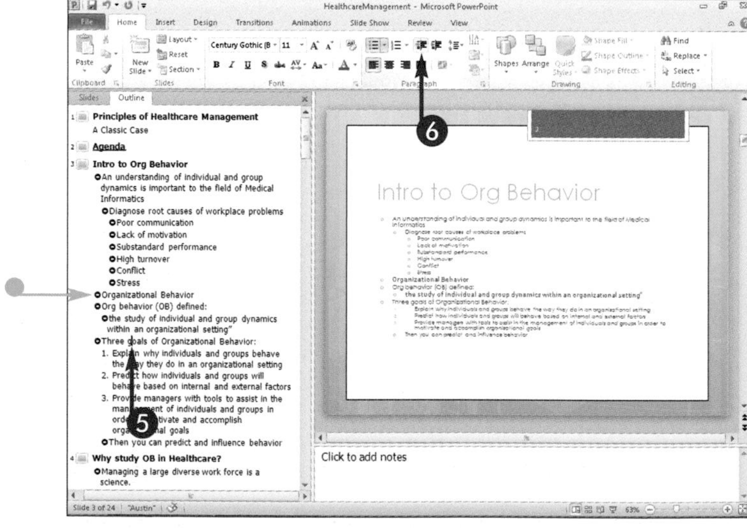

- The heading moves up one level in the outline hierarchy. Because it was a second level item, it became a slide when promoted to the top level.

7 Click a bullet to select a bullet item, or drag across multiple bullet items.

If you click ( ) to select the whole slide, or drag across multiple bullet items, PowerPoint promotes or demotes each line in the selection by one level.

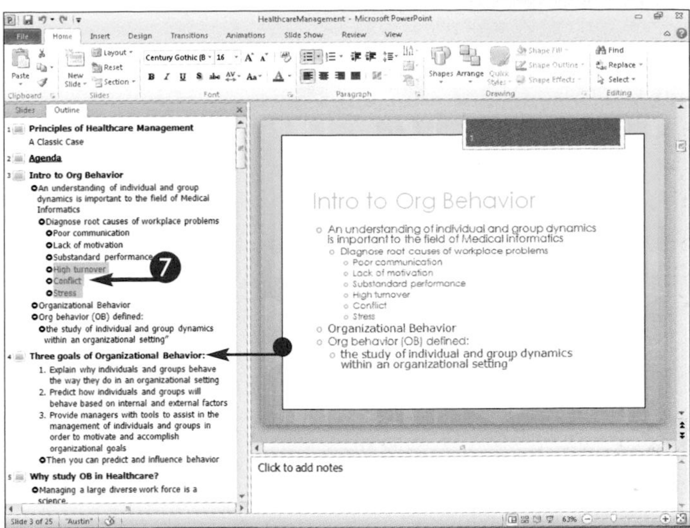

8 Right-click the selection.

9 Click **Promote** ( ) or **Demote** ( ).

In this example, Demote was clicked.

- PowerPoint promotes or demotes the text in the outline.

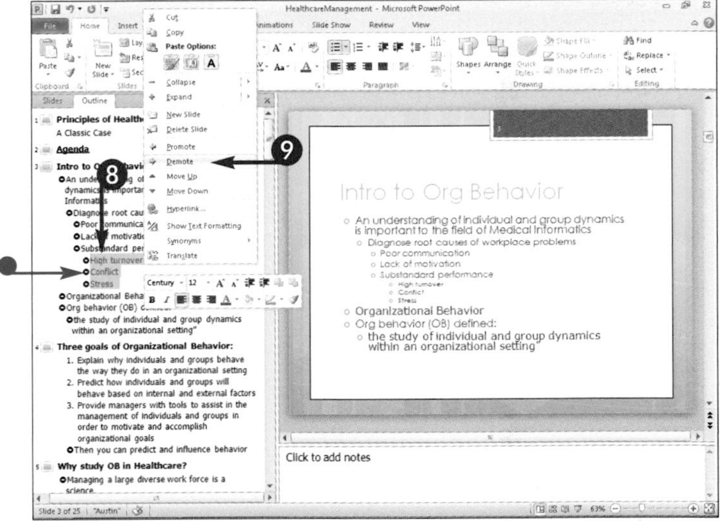

Is there a keyboard shortcut for promoting or demoting headings in a PowerPoint outline?

Yes. Click a heading or bullet item in the Outline pane. Press Tab to demote the text, or press Shift + Tab to promote it.

Can you promote and demote headings directly on a slide?

Yes. However, you cannot promote or demote a slide title. Click in a bullet list item on the slide and click either ( ) or ( ) in the Paragraph group on the Home tab. The change in promotion or demotion occurs both on the slide and in the outline.

Collapse and Expand an Outline

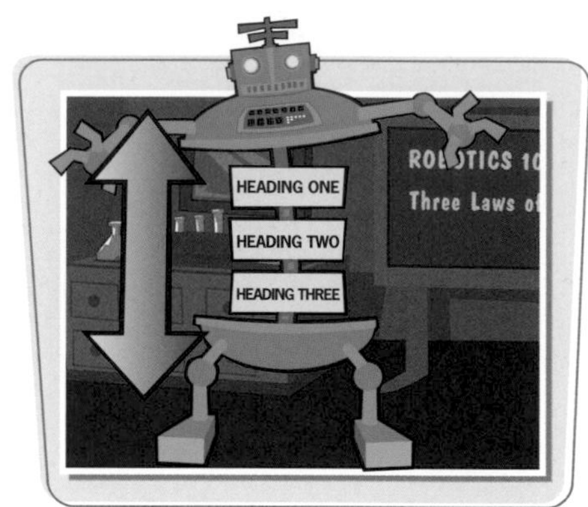

With a lengthy presentation, you can sometimes work more effectively if you collapse an outline so you see only slide titles or expand it to look at the details on one or more slides. Collapsing parts of the outline helps you scroll through the presentation easily and helps you identify outline items quickly.

You can collapse or expand multiple slides. Simply select multiple slides before performing these steps.

Collapse and Expand an Outline

1. Click the **Outline** tab.
2. Right-click any text within a slide that has details beneath it.

   The submenu appears.
3. Click the **Collapse** .
4. Click **Collapse** to collapse your selection.

- Click **Collapse All** to collapse all slides in the presentation.

  PowerPoint collapses all details and displays a gray underline under the title.

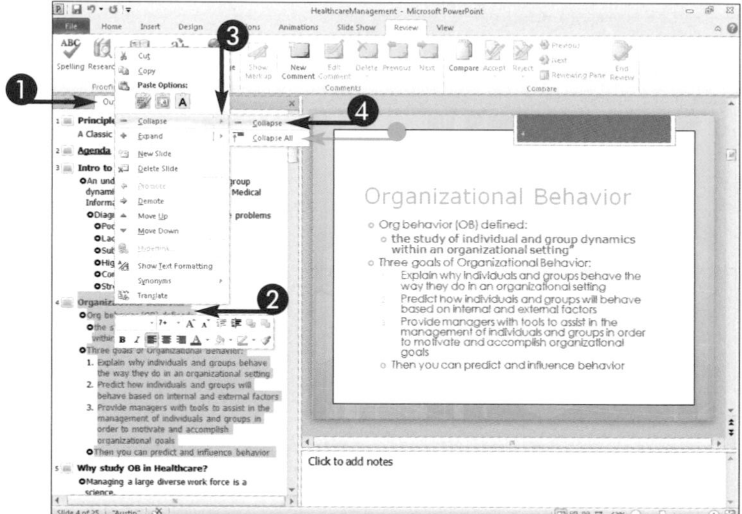

5. Right-click a collapsed slide title.
6. Click the **Expand** .
7. Click **Expand**.

- Click **Expand All** to expand all slides in the presentation.

  The slide details reappear.

Note: You can also double-click for any slide to collapse or expand it.

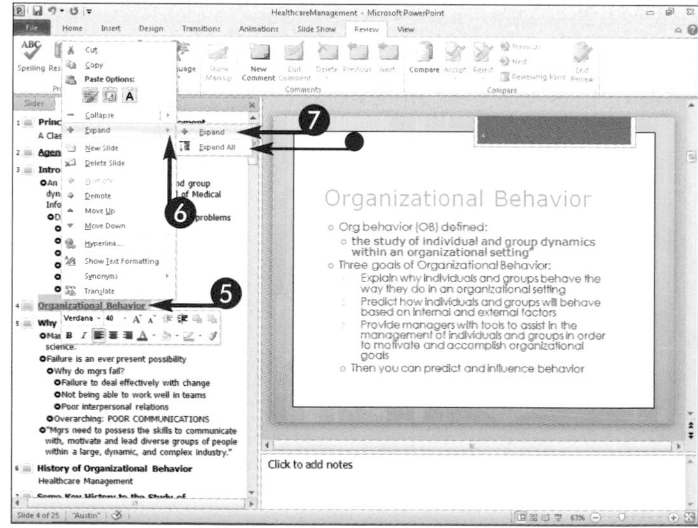

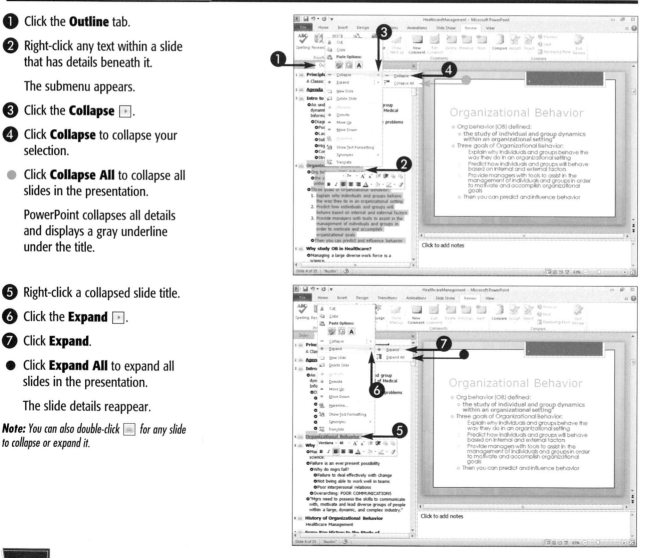

Edit Outline Content

Rarely does a first draft become a final presentation. You can edit the text in your presentation to make it as professional as possible. You typically want to change your presentation text to polish it, or fix typos and other errors. Editing an outline is much like editing text anyplace else in PowerPoint or in any other application.

Edit Outline Content

1. Click the **Outline** tab.
2. Click the point where you want to add or delete text.
3. Type to add text, or press Delete or Backspace to delete the text.

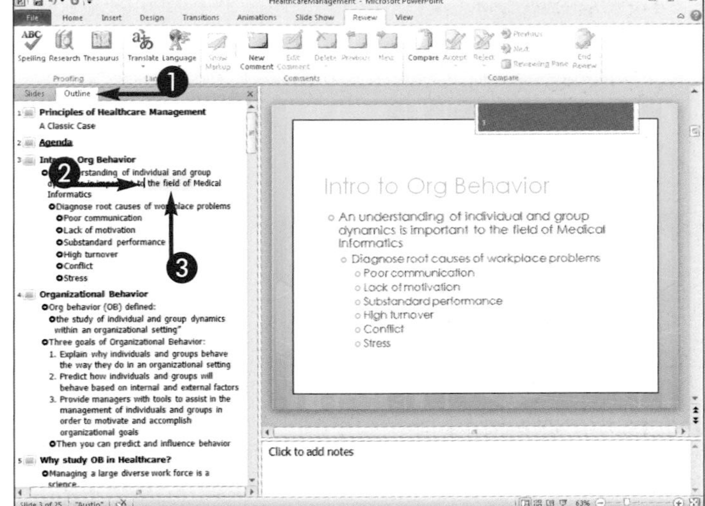

- The outline reflects the changes you made.

4. Click the bullet for any bullet item to select the entire bullet.

- Optionally, you can click ▭ to select an entire slide.

5. Press Delete.

   The entire slide or the full bullet item is deleted.

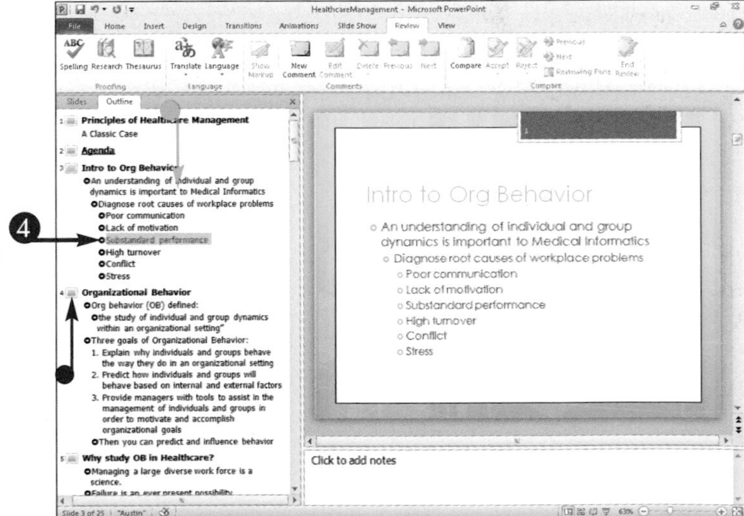

Insert Slides from an Outline

You need not reinvent the wheel if you have already written an outline in Microsoft Word or a text editor such as Notepad. To save time, you can import an outline from another file to supply all or part of the content for a new presentation. Then you can edit and format it as usual.

Insert Slides from an Outline

1. Click the **File** tab.
2. Click **Open**.

Note: *If you are creating a new presentation, import your outline to a new, blank presentation. See Chapter 3.*

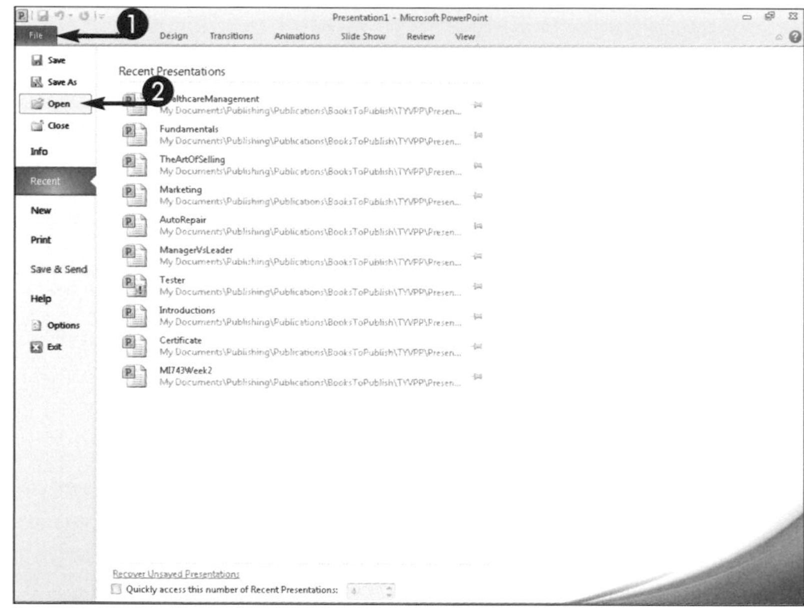

The Open dialog box appears.

3. Click the folder that holds the outline file you want to import.
4. Click ▾ on the drop-down list.
5. Click **All Outlines**.

PowerPoint shows all text-oriented files, such as Word files (DOCX), text files (TXT), and rich text files (RTF) — any file type can hold an outline.

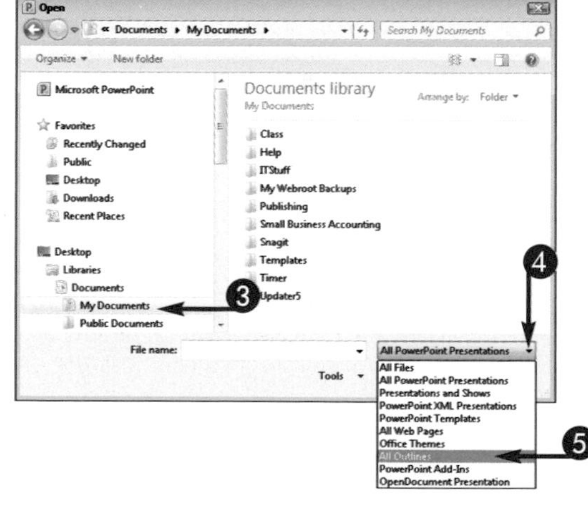

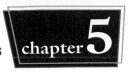

6 Click the outline file you want to import.

In this example, HealthcareManagementDOC was clicked.

7 Click Open.

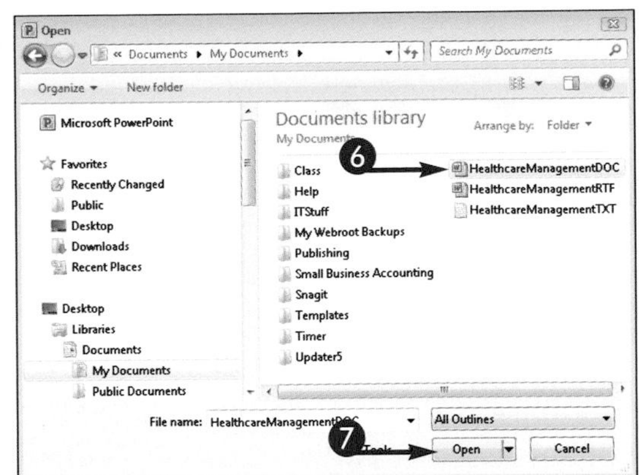

The new presentation appears in Normal view.

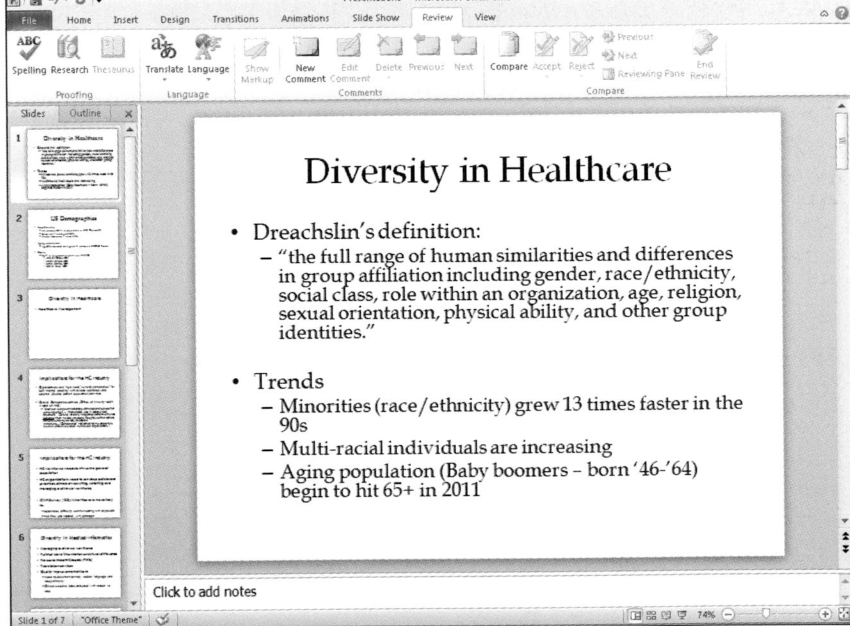

TIPS

Can I change and format an imported presentation?

Yes. Once the imported presentation content appears in PowerPoint, you can edit it just as you would any other presentation. Changes you make in PowerPoint do not affect the original outline document.

How does PowerPoint know where to start each slide?

Each top-level heading in the imported outline becomes the title for a new slide. So, be sure to review the outline before importing it. Promote each heading that you want as a slide title to the top level in the outline.

CHAPTER

Working with Layouts and Placeholders

Slide layouts consist of different combinations and arrangements of placeholders. Placeholders hold text, graphics, charts, tables, SmartArt, and multimedia. They help you build slides easily. You can use the various slide layouts and place contents into a slide's placeholders to create your presentation. This saves you the time and trouble of designing slides from scratch.

Understanding Layouts and Placeholders

Many presentation slides combine a slide title, graphic elements, and slide text in the form of a bulleted list or table. Your selection of slide layout determines where the title, graphics, and text appear. You can create a presentation quickly using the available standard slide layouts.

Types of Slide Layouts

The Slide Layout gallery enables you to choose a layout for a slide. Some layouts hold only text, such as the Title Slide, Section Header, and Title Only layouts. Other layouts include a title, plus content placeholders. Layouts that feature placeholders include Title and Content, Two Content, Comparison, and Content with Caption.

Placeholders

Each slide layout has an arrangement of placeholders. Text placeholders accept only text. Content placeholders accept either text or a graphic element. A content placeholder contains icons that help you insert graphics. You can move placeholders to design slides that suit your particular needs.

The Slide Layout Gallery

Clicking the bottom portion of the New Slide button opens the Slide Layout gallery. Clicking the Layout button on the Home tab also displays this gallery. Use the gallery to insert a slide with a particular layout. If you click the main portion of the New Slide button, PowerPoint inserts a slide with the same layout as the most recently inserted slide.

Slide Layouts Remain Flexible

You can adjust a layout to meet your particular needs. You can drag the handles of a placeholder to resize the placeholder. To move a placeholder, click its border and then drag it to another location. If a placeholder has no content in it, it is not visible when you print or show your presentation.

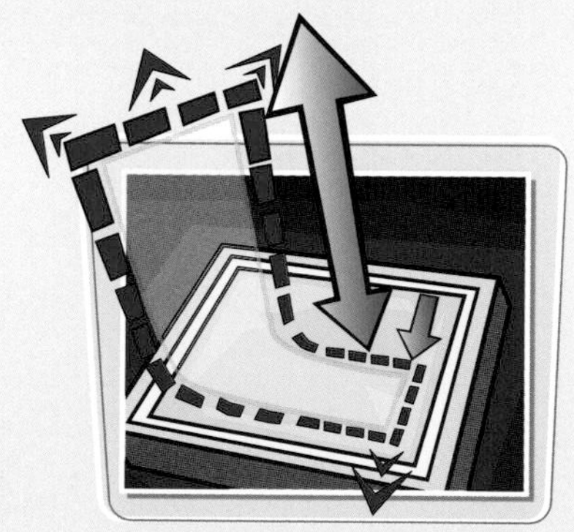

Insert a New Slide with the Selected Layout

To insert a new slide with a particular layout, you can click the bottom portion of the New Slide button and choose the desired layout from the Slide Layout gallery. Clicking the top portion of the New Slide button inserts a slide with the same layout as the last slide you inserted. PowerPoint inserts slides after the currently selected slide.

Insert a New Slide with the Selected Layout

1. Select a slide.

Note: To learn how to select a slide, see Chapter 4.

2. Click the **Home** tab.
3. Click the bottom portion of the **New Slide** button.

   The layout gallery appears.

4. Click the desired layout.

   In this example, Comparison was clicked.

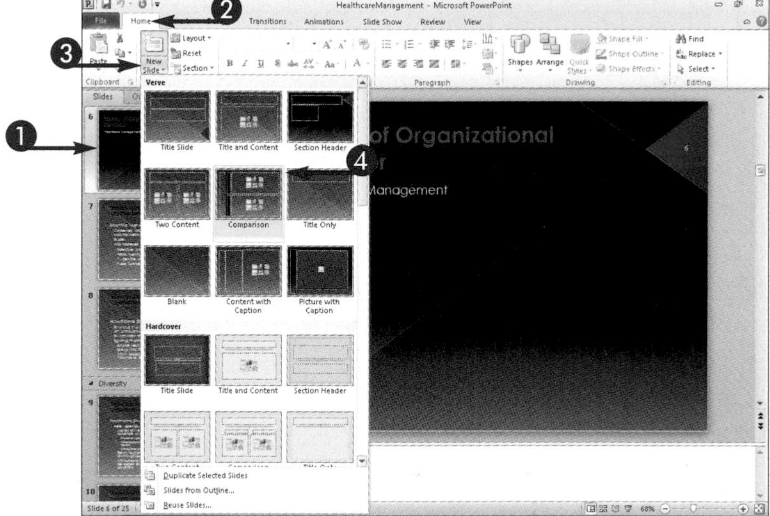

- The new slide with the specified layout appears in the presentation.

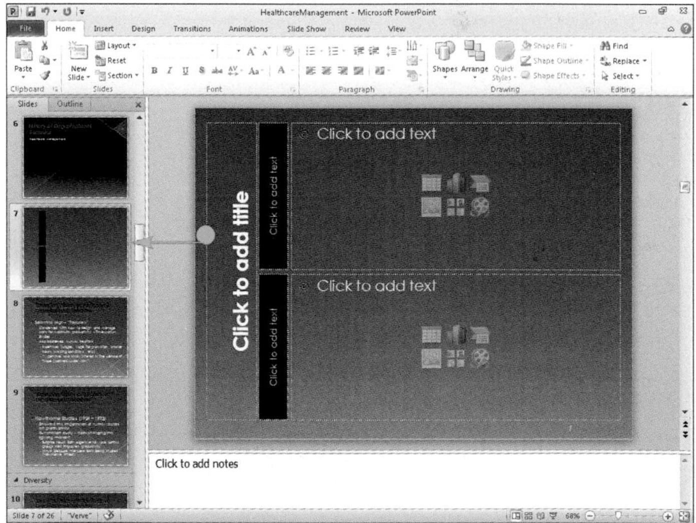

Change a Slide Layout

If you decide a slide's original layout no longer works, you can apply a different slide layout in Normal view or Slide Sorter view.

If you select a layout that does not include an element from the original layout — such as a chart that you have set up — PowerPoint keeps that additional element on the slide, even with the new layout.

Change a Slide Layout

1. Select the slide whose layout you want to change.

***Note:** To learn how to select a slide, see Chapter 4.*

2. Click the **Home** tab.
3. Click the **Layout** button.

   The Layout gallery appears.

4. Click a slide layout from the gallery.

   In this example, Title and Content was clicked.

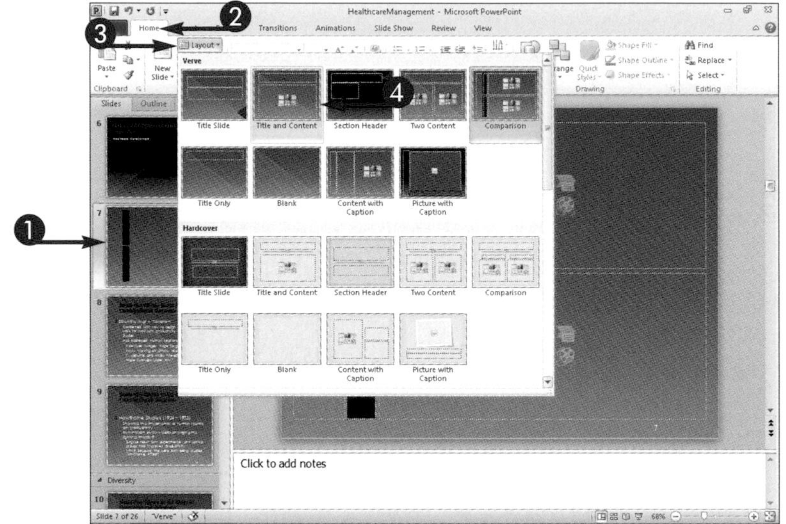

- The slide changes to the selected layout.

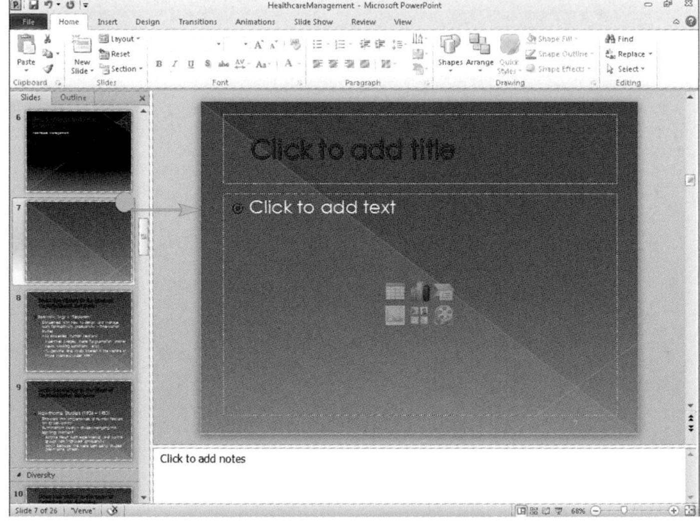

Using Layouts with a Content Placeholder

Content placeholders appear on most of the slide layouts that you will use. You can use content placeholders to build your presentation effectively and efficiently. They enable you to insert text or one of six graphical objects so that you can make your presentation pop esthetically and communicate visually.

Bulleted List

Click the **Click to add text** text and then type a list of items; press Enter at the end of each item.

Tables

Click the **Insert Table** icon ( ) to create a table — you specify the number of columns and rows in the table.

Charts

Click the **Insert Chart** icon ( ) to generate a chart using a chart type that you specify, and data that you type into an Excel worksheet.

Click to add title

• Click to add text

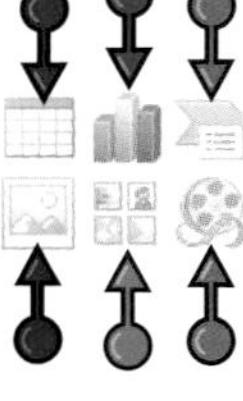

SmartArt

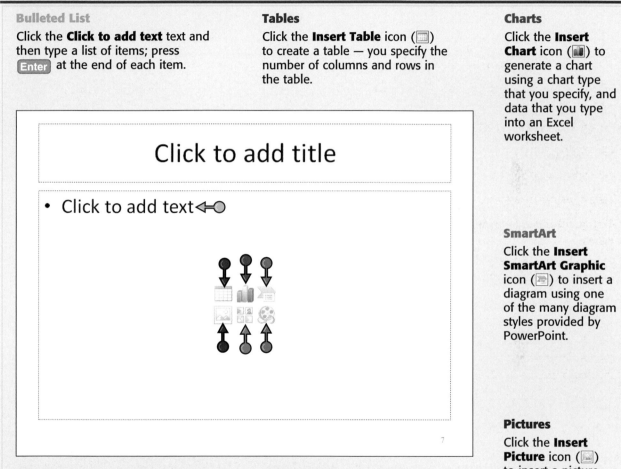

Click the **Insert SmartArt Graphic** icon ( ) to insert a diagram using one of the many diagram styles provided by PowerPoint.

Pictures

Click the **Insert Picture** icon ( ) to insert a picture file such as a bitmap or JPEG you have stored on your computer or other storage media.

Clip Art

Click the **Insert Clip Art** icon ( ) to select an image from the built-in clip art collection, or import clip art from Microsoft Office Online.

Media Clips

Click the **Media Clip** icon ( ) to insert a video file that plays on command during the slide show.

Insert a Table

You can use a table to arrange information in rows and columns for easy data comparison. For example, you might list age groups in the far left column of a table, and then compare population demographics between males and females in two other columns. You can use a content placeholder to insert a table, and then type data into the table cells.

Insert a Table

Insert a Table

1. Select a slide with a content placeholder.

***Note:** To learn how to select a slide, see Chapter 4.*

2. Click .

   The Insert Table dialog box appears.

3. Click and type the number of columns you want in your table.

4. Click and type the number of rows you want in your table.

***Note:** Alternatively, you may click to select the number of columns and rows.*

5. Click **OK**.

   The table appears on the slide.

***Note:** By default, most of the table styles assume you will enter column headings in the top row of the table.*

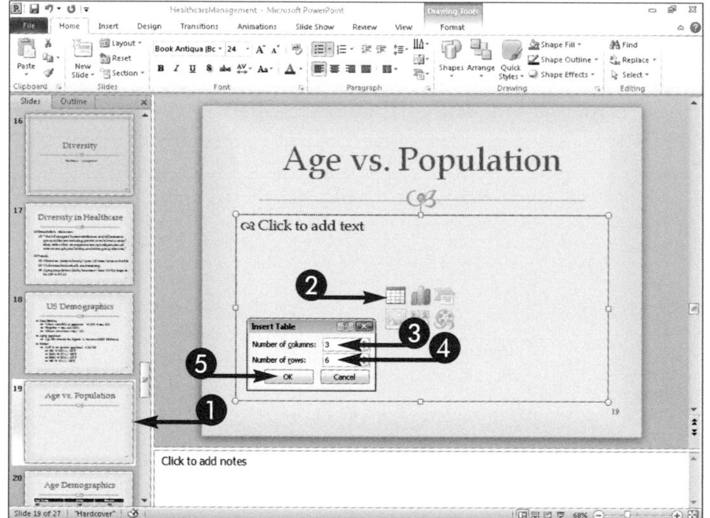

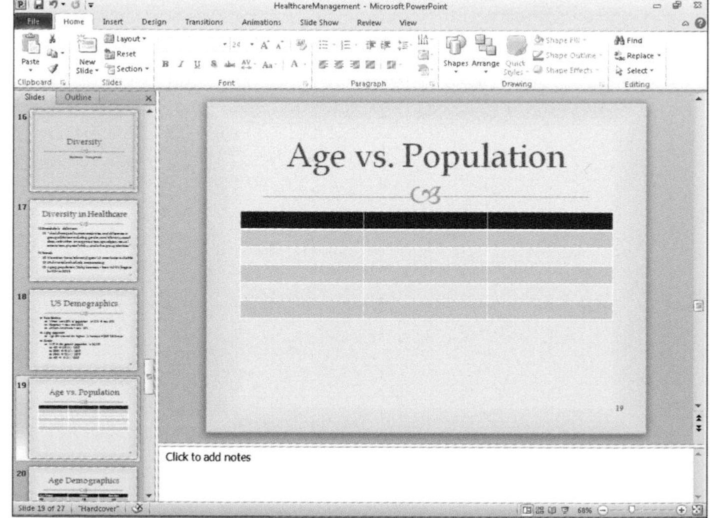

Type Text in a Table

1. Click in the first cell and type a column heading.

   In this example, Age Group was typed.

2. Press Tab.

- The insertion point moves to the next cell.

***Note:** You can also click in a cell to type data into it.*

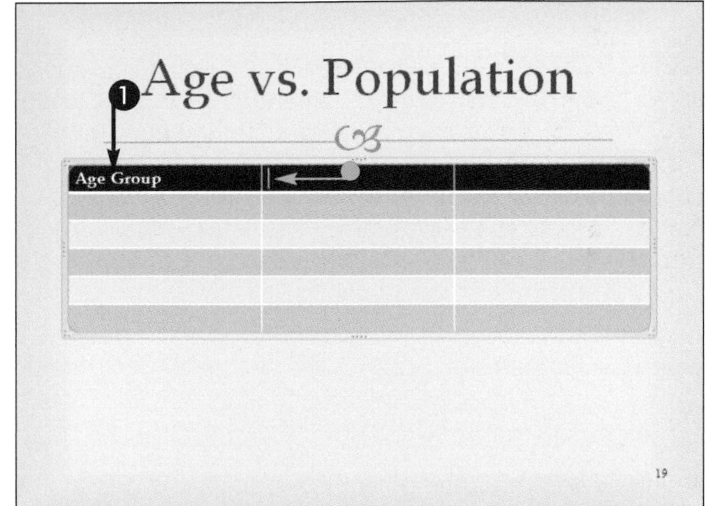

3. Continue adding column headings and cell entries by repeating Steps **1** and **2**.

4. Click outside the table when finished.

   The finished table appears on your slide.

- To make a change in table data, click in the cell, edit your entry, and then click outside the table when finished.

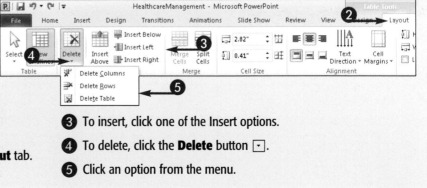

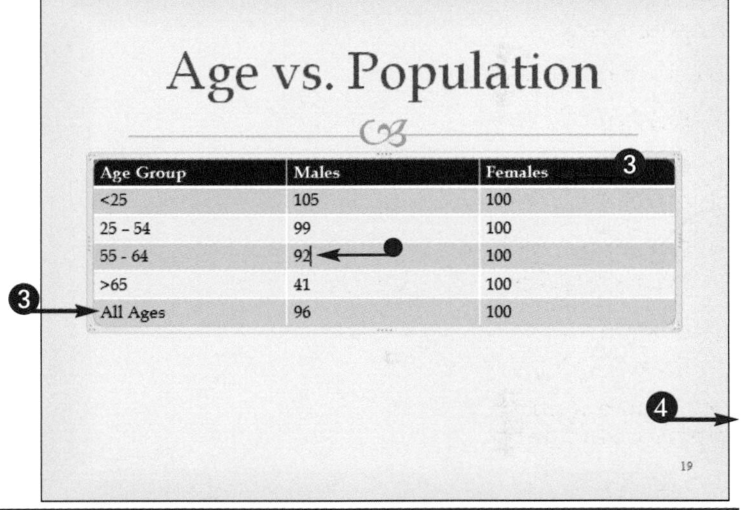

Age Group	Males	Females
<25	105	100
25 – 54	99	100
55 - 64	92	100
>65	41	100
All Ages	96	100

Can I add and delete rows or columns to tables?

Yes. You can insert and delete rows or columns by following these steps:

1. Click a cell in the row or column targeted for deletion or insertion.

2. Click the **Table Tools Layout** tab.

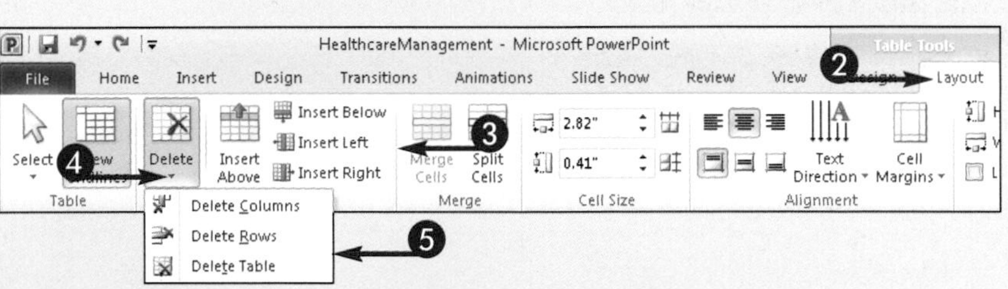

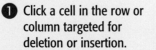

3. To insert, click one of the Insert options.

4. To delete, click the **Delete** button.

5. Click an option from the menu.

Format a Table

When you insert a table, PowerPoint automatically applies a style to the table based on the theme of the slide. You can add visual punch to your presentation by changing the format of your table. You can add and delete rows and columns, format text and background, and change the style of the table.

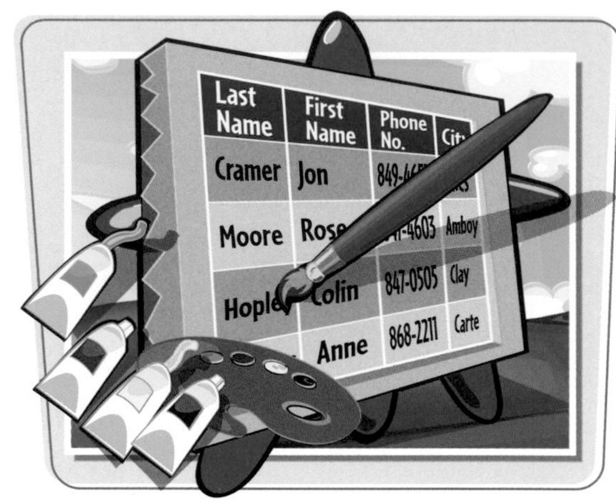

Format a Table

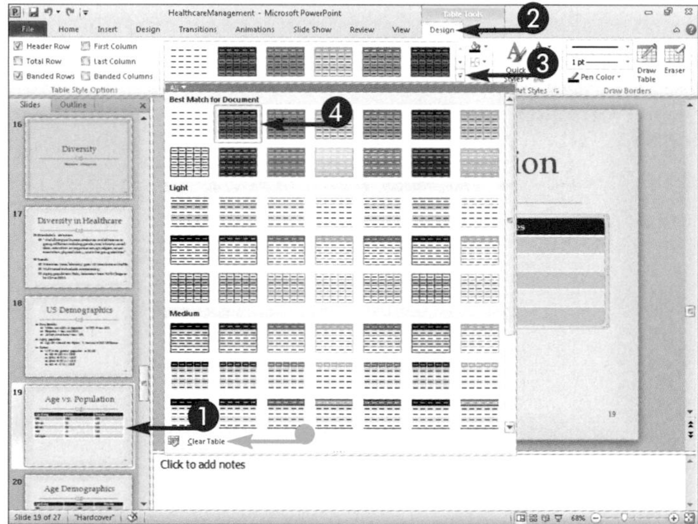

1. Select a slide with a table.

***Note:** To learn how to select a slide, see Chapter 4.*

2. Click the **Table Tools Design** tab.
3. Click the **Table Styles** ▾.
4. Click a style from the gallery.

- You can click **Clear Table** to remove any previously applied styles.

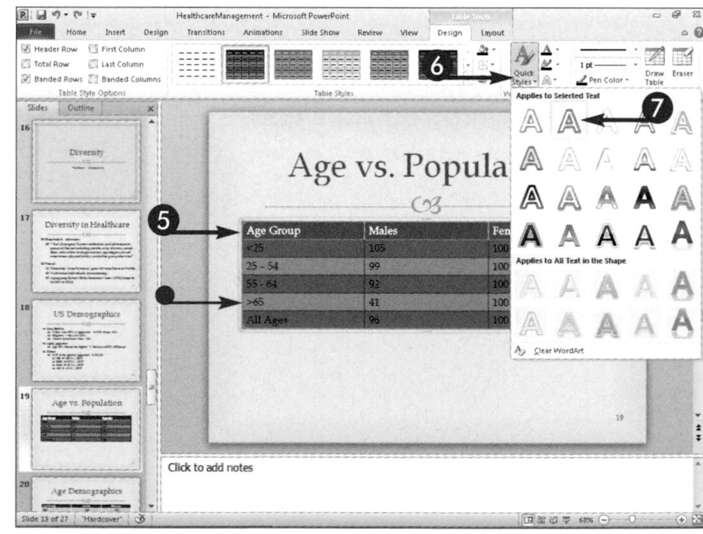

- The style is applied to the table.

5. Click and drag across table cells to select them.

   In this example, the column headings were selected.

6. Click the **Quick Styles** ▾.
7. Select a style from the gallery.

- The style is applied to the selection.

8. Click and drag across table cells to select them.

   In this example, the body of the table was selected.

9. Click the **Borders** button.
10. Click a border from the menu.

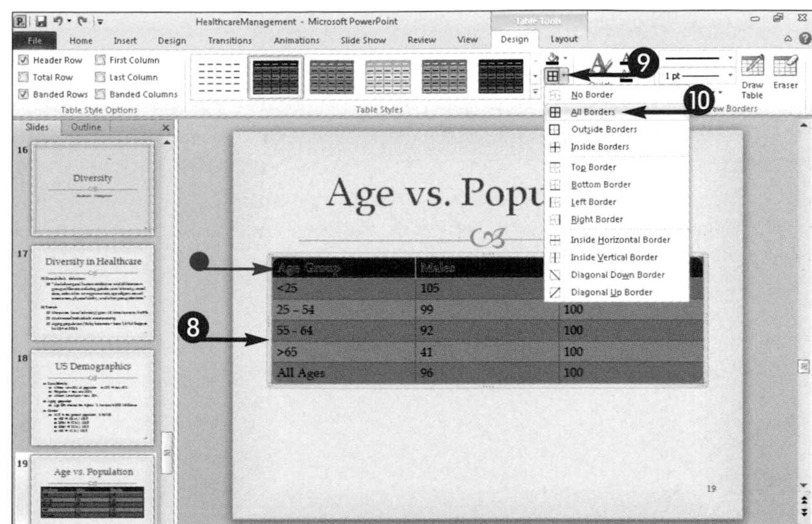

11. Click the **Home** tab.
12. Click the **Italics** button.
13. Click the **Center** button.

- The formatting changes are applied to the selection.

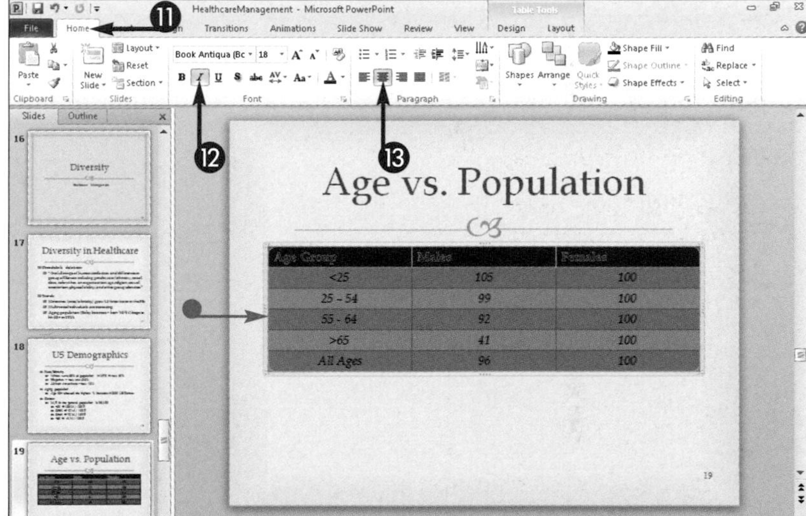

TIP

Can I make size adjustments to the table?

Yes. You can resize your table as follows:

1. Click in a table.
2. Position the mouse pointer over a handle.
3. Click and drag the handle to size the table.
4. To resize the rows and columns, position the pointer over a cell border separating rows or columns.
5. Click and drag the cell border to size the table.

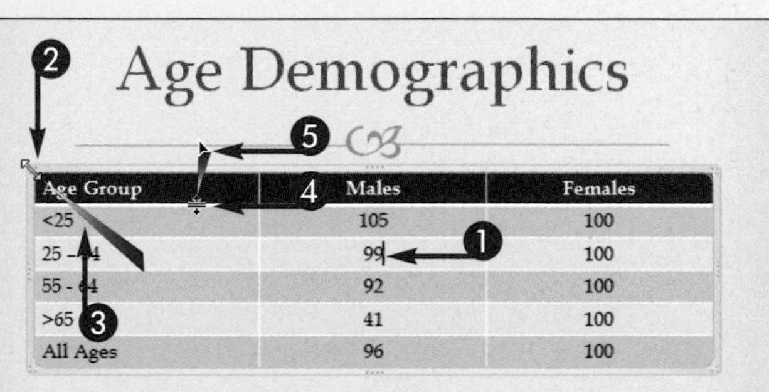

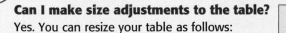

Insert a Chart

Charts present information visually and make your presentation esthetically pleasing. They give an instant impression of trends, or they compare sets of data, such as sales growth over a several-year span. You can add these visual-analysis tools to your presentation to quickly convey summarized information to your audience. PowerPoint allows you to choose the chart type and then type chart data in a spreadsheet.

Insert a Chart

Create a Chart

1. Select a slide with a content placeholder.

Note: *To learn how to select a slide, see Chapter 4.*

2. Click [chart icon].

   The Insert Chart dialog box appears.

3. Click a chart type category.
4. Click a specific chart type.
5. Click **OK**.

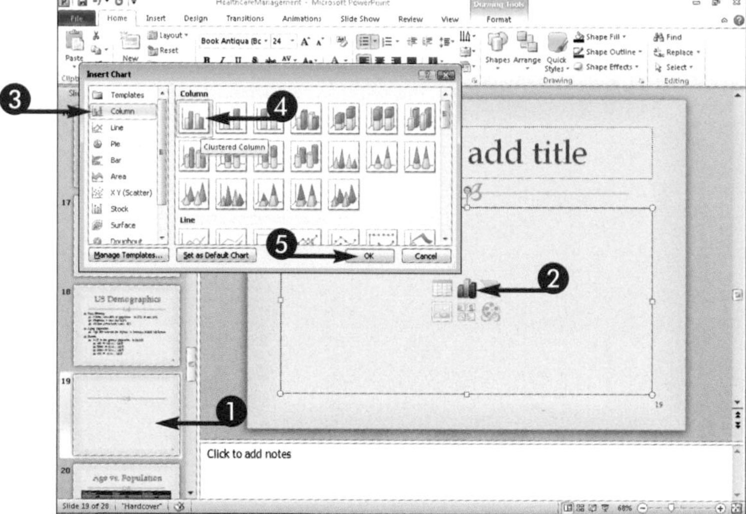

The chart appears, along with placeholder data in a separate Microsoft Excel window.

Note: *Entering data into Excel is similar to entering data into a PowerPoint table.*

6. Click in the grid to activate the Excel worksheet.
7. Delete superfluous information in rows or columns.

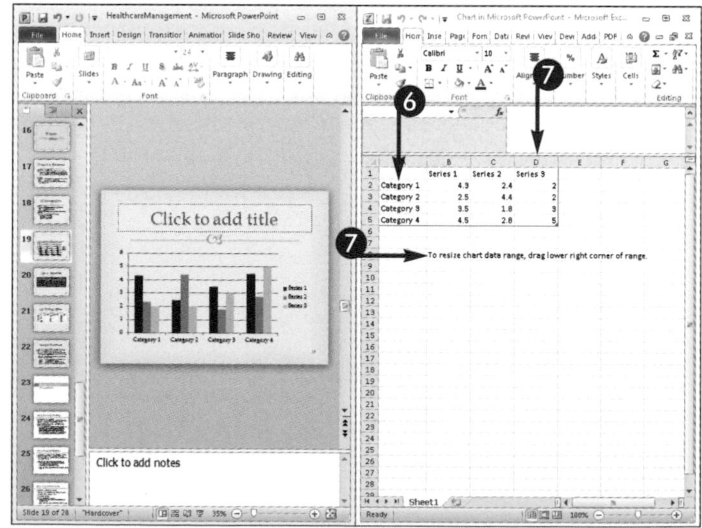

Enter Chart Data

1. In the Excel worksheet, type column headings in Row 1
2. Type row labels in Column A.

   The blue border around the table should automatically expand as you enter information.
3. Type your data values in the cells.
4. Click the **Close** button (⊠) to close the Excel worksheet.

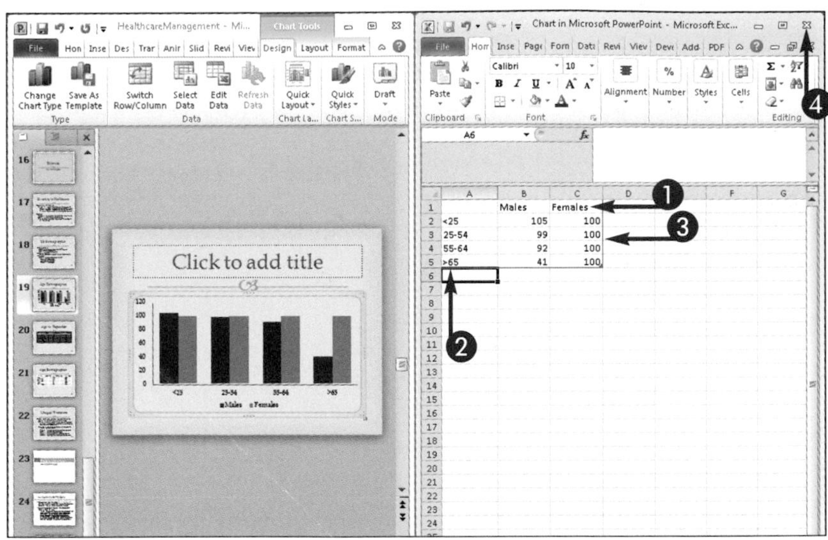

- The Excel worksheet window closes and the chart appears on the slide.

5. Click the title placeholder.
6. Type a title.

   In this example, Age Demographics was typed.
7. Click outside the chart when finished.

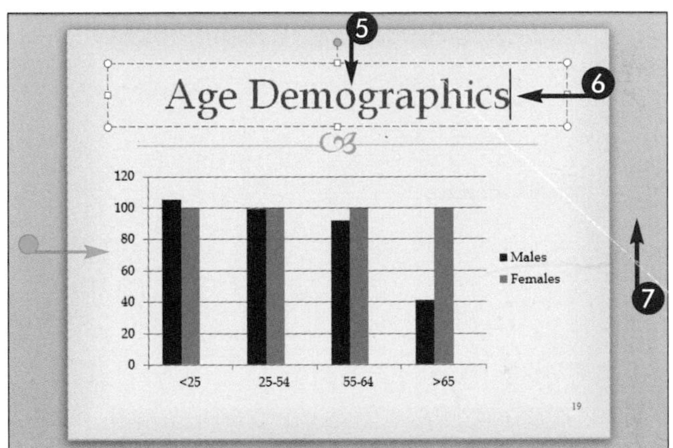

Can I change the type of chart?

Yes. Follow these steps:

1. Click anywhere in the chart.
2. Click the **Chart Tools Design** tab.
3. Click **Change Chart Type**.
4. Click a chart type category.
5. Click a specific chart type.
6. Click **OK**, and PowerPoint changes the chart type to the one you selected.

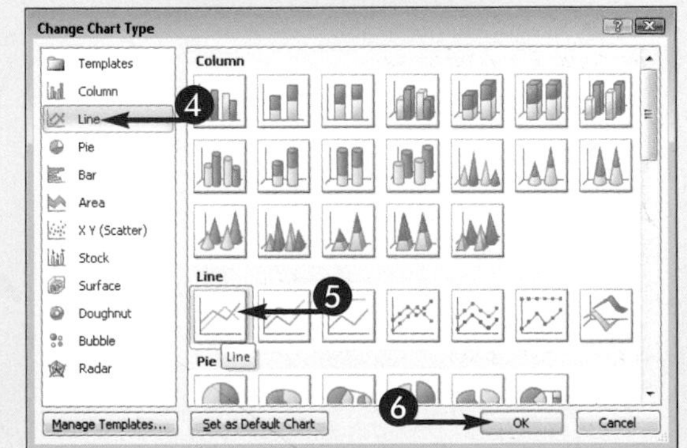

Format a Chart

When you insert a chart, PowerPoint automatically applies a style to the table based on the theme of the slide. Charts present information visually, so choice of color is important. The chart matches the theme of your presentation, but you can change the formatting of charts to give them a different appearance, convey a particular mood, or to make a specific data stand out.

Format a Chart

1. Click anywhere on a chart.
2. Click the **Chart Tools Design** tab.
3. Click the **Chart Styles** ⊽.
4. Click a chart style from the gallery.

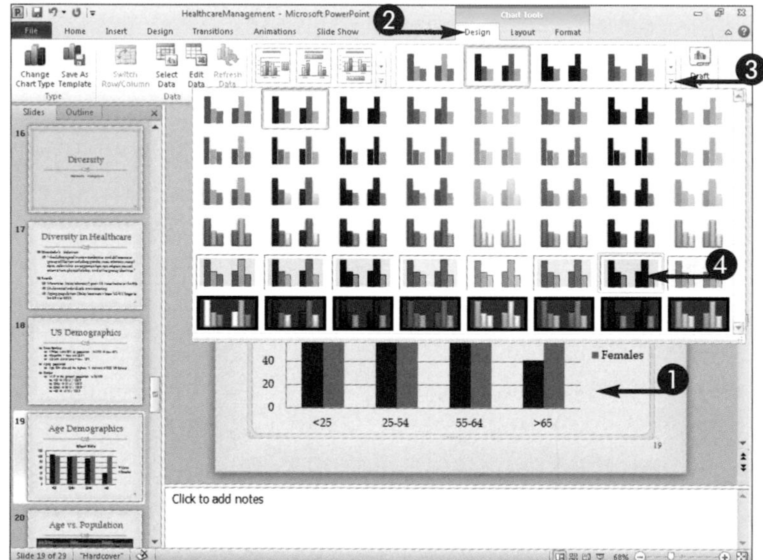

- The chart reflects the change in chart style.

5. Click the **Chart Layouts** ⊽.
6. Click a chart layout from the gallery.

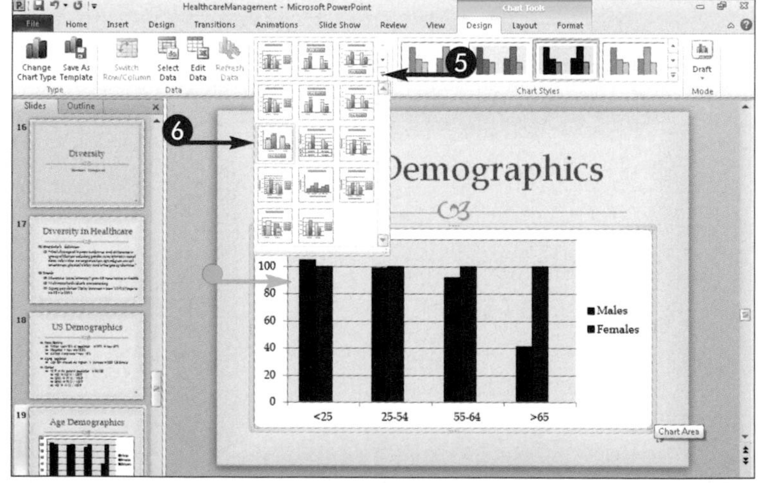

- The chart reflects the changes to chart layout.

7. Click a data point twice (not double-click).

   In this example, the column under 41 was clicked.

8. Click the **Chart Tools Format** tab.
9. Click **Shape Fill**.
10. Click a color from the gallery.

- Note the options for specialized fills.

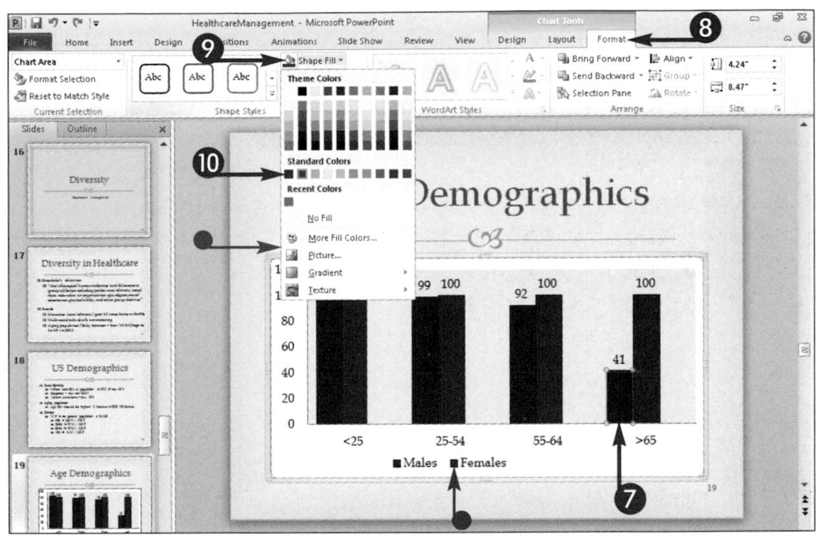

- The single data point changes color.

11. Click the chart background.
12. Click the **Shape Styles** ▾.
13. Click a shape style.

- You can change the color by clicking **Shape Fill**.
- You can change the border color by clicking **Shape Outline**.
- The chart reflects the changes to shape style.

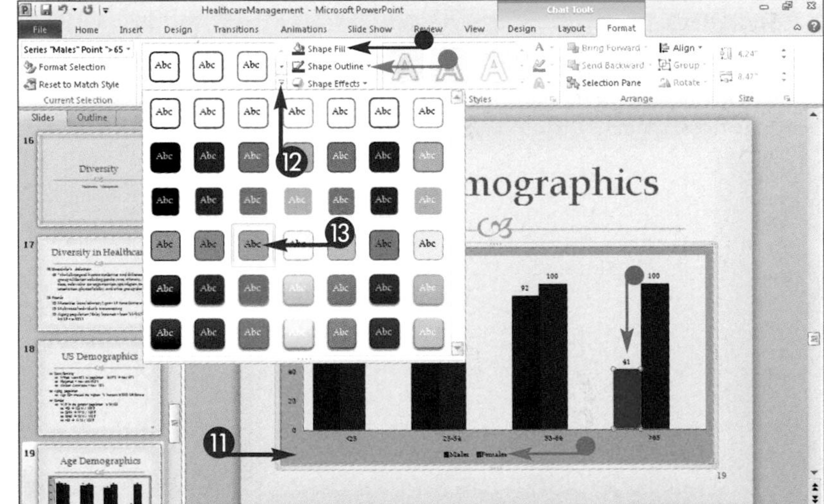

Can I format the numbers on the axis?

Yes. You can format text in a chart just like other text in PowerPoint by using the Home tab.

1. Click the chart to select it.
2. Click an axis.
3. Click the **Home** tab.
4. Click the **Font Size** ▾ and select a font size from the drop-down list.

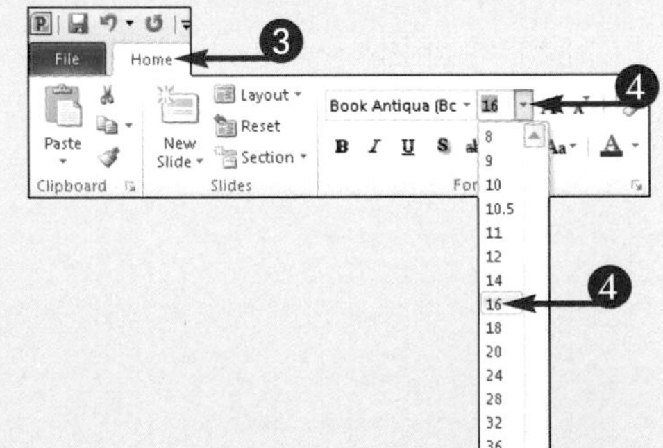

Edit Chart Data

It is not unusual for chart data to change from time to time. You can edit chart data so that you can keep the chart up to date with the most recent information. If you decide not to include all of the data in the data table, you can select data manually so your chart only reflects the data you choose.

Edit Chart Data

1. Click anywhere on a chart.
2. Click the **Chart Tools Design** tab.
3. Click **Edit Data**.

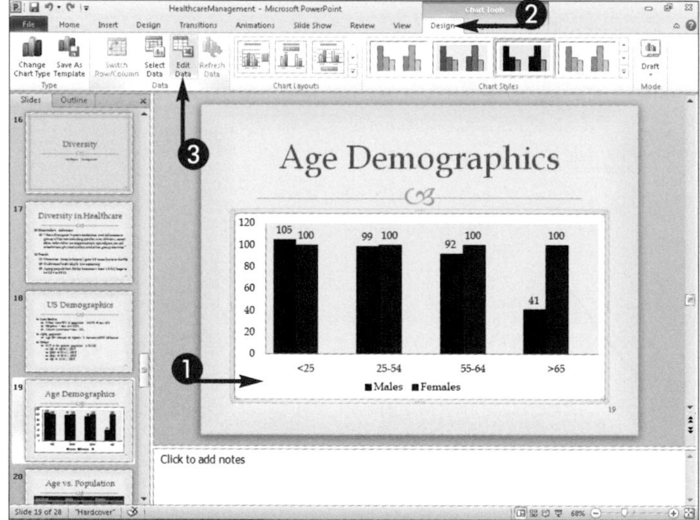

The chart appears side by side with the data in a Microsoft Excel window.

4. Type a column heading in Cell D1.
5. Type a row label in Cell A6.
6. Click in the cell and type data values for the new row and column.

Note: *The blue border around the table adjusts automatically.*

- The chart automatically updates with a new series for the added column.
- The chart automatically updates with a new category for the added row.

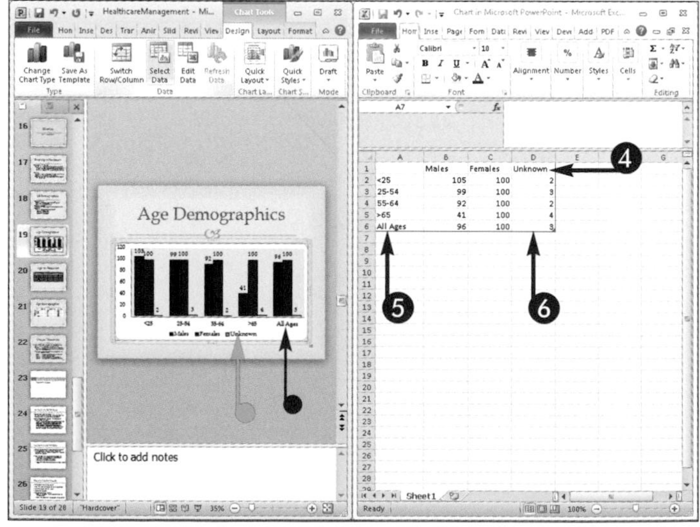

7. Click **Select Data**.

   The Select Data Source dialog box appears.

8. Click and drag across the cells that contain the data you want in your chart.

   In this example, Cells A1 through D5 were dragged.

9. Click **OK**.

10. Click ☒ to close the Excel spreadsheet.

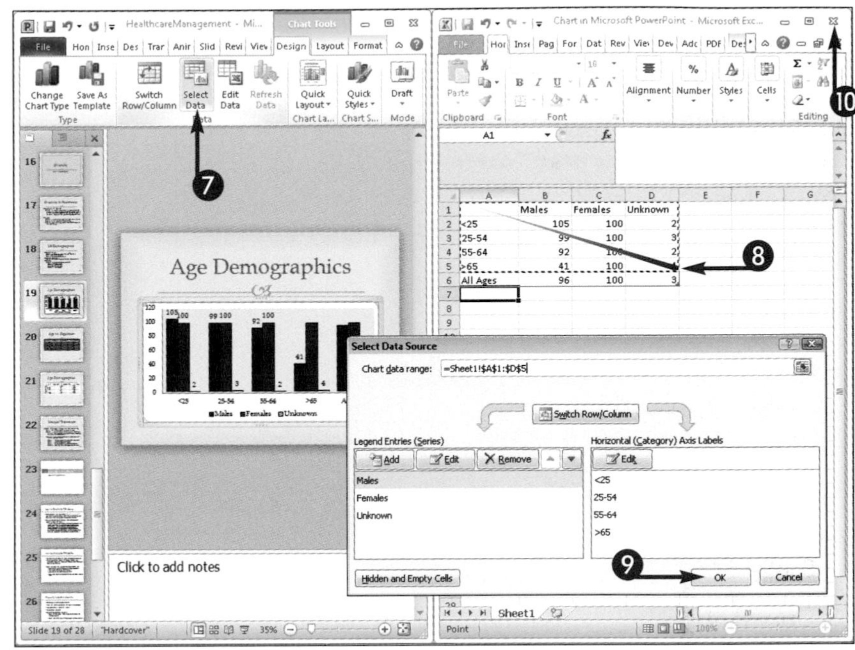

The chart reflects the changes that you made to the data selection.

The All Ages category was excluded from the data and is consequentially excluded from the chart.

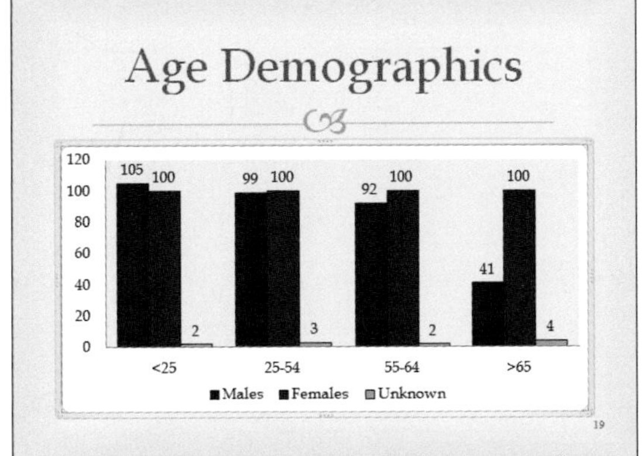

TIPS

If my chart layout has a chart title, how do I change what it says?

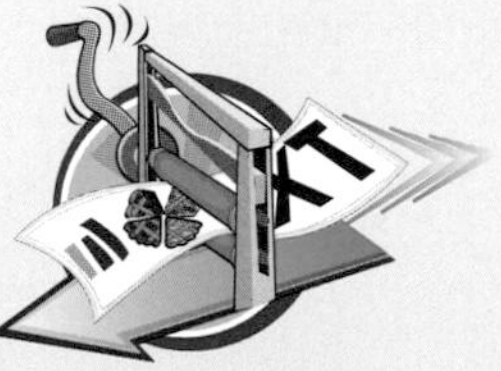

Chart titles and axis titles act very much like text placeholders. Click anywhere on the chart to select it. Click the chart title to select it, and then click it again to put the insertion point where you want to make your changes. Delete what is there and type what you want.

Can I change the color of an entire data series at one time instead of one data point at a time?

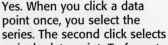

Yes. When you click a data point once, you select the series. The second click selects a single data point. To format an entire series, click a data point only once, and then make your formatting changes. PowerPoint applies the changes to the entire series.

Insert Pictures and Clip Art

You can illustrate and enhance your presentation using graphics such as pictures and clip art. Pictures include digital camera shots and scanned images. PowerPoint includes a gallery of various clip art graphics such as photos, line drawings, and bitmaps. You can even download more clip art from Microsoft Office Online.

Insert Pictures and Clip Art

1. Select a slide with a content placeholder.

Note: *To learn how to select a slide, see Chapter 4.*

2. Click the [picture icon].

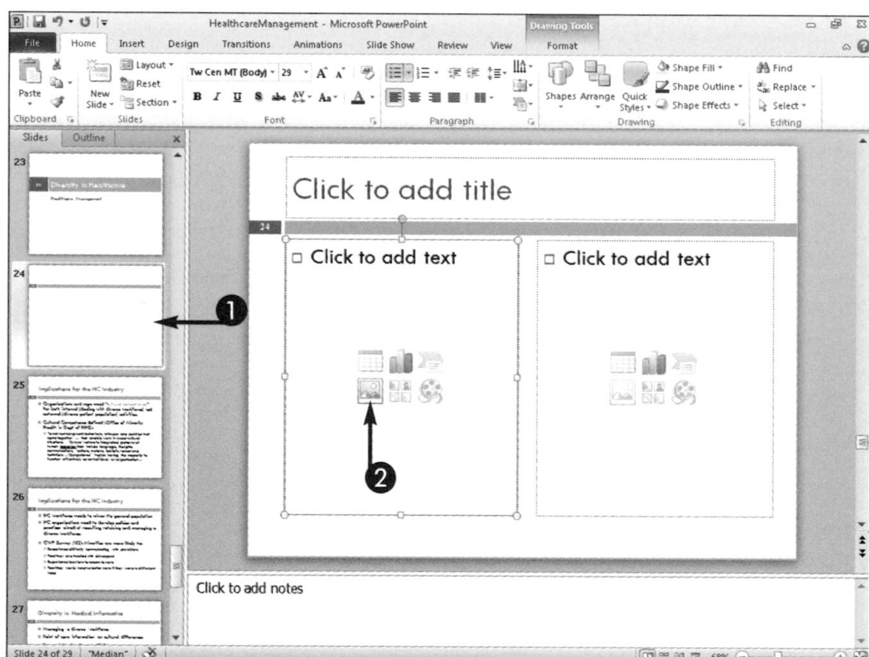

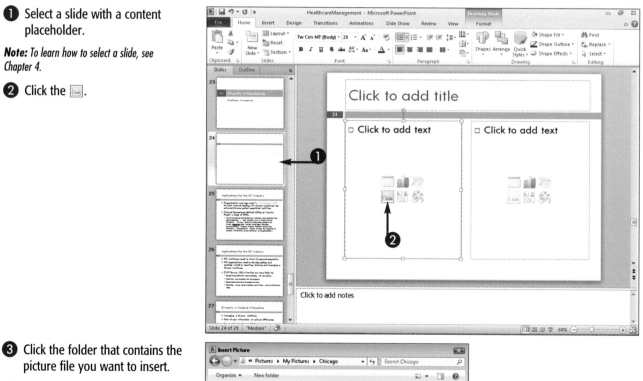

3. Click the folder that contains the picture file you want to insert.
4. Click a picture file.
5. Click **Insert**.

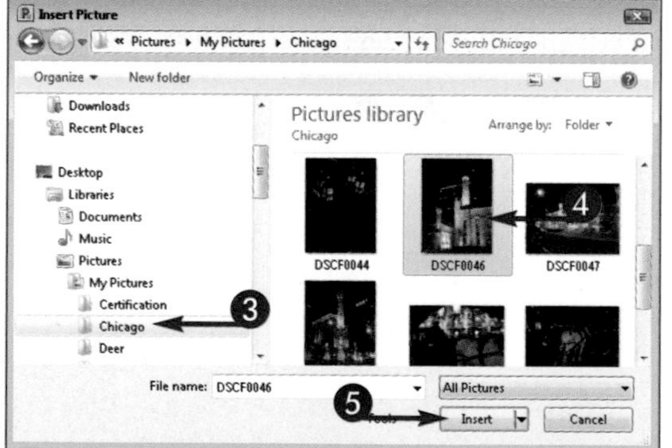

- The selected picture is inserted into the placeholder.

6. Click .

   The Clip Art task pane appears.

7. Type a term that describes the clip art image you want in the Search for text box.

   In this example, people was typed.

8. Click the **Results should be** .

9. If it is not already selected, click **All media file types** (changes to).

10. Click **Go**.

    Clip art graphics matching the search term appear.

11. Click an icon to select the clip art.

- PowerPoint inserts the clip art.

Note: *You can resize the clip art as desired. See Chapter 9 to learn how.*

12. Click to close the Clip Art task pane.

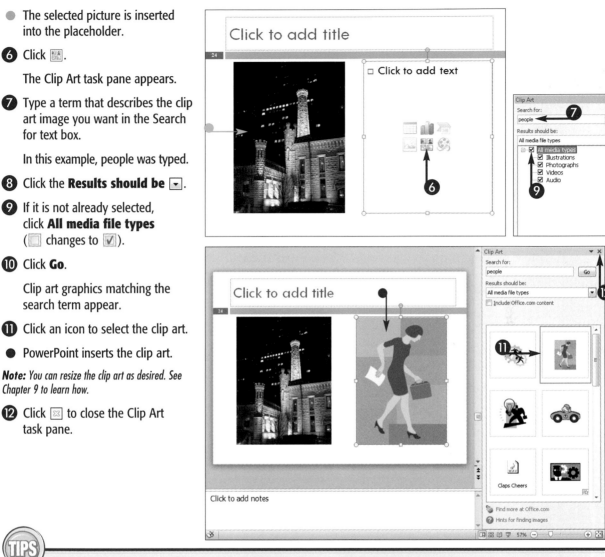

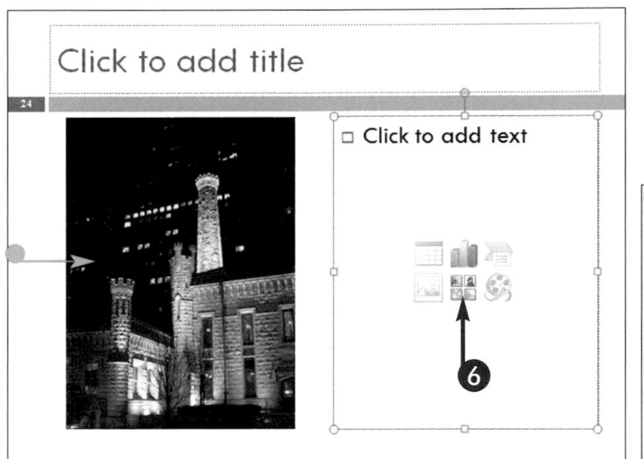

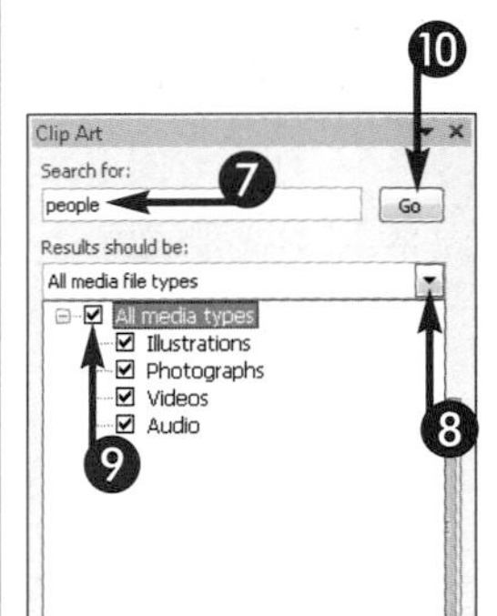

What is the purpose of Include Office.com content in the Clip Art task pane?

PowerPoint stores many clip art graphics files on your computer when you install it (assuming you do not intentionally remove that option). If you click **Include Office.com content** before you click **Go**, PowerPoint searches Office.com for even more clip art.

I see a Clip Art button on the Insert tab of the Ribbon. What does it do?

Click **Clip Art** on the Insert tab when you want to position clip art somewhere other than in a placeholder. It opens the Clip Art task pane so that you can place clip art graphics anywhere on a slide. After you insert the clip art, you can size it and position it on the slide as needed.

Insert Media Clips

Media clips include videos and animation clips that you can play during an on-screen slide show. This is a great way to present an instructional segment, or show interesting or funny video captures to make your presentation exciting.

PowerPoint recognizes media clips in a variety of different formats, such as Windows Media Video (WMV) files and Movie Pictures Experts Group (MPEG) movie files.

Insert Media Clips

1. Select a slide with a content placeholder.

Note: *To learn how to select a slide, see Chapter 4.*

2. Click the **Insert Media Clip** icon ( ).

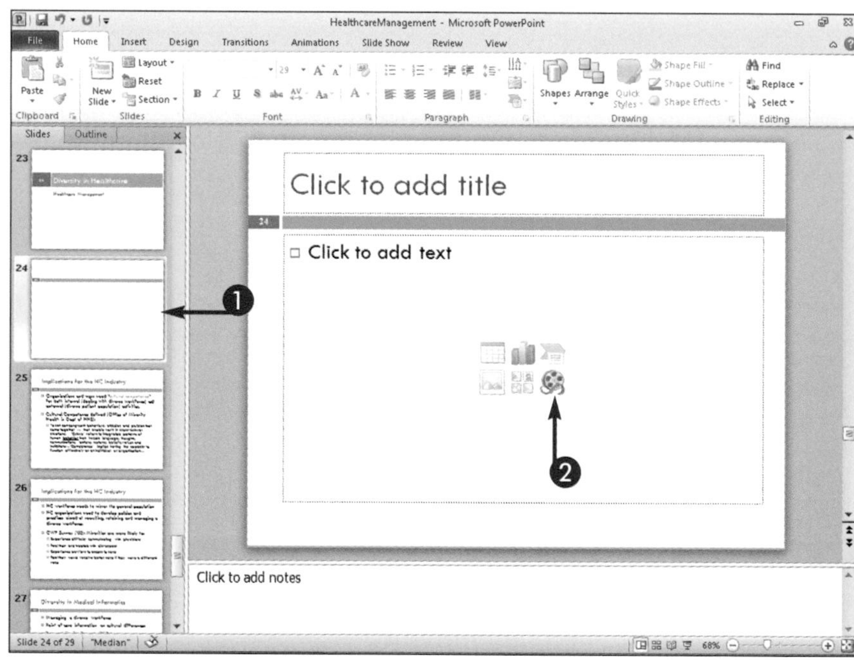

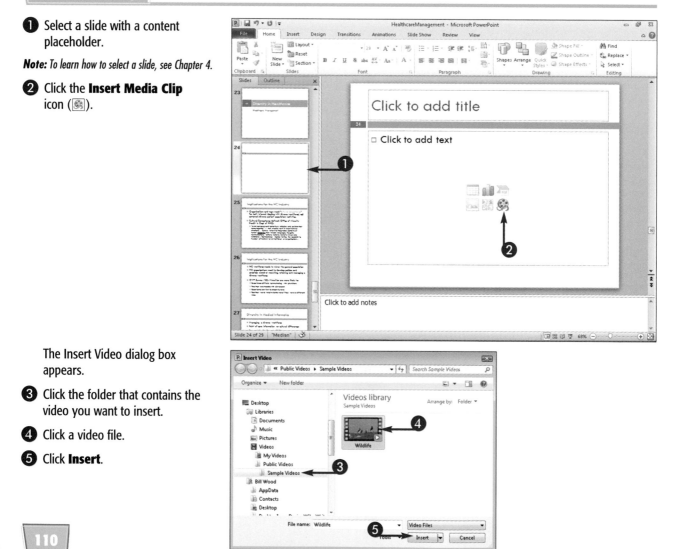

The Insert Video dialog box appears.

3. Click the folder that contains the video you want to insert.
4. Click a video file.
5. Click **Insert**.

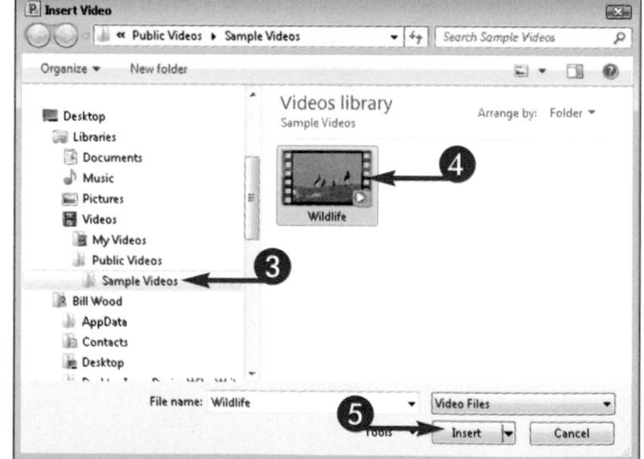

- The video clip appears on the slide along with a control bar.

6. Click the **Video Tools Playback** tab.
7. Click **Play** (▶ changes to ⏸).

   The video begins to play.

- You can also click the **Play/Pause** button to start and stop the video.
- The slide shows the progress of the video playing. Click anywhere on the slide to jump to any part of the video.
- You can click the **Move Forward** and **Move Back** buttons to jump back or forth 0.25 seconds while the video is either playing or paused.
- You can use the **Volume** button to adjust the sound.

8. Click **Pause** (⏸ changes to ▶).

   The video stops playing.

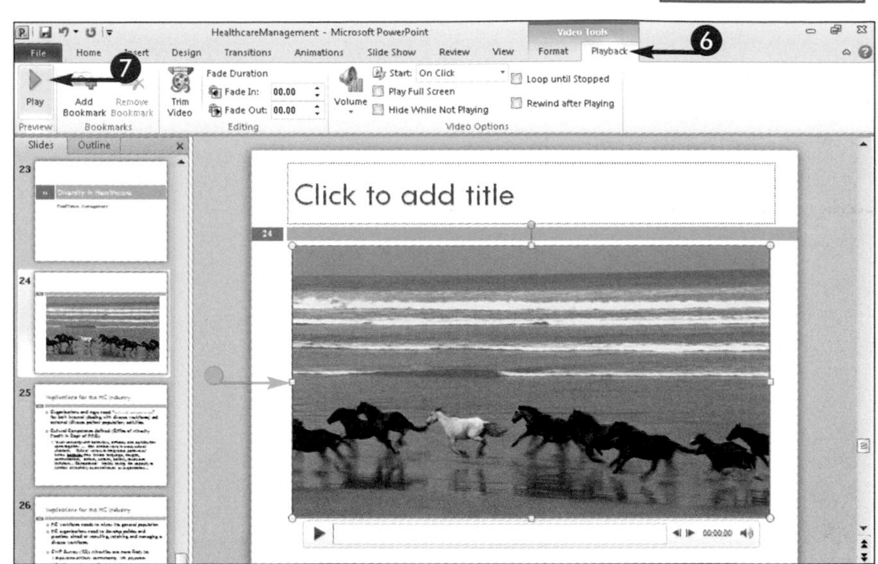

Can I insert a sound file instead of a video file?

Yes. You can insert a sound file by following these steps.

1. Click a placeholder border to select it.
2. Click the **Insert** tab.
3. Click **Audio**.
4. In the **Insert Audio** dialog box, click the folder containing the audio file.
5. Click the audio file.
6. Click **Insert**.

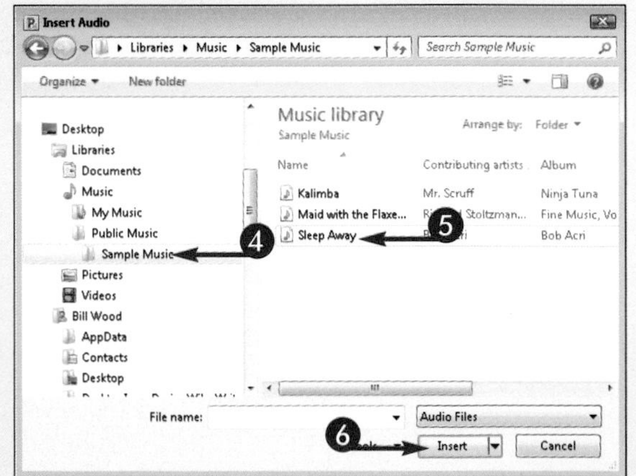

Insert a SmartArt Graphic

You can use SmartArt Graphics or SmartArt diagrams to illustrate a process or structure. For example, a diagram can show the workflow of a procedure or the hierarchy in an organization. Some SmartArt layouts are text only, and others involve text and pictures. PowerPoint offers many SmartArt layouts to help you communicate with your audience graphically.

Insert a SmartArt Graphic

1. Select a slide with a content placeholder.

Note: *To learn how to select a slide, see Chapter 4.*

2. Click .

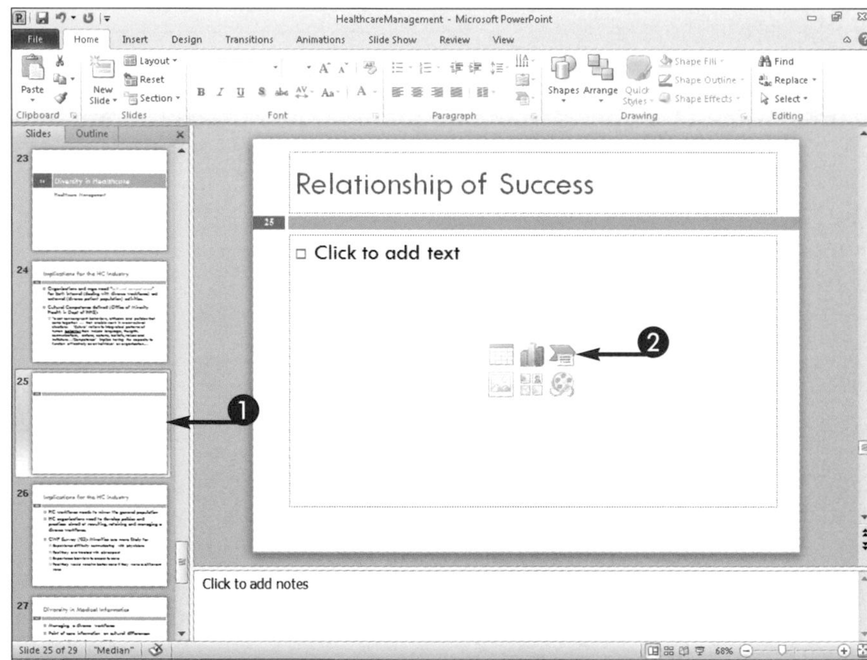

The Choose a SmartArt Graphic dialog box appears.

3. Click a diagram category.

- You can drag the scroll bar to see all the layouts in the selected category.

4. Click a specific diagram layout.

   In this example, Gear was clicked.

5. Click **OK**.

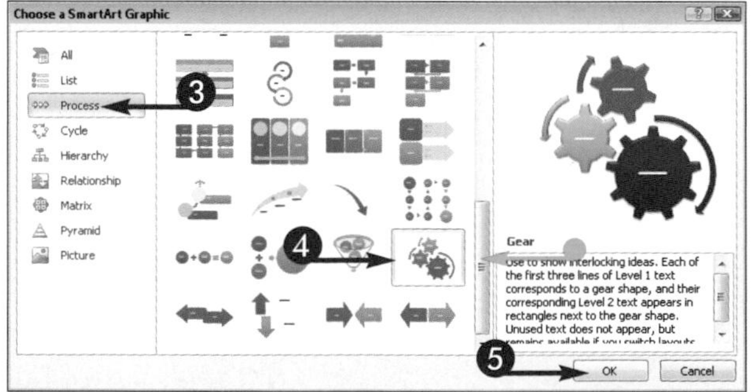

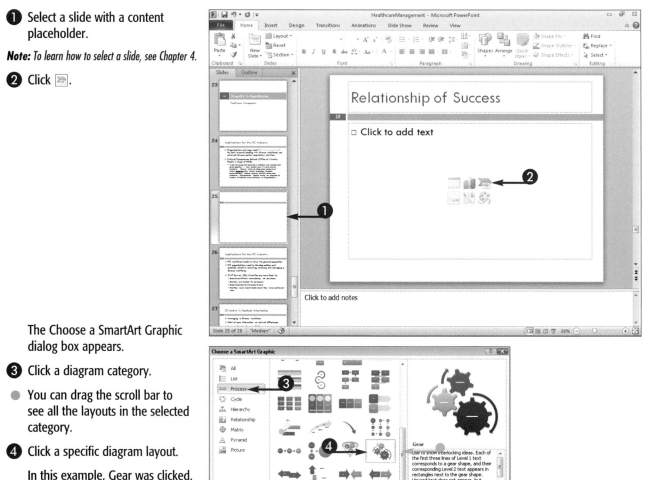

The dialog box closes and the SmartArt Graphics diagram appears on the slide.

6. Click [icon] to open the Text Pane.

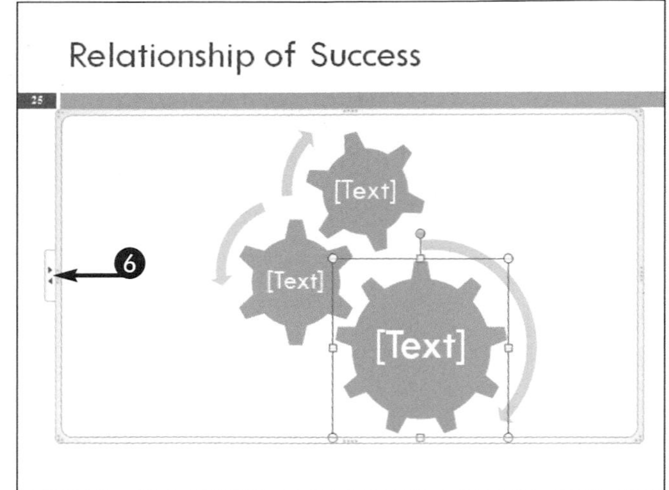

The Text Pane appears.

7. Click **[Text]** next to one of the bullets and type the text for the element.

Note: *[Text] disappears and the insertion point takes its place next to the bullet.*

Note: *You can also edit text directly in the graphical element.*

8. Repeat Step **7** to type text in the remaining graphical elements.

9. Click outside the SmartArt Graphic when finished.

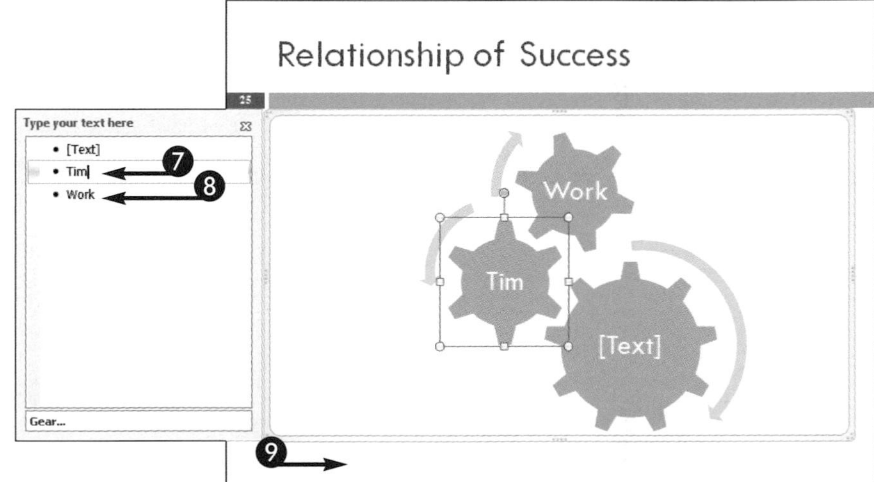

How do I add more elements in the SmartArt Graphics diagram?

Follow these steps to add additional elements.

1. Click an element next to where you want the additional element.
2. Click the **SmartArt Tools Design** tab.
3. Click the **Add Shape** [▾].
4. Click a command from the menu.

- An element is inserted.

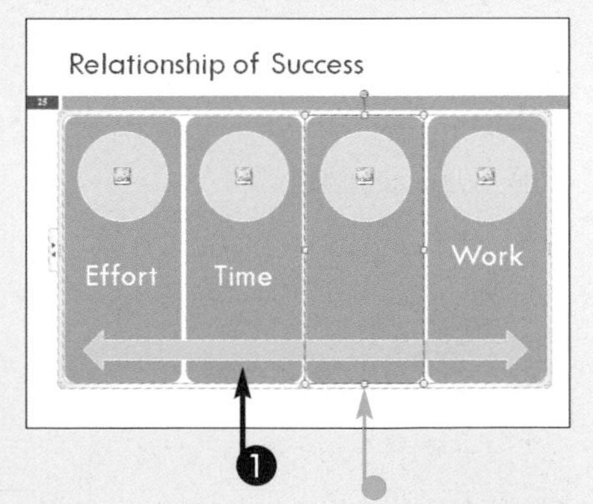

Edit SmartArt

After you create a SmartArt Graphic, you can change its look and contents at any time. For example, you can change a SmartArt Graphic to a different layout, edit the text, change its color, give it a 3-D effect, or even mix different shapes. This versatility allows you to create the perfect diagram that sends a specific message to your audience.

Edit SmartArt

1. Click anywhere in the SmartArt Graphic to select it.
2. Click the **SmartArt Tools Design** tab.
3. Click **Text Pane** or ⁝ on the SmartArt Graphic if the Text Pane is not open.

   The Text Pane appears.
4. Click any text in the Text Pane or on any element to edit the text.

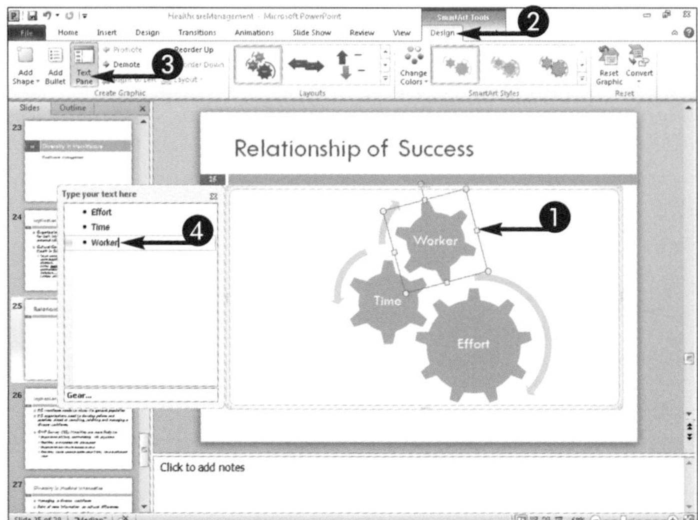

5. Click the **SmartArt Styles** ▾.

   The SmartArt Styles gallery appears.
6. Click a style from the gallery.

- The SmartArt Graphic changes style.

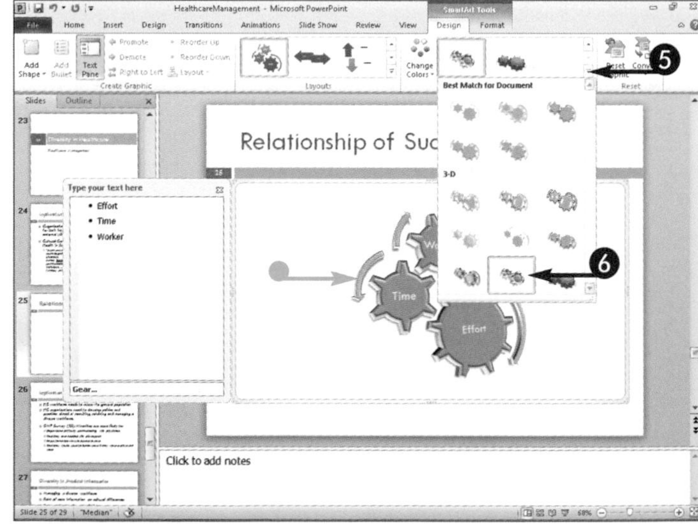

❼ Click the **SmartArt Layout** ⊡.

The SmartArt Layout gallery appears.

❽ Click a layout from the gallery.

● The SmartArt Graphic changes layout.

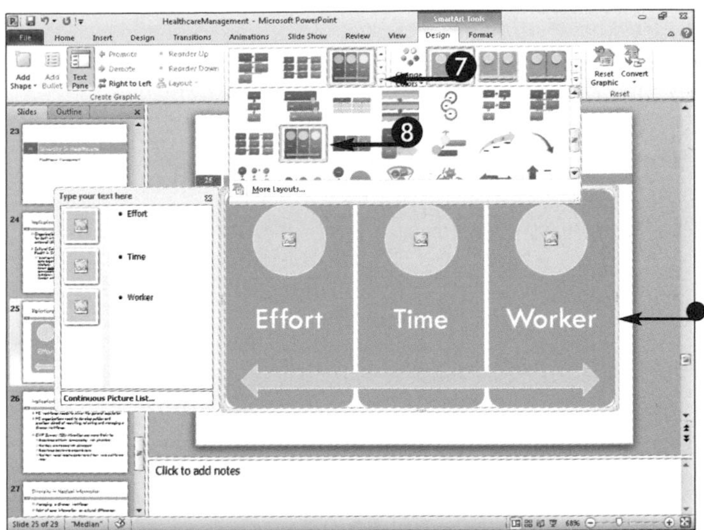

❾ Click a single element to select it.

❿ Click **Smaller** or **Larger** to change the element's size.

⓫ Click **Shape Fill** and select a color from the menu to change to the element's color.

⓬ Click **Shape Outline** and select a command from the menu to change the element's border.

● The element reflects the changes you made.

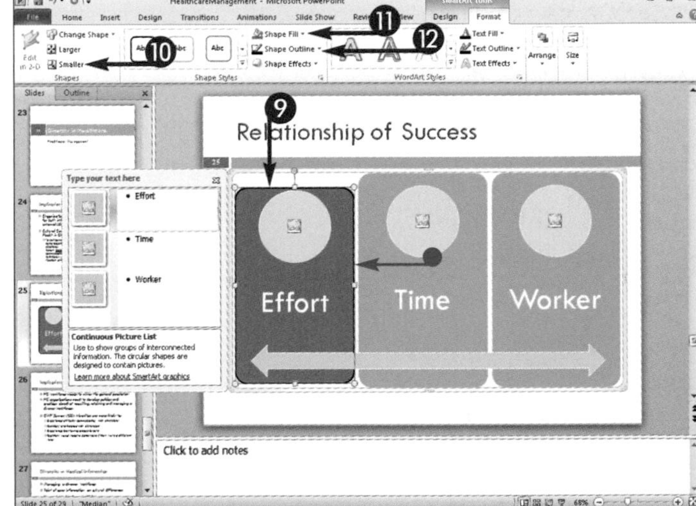

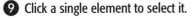

TIP

Are there color themes for the SmartArt Graphics?

Yes. Follow these steps to choose from a variety of color themes.

❶ Click a SmartArt Graphic to select it.

❷ Click the **SmartArt Tools Design** tab.

❸ Click **Change Colors**.

❹ In the Primary Theme Colors gallery, click a color theme from the gallery.

The SmartArt Graphic changes colors to the theme you choose.

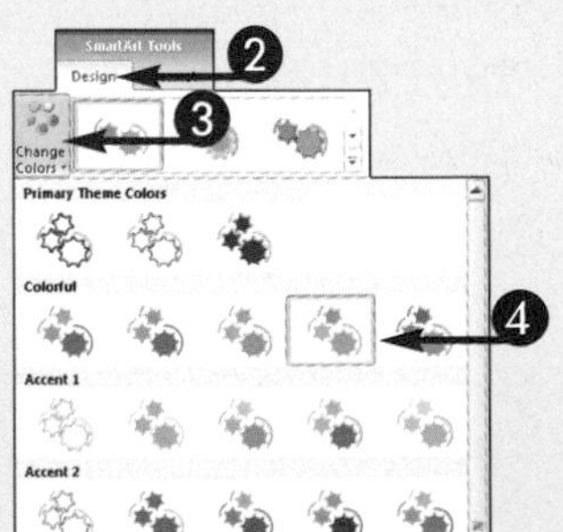

Insert a Slide from Another File

You can insert a slide from one presentation file into another. This can be a great timesaver when you have created a slide with a highly detailed chart, table, or diagram in another presentation. Importing the slide from the other presentation saves you the trouble of reentering data and reformatting the object on the slide.

Insert a Slide from Another File

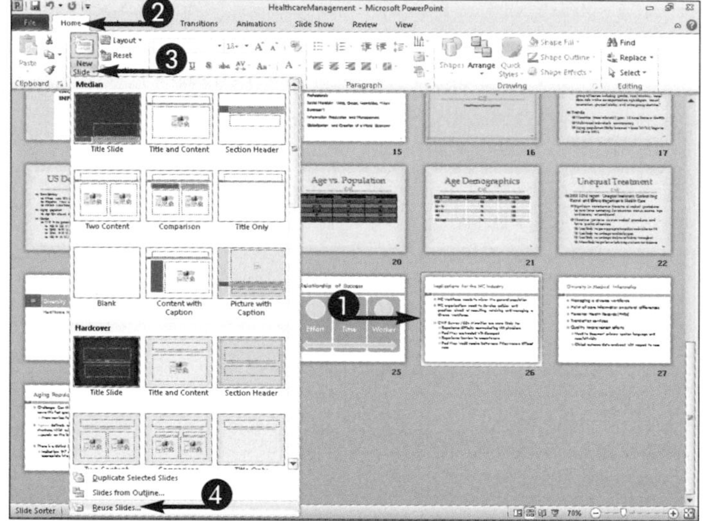

1. In either Normal or Slide Sorter view, select the slide after which you want to insert the new slide.

Note: *See Chapter 1 to learn how to switch views.*

2. Click the **Home** tab.
3. Click the bottom portion of the **New Slide** button.

   The layout gallery appears.

4. Click **Reuse Slides**.

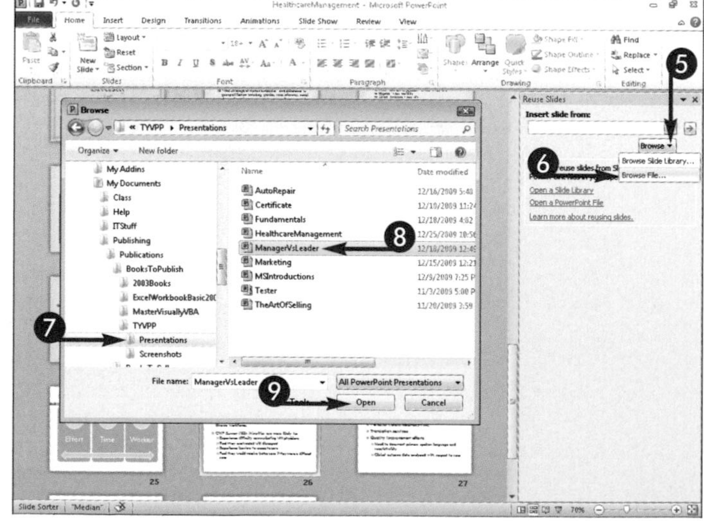

The Reuse Slides task pane appears.

5. Click the **Browse** drop-down list.
6. Click **Browse File**.

   The Browse dialog box opens.

7. Click the folder that contains the presentation file you want to view.
8. Click the presentation file that contains the slide you want to insert.
9. Click **Open**.

- PowerPoint places the path to the file in the Insert slide from text box.
- The slides of the selected presentation file are shown in the Reuse Slides task pane.

10 Drag the scroll bar to find the slide you want to insert.

11 Click the slide you want to insert.

In this example, the Leaders and Managers slide was clicked.

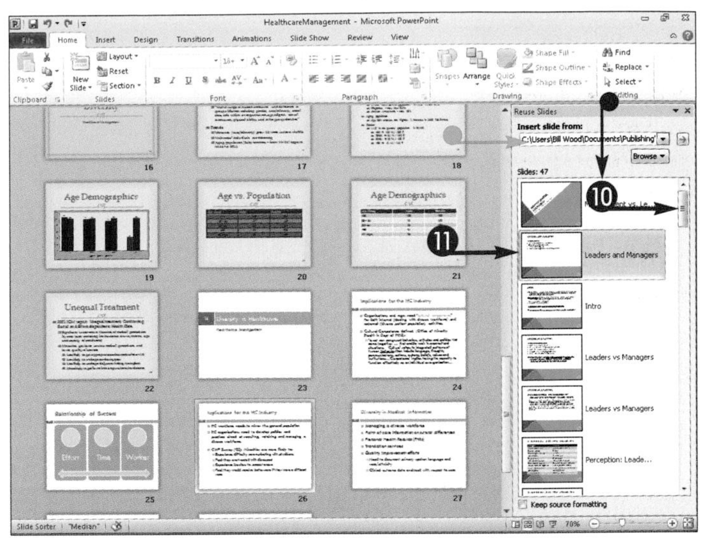

- The slide you clicked is inserted after the slide you originally selected.

Note: *If you have two presentations open, you can drag slides from one to another.*

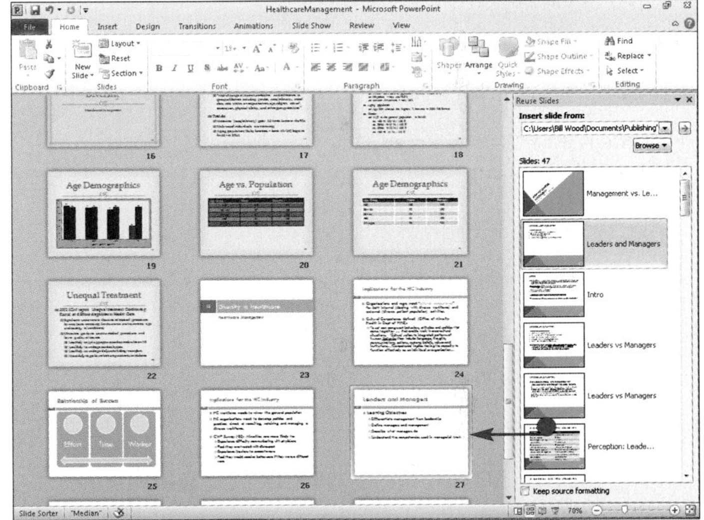

TIPS

When I look at the slides in the Reuse Slides task pane, I cannot tell what they say. Is there a way to get a better look?

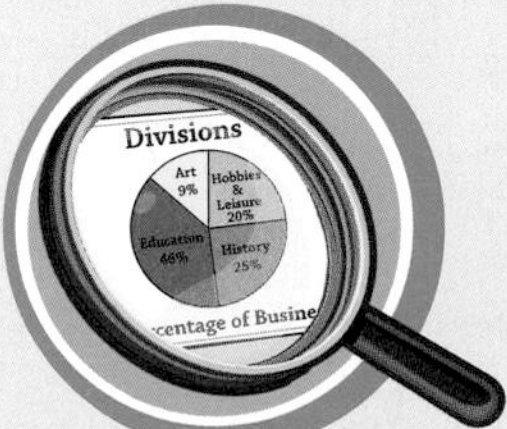

Yes. Move the pointer over the slide thumbnail (rather than the slide title), and an enlarged thumbnail will pop up to provide enhanced visibility and readability.

I cannot find the slide I want in the file I opened in the Reuse Slides task pane. Can I go back and open another file?

Yes. Click the **Browse** button drop-down list in the Reuse Slides task pane again, and then click **Browse File**. The Browse dialog box reappears so that you can select another file.

CHAPTER 7

Using Themes

You can use PowerPoint's built-in themes to add a professional-looking design to your presentation. Although it is possible to design slides by applying slide backgrounds manually or formatting elements one by one, people most commonly use slide themes built into PowerPoint.

Understanding Themes

Office Document Themes apply various types of formatting to make your slides look attractive.

Theme Elements

By default, each new presentation you create uses a blank design theme. When you choose a specific theme, PowerPoint applies a set of colors, fonts, and placeholder positions to the slides. The theme also can include a background color, background graphics, and background graphic effects.

Apply Themes

You can apply a theme to a single slide, a section, or the entire presentation. Generally it is better to use one theme for a section or an entire presentation so that the slides have a consistent look and feel. However, occasionally you might choose to apply a different theme to a particular slide for emphasis.

Modify Themes

Although PowerPoint provides professionally designed slide themes, you can tailor existing themes to meet your specific needs. You can change the background or background color, color theme, or font theme. Once you design a favorite theme, you can add it to the theme gallery to use again.

Themes and Masters

Slide masters determine where placeholders and objects appear on each slide layout. Each theme has a master for the Title Slide, Title and Content Slide, and so on. After you apply a theme, you can modify the masters. Any changes you make appear in presentation slides made with that master.

Control Design Aspects with Themes

PowerPoint themes control several design aspects of your slides. The theme determines where PowerPoint positions placeholders, the font theme (font and font size), the color theme, and the slide background.

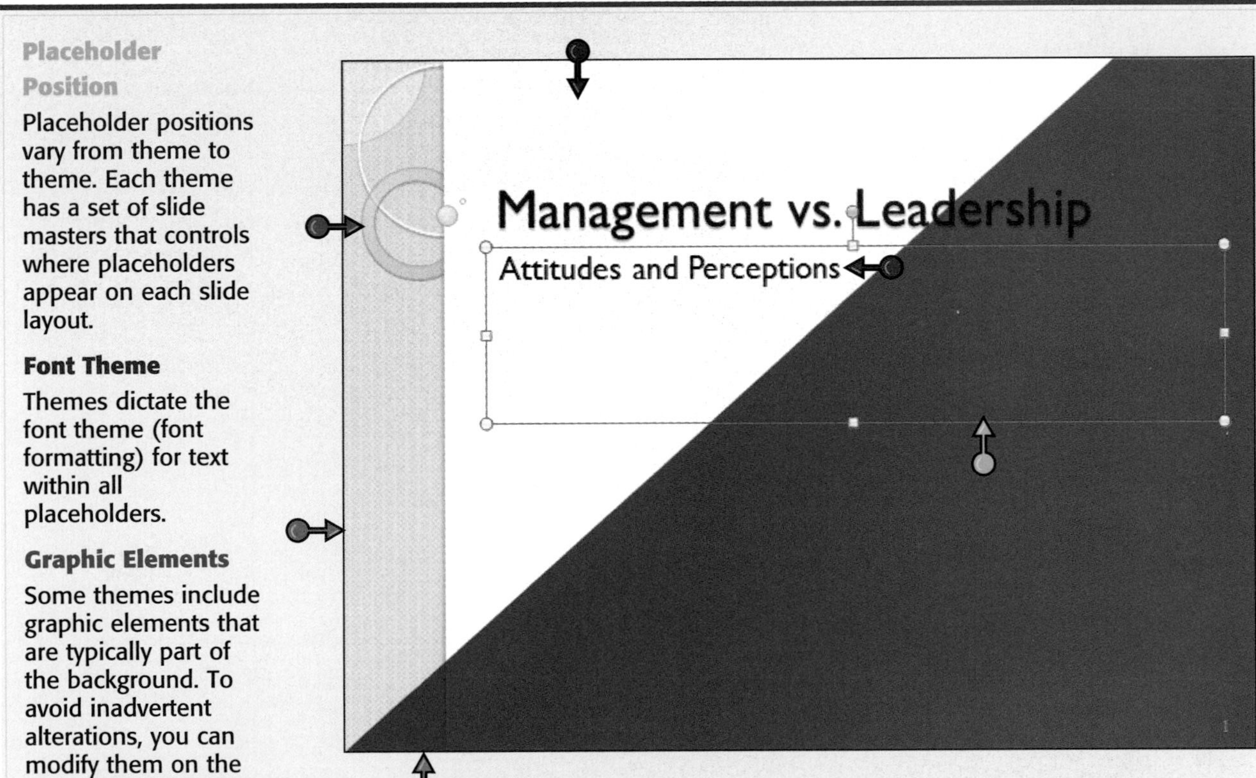

Placeholder Position

Placeholder positions vary from theme to theme. Each theme has a set of slide masters that controls where placeholders appear on each slide layout.

Font Theme

Themes dictate the font theme (font formatting) for text within all placeholders.

Graphic Elements

Some themes include graphic elements that are typically part of the background. To avoid inadvertent alterations, you can modify them on the slide masters, but not on individual slides.

Color Theme

Themes control the colors automatically applied to slide text, background, and objects such as tables, charts, and SmartArt Graphics. You can change colors on individual slides.

Background

Themes specify the background applied to slides. The background might be a solid color, a gradient, or a pattern, and may include graphics.

Effects

Effects give a dimensional appearance to graphics by adding shadows, transparency, 3-D, and more. A theme may apply a particular style of effects to graphics.

Apply a Theme to Selected Slides

You can apply a different theme to the currently selected slide(s) in either Normal or Slide Sorter view. If you apply a different theme to a single slide, be sure it complements the design used on other slides. As you advance slides, the transition from one theme to another affects your viewers.

Apply a Theme to Selected Slides

1. Select a slide(s) in Normal or Slide Sorter view.

Note: *To select multiple slides, click the first slide, and then press* Ctrl *while clicking additional slides.*

2. Click the **Design** tab.
3. Click the **Themes** gallery (▾).

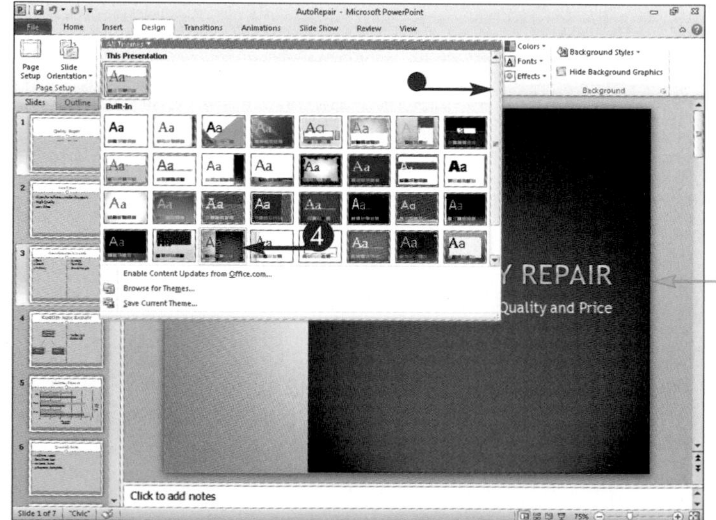

The gallery of themes appears.

4. Position your mouse pointer (↖) over a theme thumbnail.

- If the PowerPoint Live Preview feature is enabled, it shows the new design in the Slide pane.
- You can use the scroll bar to see all the themes.

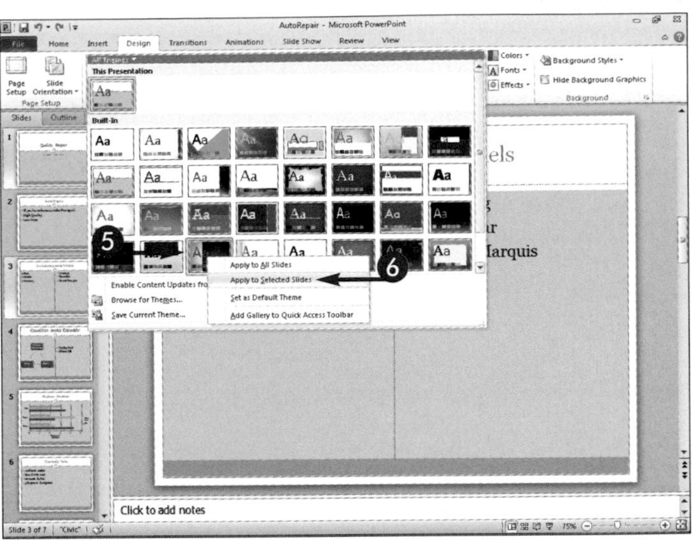

5 Right-click a theme.

The shortcut menu appears.

6 Click **Apply to Selected Slides**.

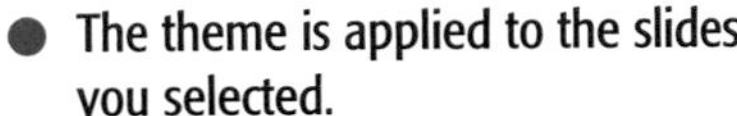

- The theme is applied to the slides you selected.

TIPS

If I change a few slides to use a different theme, can I use the master slide features for those slides?

Yes. When you apply a theme to a presentation, PowerPoint creates a set of masters for that theme. If you apply yet another theme to your presentation, you end up with two sets of masters that you can modify when you view the slide masters. In Chapter 8, you learn about using slide masters.

Why does my shortcut menu sometimes have an option called Apply to matching slides?

Apply to matching slides appears on the Themes shortcut menu if you are using more than one theme. You can apply your chosen theme to all slides that have the same theme as the currently selected slide.

Apply a Theme to All Slides

You can apply one theme to all the slides in a presentation to give them a consistent, professional look. While the slide layouts may vary, the theme supplies common colors, fonts, and more. This allows you to focus on content rather than design and formatting.

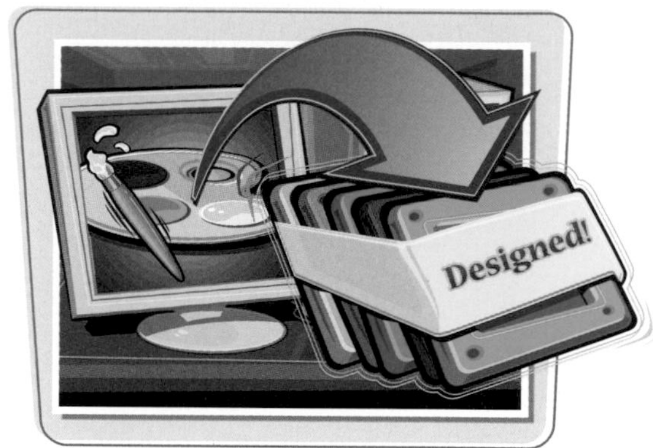

Apply a Theme to All Slides

1. Click the **Design** tab.
2. Click the **Themes** gallery ▾.

The gallery of themes appears.

- You can use the scroll bar to see all the themes.

3. Click a theme.

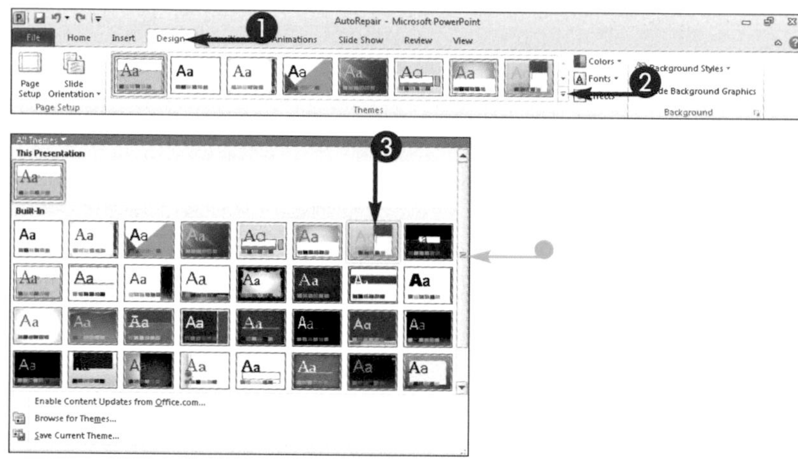

- PowerPoint applies the theme to all slides in the presentation.

Note: *You also can right-click a thumbnail in the gallery and then click **Apply to All Slides**.*

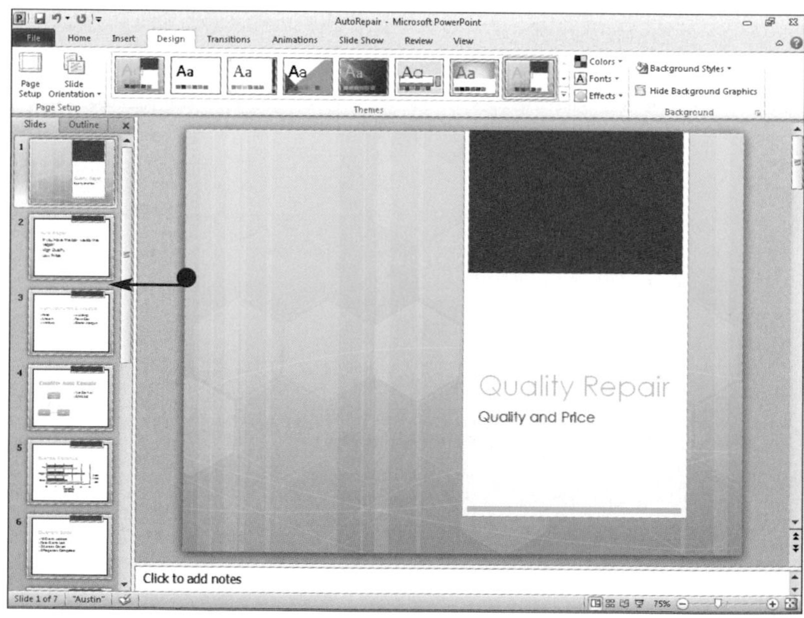

Apply a Theme to a Section

It is not unusual to change topics during a presentation. For example, a person teaching a class about Microsoft Office would change topics when moving from PowerPoint to Excel. You can apply one theme to all the slides in a section to give each section a consistent look, yet make it obvious that a portion of a presentation is a specific topic.

Apply a Theme to a Section

1. Click a section heading.

   In this example, the Competency section was clicked.

2. Click the **Design** tab.
3. Click the **Themes** gallery ▾.

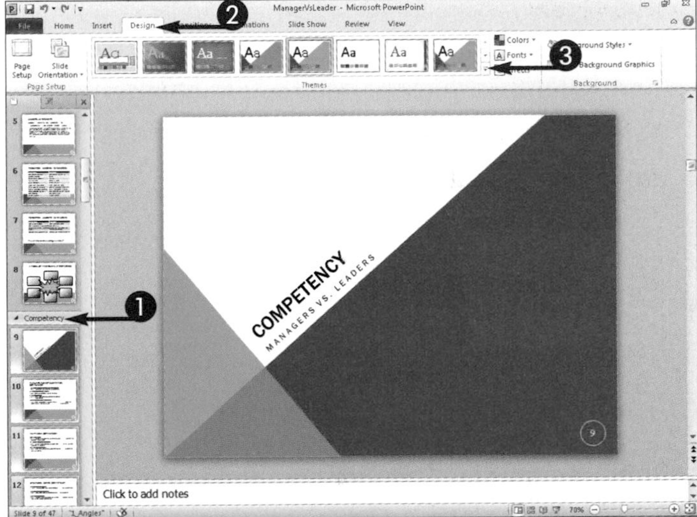

The gallery of themes appears.

- You can use the scroll bar to see all the themes.

4. Click a theme.

- PowerPoint applies the theme to all slides in the section.

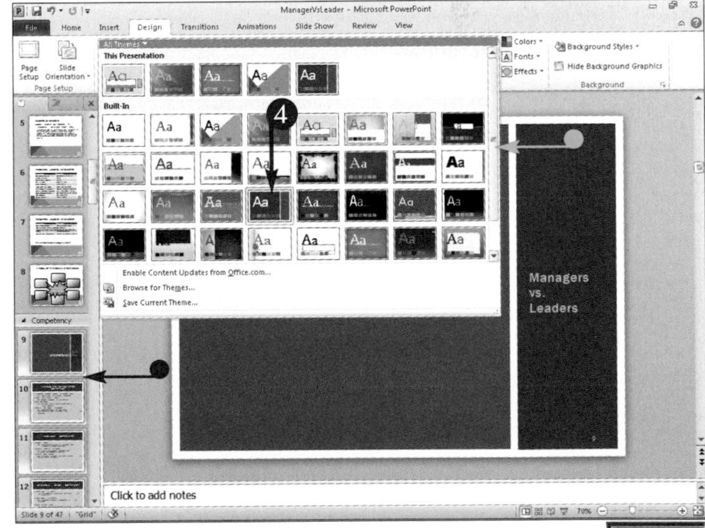

Change Theme Colors for Selected Slides

Each theme includes theme colors. You can add variety or emphasize particular slides by changing the theme colors of only those particular slides. When you change theme colors, the other aspects of the theme, such as placeholder position and background objects, stay the same. Only the colors change.

You can change theme colors on one or more slides in Normal view or Slide Sorter view.

Change Theme Colors for Selected Slides

1. Select a slide(s) in Normal or Slide Sorter view.

Note: To select multiple slides, click the first slide, and then press Ctrl while clicking additional slides.

2. Click the **Design** tab.
3. Click **Colors**.

   The gallery of colors appears.

- You can use the scroll bar to see all the color schemes.

4. Right-click the color scheme.

   In this example, Concourse was right-clicked.

5. Click **Apply to Selected Slides**.

- The theme colors change is applied to the slides you selected.

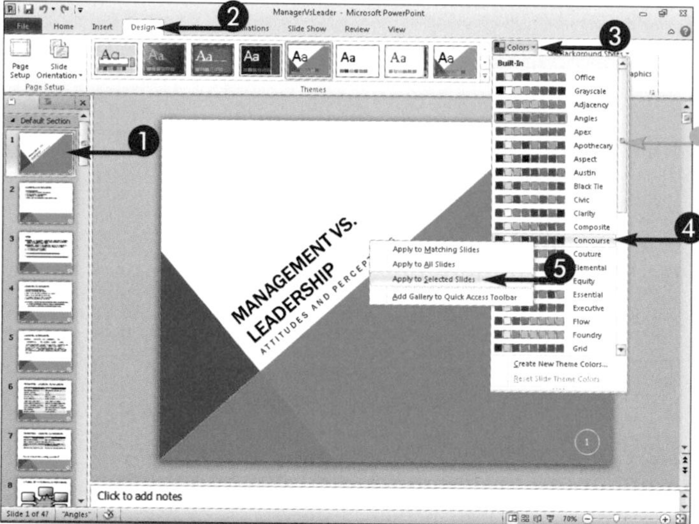

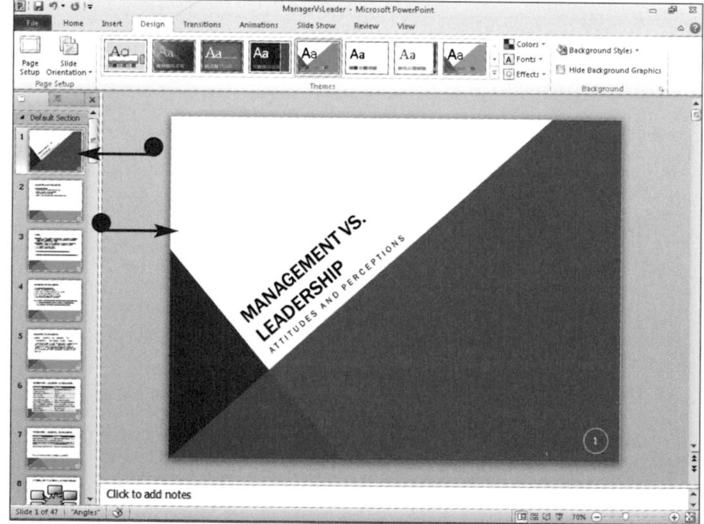

Change Theme Colors for All Slides

You can change the theme colors for a particular theme or for all the slides in a presentation. Changing colors can give a completely different feel to your presentation, while retaining your theme's look and other attributes.

Changing the theme colors also can help you get more attractive results when displaying the slide show or printing the presentation.

Change Theme Colors for All Slides

1. Select a slide designed with the theme you want to change.
2. Click the **Design** tab.
3. Click **Colors**.

   The gallery of colors appears.

   - You can use the scroll bar to see all the color schemes.

4. Click a color scheme.

   In this example, Adjacency was clicked.

Note: If your presentation has multiple themes, only the theme of the selected slide changes colors.

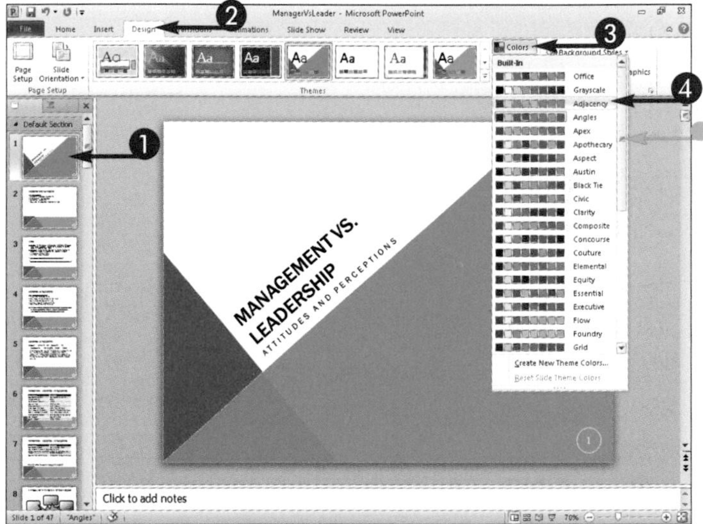

- The selected color scheme is applied to all slides using the theme.

  To change the color theme for all slides in a presentation, you can right-click a color scheme in the gallery and then click **Apply to All Slides**.

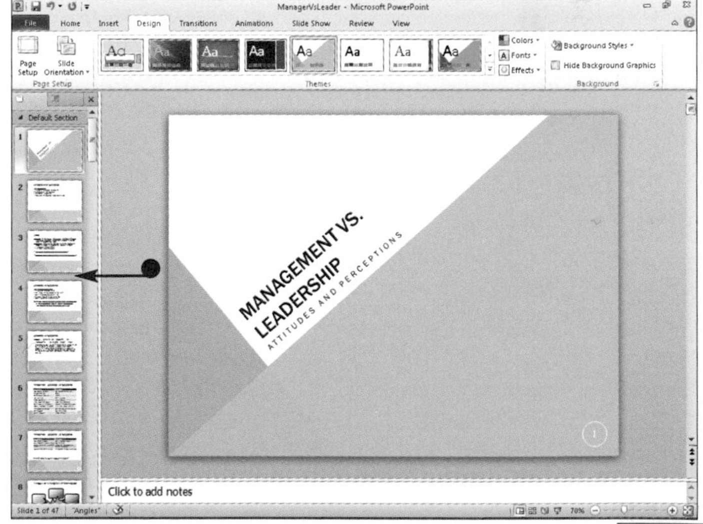

Modify a Font Theme

Each theme uses a particular font theme that defines the fonts used for headings and placeholder text. You can change the font theme for a particular theme or for the entire presentation.

You cannot change the font theme for individual slides. PowerPoint always applies the font theme to all the slides in the presentation.

Modify a Font Theme

1. Select a slide designed with the theme you want to change.
2. Click the **Design** tab.
3. Click **Fonts**.

   The gallery of font themes appears.

- You can use the scroll bar to see all the font themes.

4. Click a font theme.

Note: *If your presentation has multiple themes, only the theme of the selected slide changes fonts.*

- PowerPoint applies the font theme to all slides using the theme.

  To change the font theme for all slides in a presentation, you can right-click a font theme in the gallery and then click **Apply to All Slides**.

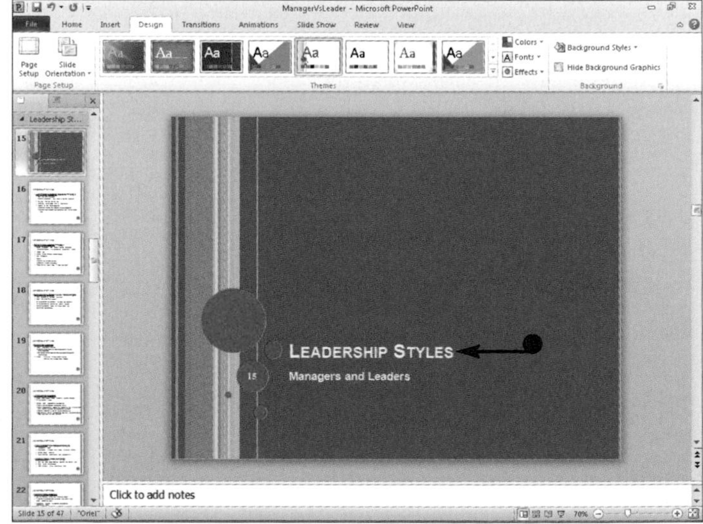

Modify the Background

A theme applies a background (sometimes plain white) on which all slide elements sit. You can change the background for one slide, a theme, or throughout the presentation to change the look.

For example, while a plain white background may work best for printing, you may prefer to add a background color or pattern for slide show playback.

Modify the Background

1. Select slide(s) in Normal or Slide Sorter view.

Note: To select multiple slides, click the first slide, and then press Ctrl *while clicking additional slides.*

2. Click the **Design** tab.
3. Click **Background Styles**.

   The gallery of backgrounds appears.

4. Right-click a background style.
5. Click **Apply to Selected Slides**.

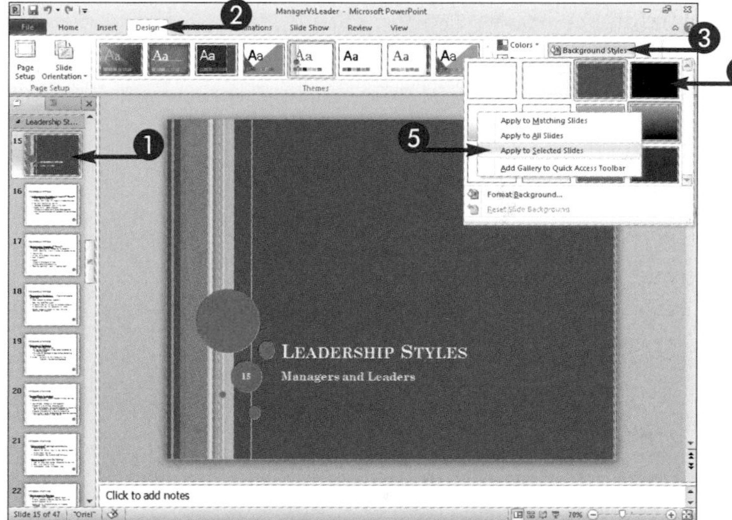

- PowerPoint applies the background style to the slides.

  To change the background for all slides whose theme matches the theme of the selected slide(s), you can right-click a background in the gallery and then click **Apply to Matching Slides**.

  To change the background for all slides in a presentation, you can right-click a background in the gallery and then click **Apply to All Slides**.

Apply a Texture or Picture Background

You can push design limits even further by using either a texture or a digital picture as a background. For example, you can use a digital photo of a new product as a slide background for a presentation introducing the new product.

You can apply a texture or picture background to selected slides or the entire presentation.

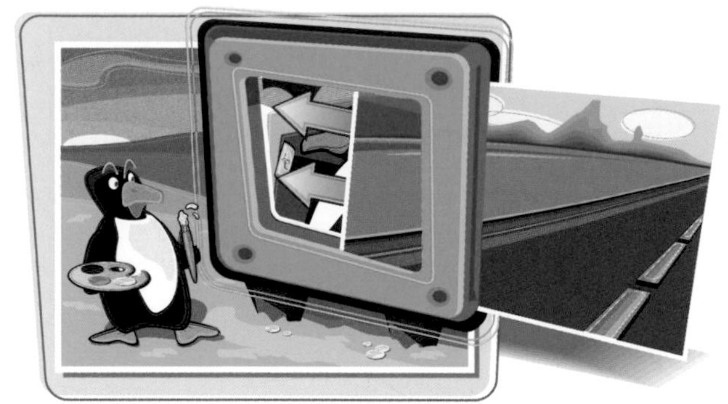

Apply a Texture or Picture Background

Apply a Texture

1. Select slide(s) in Normal or Slide Sorter view.

Note: *To select multiple slides, click the first slide, and then press* Ctrl *while clicking additional slides.*

2. Click the **Design** tab.
3. Click **Background Styles**.
4. Click **Format Background**.

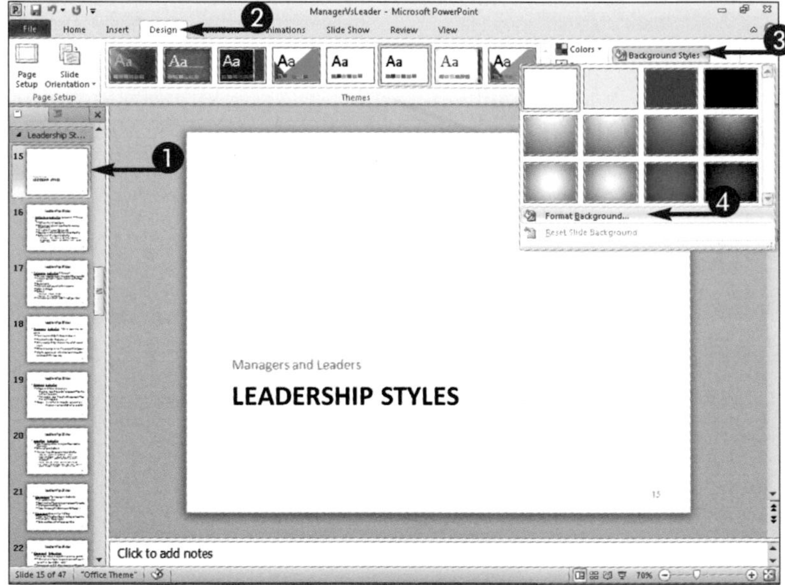

The Format Background box appears.

5. Click **Picture or texture fill** (◎ changes to ◉).
6. Click the **Texture** ▾.

   A gallery of textures appears.

7. Click a texture.

- The texture is applied to the selected slide(s).

8. Click the **Close** button (☒) on the Format Background dialog box.

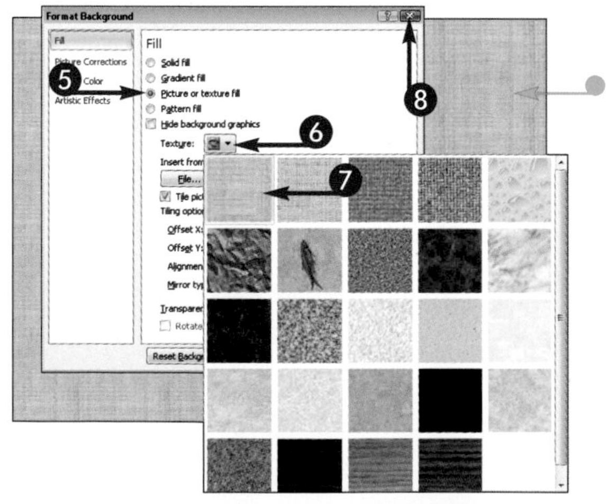

Insert a Picture

1. Perform Steps **1** to **5** on the facing page.
2. Click **File**.

   The Insert Picture dialog box appears.
3. Click the folder that contains the picture file you want to insert.
4. Click the picture file.
5. Click **Insert**.

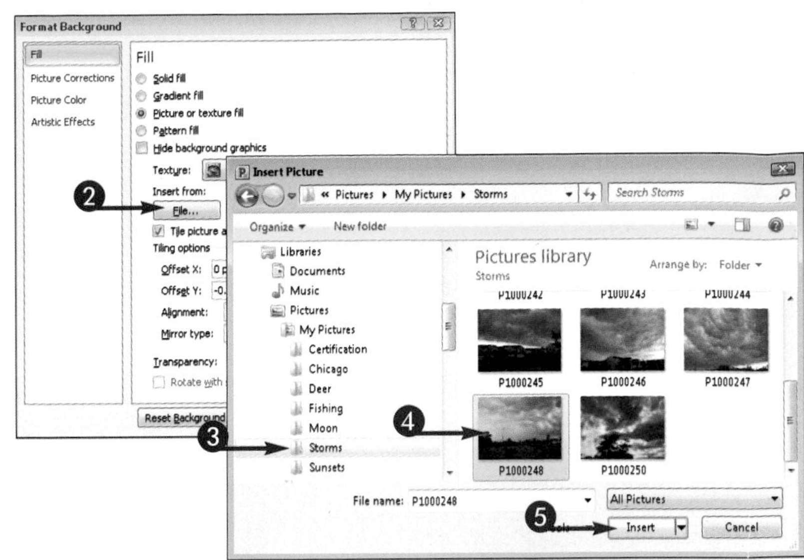

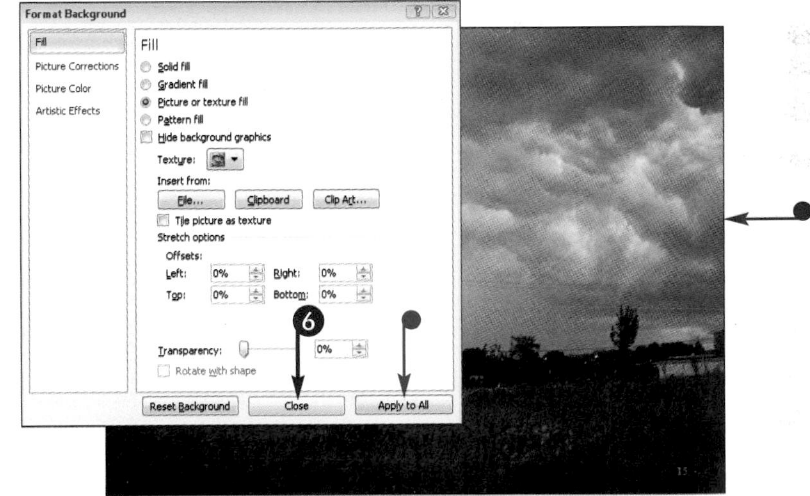

- The Insert Picture box closes and the picture becomes the background.
- Click **Apply to All** to apply the background change to all slides in the presentation.

6. Click **Close**.

TIP

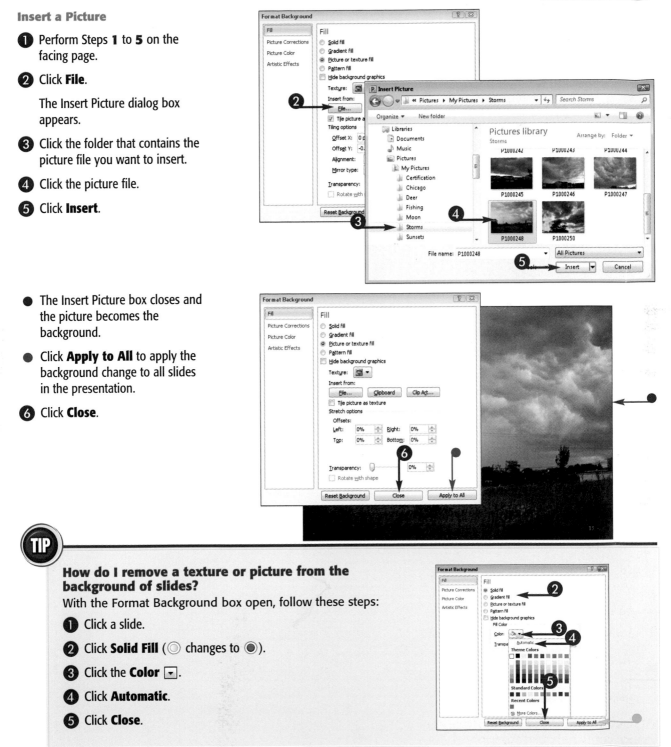

How do I remove a texture or picture from the background of slides?

With the Format Background box open, follow these steps:

1. Click a slide.
2. Click **Solid Fill** (◎ changes to ◉).
3. Click the **Color** ▾.
4. Click **Automatic**.
5. Click **Close**.

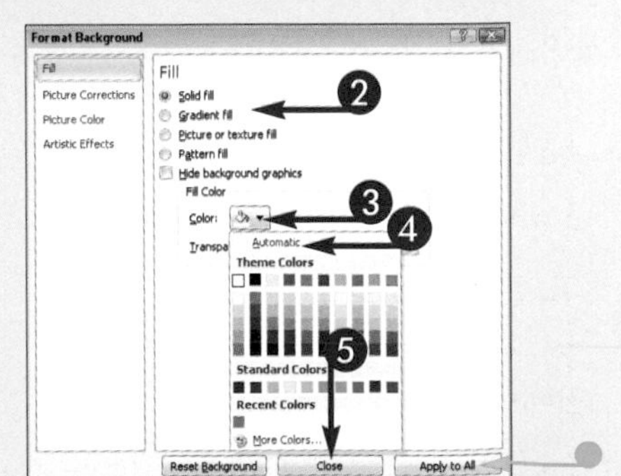

Save Your Own Theme

If you applied a color theme, font theme, and background that really work together, you can save that combination as a theme. This enables you to quickly apply that combination to other presentations.

Any changes you made, such as color theme, font theme, or a background image or pattern, are saved as part of your theme.

Save Your Own Theme

1. Click the **Design** tab.
2. Click the **Themes** gallery ▾.

   The gallery of themes appears.

- All your saved themes will appear under Custom.

3. Click **Save Current Theme**.

The Save Current Theme dialog box appears.

4. Type a file name.

   In this example, MyTheme3 was typed.

- Do not change the folder location. Your themes appear in the gallery of themes because they are in this default folder location.

5. Click **Save**.

   PowerPoint adds the theme to the gallery in the section labeled Custom.

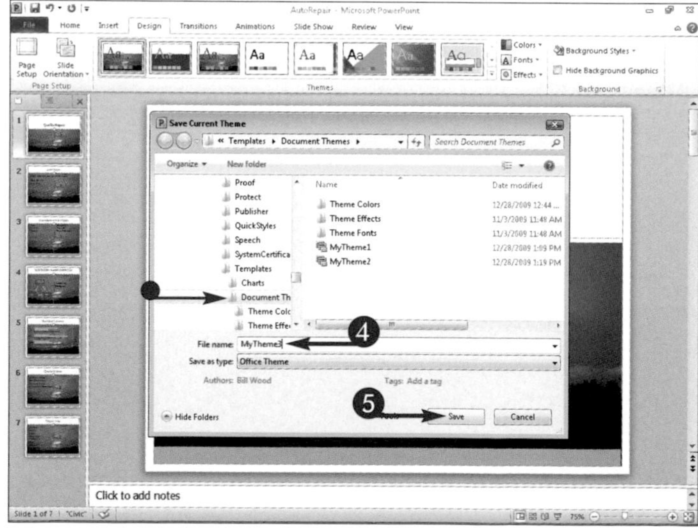

Make a Theme the Default for New Presentations

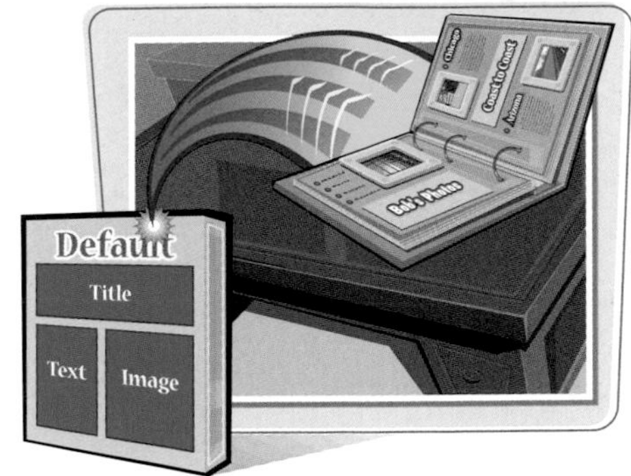

By default, a new presentation has a blank background and uses the Calibri font in varying sizes depending on the placeholder. You can make your favorite theme the default for new presentations so it is automatically applied to future presentations.

You can make any theme the default for every new presentation you create.

Make a Theme the Default for New Presentations

1. Click the **Design** tab.
2. Click the **Themes** gallery ▾.

   The gallery of themes appears.
3. Right-click the theme to set as the default.
4. Click **Set as Default Theme**.

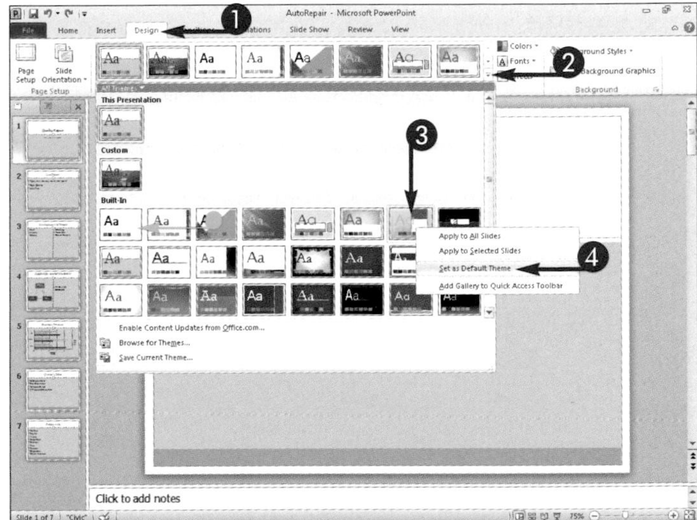

The theme immediately becomes the default theme. Any blank presentation you create uses that theme.

To return to the original default theme, set the Office Theme as the default. If you position your mouse over a theme in the gallery, a ScreenTip with the theme name appears.

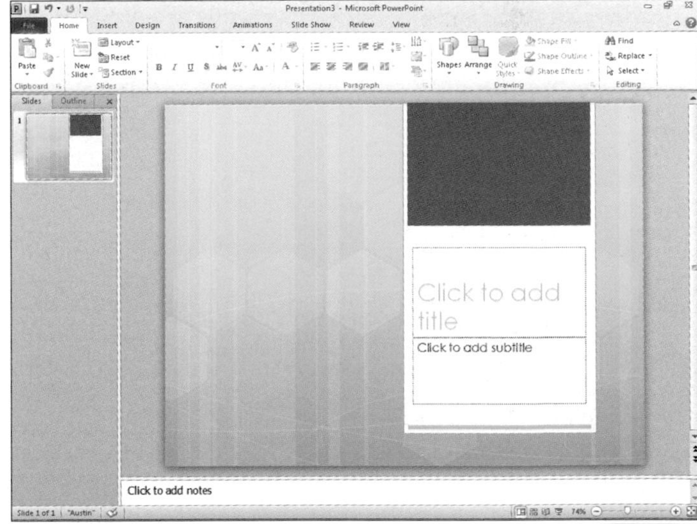

Save a Template

A *template* is a boilerplate presentation that you use repeatedly, but change certain items from use to use. It includes both a presentation design and reusable template content, such as bulleted lists you would use often in a sales presentation. You can save any presentation as a template so that you can create new presentations using the template's formatting and contents.

Save a Template

❶ Click the **File** tab.

❷ Click **Save As**.

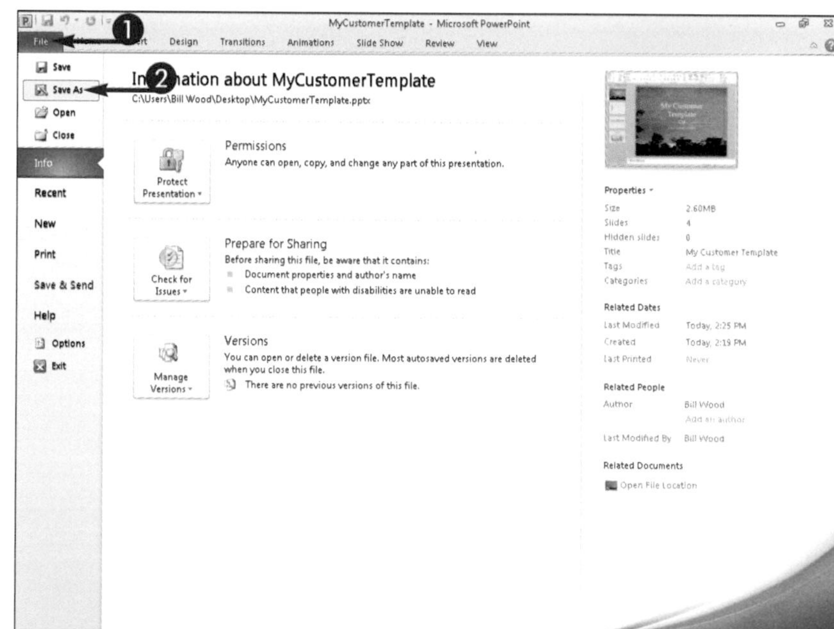

The Save As dialog box appears.

❸ Click the **Save as type** ▾.

❹ Click **PowerPoint Template**.

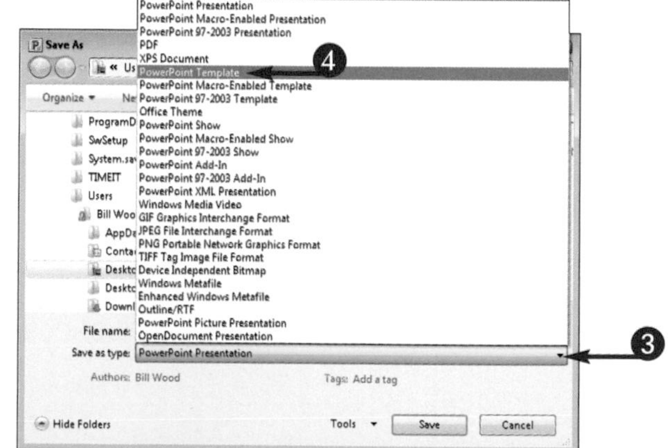

- Do not change the folder location. Your templates appear in the PowerPoint templates because they are in this default folder location.

5. Type a file name.

   In this example, MyCustomerTemplate was typed.

6. Click **Save**.

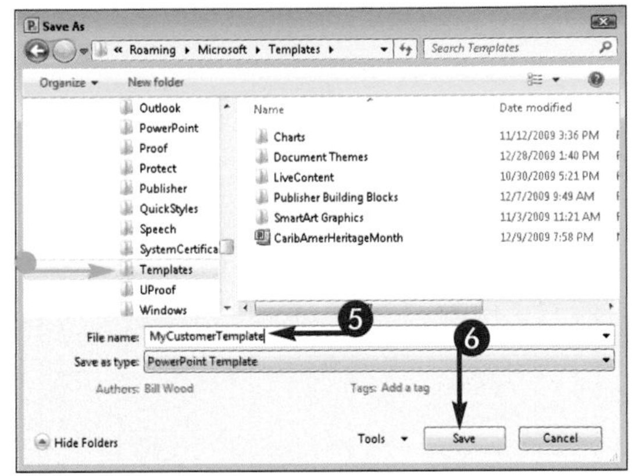

7. Click the **File** tab.

8. Click **New**.

9. Click **My templates**.

   The New Presentation dialog box appears.

- Your template appears here.

Note: *To create a new presentation with a template, click the template, and then click* ***OK****. For more on using templates, see Chapter 3.*

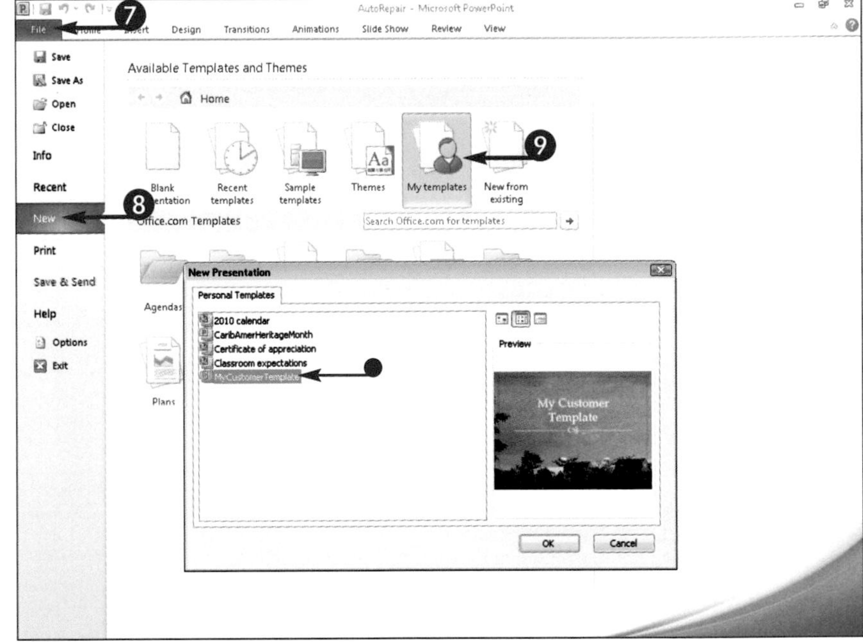

TIPS

I like some of the templates on Microsoft Office Online. Are other templates available?

Yes. Many PowerPoint templates are available online. You can download some for free, but must purchase others. Type **PowerPoint Templates** in your favorite Internet search engine to find other templates.

Can I customize anything when creating a template?

Yes. The point of a template is to reuse features that do not change from use to use, such as quotes, charts, tables, and backgrounds. Things that may change from use to use are table data, chart data, the title of the presentation, and the name of the company or audience members. You design a template like any other presentation.

CHAPTER

Using Masters

Masters enable you to make global settings for your slides, such as inserting your company logo or a page number on every slide. When you change a master, all slides based on that master change, too.

Understanding Masters

PowerPoint offers three master views. Each enables you to set up the basic infrastructure for your slides to save you from having to arrange and design elements on every slide.

Work with Three Kinds of Masters

PowerPoint uses the Slide Master set, Handout Master, and Notes Master to control page layouts. The Slide Master set consists of an overall theme master and a master for each slide layout. Changes made to masters are applied to corresponding presentation slides. The Handout Master controls the layout of printed handouts. The Notes Master controls how printed notes pages look.

Using Masters to Make Global Changes

When you change a master, such as increasing the font size for slide titles or adding a graphic, PowerPoint applies that change to all corresponding slides in the presentation. This saves you time and gives your presentation a consistent look and feel.

How Masters Relate to the Theme

Masters are based on themes. When you apply a theme to your presentation, PowerPoint automatically creates a set of slide masters with that theme. If you change a slide master, you can then save it as theme, which preserves the new master. If you apply more than one theme to your presentation, you will have multiple master sets — one for each theme.

Overriding Master Settings

When you make changes to individual presentation slides in Normal view, for example changing the font, that change takes precedence over master settings. You can also omit the graphics placed on a slide master from individual presentation slides — you use the Background group on the Design tab of the Ribbon.

Understanding Slide Master Elements

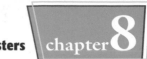

You can use Slide Master view to create global design settings for your slides. The Slide Master and Layout Masters contain placeholders where you can set formatting for common text elements. They also contain various placeholders for footer information, a date, and slide numbers.

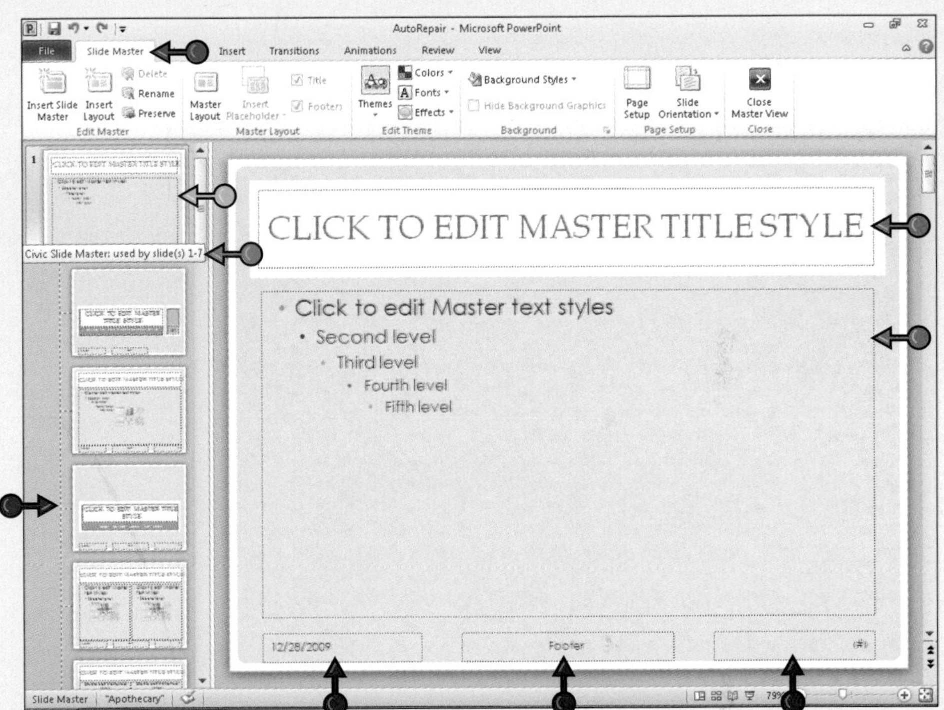

Slide (Theme) Master

The Slide Master is shown in the left pane and a set of masters is created for each theme you apply to a presentation. It is connected with the related Layout Masters with a dotted line. Any changes made on the Slide Master are seen on all presentation slides based on it.

Layout Masters

Layout Masters represent the various slide layouts that you can insert into a presentation, such as Title Slide, Title and Content, and Two Content. Layout Masters are associated with a Slide Master. Changes on a Layout Master affect only those presentation slides with its particular layout.

Slide Master View Tab

Use the Slide Master tab to create, delete, preserve, or rename Slide Masters or Layout Masters. You can also change or insert placeholders and backgrounds, or change color themes and font themes.

Placeholders

You can select a text or content placeholder and apply formatting changes. That formatting becomes the default style for that placeholder on all slides using the layout.

Footer, Date, and Slide Numbers

The Date placeholder positions the date on each slide, and the Page (#) placeholder provides page numbers on all slides. Use the Footer placeholder to add information, such as your company's name, to every slide.

Dependency on a Master Design

Position the mouse pointer (↖) over any slide in the Slide Master view and a ScreenTip shows you which presentation slides use that Slide Master or Layout Master design.

Open and Close Slide Master View

You work with the Slide Master and Layout Masters in Slide Master view. Display Slide Master view using the View tab. Opening Slide Master view automatically displays tabs for working with the Slide Master set.

After you make changes to the Slide Master set and close the Slide Master view, PowerPoint redisplays whatever view you had open previously — either Normal view, Slide Sorter view, or Notes Page view. Your global changes appear there.

Open and Close Slide Master View

1. Click the **View** tab.
2. Click **Slide Master**.

Slide Master view and the Slide Master Ribbon tab appear.

3. Click the **Slide Master** tab.
4. To close the Slide Master view, click **Close Master View**.

Slide Master view closes and PowerPoint restores the previous presentation design view — Normal, Slide Sorter, or Notes Page.

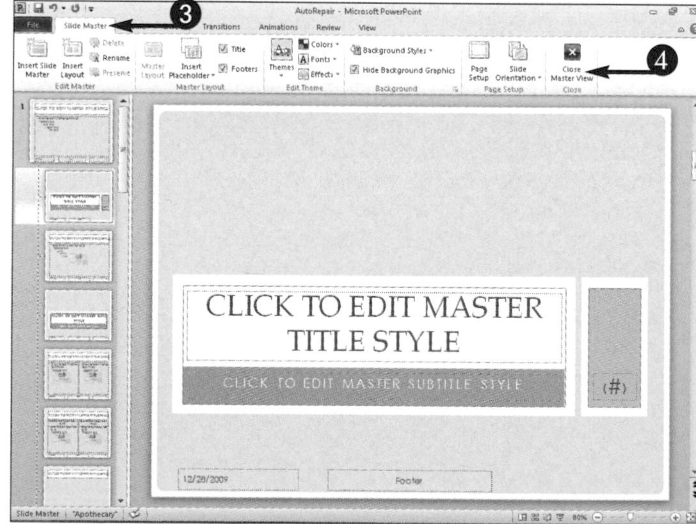

Remove a Placeholder

The Layout Masters contain placeholders for the slide title, text or graphic content, date, footer, and slide numbers. If you are not using a particular placeholder, you can remove it from the Layout Masters.

Deleting a placeholder from the Slide Master at the top does not delete it from the Layout Masters, though formatting changes made to placeholders on the Slide Master do affect the formatting of associated presentation slides.

Remove a Placeholder

1. Display Slide Master view.

Note: *To access Slide Master view, see the section "Open and Close Slide Master View."*

2. Click the Layout Master that contains the placeholder you want to remove.
3. Click the border of a placeholder to select it.
4. Press Delete.

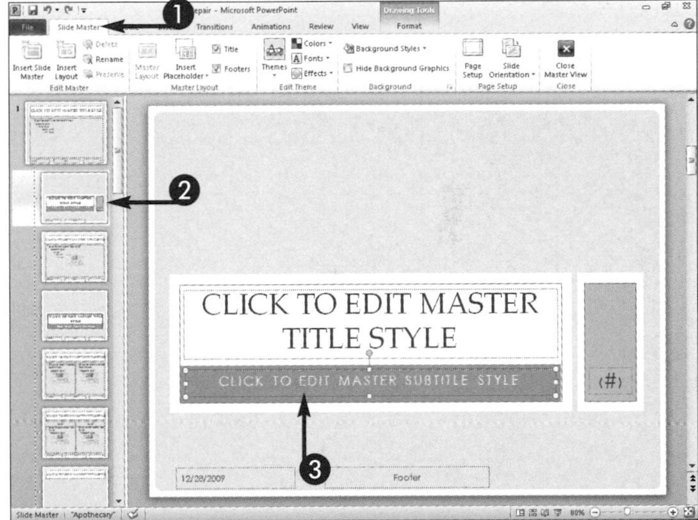

- The placeholder is deleted.

Note: *If you delete a placeholder from a Layout Master, PowerPoint does not delete the placeholder on existing presentation slides, though it does affect its formatting. Slides inserted in the presentation after you make this deletion from the Layout Master will not contain the placeholder.*

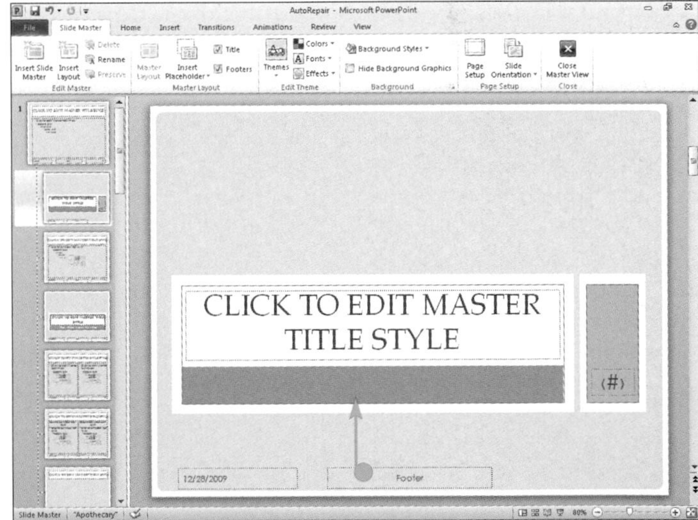

Insert a Placeholder

You can insert a new placeholder in any Layout Master in Slide Master view. You can insert placeholders for text or content, plus other types of placeholders like picture or chart placeholders.

Note that you also can resize, reposition, or reformat any placeholder at any time. Formatting changes affect existing presentation slides. Click the placeholder's border to select it, and then make the desired changes.

Insert a Placeholder

1. Display Slide Master view.

Note: To access Slide Master view, see the section "Open and Close Slide Master View."

2. Click a Layout Master.
3. Click the **Insert Placeholder** ▾.
4. Click a placeholder type.

   In this example, Picture was clicked.

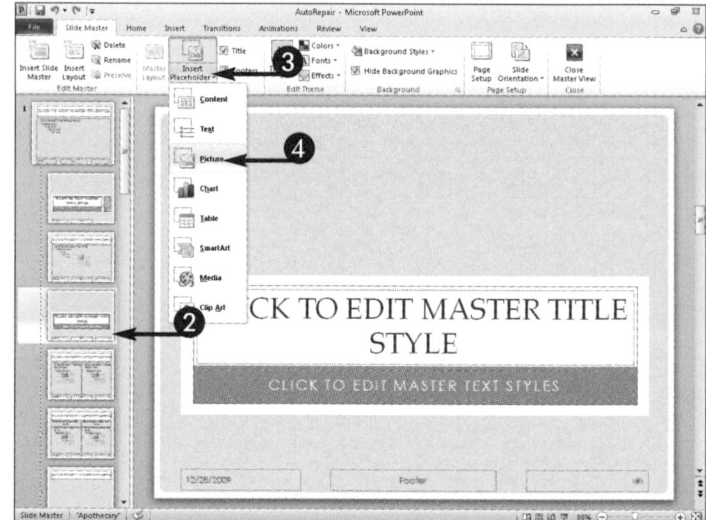

   The crosshair pointer (+) appears.

5. Click where you want the upper-left corner of the placeholder and drag across the slide to where you want the lower-right corner of the placeholder.

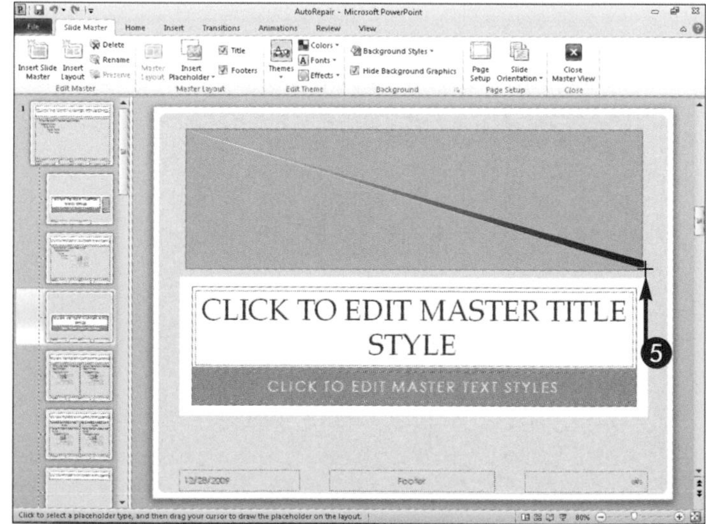

- When you release the mouse button, the placeholder appears.

6. With the new placeholder still selected, click the **Home** or **Animations** tab.

   In this example, the Home tab was clicked.

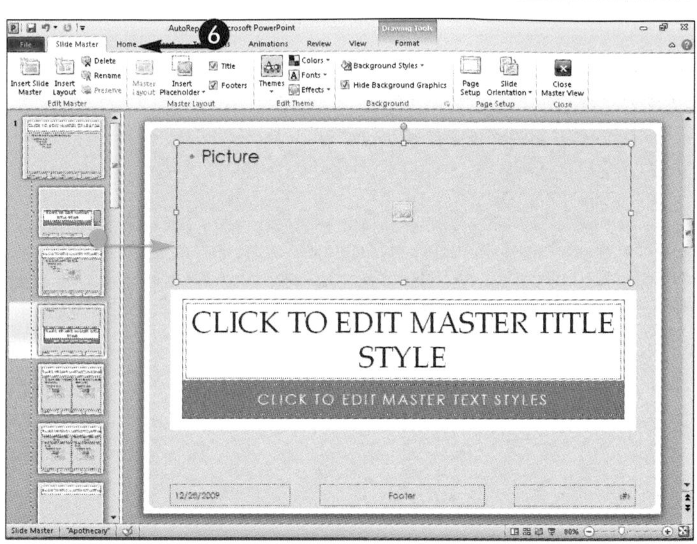

7. Use the tools found on the tab to format the placeholder.

8. Click outside the placeholder when finished.

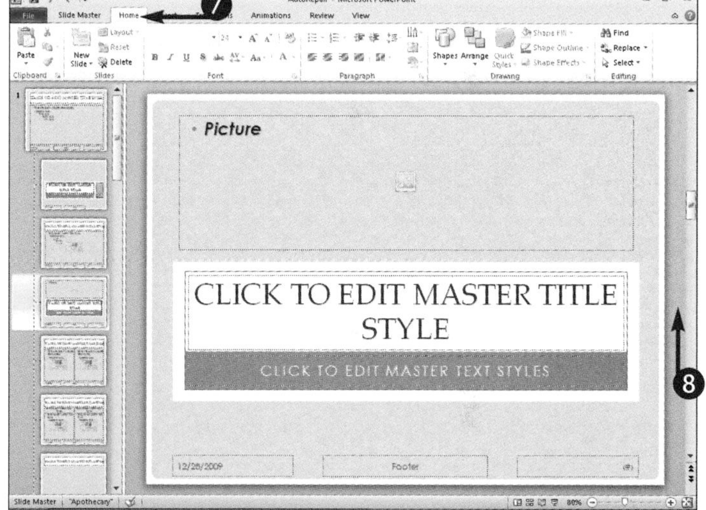

TIPS

Is there an easy way to reinstate a placeholder that I deleted from the Slide Master?

Yes. Click the **Slide Master** thumbnail at the top of the left pane in Slide Master view. Click the **Slide Master** tab on the Ribbon and then click the **Master Layout** button. In the Master Layout dialog box, click the check box for the deleted placeholder (☐ changes to ☑) and then click **OK**. PowerPoint reinstates the placeholder.

How do I move or resize a placeholder?

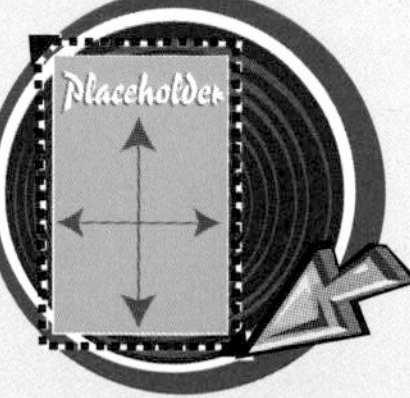

Click the placeholder border to select it. To move the placeholder, move ⇖ over the border and drag it. To resize the placeholder, move the ⇖ over one of the handles, and drag it.

Add a Footer

The Slide Master set has placeholders for footers that are used to show information such as your company name on slides. You can reposition the footer placeholders on the Slide Master or Layout Masters.

If you add a footer to the Slide Master, it appears on all slides. Add a footer to a Layout Master, and it appears only on presentation slides with that layout. Adding a footer to selected presentation slides in Normal view affects only those slides. You can also use footers in Handout view or Notes Page view.

Add a Footer

1. Display Slide Master view, Normal view, Handout view, or Notes Page view.

Note: *To access Slide Master view, see the section "Open and Close Slide Master View."*

In this example, Slide Master view is displayed.

2. Click the Slide Master or one of the Layout Masters.

In this example, the Section Header Layout Master was clicked.

3. Click the **Insert** tab.
4. Click **Header & Footer**.

The Header and Footer dialog box appears.

5. Click **Footer** (☐ changes to ☑).
6. Type your information in the text box.
7. Click **Apply**.

- You can click **Apply to All** to add the footer to the entire Slide Master set.

Note: *Adding the footer to the entire Slide Master set also applies the footer to all presentation slides.*

- The footer appears on the Layout Master and any presentation slides that share its layout.

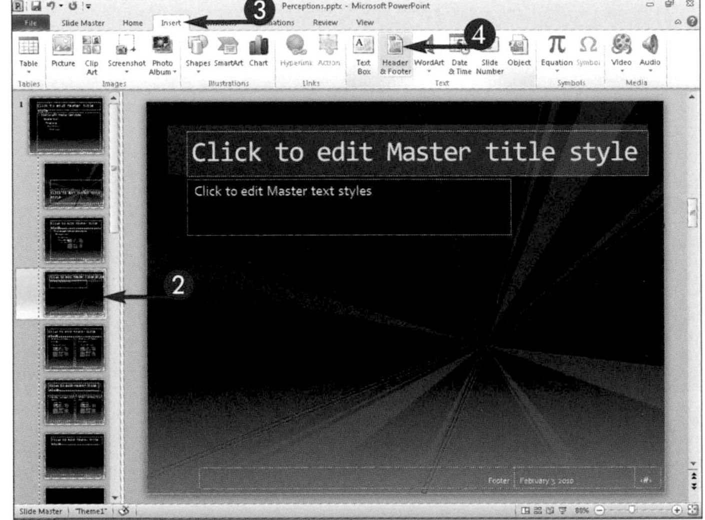

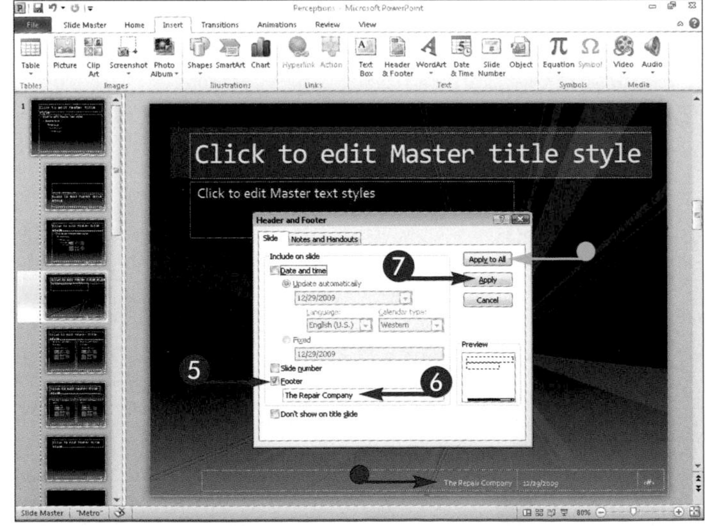

Add a Date

The Slide Master set includes a placeholder for a date. You can add a particular date or one that shows the computer's system date. You can reposition the date placeholders on Slide Master or Layout Masters.

Adding a date to Slide Master affects all slides. Adding a date to a Layout Master affects only presentation slides with its layout. You can also add a date to particular presentation slides in Normal view, or to all pages of Handout view or Notes Page view.

Add a Date

1. Display Slide Master view, Normal view, Handout view, or Notes Page view.

Note: *To access Slide Master view, see the section "Open and Close Slide Master View."*

In this example, Slide Master view is selected.

2. Select the slide(s) in which you want to show the date.

Note: *To select multiple slides, click the first slide, and then press* Ctrl *while clicking additional slides.*

3. Click the **Insert** tab.
4. Click **Date & Time**.

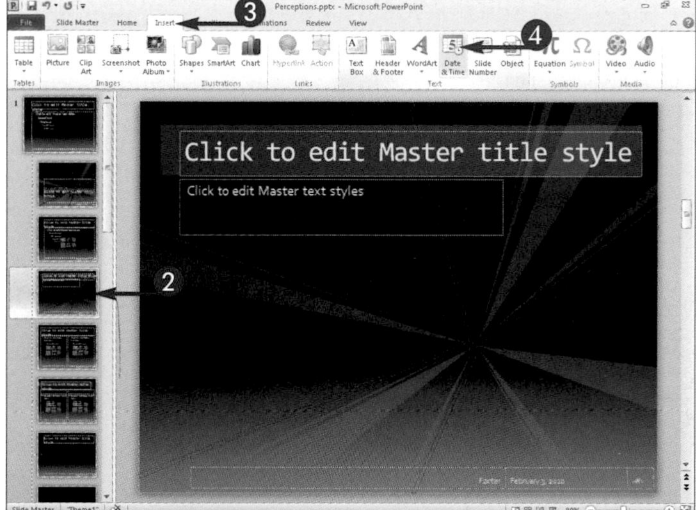

The Header and Footer dialog box appears.

5. Click **Date and time** (☐ changes to ☑).
6. Click the **Update automatically** option (◯ changes to ◉).
7. Click ▾ on the format drop-down list.
8. Click a format.
9. Click **Apply**.

- You can click **Apply to All** to add the date to all presentation slides.
- The date appears on the selected slides.

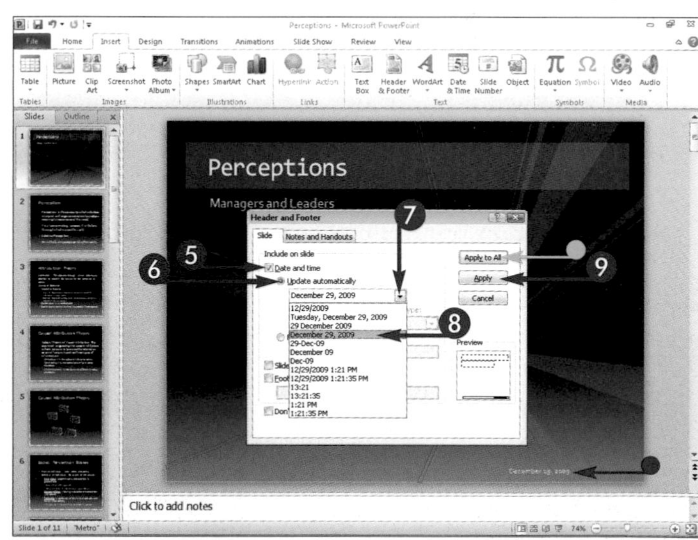

Set Up Slide Numbers

You can have PowerPoint automatically number the presentation slides with the option to not include a slide number on the title slide. You can reposition the slide number placeholders on the Slide Master or Layout Masters.

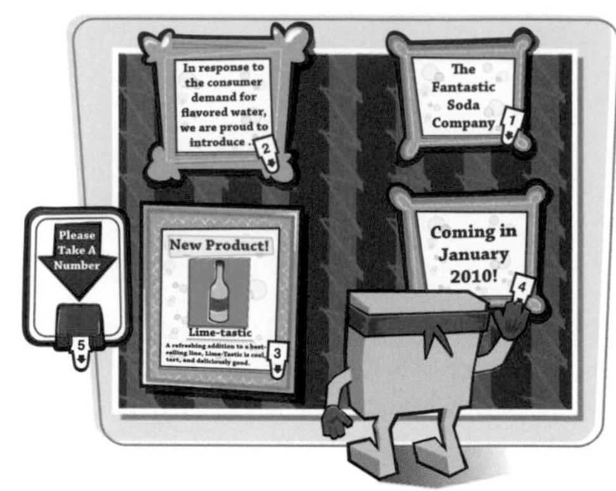

You can set up slide numbers on the Slide Master, which affects all slides; Layout Masters, which affects only slides with respective layouts; or on particular presentation slides in Normal view.

Set Up Slide Numbers

1. Display Slide Master view, Normal view, Handout view, or Notes Page view.

Note: To access Slide Master view, see the section "Open and Close Slide Master View."

In this example, Normal view is displayed.

2. Select a slide(s) if you do not want numbers on every slide.

Note: To select multiple slides, click the first slide, and then press Ctrl *while clicking additional slides.*

3. Click the **Insert** tab.
4. Click **Slide Number**.

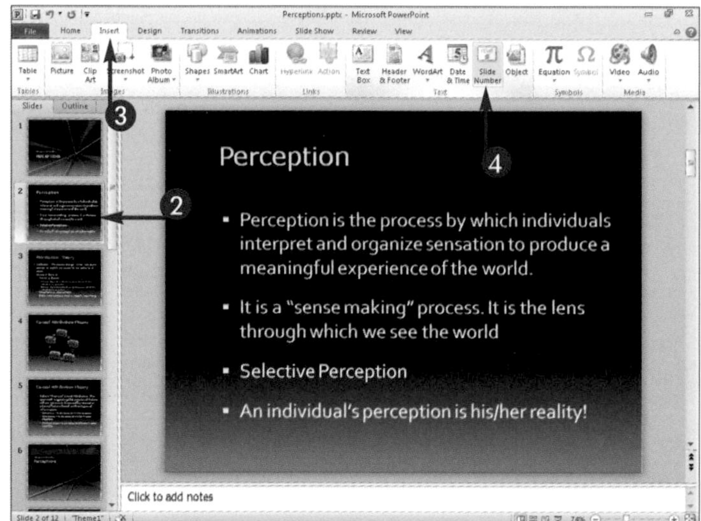

The Header and Footer dialog box appears.

5. Click **Slide Number** (☐ changes to ☑).
6. Click **Don't show on title slide** (☐ changes to ☑).
7. Click **Apply to All**.

- You can click **Apply** to apply slide numbers only to selected slides.
- Slide numbers appear on all presentation slides except the title slide.

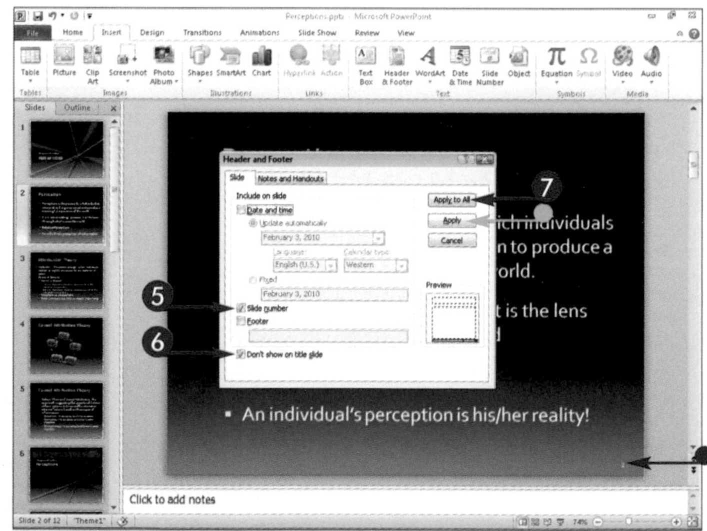

Insert a Graphic in Slide Master View

You can use Slide Master view to insert a graphic that appears on every slide. For example, your organization or company might want its logo on all slides for professionalism and consistency.

You can resize or reposition a graphic on a master, such as a graphic placed on a slide. See Chapter 9 for more about resizing and repositioning graphics.

Insert a Graphic in Slide Master View

1. Display Slide Master view.

Note: *To access Slide Master view, see the section "Open and Close Slide Master View."*

2. Click the Slide Master.
3. Click the **Insert** tab.
4. Click **Picture**.

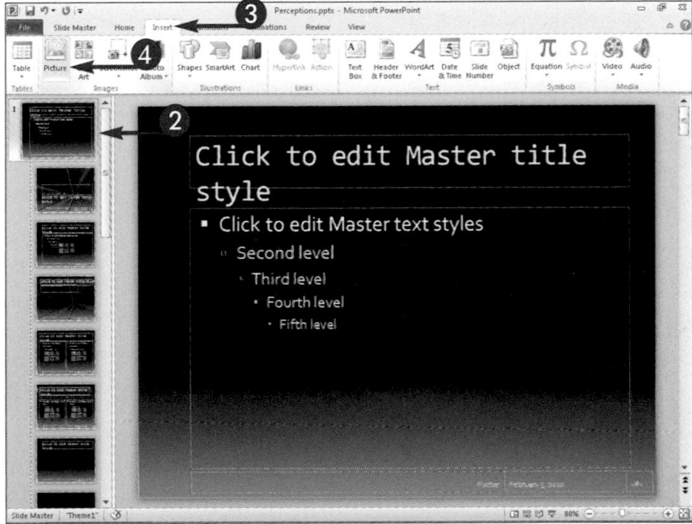

The Insert Picture dialog box appears.

5. Click the folder that contains the picture file you want to insert.
6. Click the graphics file you want to insert.
7. Click **Insert**.

The dialog box closes and the picture appears on the master, where you can move and resize it as needed.

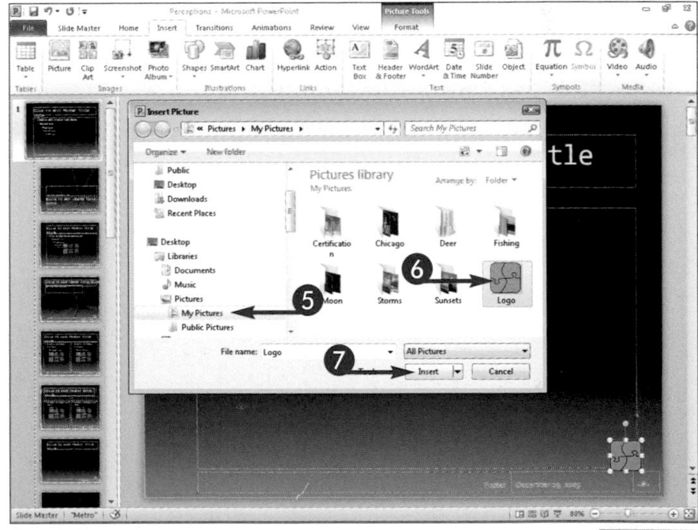

Work with Multiple Masters

You may decide to use a few different looks in your presentation. For example, you may have a Human Resources presentation with a section on employee benefits and a section on company policies. You may decide to use different themes for visual differentiation between sections.

How Multiple Masters Occur in a Presentation

When you apply more than one theme within a single presentation, PowerPoint creates a Slide Master and associated Layout Masters for each theme. Masters are based on themes, so you cannot change the theme of a set of masters, though you can create a new blank Slide Master set to design it from scratch.

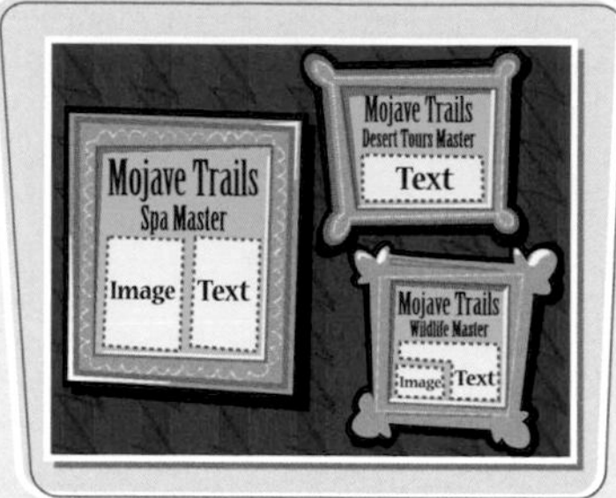

Manage Your Theme with Multiple Masters

If you use multiple themes (and therefore multiple masters), make sure the themes are complementary. You can do this by selecting slide designs with similar color themes and font themes, plus graphics and backgrounds that work well together.

Use Multiple Masters with Slides

If your presentation has multiple masters, you can apply the different master designs to presentation slides selectively. In Normal view, select a slide, and then use the Layout button on the Home tab to choose a layout and master combination. The layouts are organized by the Slide Master name.

How to Use Multiple Masters

Changes made on the Layout Master of one set of masters do not affect the same layout on another set of masters. Those changes only affect presentation slides with that particular layout/master combination. For changes you want applied to all slides, you must change each Slide Master.

Insert a New Blank Master

You can insert a blank master and customize it in Slide Master view. Then you can use various methods to reformat text, change the background, add graphics, and so on.

Chapter 4 gives procedures for formatting text, and Chapter 9 provides information on working with graphics. By changing various elements, you can create a unique master design within a presentation.

Insert a New Blank Master

1. Display Slide Master view.

Note: To access Slide Master view, see the section "Open and Close Slide Master View."

2. Click **Insert Slide Master**.

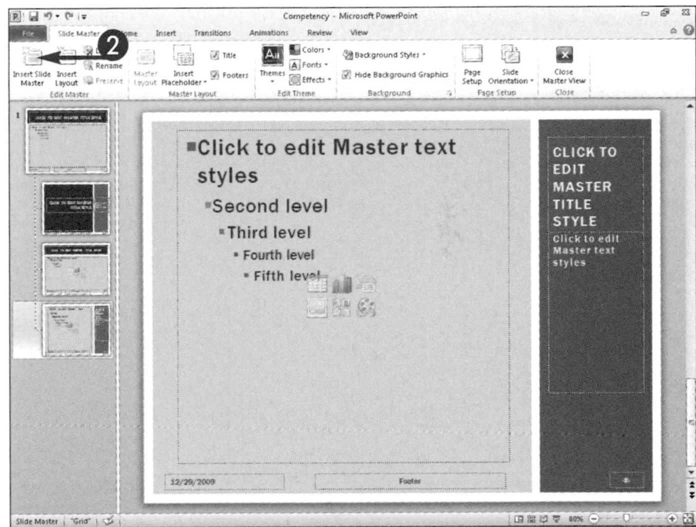

- A new Slide Master set (set of masters) appears.
- PowerPoint numbers each master, and displays the number on the Slide Master thumbnail.
- Selecting a theme from the Themes button creates a set of masters with that particular theme.

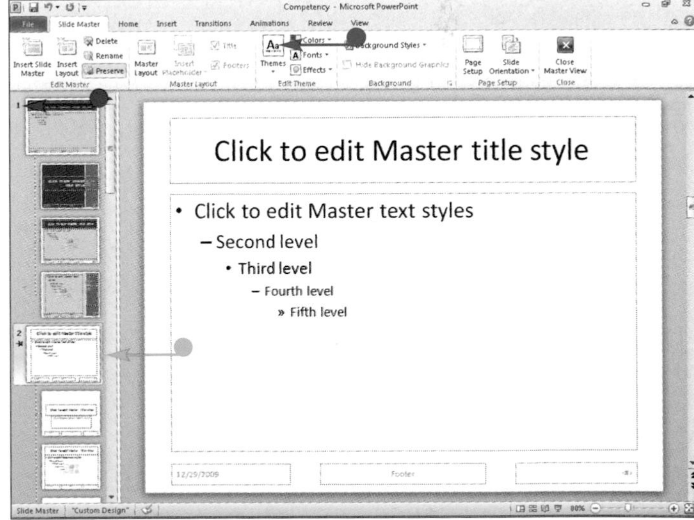

Preserve a Master

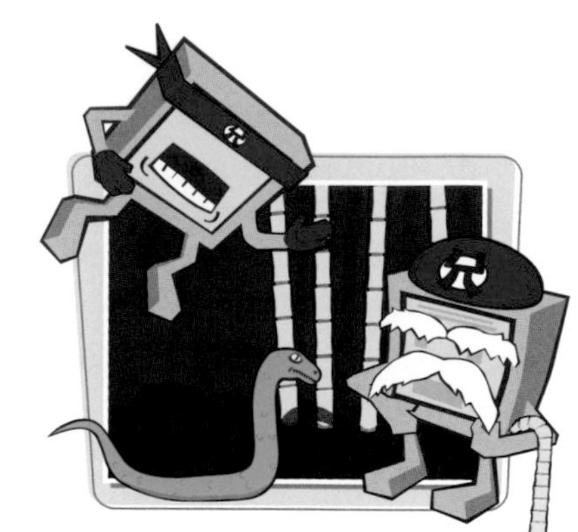

PowerPoint removes a Slide Master set if you delete all the presentation slides that use it. You can preserve a Slide Master set so it is never automatically removed from the presentation. That way you can use it for future presentation slides.

Keep in mind that even if it is preserved, you can still manually delete the set of masters in Slide Master view — simply delete the Slide Master.

Preserve a Master

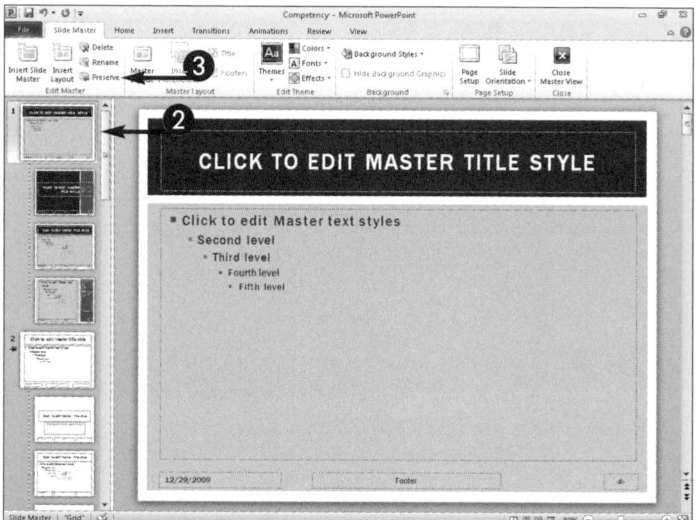

1. Display Slide Master view.

Note: *To access Slide Master view, see the section "Open and Close Slide Master View."*

2. Click the Slide Master you want to preserve.
3. Click **Preserve**.

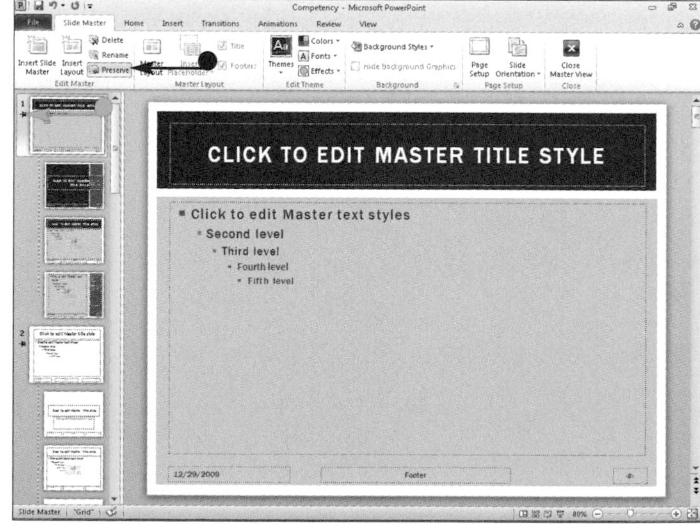

- PowerPoint preserves the master and a pushpin appears on the Slide Master thumbnail.
- The Preserve button on the Ribbon becomes highlighted.

Note: *To reverse the process, perform Steps* **1** *to* **3** *again so the Preserve button is no longer highlighted.*

Rename a Master

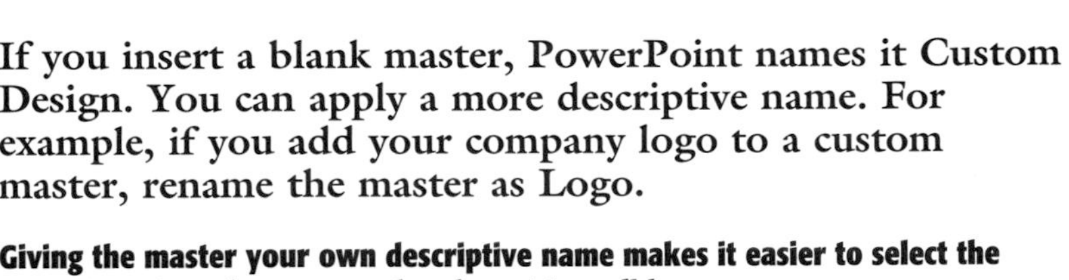

If you insert a blank master, PowerPoint names it Custom Design. You can apply a more descriptive name. For example, if you add your company logo to a custom master, rename the master as Logo.

Giving the master your own descriptive name makes it easier to select the correct master when you apply a layout to a slide.

Rename a Master

1. Display Slide Master view.

   ***Note:** To access Slide Master view, see the section "Open and Close Slide Master View."*

2. Click the Slide Master you want to rename.
3. Click **Rename**.

   The Rename Layout dialog box appears.

4. Type a name.

   In this example, Logo was typed.

5. Click **Rename**.

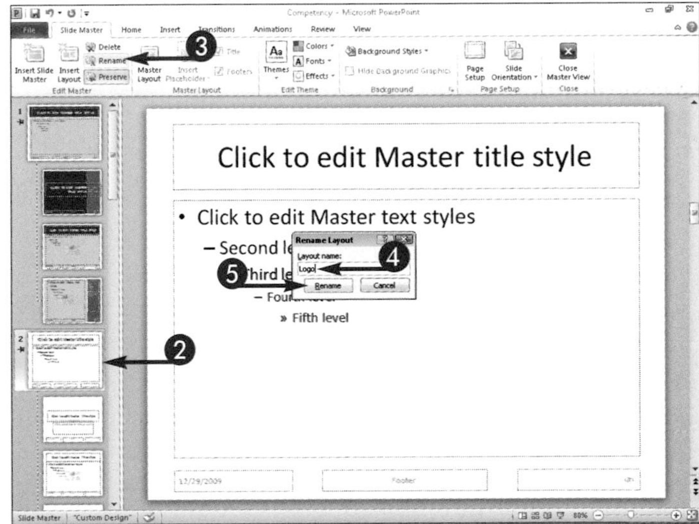

The dialog box closes, and PowerPoint renames the master.

- Position the pointer over the Slide Master thumbnail in the left pane of Slide Master view to see a ScreenTip with the new name.

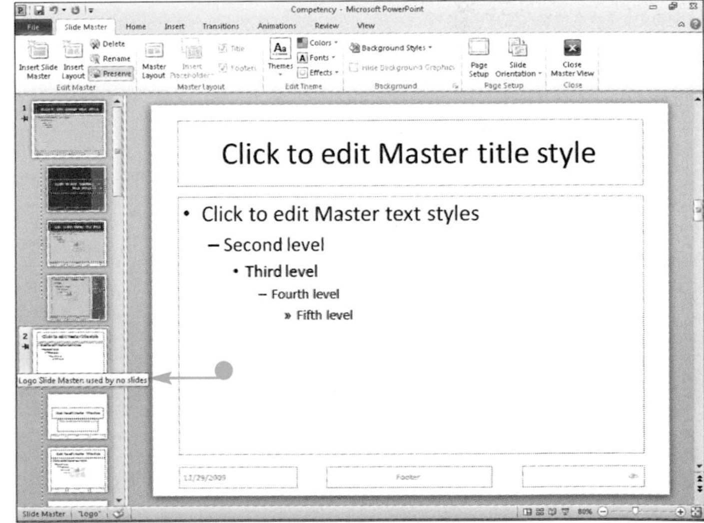

Work with the Notes Master

Changes in the Notes Master affect the Notes Page view and printing the Notes Page view. The Notes Master has a placeholder for the slide and one for the Notes area, as well as placeholders for header, footer, date, and slide number.

You can modify the format of Notes text, move placeholders around, delete placeholders, and enter headers and footers. See Chapter 14 for information about printing Notes.

Work with the Notes Master

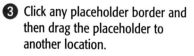

1. Click the **View** tab.
2. Click **Notes Master**.

The Notes Master view appears.

3. Click any placeholder border and then drag the placeholder to another location.
4. Click any placeholder border and resize it by dragging one of the handles.

You can use the commands on the Insert tab to add the header, footer, date, or slide number as described earlier in this chapter.

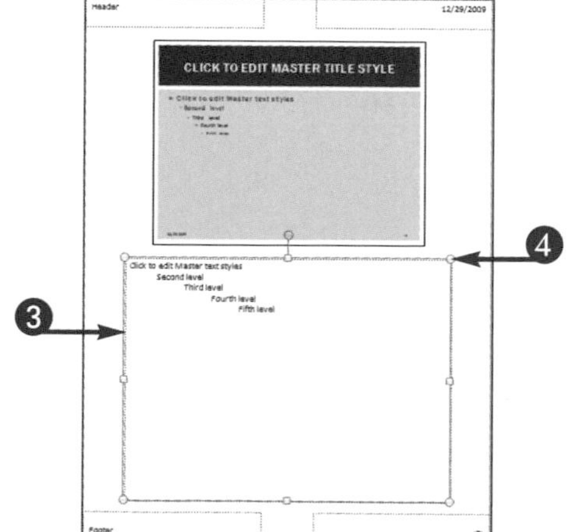

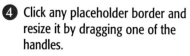

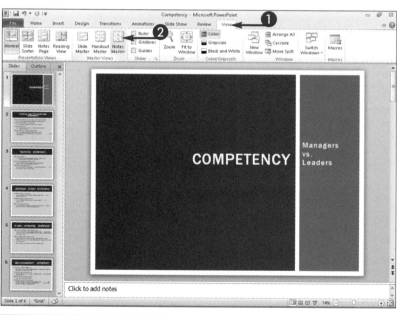

In this example, the notes text placeholder was moved and resized, and the page placeholder was moved to the top, next to the date.

5. Click any placeholder border to select it.

6. Use tools on the Home tab or Drawing Tools Format tab to change the font formatting or text box formatting.

   In this example, the Notes text box was selected and the Italics button (I) and Bold button (B) on the Home tab were clicked.

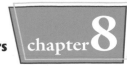

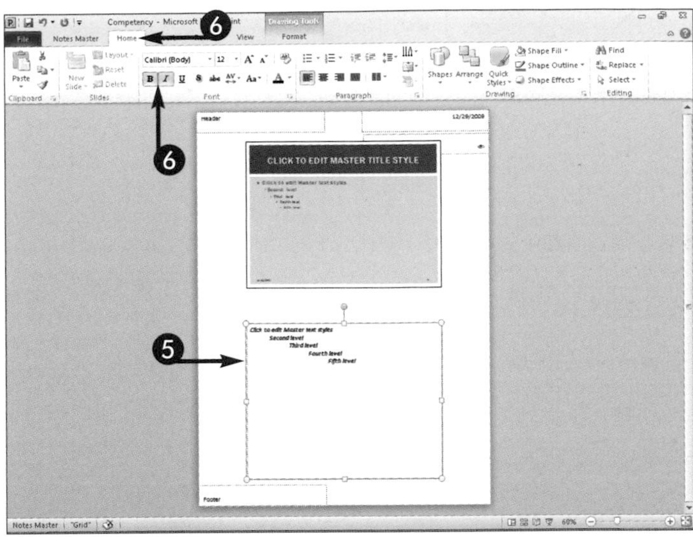

7. Click the **Notes Master** tab.

8. Click to enable or disable items in the Placeholders group as needed (☐ changes to ☑).

***Note:** Unselected (☐) placeholders disappear from the master. Selected (☑) items appear on the master.*

9. Click **Close Master View**.

   Notes Master view closes and PowerPoint displays the previously used view.

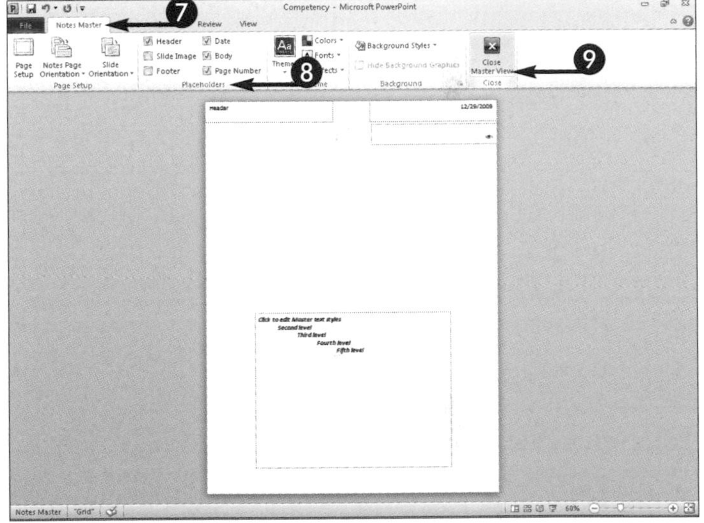

TIPS

Is there a way to print just Notes, and not slides?

Yes. Strangely, if you remove the slide placeholder from the Notes Master, the slide images still appear on the Notes Page view. You must display the Notes Page view and go to each individual page and delete the slide placeholder. Then the Notes pages print without the slides.

Can I format the font for the header, footer, date, and page number?

Yes. Format the header, footer, date, and page number placeholders just like any other placeholder. Click the border of the placeholder, and then use commands from the Home tab or Drawing Tools Format tab to format the text or the placeholder itself.

Work with Handout Master

In Handout Master view, you can choose a handout layout, as well as work with header and footer placeholders to control the appearance of your printed handouts. Any formatting you do on the Handout Master appears in Handout view.

You can also use commands on other tabs in Handout Master view to change the handout's appearance.

Work with Handout Master

1. Click the **View** tab.
2. Click **Handout Master**.

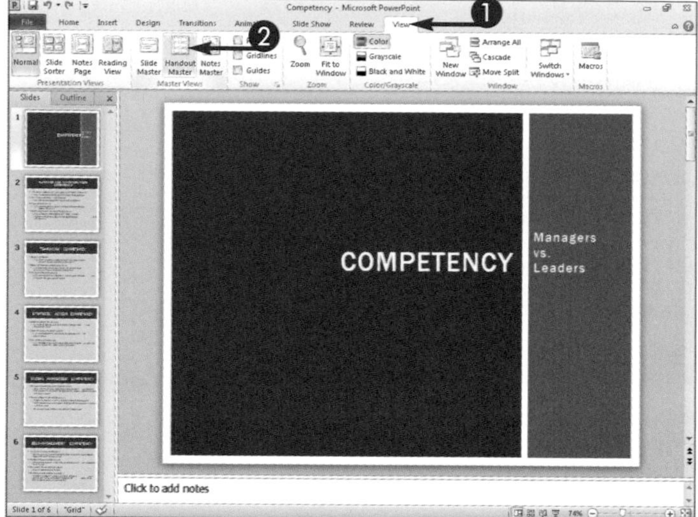

3. Click the **Handout Master** tab.
4. Click items in the Placeholders group to hide them from the Handout Master (☑ changes to ☐).

- You can click the **Fonts** ▾ and pick a font theme from the drop-down list to change the font.

5. Click **Close Master View**.

   The Handout Master view closes.

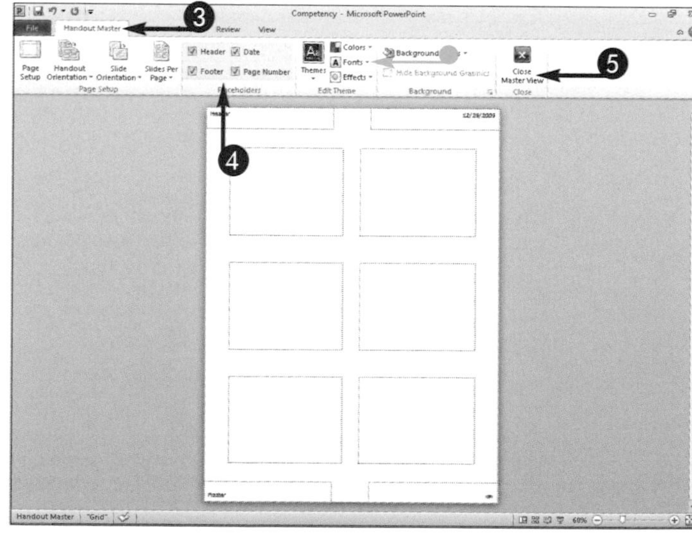

Omit Master Graphics on a Slide

Although inserting a graphic on the Slide Master or a Layout Master causes the graphic to appear on every presentation slide based on the master, you can override this on individual presentation slides. You might do this because the master graphics overlap with other objects on an individual presentation slide.

Omit Master Graphics on a Slide

1. Select slide(s) in Normal or Slide Sorter view.

Note: To select multiple slides, click the first slide, and then press Ctrl *while clicking additional slides.*

2. Click the **Design** tab.
3. Click **Hide Background Graphics** (☐ changes to ☑).

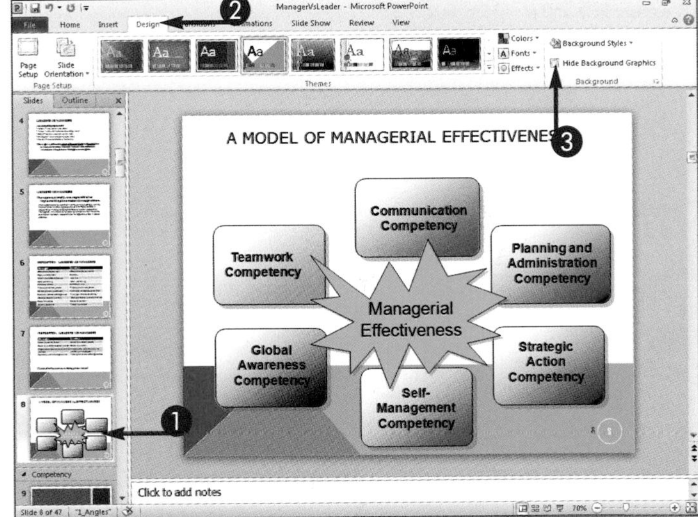

- The master graphics are hidden from the slide.

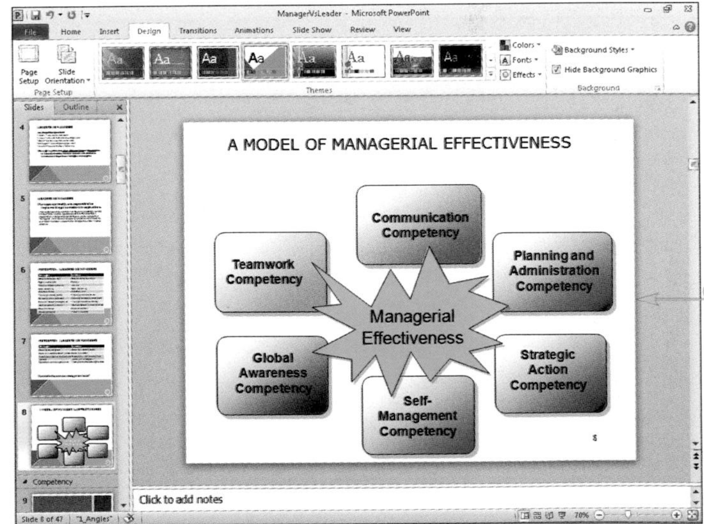

Create a Custom Slide Layout

You need not add an entire additional master into a presentation to add some customization. You can work in Slide Master view to add a new slide layout to the current master. For example, if you want to create a slide layout with three content placeholders, you can do so and then apply the new layout to slides in your presentation.

Create a Custom Slide Layout

1. Click the **View** tab.
2. Click **Slide Master**.

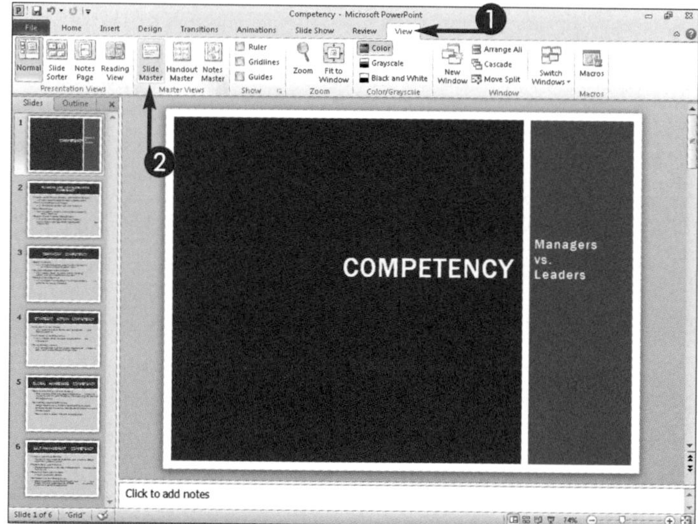

Slide Master view appears.

3. Click in between master slide thumbnails where you want insert the new slide layout.
4. Click **Insert Layout**.

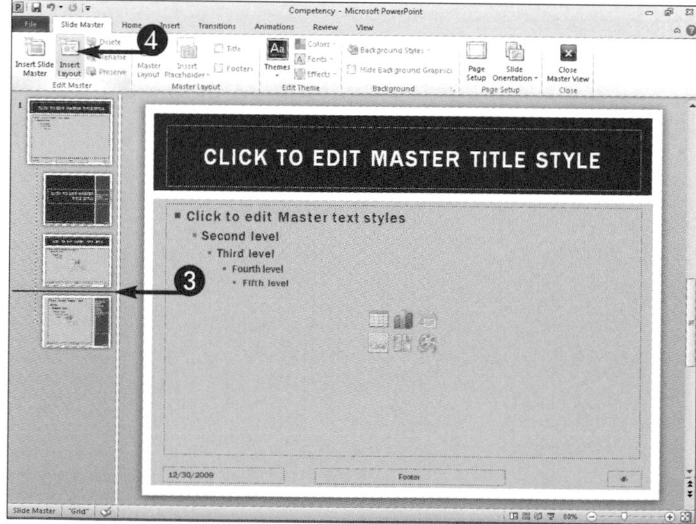

- The new custom Layout Master appears in the pane at the left, selected so that you can edit it.

5. Click [▾] on the **Insert Placeholder** button.
6. Click a layout type.
7. Drag the placeholder onto the slide.

   In this example, a text placeholder and a table placeholder were inserted, and now a chart placeholder is being inserted.

***Note:** See "Insert a Placeholder" earlier in this chapter.*

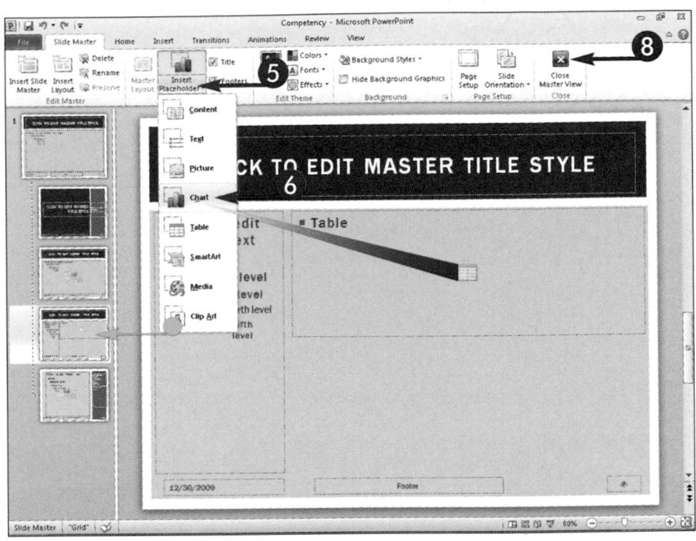

8. Click **Close Master View** when finished.

   Slide Master view closes and PowerPoint displays the previous view.

9. Click the **Home** tab.
10. Click the **New Slide** [▾].

    The gallery of layouts appears.

- Your custom layout appears in the gallery.

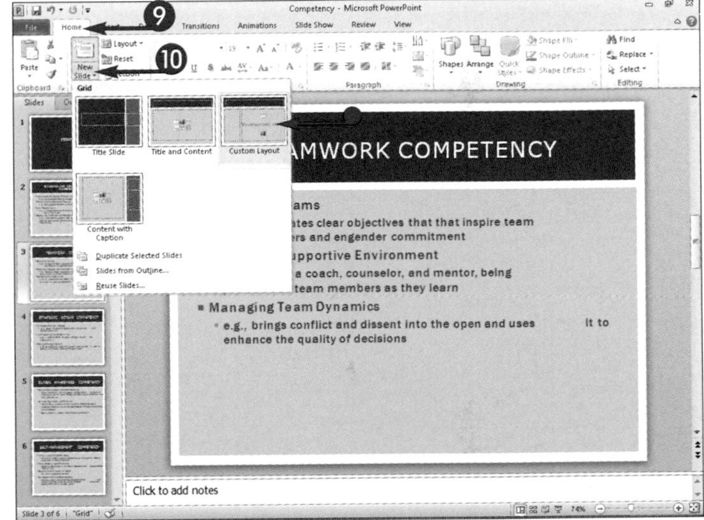

TIPS

Can I assign a unique name to my custom Layout Master?

Yes. Your custom Layout Master handles just like any other Layout Master. See "Rename a Master" earlier in this chapter to review how to rename your custom Layout Master.

Can I change the background for my custom slide layout?

Yes. In Slide Master view, click the Layout Master thumbnail that you want to change. Use the commands in the Background group on the Slide Master tab to make background changes. See Chapter 7 for more on changing backgrounds of slides.

CHAPTER

Adding Graphics and Drawings

Adding graphic elements such as photographs, WordArt, and shapes to your slides can enhance the attractiveness and effectiveness of your presentation. You can place graphic elements anywhere on a slide — you are not bound by slide placeholders. You can also use color and various formatting options to make your presentation picture-perfect.

Insert Clip Art

PowerPoint provides clip art in the form of picture, illustration, sound, and movie (animation) files. You can search for clip art by keyword or phrase and can even find clip art online. You can insert clip art anywhere on your slide without using an existing content placeholder — giving you complete flexibility working with it.

Insert Clip Art

1. Select a slide in Normal view.

Note: *To navigate to and select a slide, see Chapter 4.*

2. Click the **Insert** tab.
3. Click **Clip Art**.

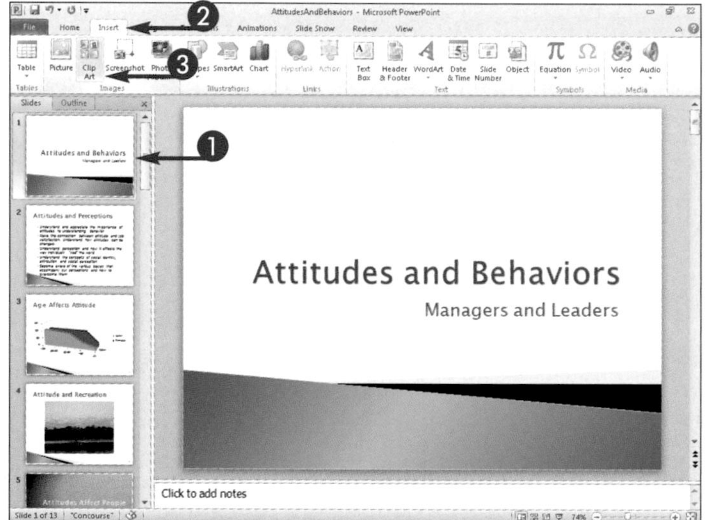

- The Clip Art task pane appears.

4. Type a search term.
5. Click the **Results should be** ▾.
6. Select the type of clip art you want to see (☐ changes to ☑).

   In this example, All media types was selected.

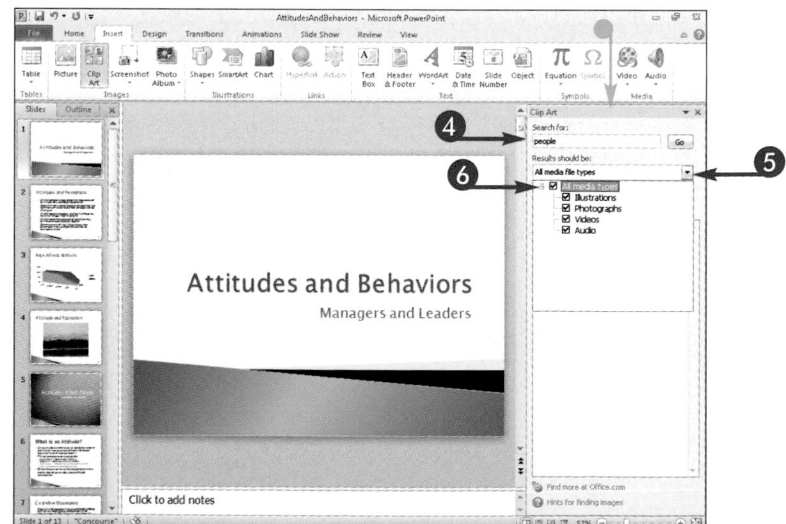

- Click **Include Office.com content** to include clip art from Office.com (☐ changes to ☑).

7 Click **Go**.

Clip art graphics matching the search term appear.

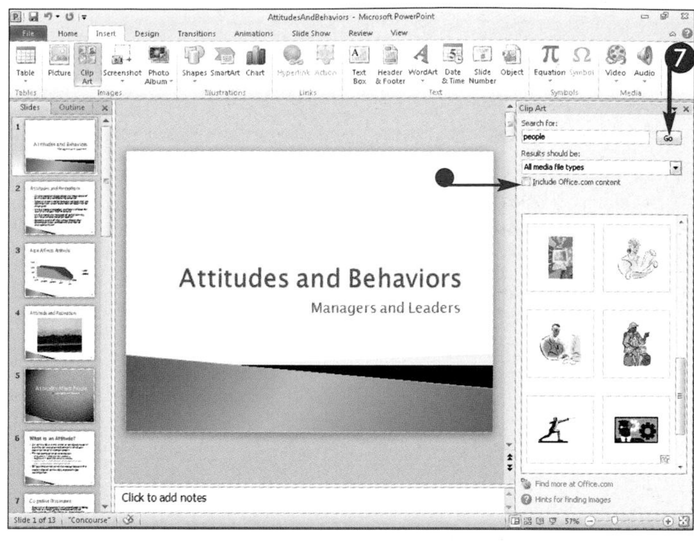

- A star in the lower-right corner of the clip art thumbnail denotes that it has animation; it prints like an illustration, but moves during the slide show.

8 Click and drag to scroll through and view the clip art.

9 Click the clip art of your choice.

- The clip art appears on the slide.

Note: *See the sections "Move Objects" and "Resize Objects" in this chapter to learn how to size and position the clip art.*

10 Click the **Close** button (☒).

The Clip Art task pane closes.

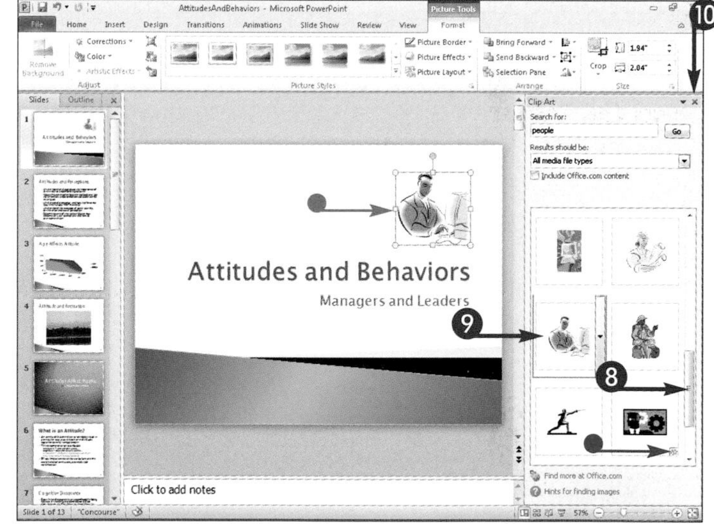

TIPS

How can I use Microsoft's online site to find clips?

After you display the Clip Art task pane, click the **Find more at Office Online** link. The Web browser launches and displays clip art information on Microsoft Office Online. Here, you can download clip art and get information about clip art.

What happens if I insert a sound clip?

When you insert a sound clip on a slide, a small megaphone icon appears on the slide. On the Audio Tools Playback tab, you can set it up so the sound plays automatically or only when you click the icon. See Chapter 12 for more about inserting sound and movie clips.

Draw a Shape

There are many predefined shapes that you can easily draw on a slide to add visual spice. You can choose these shapes from a gallery and draw them with a simple click and drag. You can change shape formatting and some shapes can even run actions.

You can draw circles, rectangles, connector lines, and other shapes that are useful in creating flow charts.

Draw a Shape

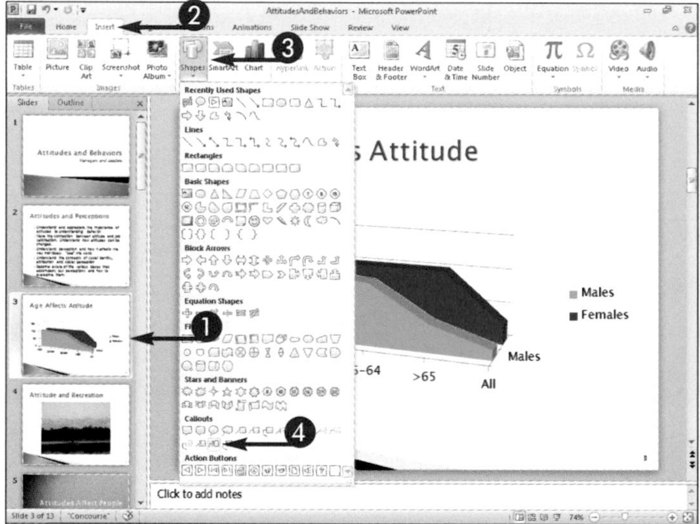

1. Select a slide in Normal view.

***Note:** To navigate to and select a slide, see Chapter 4.*

2. Click the **Insert** tab.
3. Click **Shapes**.

   The gallery of shapes appears.

4. Click the shape you want to draw.

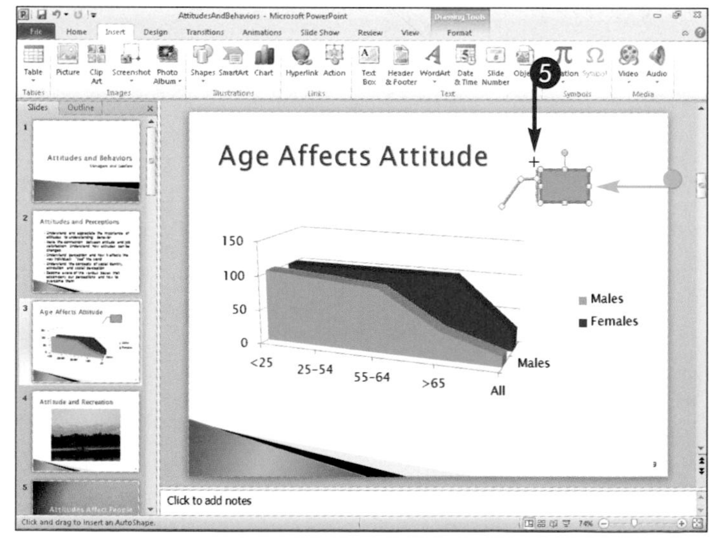

The gallery closes, and the mouse pointer (↖) changes to a crosshair pointer (+).

5. Click the slide to insert the shape.

- When you release the mouse button, the shape appears.

***Note:** You may also click and drag the shape to size while inserting it.*

***Note:** Use the Rectangle or Oval shape to draw a square or circle. Press and hold Shift as you drag.*

Add a Text Box

You can add a text box anywhere on a slide. A text box differs from a placeholder because it does not automatically produce a bulleted list. A text box is great for free-form text and automatically enlarges, shrinks, and wraps text depending on the amount of text you type.

Keep in mind that text box contents do not appear in your presentation outline.

Add a Text Box

1. Select a slide in Normal view.

***Note:** To navigate to and select a slide, see Chapter 4.*

2. Click the **Insert** tab.
3. Click **Text Box**.

- The mouse pointer (↖) changes to an insertion cross.

4. Click and drag from where you want the left-upper corner of the text box to where you want the right side of the text box.

***Note:** Dragging establishes the box width. The height adjusts automatically based on the amount of text you type.*

- The text box appears with an insertion point inside.

5. Type your text.
6. Click anywhere outside the text box when finished.

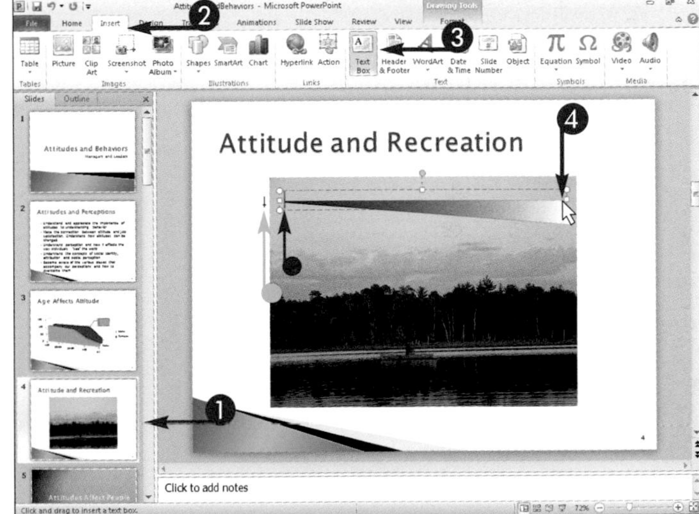

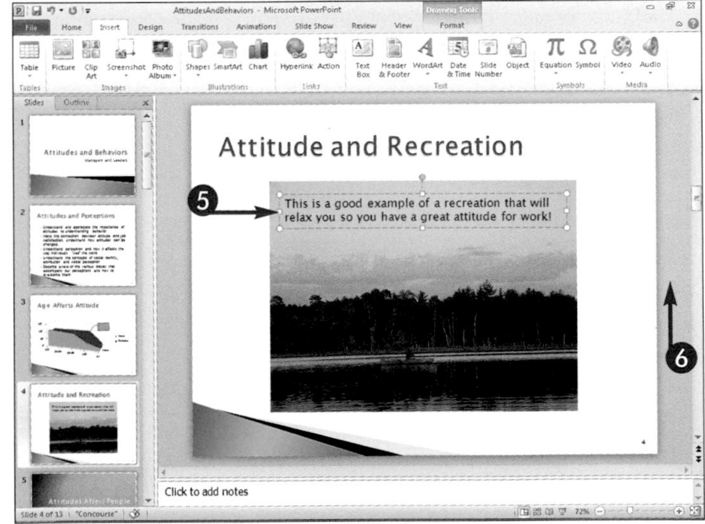

Add Text to a Shape

If you think that a plain text box lacks pizzazz, you can create a jazzier text box by adding text to a shape. The text appears within the shape, and the shape effectively becomes a text box.

Shapes do not have some of the automation that text boxes have. For example, they do not automatically enlarge or shrink based upon the amount of text you type.

Add Text to a Shape

1. Right-click the shape in which you want to add text.
2. Click **Edit Text**.

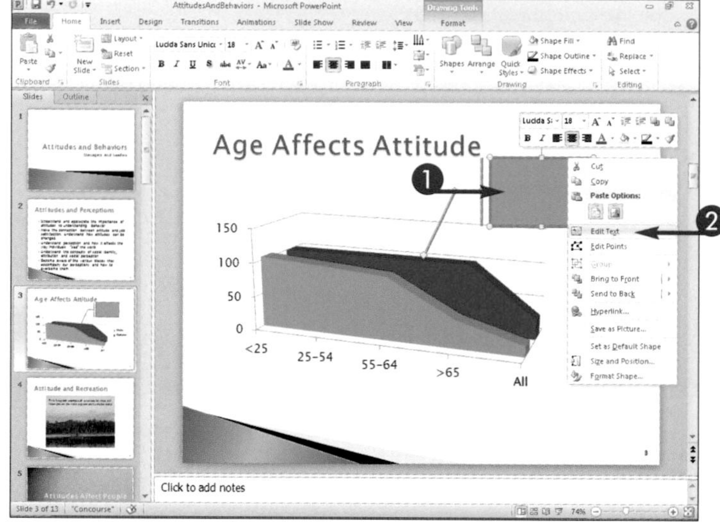

The insertion point appears inside the shape.

3. Type your text.

   In this example, Note the zero slope of this graph was typed.

4. Click anywhere outside the shape when finished.

   The text appears in the shape.

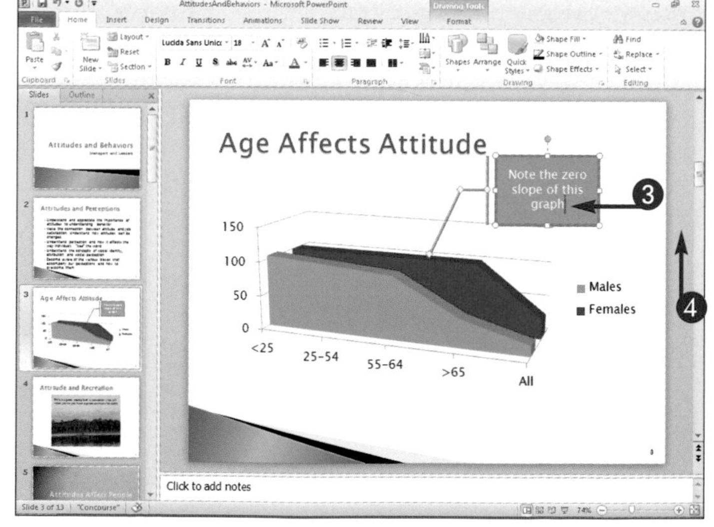

Select Objects

To change the contents of an object, format it, adjust its size, or reposition it, you first must select the object. When you select an object, PowerPoint displays that object's particular contextual tab on the Ribbon. Selecting an object is also the way you tell PowerPoint that you want to work with that object (or group of objects, if you select more than one).

The method for selecting an object varies, slightly depending on the type of object.

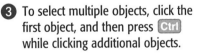

Select Objects

1. Select a slide in Normal view.

   Note: *To navigate to and select a slide, see Chapter 4.*

2. Click an object.

   - Note the contextual tab specific to the particular object you clicked.

   Note: *For objects that hold text, clicking the text displays the insertion point for editing the text. Clicking the border of an object selects the entire object, enabling you to move or format it.*

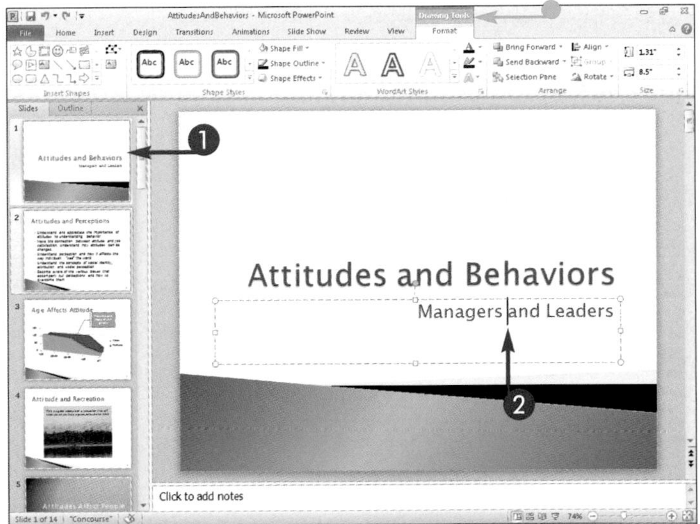

3. To select multiple objects, click the first object, and then press Ctrl while clicking additional objects.

   Note: *You may also select multiple objects by clicking and dragging on the slide around them.*

4. To select all objects on a slide, click the **Home** tab.
5. Click **Select**.
6. Click **Select All**.

   Note: *You may deselect an object from a group by clicking it while pressing Ctrl.*

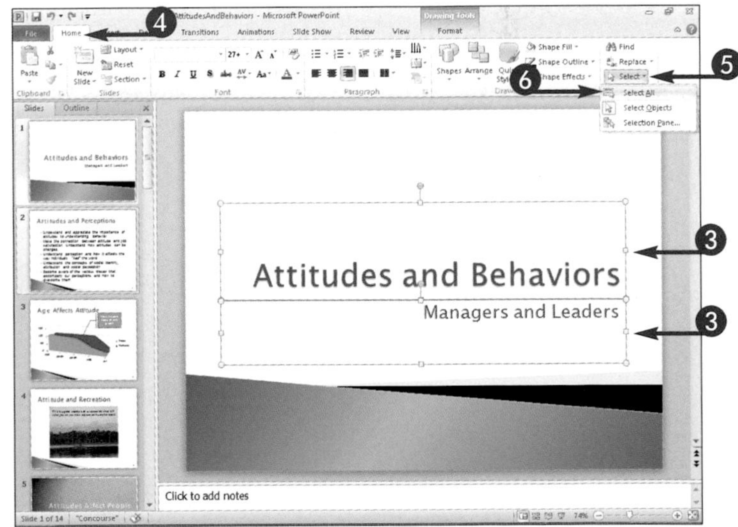

Format Objects

You can adjust the formatting of an object to make it more visually appealing or easier to see against a slide background. For example, you can add a fill color, modify the font, change the thickness or color of lines, or modify arrow styles.

Format Objects

❶ Click the object to format.

The object is selected and its particular contextual tab appears — in this example, it is the Drawing Tools Format tab.

❷ Click the **Drawing Tools Format** tab.

- Click **Shape Fill** to change the color of the object.
- Click **Shape Outline** to change the color or weight of the object's border, or change the border to dashes or dots.

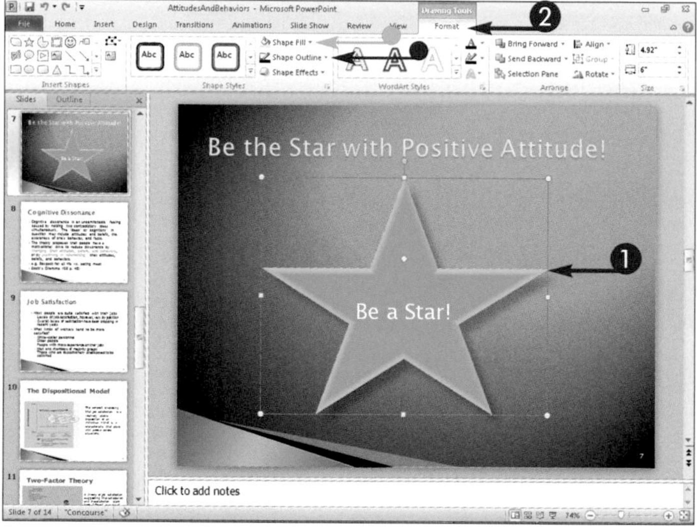

- Click the **Shape Styles** ▾ to give the entire shape a theme.
- Click **Shape Effects** to give the shape a special effect like Shadow or Reflection.
- Click the **WordArt** ▾ to give the font a special effect.
- You can use the Arrange group to arrange and align objects.

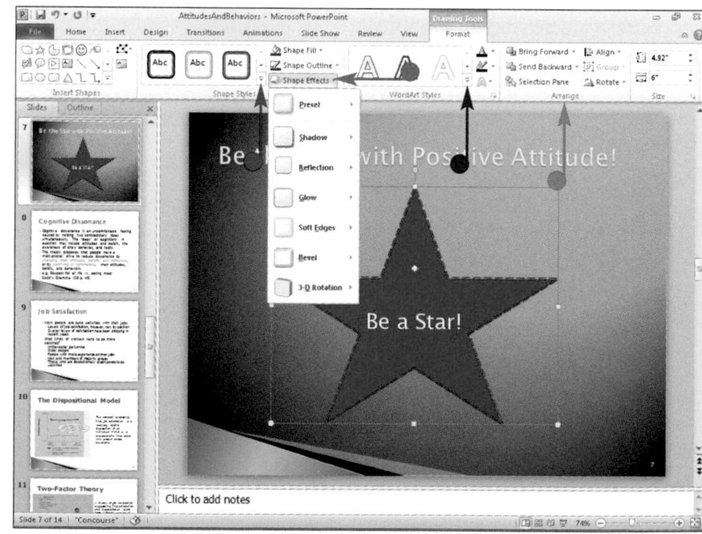

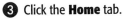

3. Click the **Home** tab.

- Use the Font group to change font appearance, such as color, font size, bold, and italics.
- Use the Paragraph group to change text alignment, line spacing, or add bullets.

4. Right-click the object.

   The shortcut menu appears.

5. Click **Format Shape**.

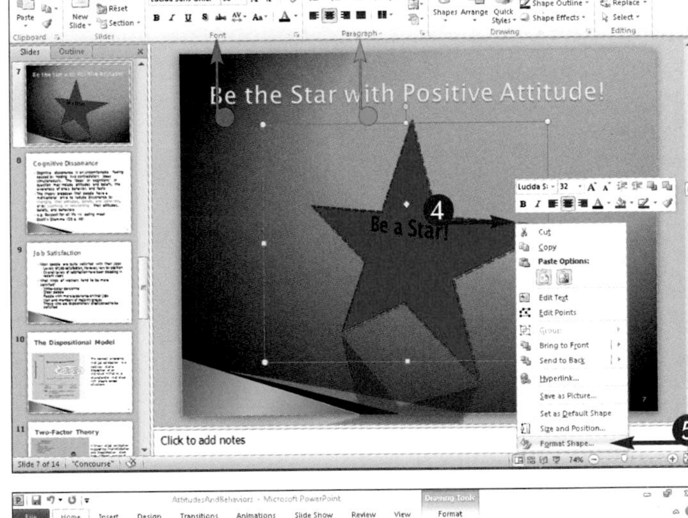

The Format Shape dialog box appears.

Any possible object formatting appears in this dialog box.

6. Click a format category.

   In this example, 3-D Rotation was clicked.

7. Use the available formatting tools to format your object.

8. Click **Close** when finished.

   The formatting is applied to the object.

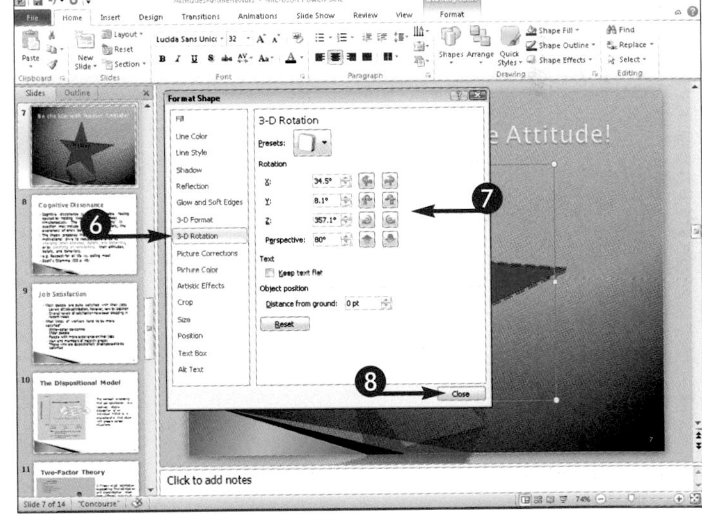

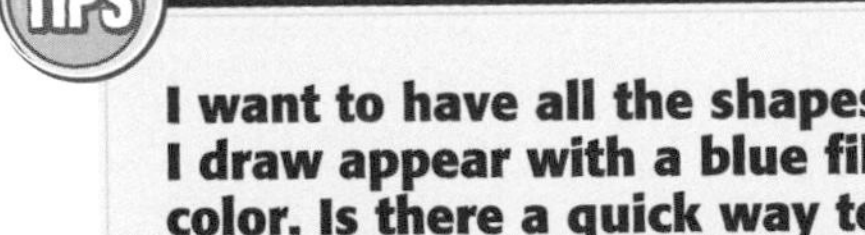

I want to have all the shapes I draw appear with a blue fill color. Is there a quick way to do that?

Yes. Draw any shape and then click **Shape Fill** on the **Drawing Tools Format** tab to select the blue fill color you want to use. Then right-click the shape and click **Set as Default Shape**. Shapes you insert will now appear in blue.

Can I make an object transparent?

Yes. Open the Format Shape dialog box, and then click the **Fill** category. Click **Solid Fill** (◎ changes to ◉), and then use the Transparency slider or spinner to adjust the transparency.

Move Objects

When you add an object, such as a picture, text box, placeholder, or shape, it may not appear in the place you want it. When you insert a slide, you may prefer to position the text and content placeholders in a different location than the standard layout. You can reposition objects on a slide so you can strategically place them.

Move Objects

❶ Click an object to select it.

❷ Position the mouse over the border of the object.

When you move the mouse over the border of a selected object, it changes to a four-headed arrow pointer.

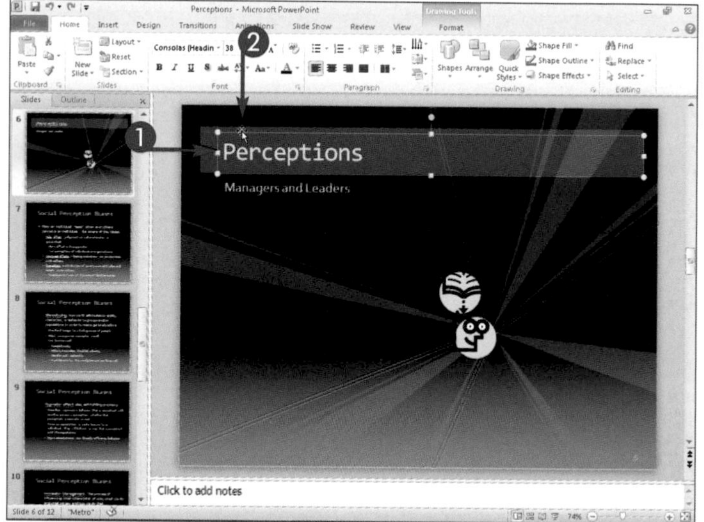

❸ Click and drag the object to a new position.

When you release the mouse button, the object appears in its new position.

❹ Click anywhere outside the shape when finished.

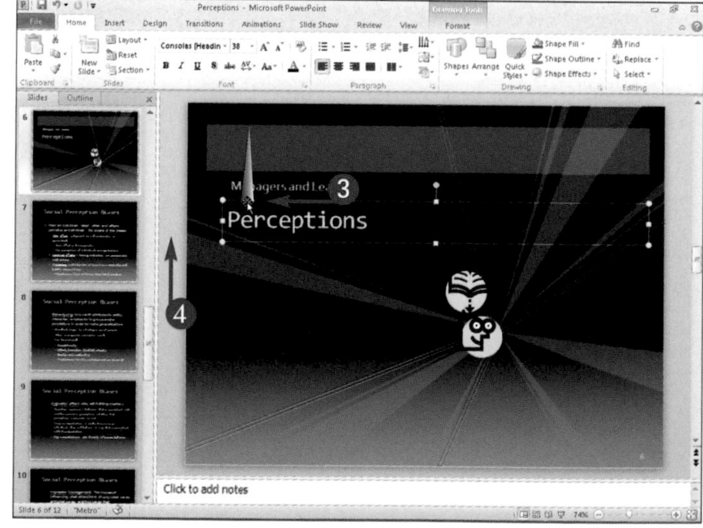

Resize Objects

Many times, after placing an object on a slide, you will want to resize it to your liking. You can resize objects such as charts, WordArt, pictures, and shapes on your slide to optimize the visual impact.

When you select an object, handles appear on the border. Drag a handle to resize an object. Dragging a corner handle while pressing Shift retains the object's original proportions.

Resize Objects

1. Click an object to select it.

- Handles appear on the border around the object.

2. Position the mouse over a handle on the border of the object.

   When you move the mouse over the border of a selected object, it changes to a two-headed arrow.

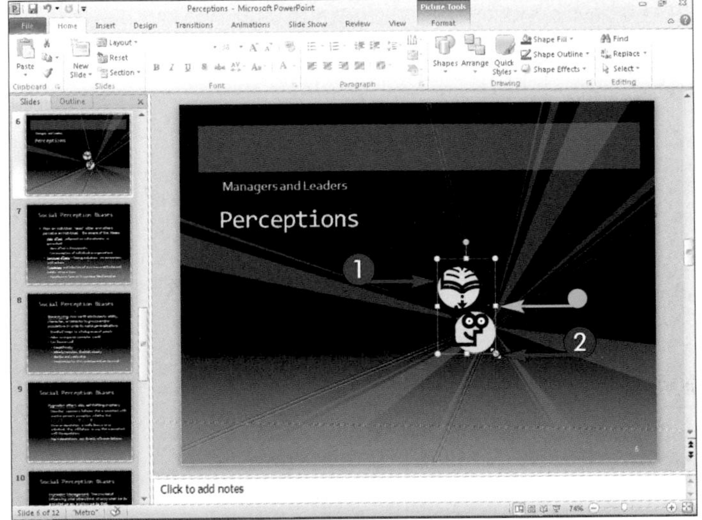

3. Click and drag outward from the object's center to enlarge it or inward to shrink it.

   When you release the mouse button, the object appears at its new size.

***Note:** Dragging a corner handle while pressing Shift retains the object's original proportions.*

4. Click anywhere outside the object when finished.

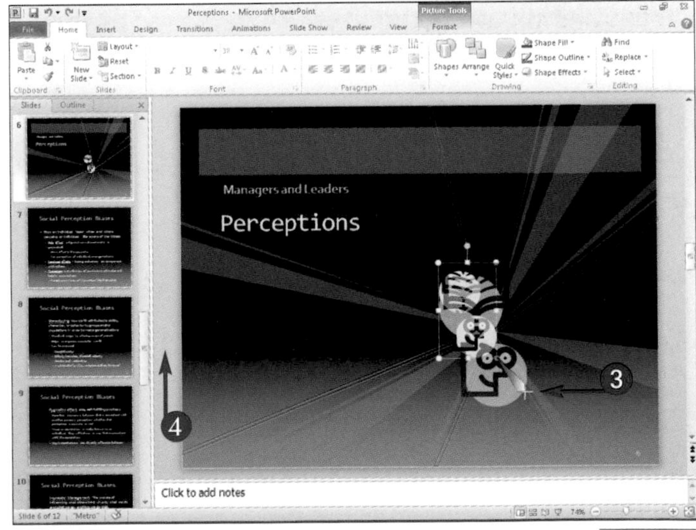

Flip and Rotate Objects

Sometimes when you combine several shapes to create a more complex graphic or want a picture to feel more dramatic, you may want to rotate it. PowerPoint enables you to rotate an object 360 degrees or quickly flip it horizontally or vertically to accomplish that dramatic effect.

The Format tab offers the flip and rotation tools. You also can drag to freely rotate an object.

Flip and Rotate Objects

Flip Objects

1. Click an object to select it.
2. Click the **Picture Tools Format** tab.
3. Click the **Rotate** button ( ).

Note: *For a SmartArt Graphic, you must first click **Align**, and then click **Rotate**.*

4. Click **Flip Vertical** or **Flip Horizontal**.

   PowerPoint flips the object 180 degrees in the selected direction.

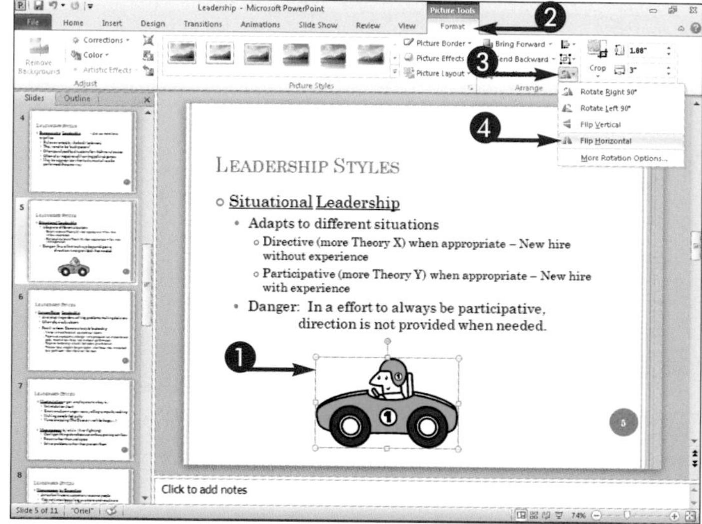

Rotate Objects

1. Click an object to select it.

   Handles appear around it, including a green rotation handle above the object.

2. Position the mouse over the green handle.

   changes to circle arrows.

3. Drag the green handle clockwise or counterclockwise.

   The object rotates as you drag. When you release the mouse, the object stays at the new angle.

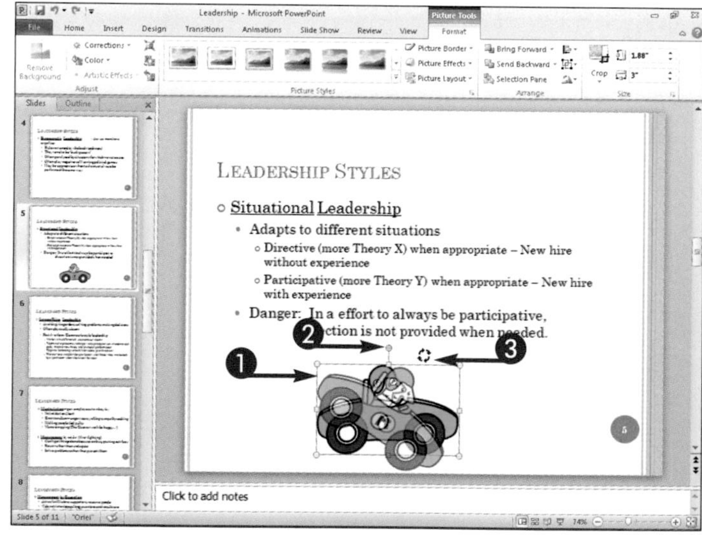

Apply a New Effect

When you select an object, Contextual tabs appear on the Ribbon to provide you with tools for formatting the object. Contextual tabs for pictures, shapes, and Clip Art include a Format tab that enables you to apply a shape effect such as a shadow, reflection, or glow. You can use shape effects to add dimension and realism to the object's appearance.

Apply a New Effect

1. Click an object to select it.
2. Click the **Home** tab.
3. Click **Shape Effects**.

   The gallery of Shapes appears.
4. Click a special effect.

   In this example, Reflection was clicked.

   The Reflections gallery appears.
5. Click a **Reflection Variation**.

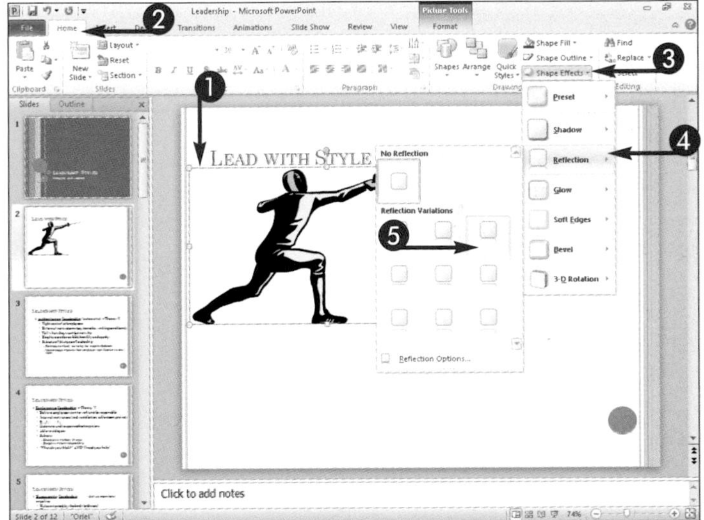

- The Special Effect is applied to the object.

6. Click anywhere outside the object when finished.

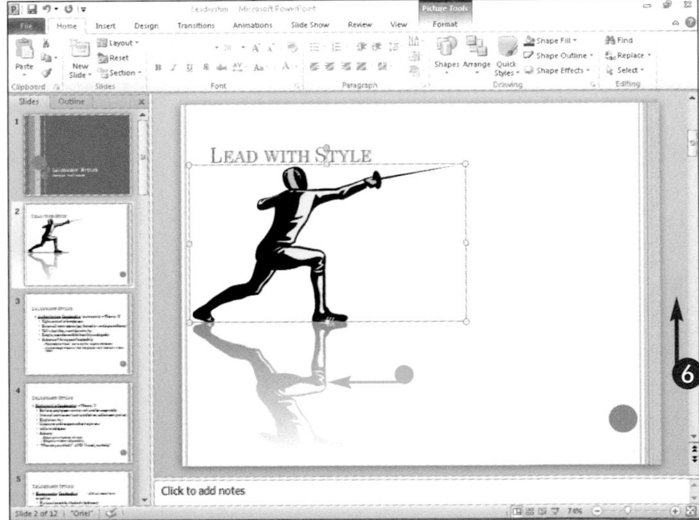

Add WordArt

The WordArt feature enables you to create special effects with text. You can bend WordArt text and apply interesting color styles. Using the WordArt feature, you can emphasize an important word or phrase, or you can create a simple logo.

WordArt is an object that you can move, resize, or format using techniques discussed earlier in this chapter.

Add WordArt

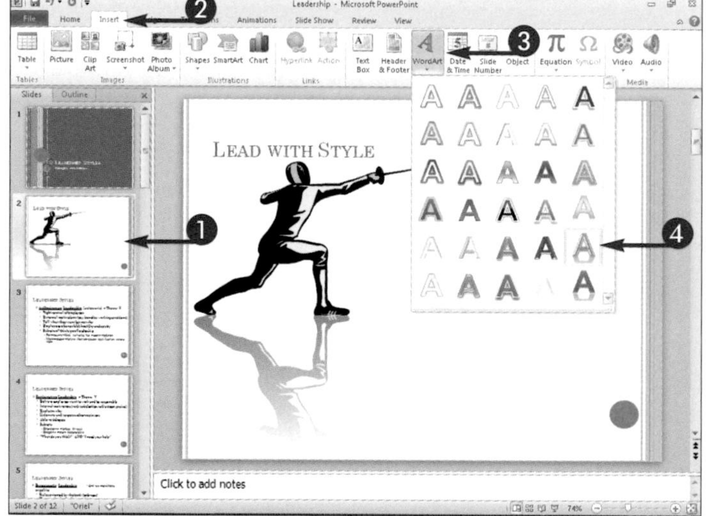

1. Select a slide in Normal view.

Note: *To navigate to and select a slide, see Chapter 4.*

2. Click the **Insert** tab.
3. Click **WordArt**.

   The WordArt gallery appears.

4. Click a WordArt style.

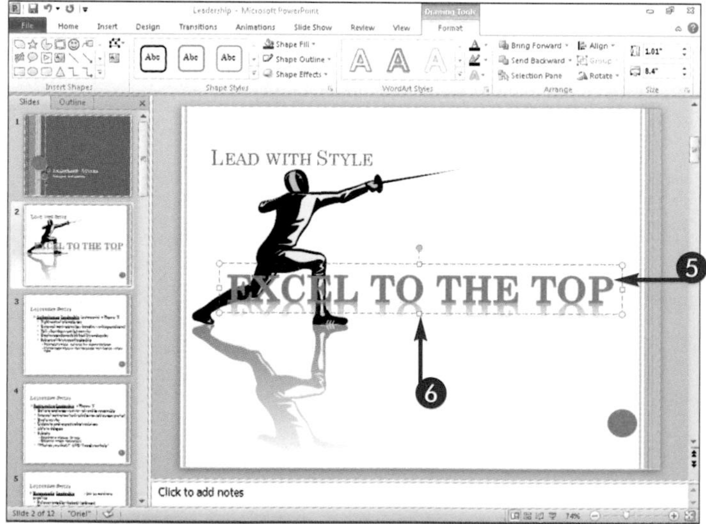

The WordArt appears on the slide ready to type a word or phrase.

5. Type a word or phrase.

   In this example, EXCEL TO THE TOP was typed.

   As you type, the WordArt text automatically sizes itself.

6. Click and drag the handles to move and size the WordArt as needed.

7. Click the **Drawing Tools Format** tab.

8. Click the **Text Effects** button (A▾).

   The gallery of Text Effects appears.

9. Click a text effect.

   In this example Transform was clicked.

   The Transform gallery appears.

10. Click a **Warp** variation from the gallery.

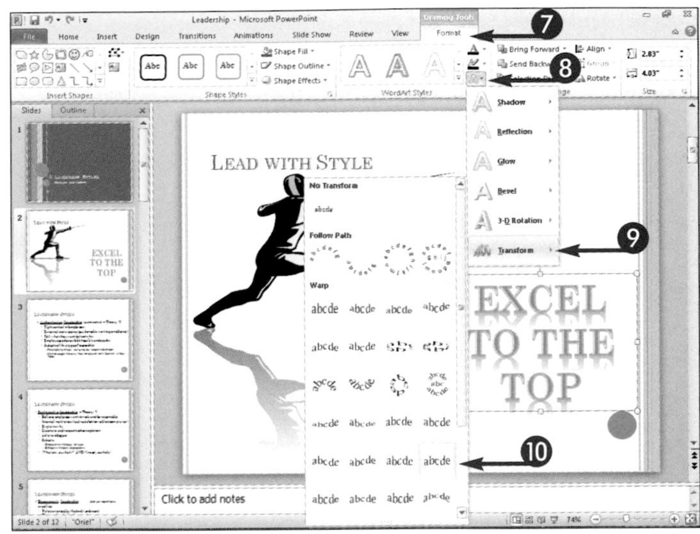

The special effect is applied to the WordArt.

- Drag the pink handles on the WordArt border to increase or decrease the effect.
- Use other tools on the Format tab to change the appearance of the WordArt.

11. Click outside the object when finished.

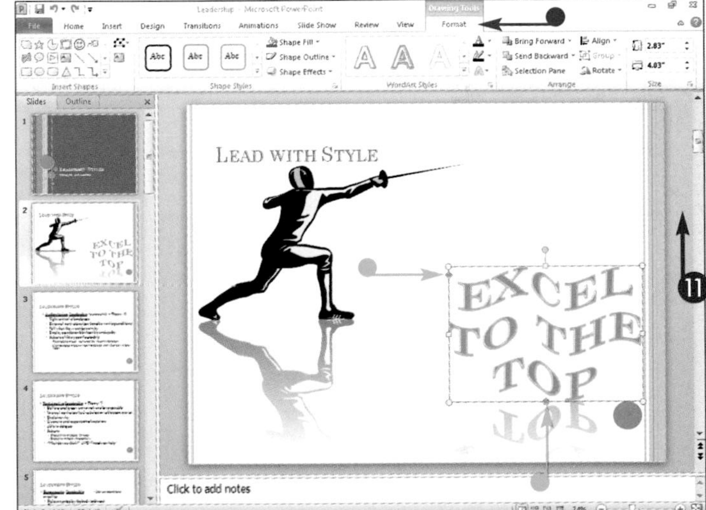

I created a WordArt object, but then realized it contains a typo. Is there any way to change it?

Yes. Click the object just like any text box or placeholder. The insertion point appears within the text of the WordArt so that you can make the necessary changes.

How do I change the style and color of the WordArt?

Click a WordArt object, and then click the **Drawing Tools Format** tab when it appears. Click the **WordArt Styles** ▾. When the WordArt gallery appears, click another WordArt style.

Insert a Hyperlink

A hyperlink enables you to perform a variety of actions when you click it during a slide show. It enables you to easily go somewhere in PowerPoint or outside of PowerPoint during a slide show. You can have a hyperlink display another slide in the current presentation, open another presentation, open a document from another application, start a blank e-mail, or open a Web page.

Insert a Hyperlink

1. Click a placeholder or text box to select it.
2. Position the insertion point where you want to insert the hyperlink.
3. Click the **Insert** tab.
4. Click **Hyperlink**.

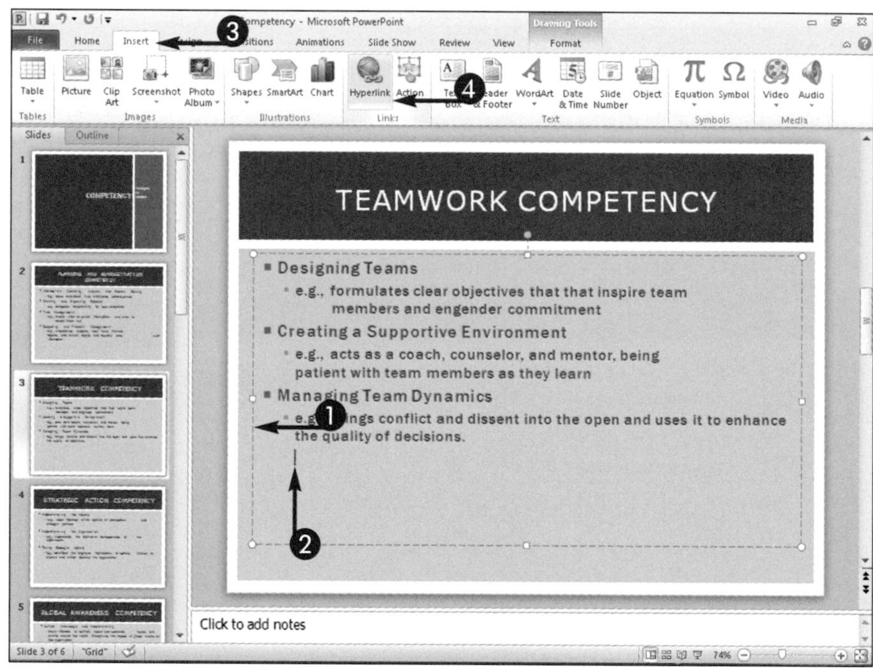

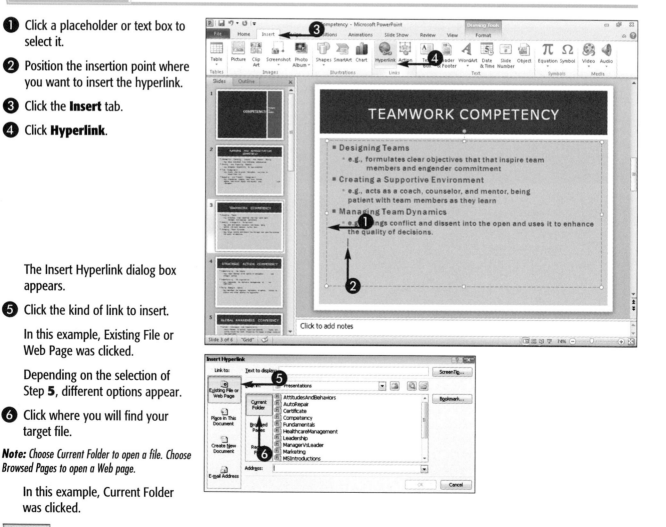

The Insert Hyperlink dialog box appears.

5. Click the kind of link to insert.

   In this example, Existing File or Web Page was clicked.

   Depending on the selection of Step **5**, different options appear.

6. Click where you will find your target file.

Note: *Choose Current Folder to open a file. Choose Browsed Pages to open a Web page.*

In this example, Current Folder was clicked.

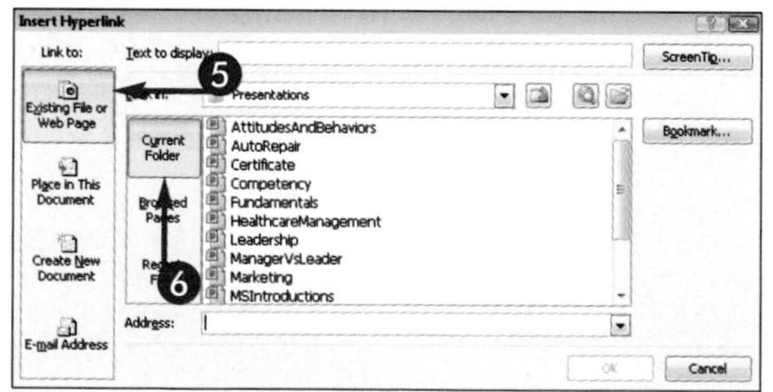

Depending on the selection of Step **6**, different options appear.

7. Click ▾ on the **Look In** drop-down list.

8. Find and click the folder that contains the file you want to open.

9. Click the file to open.

   In this example, AutoRepair was clicked.

   PowerPoint enters information in the Text to display text box and the Address text box.

10. Click the **Text to display** text box and type the text you want the hyperlink to display on the slide.

    In this example, Auto Repair Information was typed.

11. Click **OK**.

- PowerPoint places the link on your slide.

  During the slide show, click the text to follow the link.

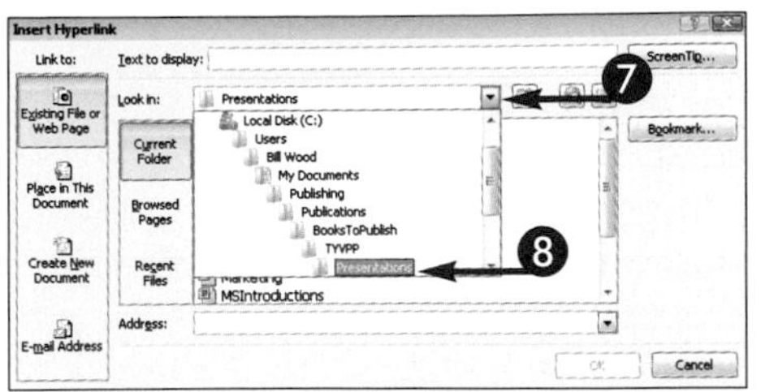

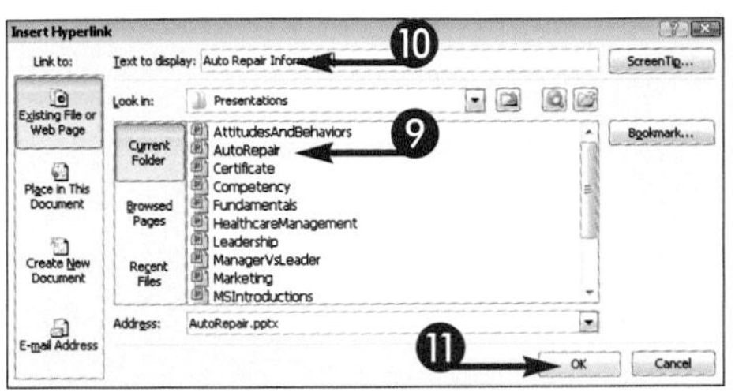

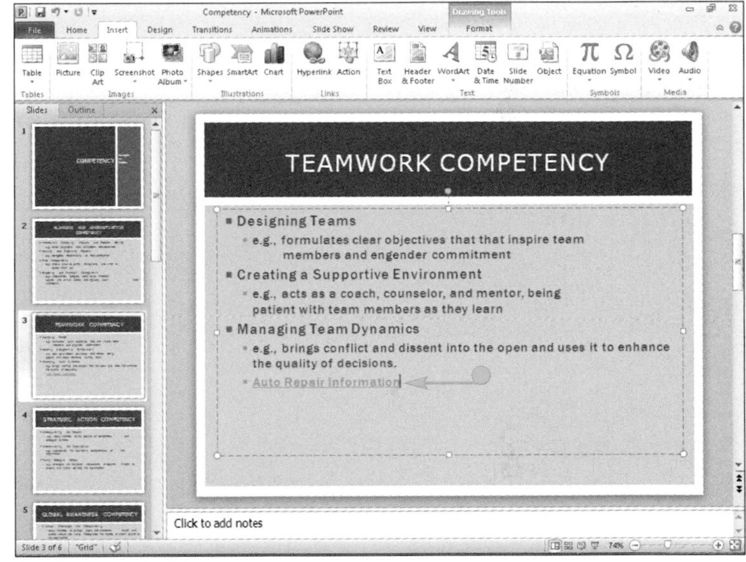

TIPS

How do I remove a link to a file but leave the link text?

Right-click the hyperlink, and click **Edit Link** on the shortcut menu. When the Edit Hyperlink dialog box opens, click **Remove Link**, and then click **OK**. The link text remains, but the link itself is removed.

How can I let the person running the presentation know what the link does without being wordy with the hyperlink text?

You can create a ScreenTip. While in the Insert Hyperlink or Edit Hyperlink dialog box, click the **ScreenTip** button and enter as much text as you like in the dialog box that appears. Click **OK** and finish creating the link from there. When the person running the show positions the ↖ over the link, the tip appears in a little box.

Group and Ungroup Objects

You may create a set of objects that you want to move or format as a unit. For example, you may draw a car using ovals and lines. You can group the objects so the collection of objects acts as a single object. After grouping objects, changes you make then apply to all the objects in the group.

Group and Ungroup Objects

Group Objects

1. Select multiple objects.

***Note:** See the section "Select Objects" earlier in this chapter to learn how to select multiple objects.*

2. Click the **Picture Tools Format** tab.

***Note:** If you see two Format tabs, click either.*

3. Click the **Group** button ().
4. Click **Group**.

   A single selection box appears around the grouped object.

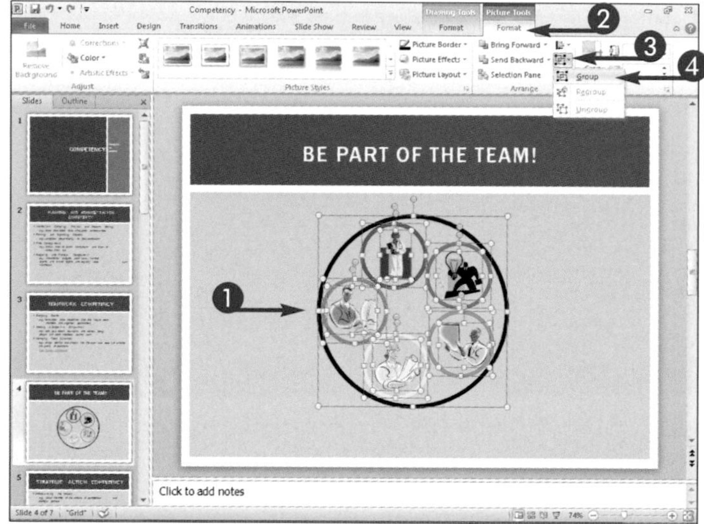

Ungroup Objects

1. Select the grouped object.
2. Click the **Picture Tools Format** tab.

***Note:** If you see two Format tabs, click either one.*

3. Click .
4. Click **Ungroup**.

   The objects separate.

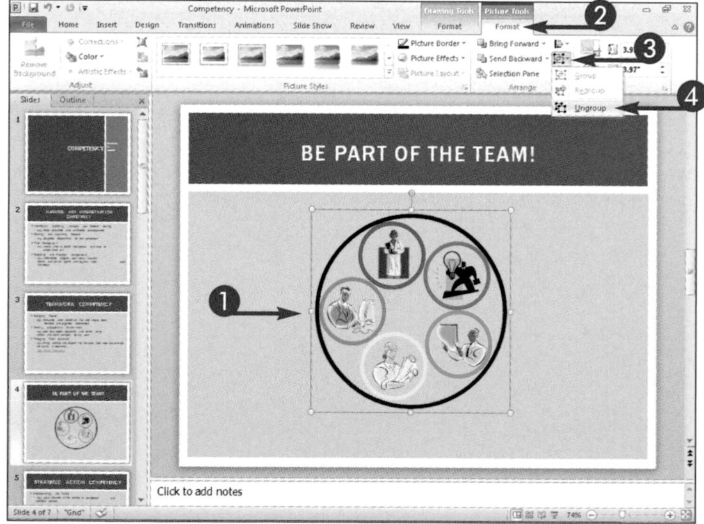

Change Object Order

When you work with multiple objects, you may want to stack them in layers so that they overlap as objects do in real life. For example, if you want to create a shadow effect for an object, the shape that you use as the shadow must be behind the object. Controlling which object appears in front of another is called *arranging* or *ordering*.

Change Object Order

1. Select an object to arrange.
2. Click the **Drawing Tools Format** tab.
3. Click the **Send Backward** ▾.
4. Click **Send Backward**.

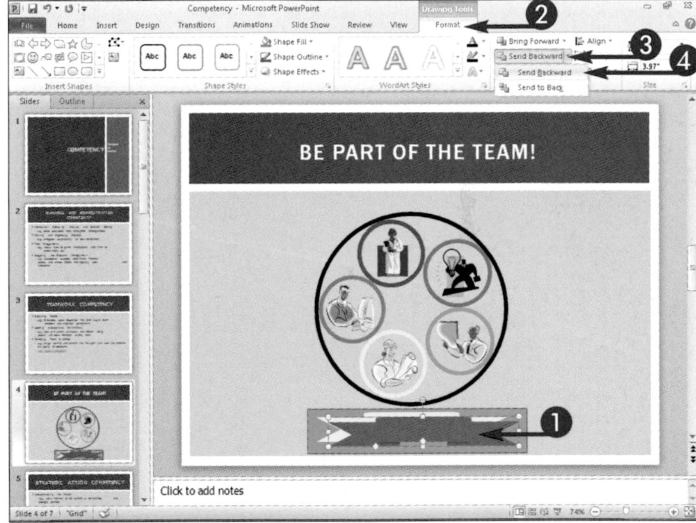

The object moves a layer back.

5. Click outside the object when finished.

***Note:** To arrange an object only one layer, click **Bring Forward** or **Send Backward**; to move an object behind or in front of everything else, click **Send to Back** or **Bring to Front**.*

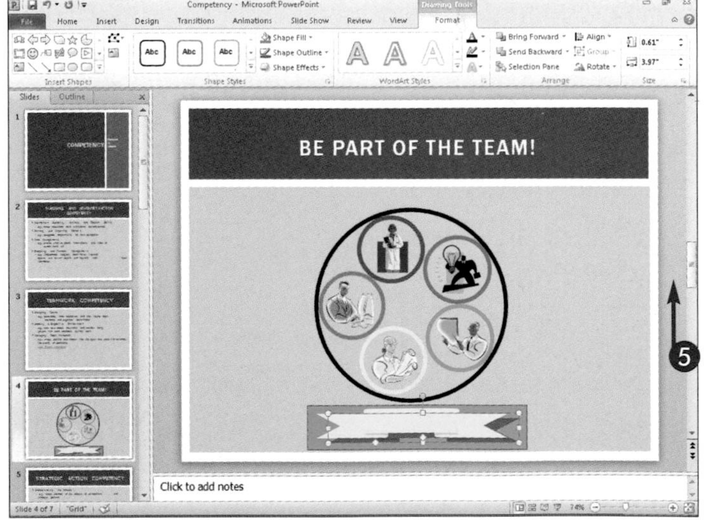

Using the Grid and Guidelines

PowerPoint offers two features that help you position and align objects with precision. The grid looks like graph paper lines on your slide when you display it. You can add individual guides at locations of your choosing. You can then position objects to align with the grid or guides.

Using the Grid and Guidelines

1. Click the **View** tab.
2. Click ⧉ on the **Show** group.

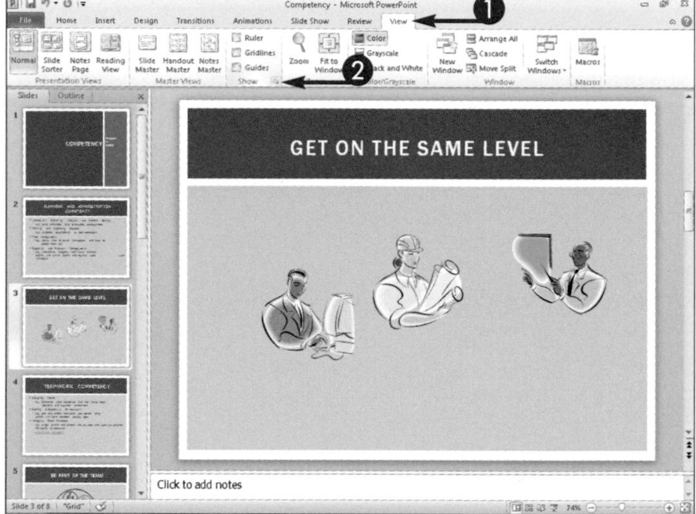

The Grid and Guides dialog box appears.

3. Click the **Display grid on screen** check box (☐ changes to ☑).

- You can change the spacing of the gridlines by making a selection from the Spacing drop-down list.

4. Click the **Display drawing guides on screen** check box (☐ changes to ☑).
5. Click **OK**.

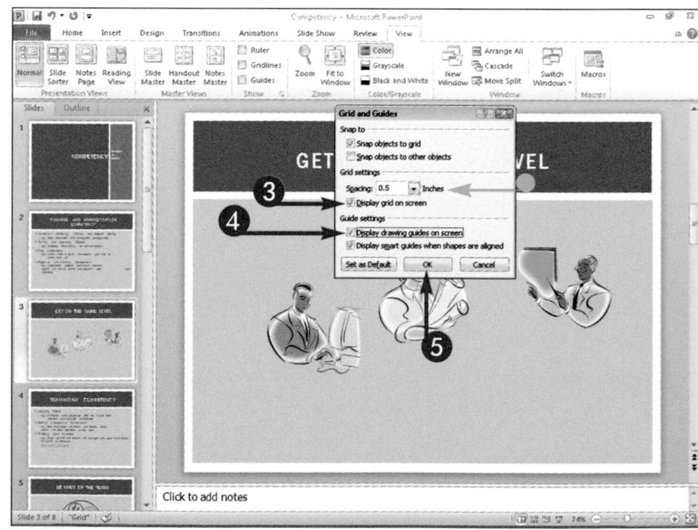

- The grid appears as dotted lines.
- The dashed guides intersect in the center of the slide.

6. Click and drag an object to align it with the grid or guide.

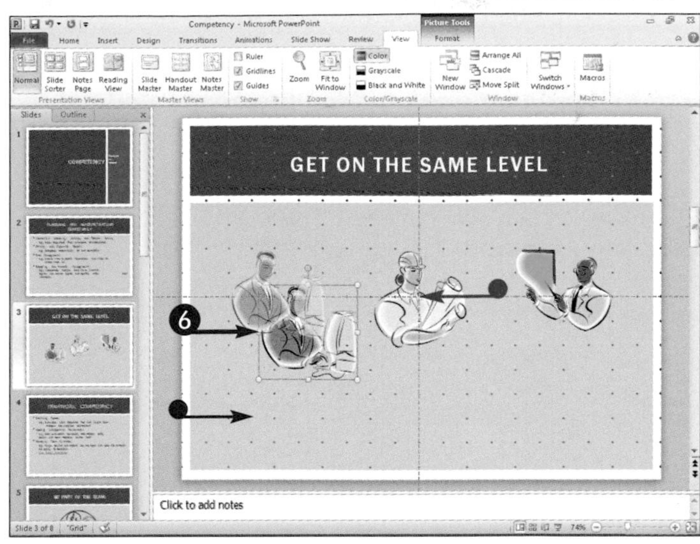

The object snaps to the gridline.

7. Click and drag a guide.

   A value showing the position of the guide appears as you drag.

8. To hide the gridlines and guides, click **Gridlines** and **Guides** in the Show group on the Ribbon (☑ changes to ☐).

   You can also hide the gridlines and guides by following Steps **1** to **5** to clear the check boxes in the Grid and Guides dialog box.

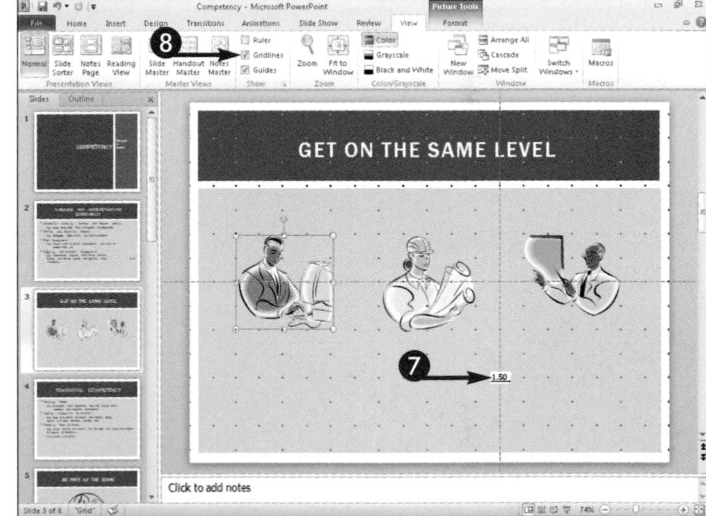

TIPS

Is there a way to stop objects from automatically snapping to gridlines?

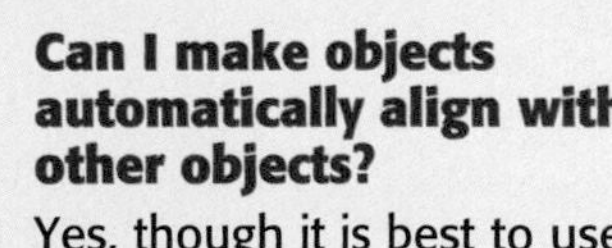

Yes. Open the Grid and Guides dialog box. Click the **Snap objects to grid** option (☑ changes to ☐), and then click **OK**. Now when you move an object, it will not automatically snap and align to the gridlines.

Can I make objects automatically align with other objects?

Yes, though it is best to use it when the snap to grid feature is off. Open the Grid and Guides dialog box. Click the **Snap objects to other objects** option (☐ changes to ☑), and then click **OK**. When you move an object in-line with another object, it will pop into place and will "stick" there.

Nudge Objects

You may want to move an object by very small increments. Using the mouse to perform delicate and precise moves can be tricky. The nudge feature enables you to move a selected object by small increments to the right, left, up, or down on the slide.

Nudge Objects

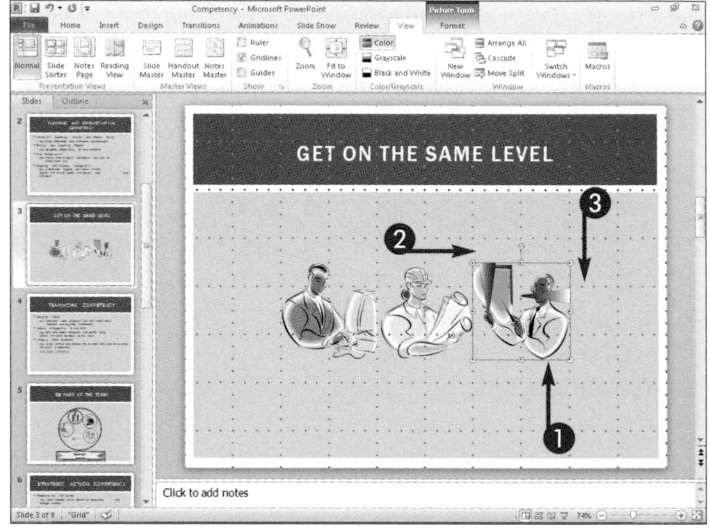

1. Select an object.
2. Press ↓, ←, →, or ↑ as many times as needed to nudge the object in the desired direction.

   Pressing an arrow nudges the object one gridline.
3. Press and hold Ctrl while pressing ↓, ←, →, or ↑ to nudge the object by very small increments.

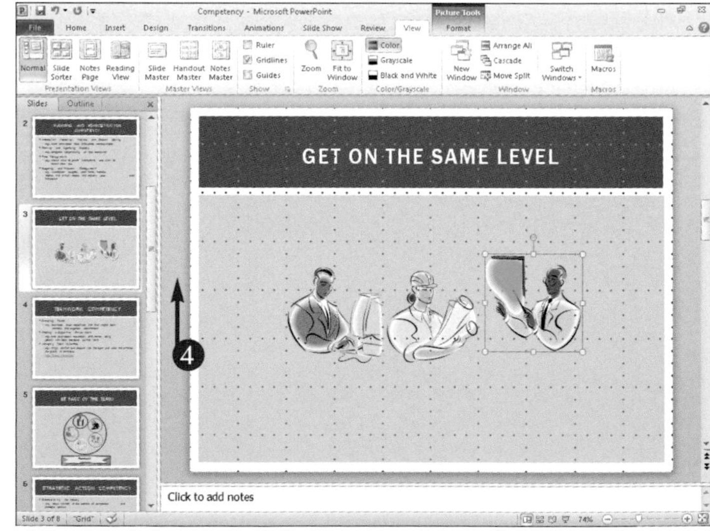

In this example, ↑ was pressed once and the object moved one gridline.

In this example, → was pressed ten times while holding the Ctrl key down and the object moved half a gridline.

4. Click outside the object to finish.

Align Objects

You can align objects relative to each other for a picture-perfect look. For example, you can make several objects align at the same position as the leftmost object, or you can distribute objects evenly relative to one another.

Align Objects

1. Select multiple objects.
2. Click the **Picture Tools Format** tab.
3. Click the **Align** button (⊫).
   - Click **Align to Slide** to align the object(s) with the slide.
4. Click the desired alignment command.

   In this example Align Top was clicked.

   The top borders of the objects align to the topmost object.

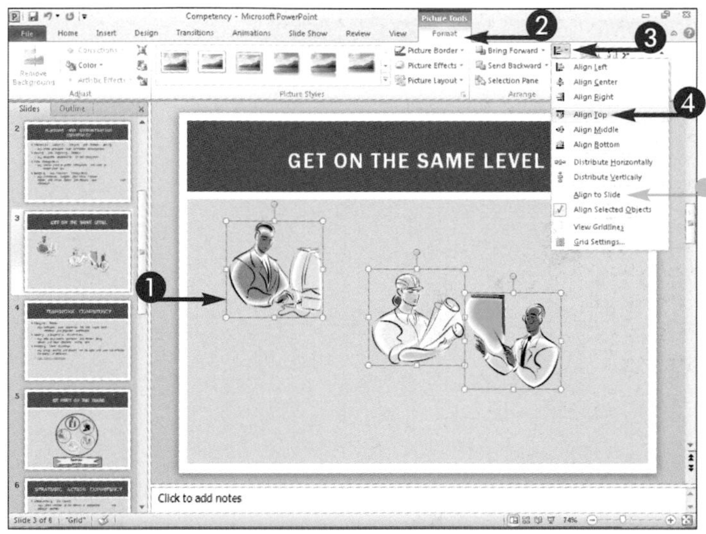

5. Click ⊫.
6. Click **Distribute Horizontally** or **Distribute Vertically**.

   In this example Distribute Horizontally was clicked.

   The objects distribute evenly horizontally.

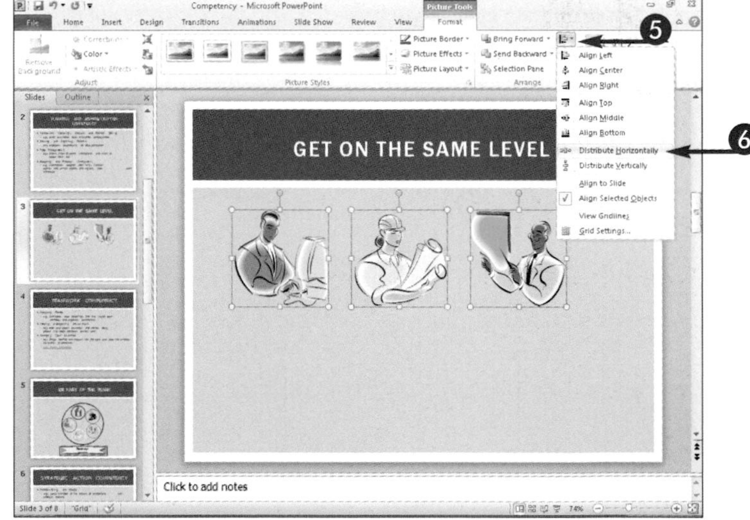

CHAPTER 10

Organizing Slides

After you have created a number of slides, you should check to ensure that the overall flow of your presentation makes sense. A great place to organize your slides is in Slide Sorter view. This view displays a thumbnail (little pictures) of each slide. You can use the thumbnails to move, delete, or copy slides with ease.

Move a Slide

A good presentation conveys a sequence of ideas in a logical progression. When creating a presentation, you often must reorganize slides to get that sequence right.

You may also want to rearrange slides based on your audience to create a variation that places the emphasis on different ideas.

Move a Slide

1. Click the **View** tab.
2. Click **Slide Sorter**.

   Slide Sorter view appears.
3. Drag a slide thumbnail to the desired location.

- A line appears to indicate the new slide position.

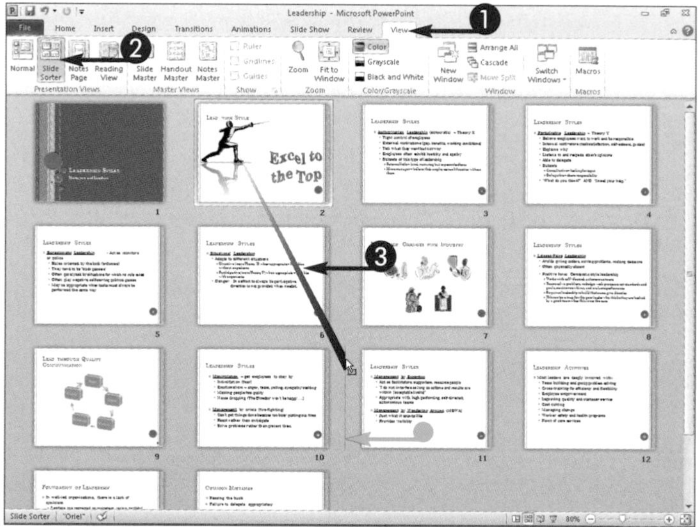

- When you release the mouse button, the slide appears in its new position.

Note: *Press and hold* Ctrl *as you drag to copy and paste the slide to the new position.*

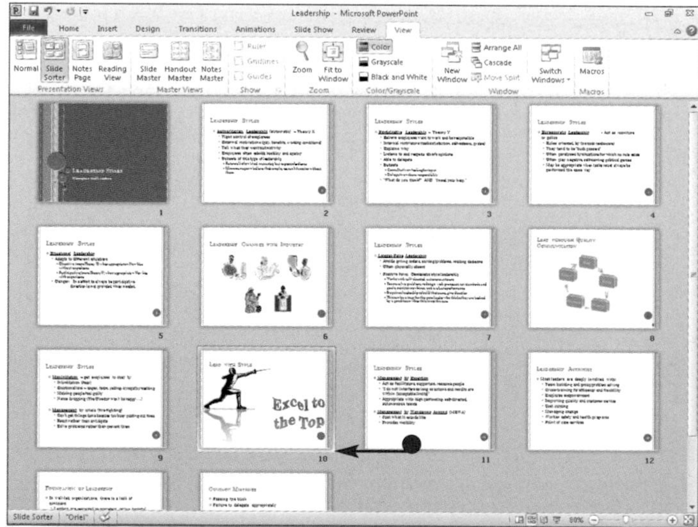

Copy and Paste a Slide

If you create presentations about similar subjects, you may want to copy a slide from one presentation to another to save time. You can simply copy and paste the slide.

You can also click and drag a slide from one presentation or to another to copy it.

Copy and Paste a Slide

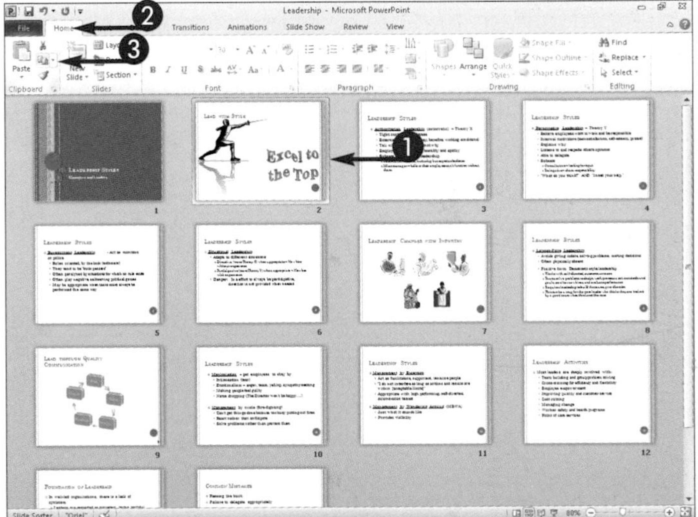

1. Select slide(s) in Normal or Slide Sorter view.

Note: To select multiple slides, click the first slide, and then press Ctrl while clicking additional slides.

2. Click the **Home** tab.
3. Click the **Copy** button ( ).
4. Open another presentation or switch to one that is already open.

Note: For help opening presentations, see Chapter 3.

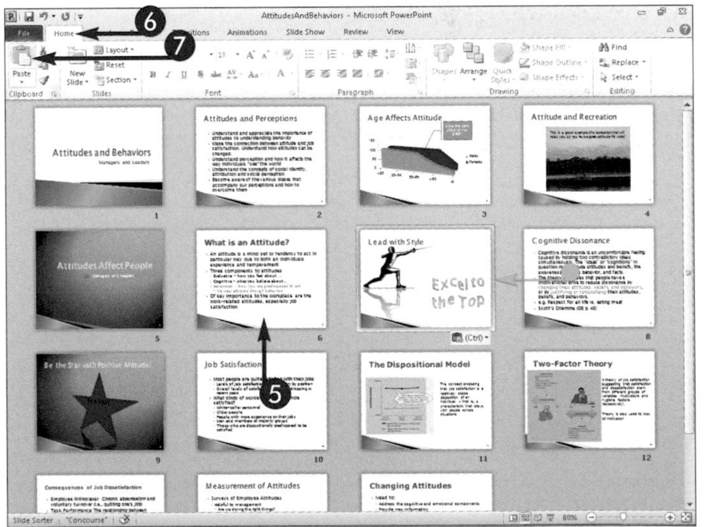

5. In Normal or Slide Sorter view, click the slide after which you want the copied slide to appear.
6. Click the **Home** tab.
7. Click **Paste**.

- The copied slide(s) appear in the presentation in the selected position.

You can change it back to its original formatting by clicking the **Paste Options** button ((Ctrl)).

Delete a Slide in Slide Sorter View

As you build your presentation, you may decide you do not need particular material. In this case, you can simply delete the slide covering that material. Deleting a slide is quick and easy.

Delete a Slide in Slide Sorter View

1. Select slide(s) in Slide Sorter view.

   In this example, slides 3, 7, 9, 11, and 12 were selected.

Note: *To select multiple slides, click the first slide, and then press* Ctrl *while clicking additional slides.*

2. Right-click any selected slide.

   The shortcut menu appears.

3. Click **Delete Slide** or press Del.

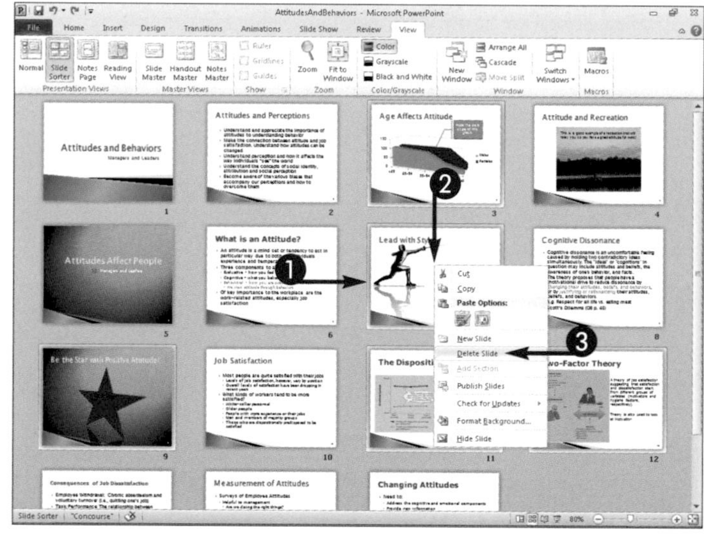

PowerPoint deletes the selected slide(s) from the presentation.

Note: *PowerPoint does not prompt you to confirm the deletion. If you want to get the slide back, click the* ***Undo*** *icon (↶) on the Quick Access Toolbar.*

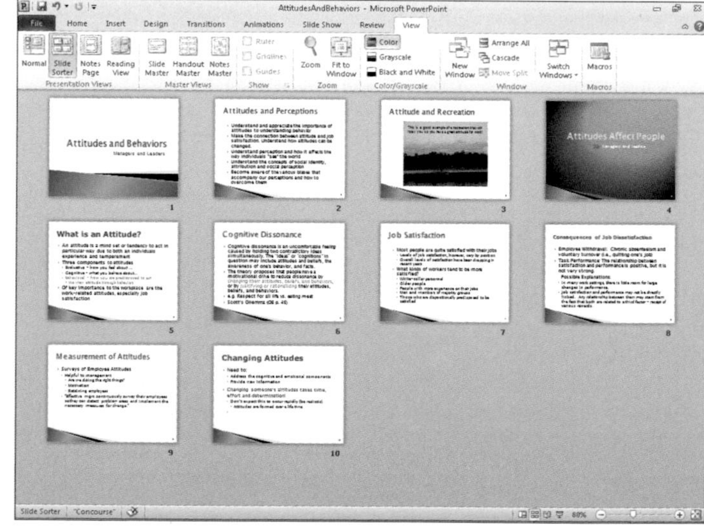

Make a Duplicate Slide

If you need to make two slides that are very similar, you can design the first, and then use the Duplicate Slide feature to duplicate it. Then you can make minor changes to the copy to create the new slide.

For example, if a slide at the beginning of a presentation lists key topics, you can duplicate it, make minor changes, and use it as a summary.

Make a Duplicate Slide

1. Select slide(s) in Slide Sorter view.

   Note: *To select multiple slides, click the first slide, and then press* Ctrl *while clicking additional slides.*

2. Click the **Home** tab.
3. Click the **New Slide** ▾.
4. Click **Duplicate Selected Slides**.

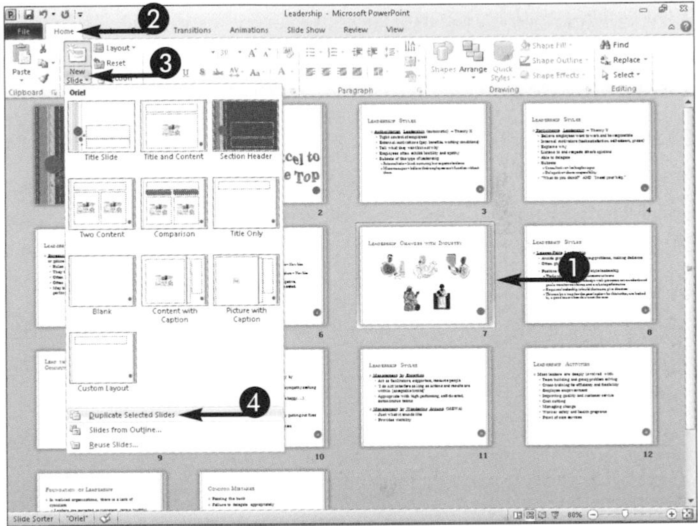

- PowerPoint duplicates the selected slide(s).

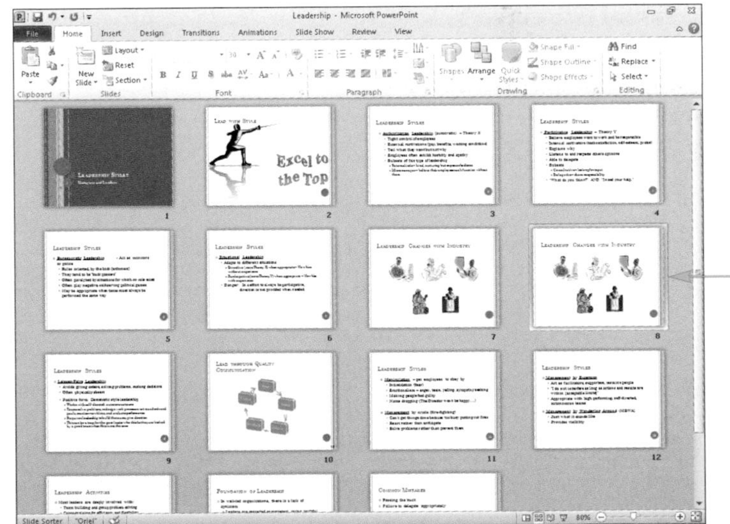

Hide a Slide

Hiding a slide prevents it from appearing during the slide show. By hiding slides, you can create an abbreviated slide show from a presentation without deleting any slides. You can hide slides, give the presentation, and then unhide them.

Hiding slides is a good way to temporarily remove them to see how your presentation flows without them.

Hide a Slide

1. Select slide(s) in Slide Sorter view.

Note: *To select multiple slides, click the first slide, and then press* Ctrl *while clicking additional slides.*

2. Click the **Slide Show** tab.
3. Click **Hide Slide**.

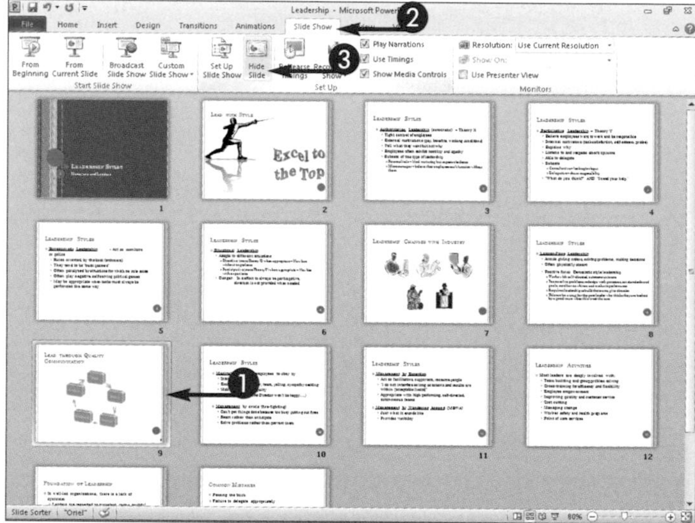

- A gray box with a diagonal line appears over the slide number, indicating the slide will not be seen during the slide show.

4. To redisplay hidden slide(s), repeat Steps **1** to **3**.

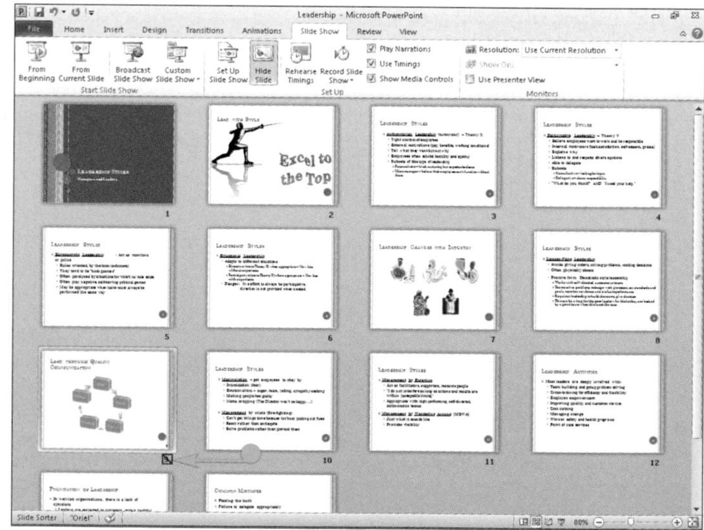

Zoom In the View

In Slide Sorter view, you can view a slide in greater or less detail by changing the zoom level. If you want to view more slide thumbnails, you can select a smaller zoom percentage so the slides are smaller. That approach can help you find a slide more quickly.

Zoom In the View

1. Display the Slide Sorter view.
2. Click the **View** tab.
3. Click **Zoom**.

   The Zoom dialog box appears.

4. Click a zoom percentage option (◎ changes to ◉).

   In this example 66% was clicked.

- You can also click the **spinner** (⬍) or type a percentage in the Percent text box.

5. Click **OK**.

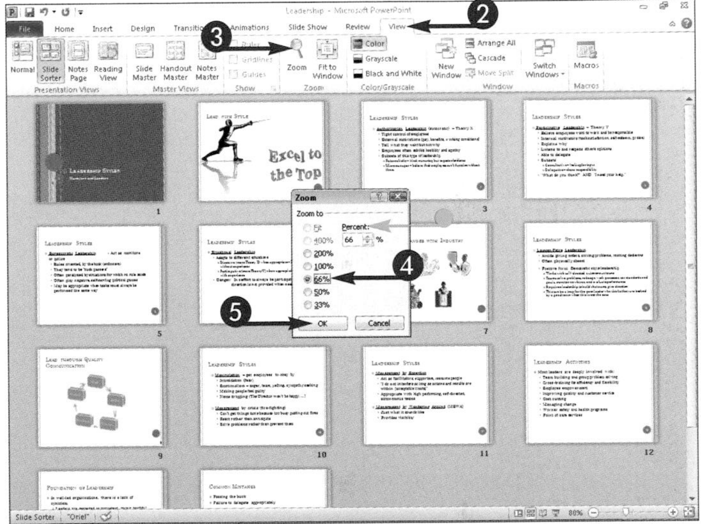

- You also can drag the Zoom slider to zoom, or click the **Zoom In** button ⊕ or the **Zoom Out** button ⊖ at the end of the slider.

PowerPoint displays the slides at the specified zoom level.

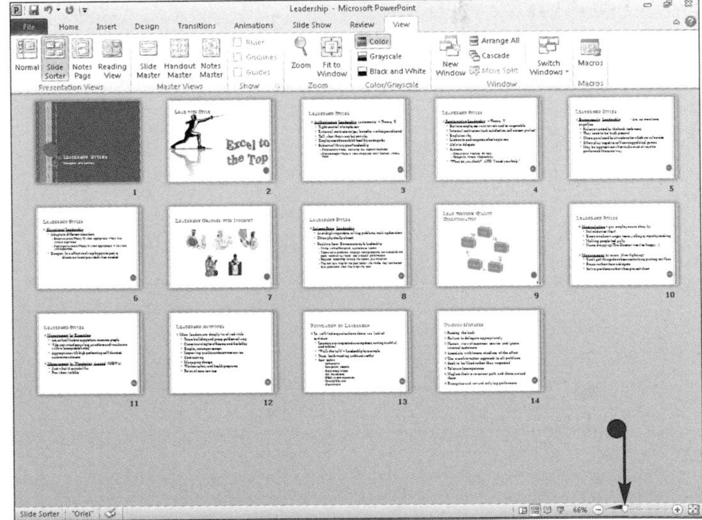

Go to an Individual Slide

When you are working in Slide Sorter view, it is sometimes useful to go to Normal view, where you can view a slide in detail. While in Slide Sorter view, you can quickly and easily show a slide in Normal view to see its detail.

Although you can select a slide and then click the Normal view icon, these steps show a faster way to display an individual slide.

Go to an Individual Slide

1. Display the Slide Sorter view.
2. Double-click the slide that you want to see in detail.

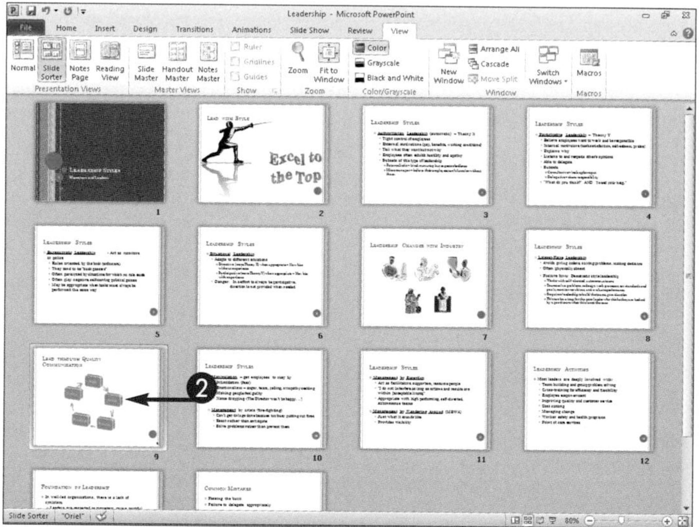

- The slide appears in the Normal view.

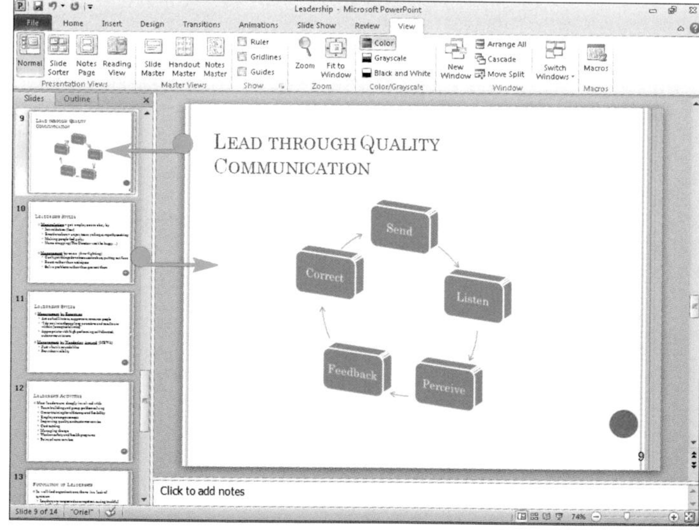

Change Slide Orientation

Typically, slide shows are presented horizontally in the landscape orientation; portrait is vertical, like a business letter. There are times when you may want your presentation in the portrait position — possibly while you print the slide show. You can change the orientation of your presentation, though changing orientation does change the proportions of objects on the slides.

Change Slide Orientation

1. Display the presentation in Normal, Slide Sorter, or Notes Page view.
2. Click the **Design** tab.
3. Click **Slide Orientation**.
4. Click an orientation.

   In this example, Portrait was clicked.

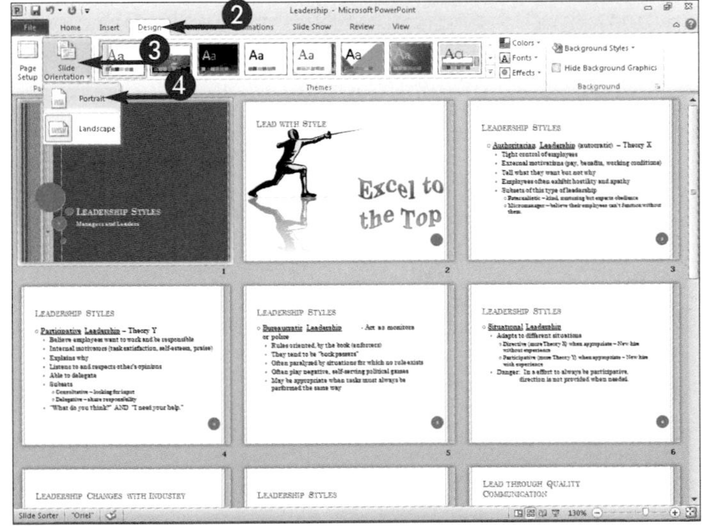

The slides change to the chosen orientation.

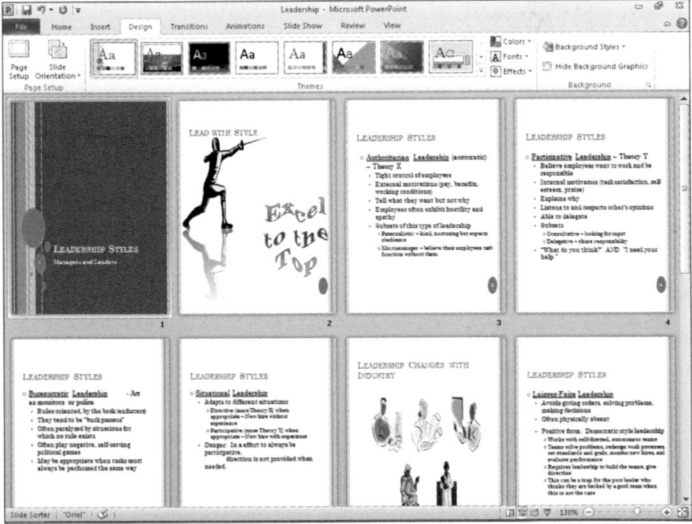

View Slides in Grayscale

In a presentation with a lot of color in the background, it can be easier to view slide content in grayscale, or black and white. You can view grayscale slides in Normal, Slide Sorter, or Notes Page view.

Grayscale presents slides in shades of gray. Black and white is more extreme because it uses no shading.

View Slides in Grayscale

1. Display the Normal view.
2. Click the **View** tab.
3. Click **Grayscale** or **Black and White**.

   In this example, Grayscale was clicked.

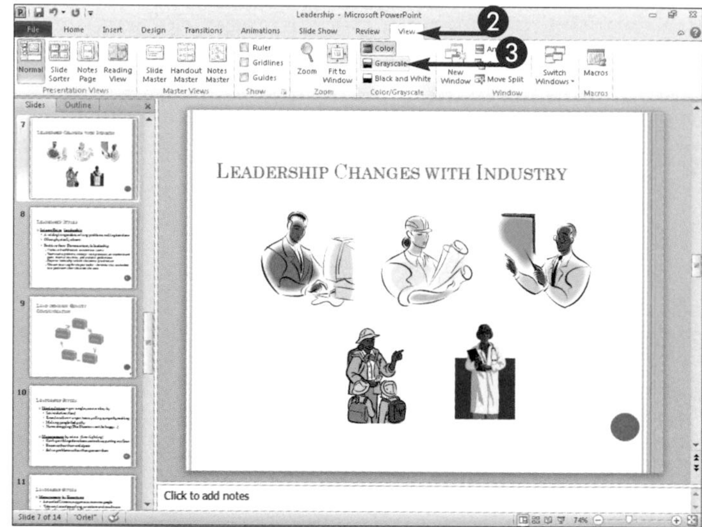

The presentation appears in grayscale and an additional tab called Grayscale appears.

4. Click the **Grayscale** tab.
5. Click an object in the presentation.
6. Click **Inverse Grayscale**.

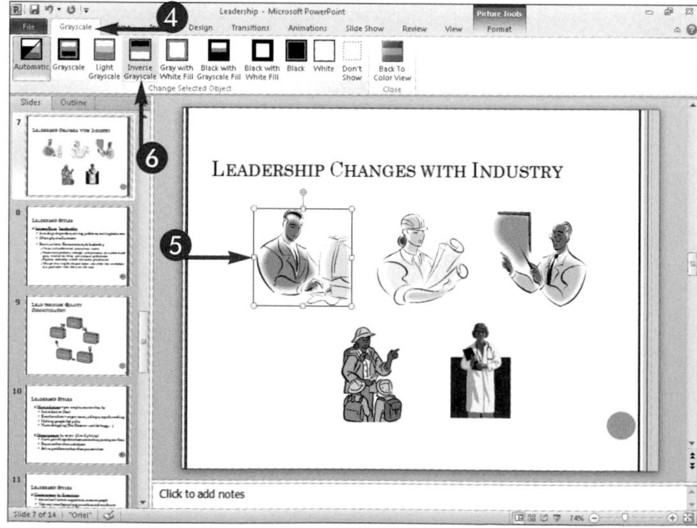

- The object changes appearance.

7. Click **Back to Color View**.

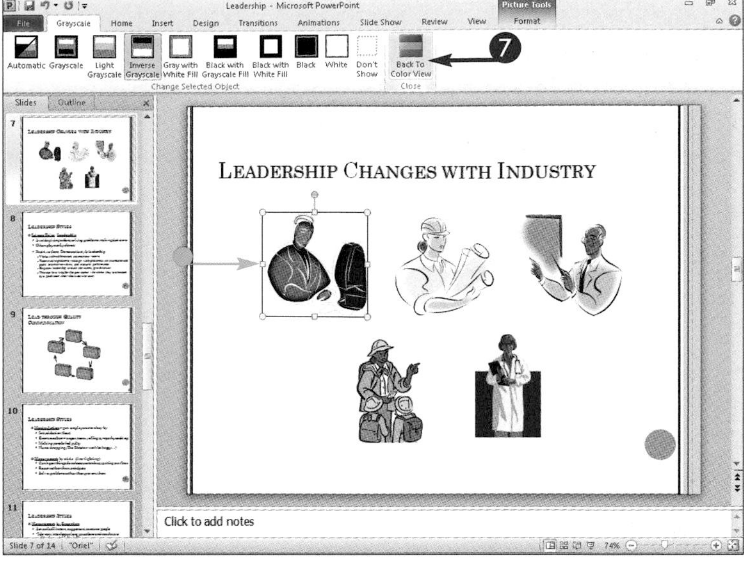

The presentation returns to color view.

TIP

Can I print in grayscale, or black and white?

Yes. If you use a black-and-white printer, PowerPoint automatically adjusts the presentation to print in grayscale. If you use a color printer, do the following:

1. Click the **File** tab.
2. Click **Print**.
3. Click **Color**.
4. Click **Grayscale** or **Pure Black and White**.
5. Click **Print**.

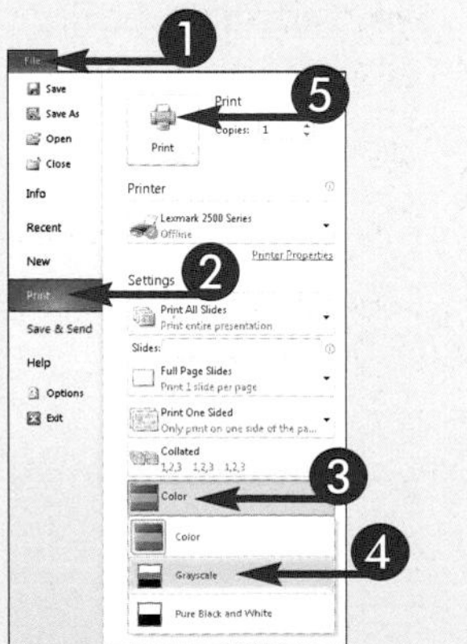

Group Slides into Sections

You may need to present multiple topics in your slide show, calling for a logical separation between topics. A presentation on Microsoft Office may need four distinct sections for the different applications. Instead of creating four presentations, you can easily separate one presentation into sections. The sections exist independently, enabling you to easily apply different themes and color schemes to each without affecting the others.

Group Slides into Sections

1. In Normal or Slide Sorter view, click the slide that you want to begin your new section.
2. Click the **Home** tab.
3. Click **Section**.
4. Click **Add Section**.

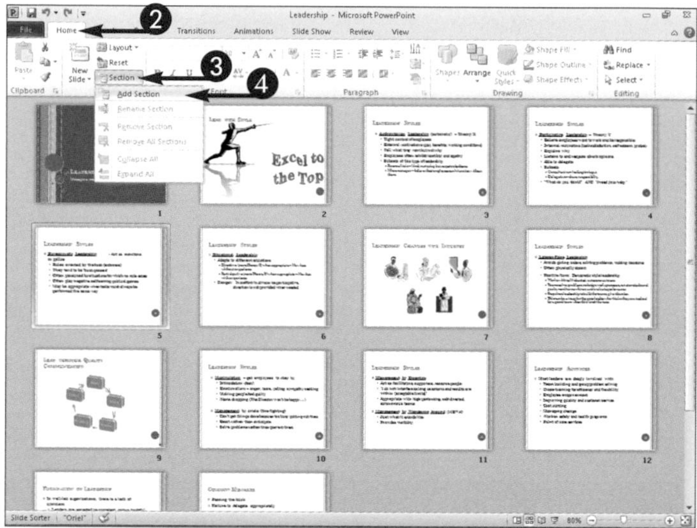

- A section is inserted before the slide that you selected.

  Note that the beginning part of the presentation becomes a section, too.

5. Click a section to rename.
6. Click **Section**.
7. Click **Rename Section**.

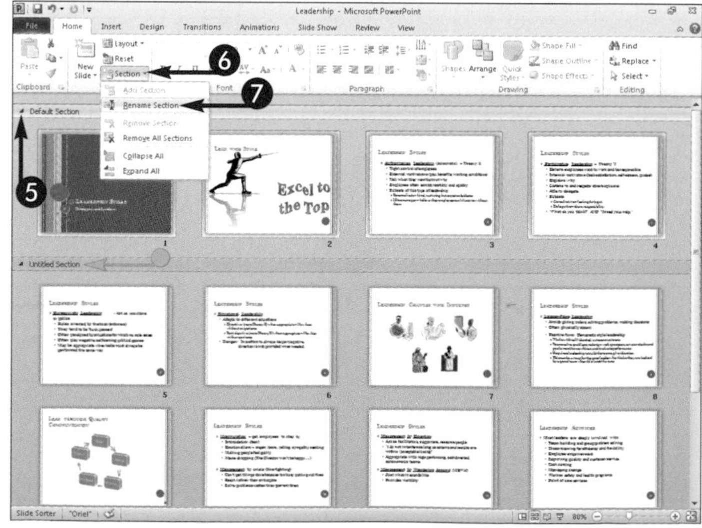

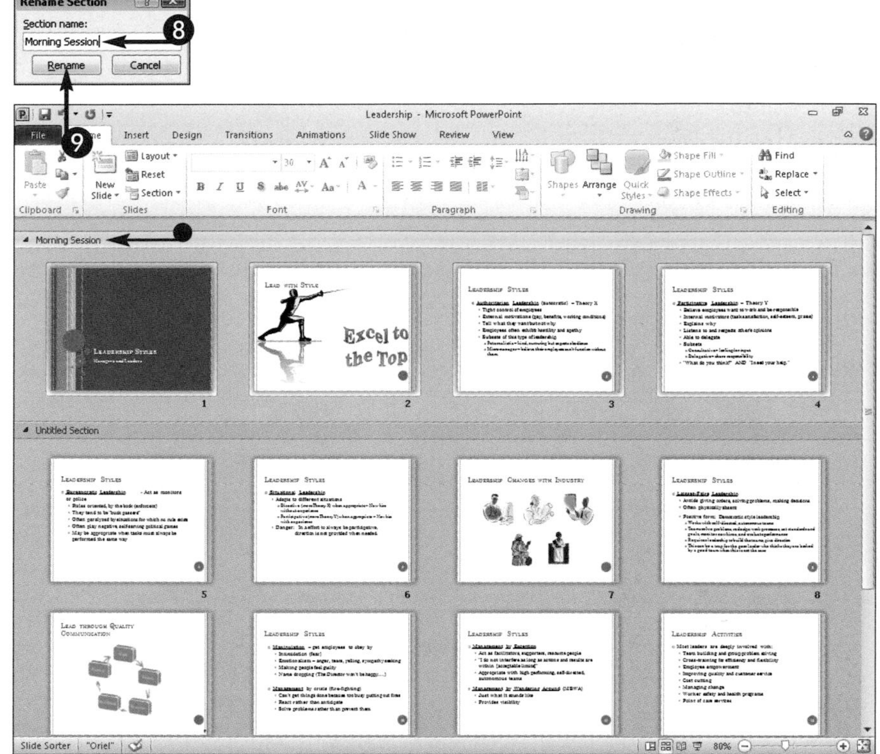

The Rename Section dialog box appears.

8 Type a new name.

In this example, Morning Session was typed.

9 Click **Rename**.

- PowerPoint renames the section.

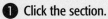

Can I get rid of a section?

Yes. You can remove a section or simply collapse it, depending on your need. To remove a section

1. Click the section.
2. Click the **Home** tab.
3. Click **Section**.
4. Click **Remove Section**.
5. To collapse or expand a section, click ◢ next to the section name.

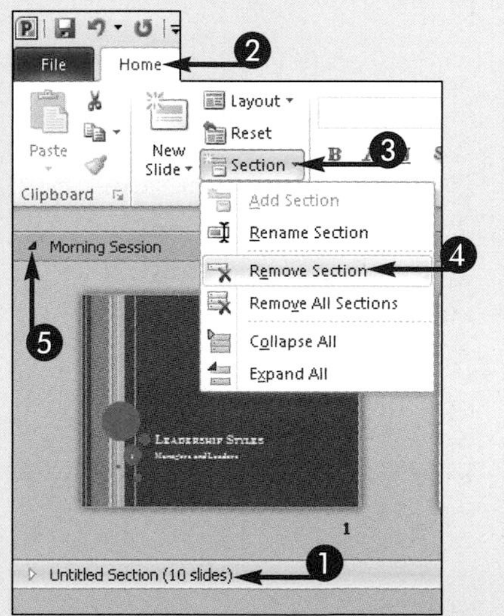

CHAPTER 11

Adding Action to Slides

Animations and transitions create action in your presentation. Animation gives movement to text and objects so the slide show does more than display static bullet points. Transitions add an interesting effect when the slide show advances from one slide to another, as opposed to simply advancing from slide to slide.

Understanding Animations and Action Buttons

In PowerPoint, *animation* refers to text or object motion on slides. *Action buttons* perform an action when clicked during a slide show. *Transitions* refer to special effects that occur while the slide show changes from one slide to another.

What Is Animation?

Without animation, all the items on a slide appear at once and remain motionless during the slide show. Adding animation to slide objects causes them to appear at different times, with special motion. For example, you might animate a set of bullet points to move onto the screen one at a time.

When to Use Animation in a Presentation

Animations help you add emphasis to text or an object on a slide. If the audience's attention drifts after a long explanation or technical discussion, animations can help audience members refocus. However, overusing animations can make your presentation seem busy and can overshadow the presentation's content.

Apply an Animation

The Animations tab on the Ribbon contains the commands for working with animation. You can apply one of several standard animations from the Animations group. Select a placeholder or other object, and then choose the desired animation. You can apply various animations to each object on the slide.

Build Custom Animations

You can apply a custom animation to text or an object. PowerPoint groups custom animations effects into four types: Entrance, Exit, Emphasis, and Motion Paths. You can work with custom animations in the Animation Pane. You can modify animation effects, timing, and triggers.

Modify Animation Effects

Custom animations also give you more control over how you start playing the animation, its direction, the amount of motion it has, and its playback speed. You can set an animation to play when you click the object during the slide show, or to play automatically.

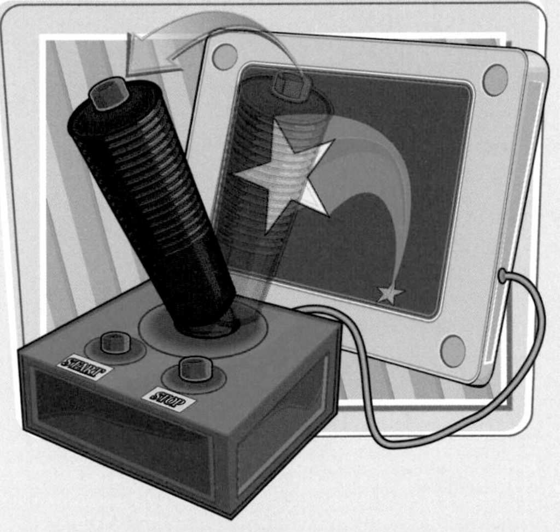

How Action Buttons Work

Action buttons provide interaction — not just action. You can draw an action button on a slide and then select the action that will occur when you click the button during the slide show. For example, clicking the action button might open a Web page or an external document such as a proposal, or show a particular slide.

Preview Animations and Action Buttons

To create a professional presentation, choose appropriate effects and always make sure they run properly. The Animation Pane offers a Play button for previewing specific animation effects. To preview an action button, you must run the slide show and click the button to verify its behavior.

Run Animations or Action Buttons during a Slide Show

You can program animations to play when a slide appears or when you click a slide. You can set up custom animations to play when a slide appears, play with a previous animation, or play after the previous animation. Finally, you can click an action button to make it perform its action.

Apply an Animation

You can use the Animations tab on the Ribbon to apply an animation to any slide object. If you select a complex object such as a SmartArt diagram or a bulleted list, you can apply the animation to each of its individual parts and control how those parts appear. The basic animations fade objects, wipe them, or fly them onto the screen.

Apply an Animation

1. Select an object to animate — you can apply an animation to multiple objects.

Note: *To select multiple objects, click the first object, and then press* Ctrl *while clicking additional objects.*

2. Click the **Animations** tab.
3. Click ▾ in the **Animations** group.

   The gallery of animations appears.

4. Click an animation.

   In this example, Fly In was clicked.

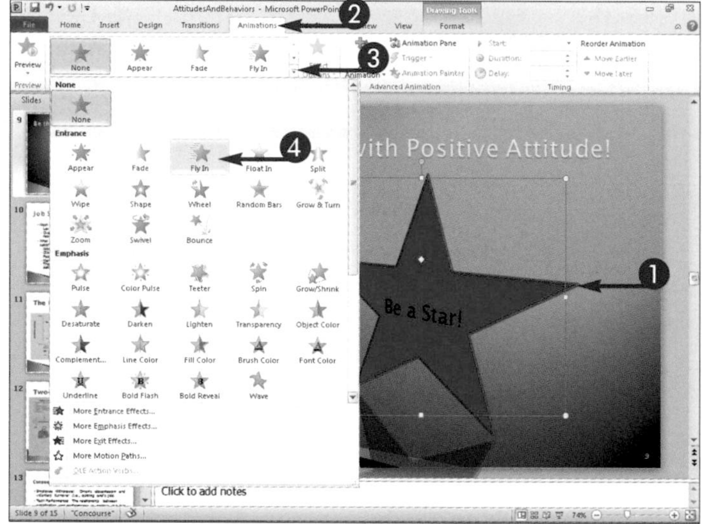

- PowerPoint applies the animation to the object and assigns it a sequence number
- PowerPoint places an animation icon next to the slide thumbnail.

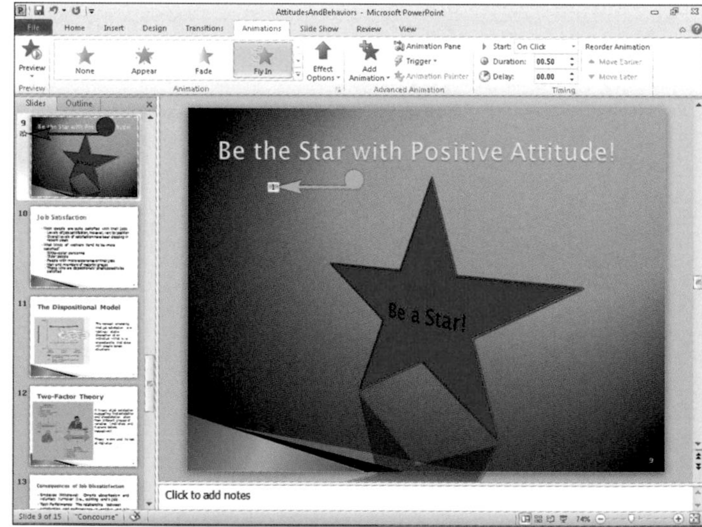

Preview an Animation

You can see all the animation in your presentation simply by running the slide show. However, you can also see the animation in individual slides in Normal or Slide Sorter view. Previewing the animation of a slide enables you to verify that the various animations work as expected and are appropriate for the slide's content.

Preview an Animation

1. Display a slide with animation in Normal or Slide Sorter view.
2. Click the **Animations** tab.
   - The sequence numbers of the slide's animations appear.
3. Click **Preview**.

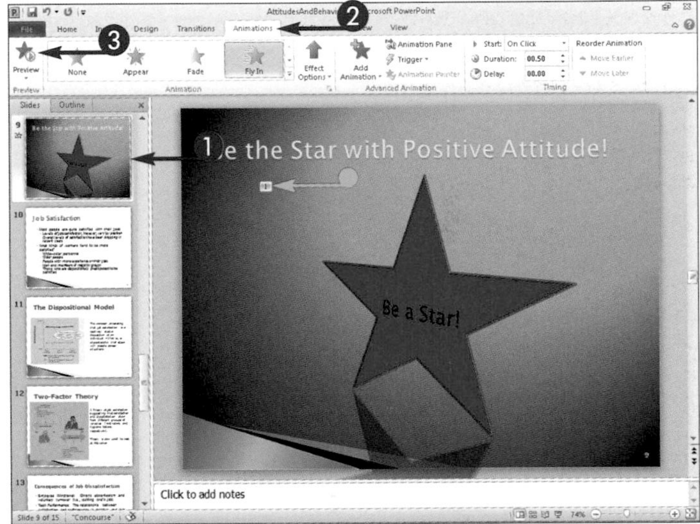

PowerPoint runs all animation on the slide.

- In this example, the star flies in from the bottom.

Note: *You also can preview the animation by running the entire slide show. See Chapter 13 to learn how to run a slide show.*

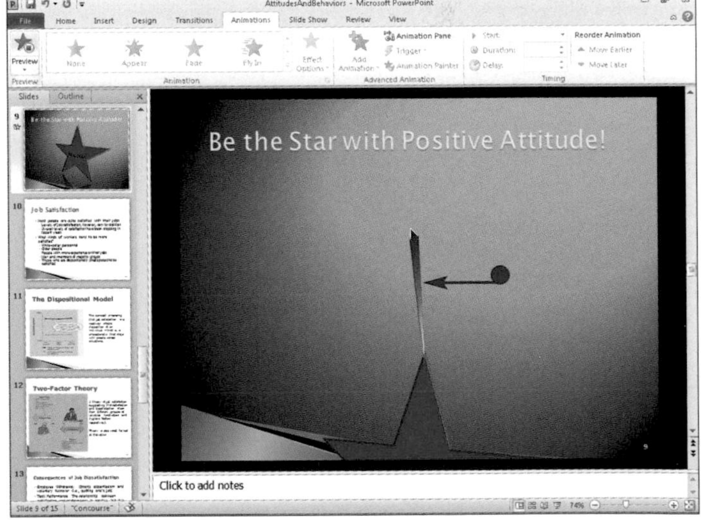

Add an Animation

You not only can apply different animations to different objects on a slide, but you can also apply multiple animations to one object. This enables you to make an object do a variety of movements, creating a complex special effect.

Simple is usually best, so try not to create too much complexity.

Add an Animation

1. Select an object that already has an animation.
2. Click the **Animations** tab.
3. Click **Add Animation**.

   The gallery of animations appears.

- Use the scroll bar to see more animations.

4. Click an animation.

   In this example, Wipe was clicked.

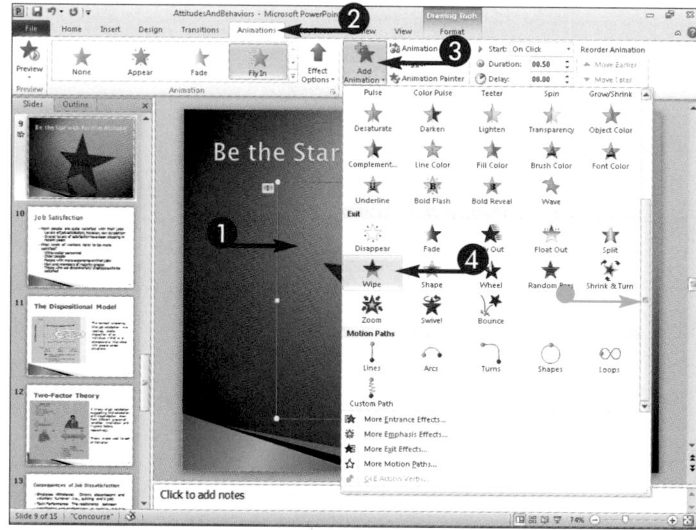

- An additional sequence number appears.

  In this example, this object has two animations that will run sequentially. The Wipe animation will run second because its sequence number is 2.

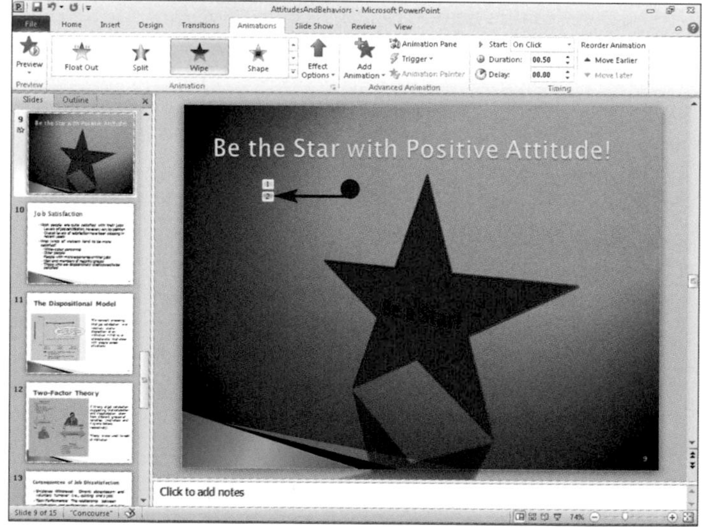

Change Animation Effects

PowerPoint gives you the flexibility to choose the motion of an animation. For example, the Fly In animation can bring the object onto the screen from any direction. It can bring the object onto the screen as one piece, in pieces simultaneously, or as pieces at separate times. You can change these effects, controlling the animation completely.

Change Animation Effects

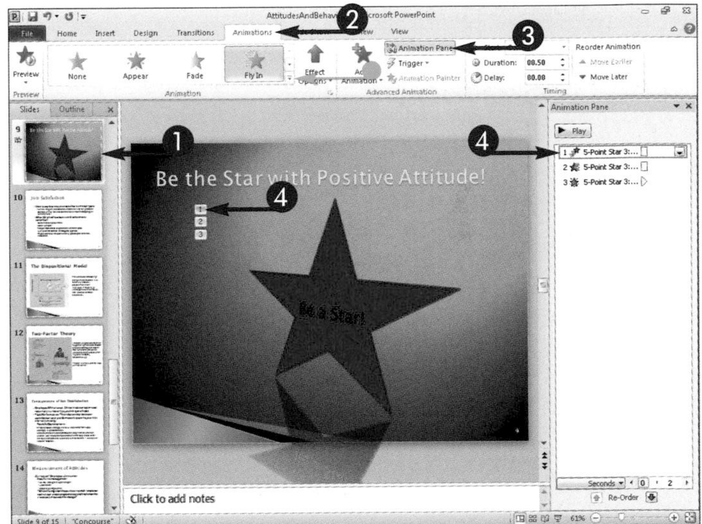

1. Select a slide with animation.
2. Click the **Animations** tab.
3. Click **Animation Pane**.

   The Animation Pane appears — all animations are listed here.
4. Click the sequence number of the animation you want to change or click it in the Animation Pane.

- To change the animation itself, simply click the Animation ▾ and select another animation from the gallery.

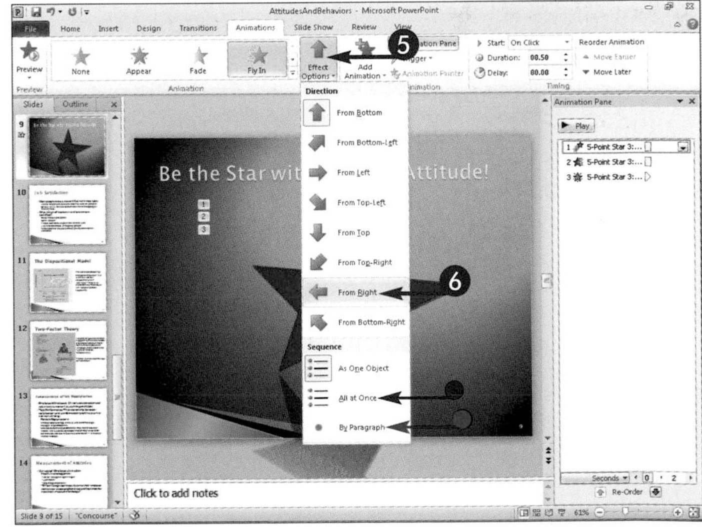

5. Click **Effect Options**.

   The gallery of effects appears.

Note: *The Effects Options are different for each animation.*

6. Click an effect from the gallery.

   In this example From Right was clicked.

- Click **All at Once** to have the pieces move independently, but at the same time.
- Click **By Paragraph** to have the pieces appear separately.

The effects for the animation are changed.

Change the Animation Trigger

Something must trigger the animation to run. The trigger can be the appearance of the slide on-screen, clicking anywhere on the slide, or clicking a particular object on the slide. You can also trigger the animation to run with or after another animation.

The default trigger is clicking anywhere on the slide.

Change the Animation Trigger

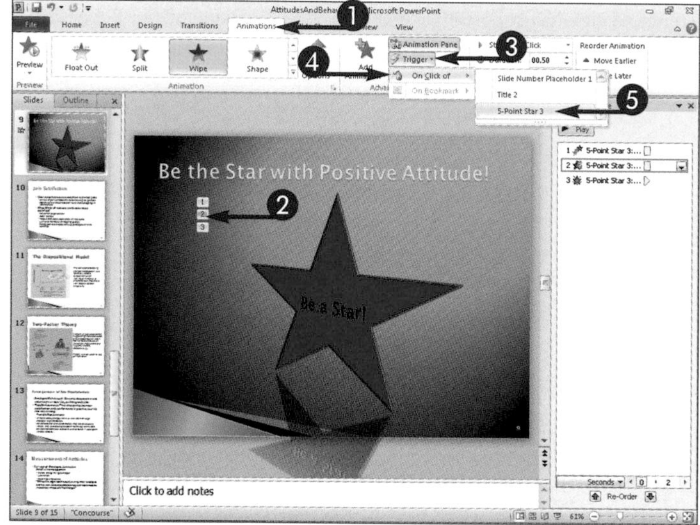

1. Click the **Animations** tab.
2. Click the sequence number of an animation or click it in the Animation Pane.
3. To run an animation when you click an object, click **Trigger**.
4. Click **On Click of**.
5. Select the object from the menu.

   In this example 5-Point Star 3 was clicked.

   The second animation will now run when you click the star.

6. Click a different animation.
7. Click ▾ on **Start** to change the trigger.
8. Click an option.

   On Click runs the animation when you click the mouse.

   With Previous runs the animation simultaneously with the previous animation.

   After Previous runs the animation automatically, but only after the time set in the Delay box.

***Note:** To run the first animation automatically when the slide first appears, set its trigger to With Previous.*

Modify Animation Timing

Sometimes you want things to happen quickly, and sometimes slow is better. You can modify the duration of your animation, and delay the time between its trigger and its appearance. This flexibility enables you to be very exacting while creating an effect that will have maximum impact on your audience.

Modify Animation Timing

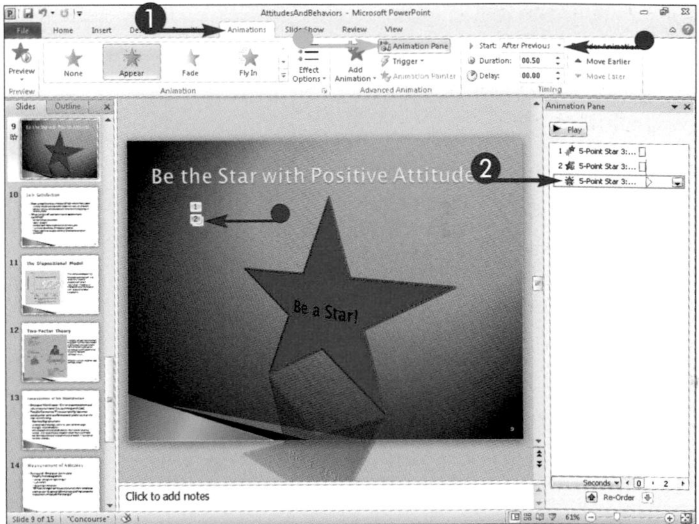

1. Click the **Animations** tab.

- Click **Animation Pane** if it is not open.

  The Animation Pane opens.

2. Click the sequence number of an animation or click it in the Animation Pane.

- The sequence number of the third animation is under the second, denoting that it runs automatically after the second because the Start box is set to After Previous.

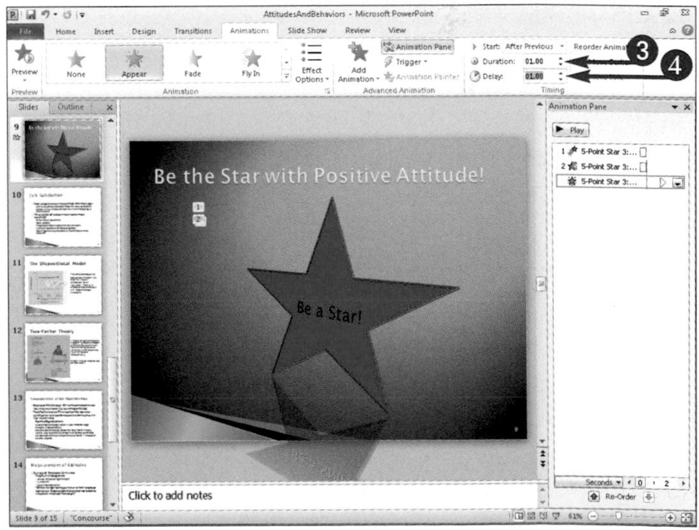

3. Click ⬍ on **Duration** or enter a number into the text box to adjust the run time of the animation.

4. Click the spinner (⬍) on **Delay** or type a number into the text box to adjust the delay between the trigger and when the animation starts.

   The Duration was set to 1.00, and Delay was set to 1.00. The third animation will now start after a 1-second delay and last for 1 second.

Reorder Animations

After applying multiple animations on a slide, you can change the order in which the animation plays on the slide during your presentation. You can change the order of the animations many ways, including running an animation of one object, then an animation of another object, and then more animation on the first object.

Reorder Animations

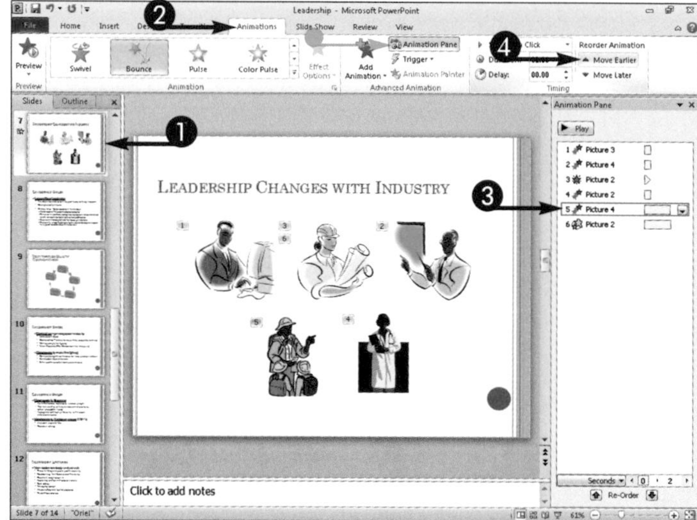

1. Select a slide with multiple animations
2. Click the **Animations** tab.
   - Click **Animation Pane** if it is not open.

   The Animation Pane opens.
3. Click the sequence number of an animation or click it in the Animation Pane.
4. Click either **Move Earlier** or **Move Later** to change the order of the animation.

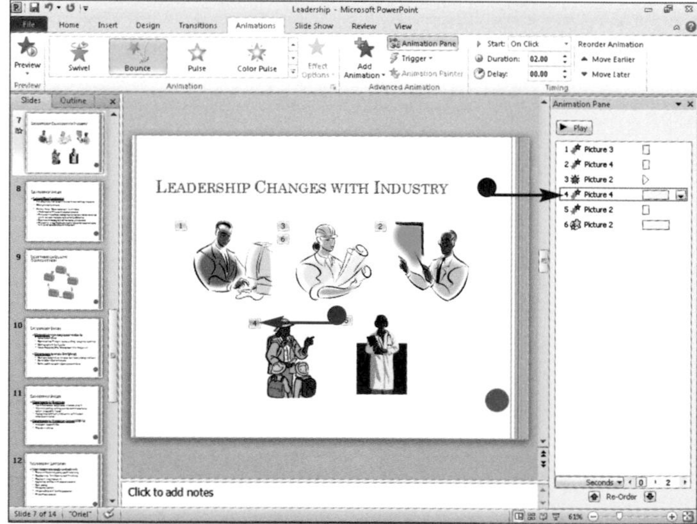

- The animation moves up or down in the list accordingly.
- The sequence number of the animation changes.

Remove an Animation

You can remove both standard and custom animations from slide objects. If you apply animations to a slide and decide they make it too complex, you need to remove the animations. You can remove the animations from the Animation gallery or the Animation Pane.

Remove an Animation

1. Click the **Animations** tab.
   - Click **Animation Pane** if it is not open.

     The Animation Pane appears listing all animations.
2. Click the sequence number of the animation you want to change or click it in the Animation Pane.
3. Click ▾ on the animation.
4. Click **Remove**.

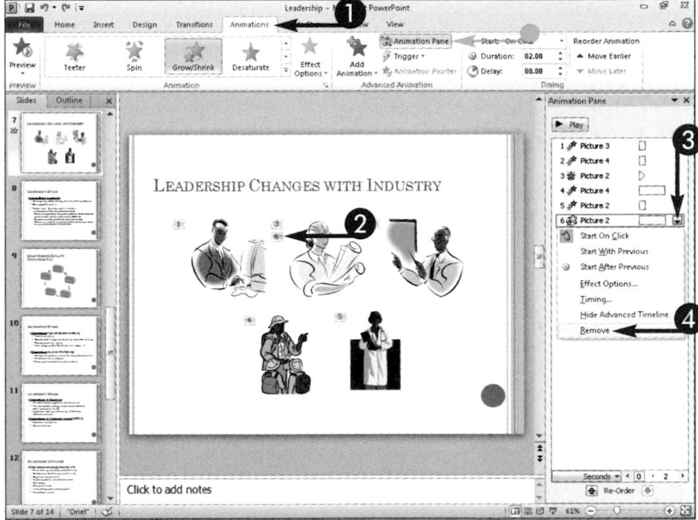

PowerPoint removes the animation from the object.

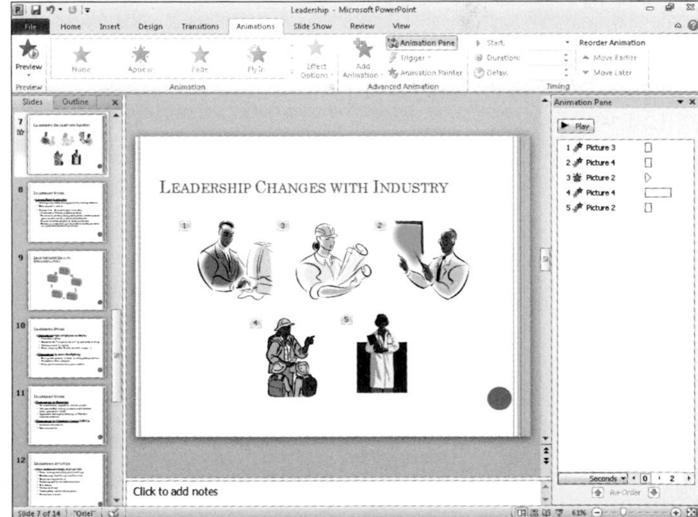

Insert an Action Button

Action buttons enable you to jump to a slide during a slide show quickly and easily. You also can use them to open a Web page, another presentation, or another type of document.

Jumping to a Web page requires an Internet connection. Any document that opens via an action button must be available on your computer.

Insert an Action Button

1. Select a slide in Normal view.
2. Click the **Insert** tab.
3. Click **Shapes**.
4. Click a button style.

   The mouse pointer turns into a crosshair (+).
5. Click where you want the button.

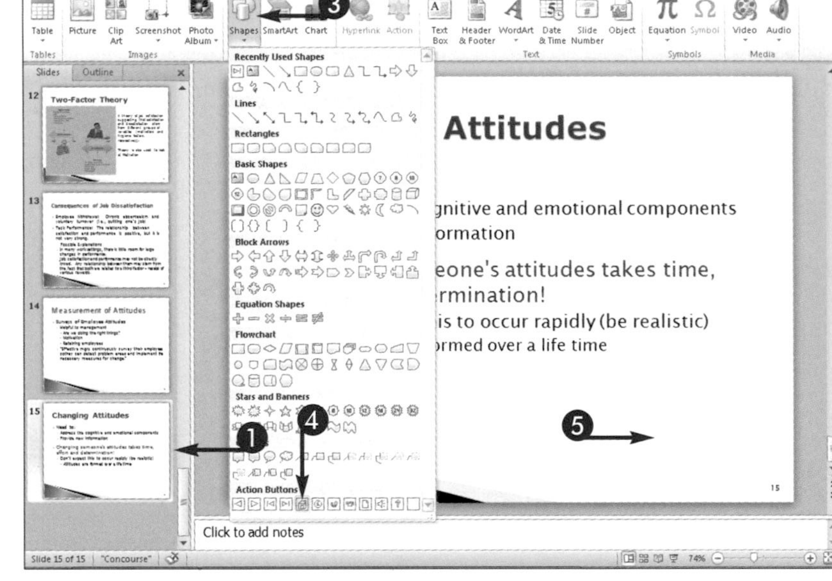

- The action button appears and the Action Settings dialog box appears.

6. Click **Hyperlink to** (◎ changes to ◉).
7. Click the **Hyperlink to** ▾.
8. Click and drag the scroll bar to scroll down.
9. Click **Other File**.

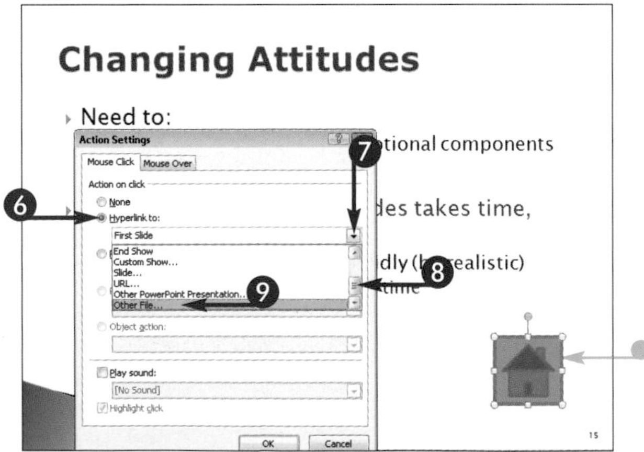

The Hyperlink to Other File dialog box appears.

⑩ Click the folder containing the file.

⑪ Click the file.

⑫ Click **OK**.

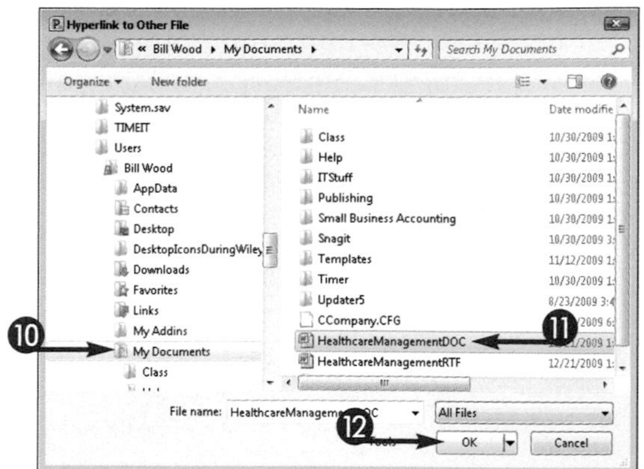

- PowerPoint inserts the path to the file into the Hyperlink drop-down list.

⑬ Click **OK**.

The selected file will open when you click the button during the slide show.

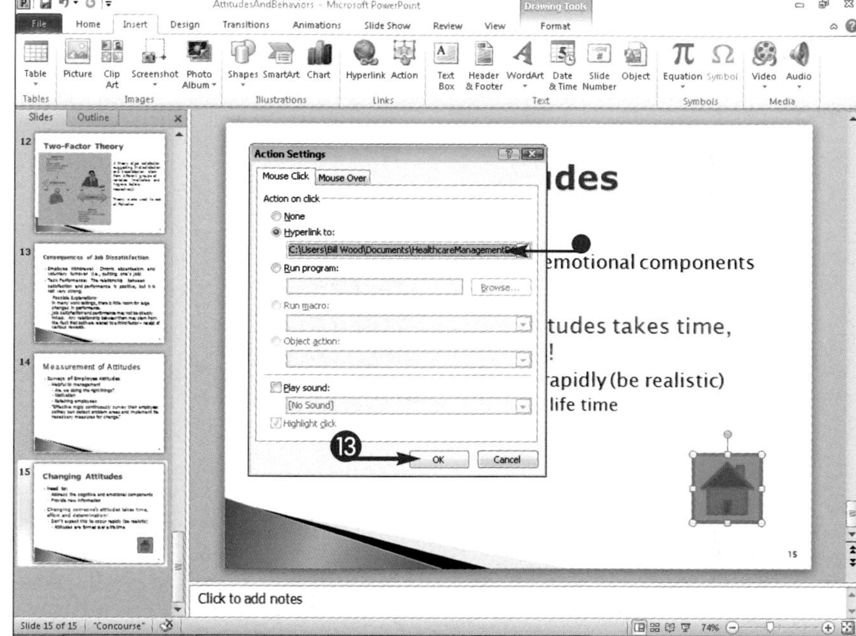

In the Hyperlink to drop-down list, what do some of the other choices do?

You can select **Slide** to go to a different slide in the current presentation; select **Other PowerPoint Presentation** to open a different slide show; or select **URL** to open a Web page. You can use your Web browser to browse to a Web page and then copy and paste a URL from it into the Hyperlink to URL dialog box.

What if I want to change what an action button does?

Right-click the action button and then click **Edit Hyperlink**. This displays the Action Settings dialog box, where you can make your changes.

Introducing Transitions

A *transition* is the switch from one slide to another, and it offers yet another opportunity to add variety to your presentation. With transitions, you can vary the way the next slide appears, such as fading from one slide to the next. You can also arrange for sounds to play when a transition occurs, adjust the runtime of a transition, or delay the start of a transition.

What Is a Transition?

A transition effect occurs when you advance a slide show from one slide to another. Movies use transitions — for example, when you see the screen dissolve from one image to another, or you see an image seem to wipe across the screen to reveal another scene.

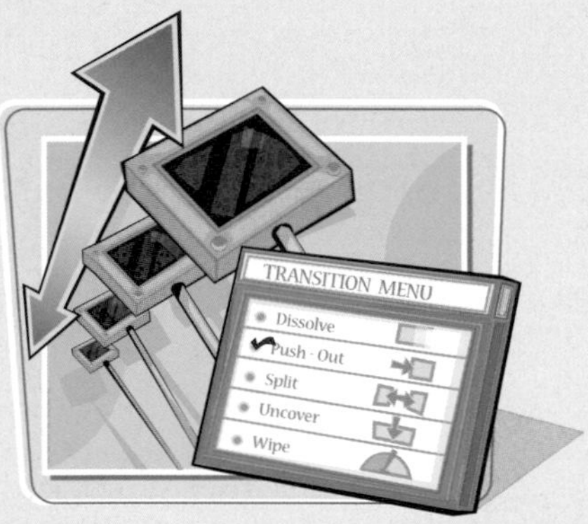

Different Ways to Advance Slides

Transitions also are used to control when slides advance. You can choose to have a slide advance on a mouse click, or to advance with preset timing. For example, if you plan to show a presentation at a kiosk or unattended computer, you might have slides advance every 30 seconds.

Control Speed

You can control how fast a transition occurs. Effects such as a fade-in can be very different depending on whether your slides fade slowly or quickly. The former gives viewers more of a separation from one topic to another; the latter keeps the presentation moving right along.

Add Sounds

Adding a sound when a transition occurs can provide emphasis or alert audience members to an important point. For example, you could display the slide that tells your viewers that you have broken last year's sales record while playing a drumroll.

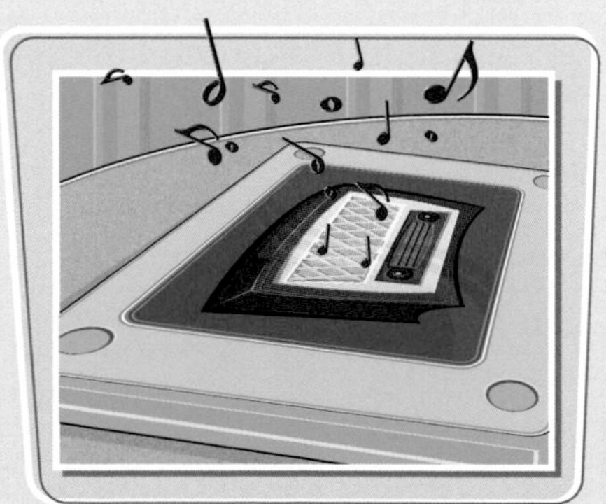

Apply a Transition

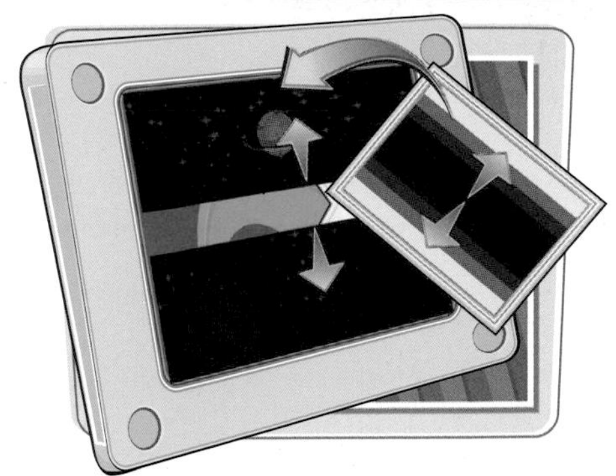

You can apply a transition to any slide in either Normal or Slide Sorter view to give your slide show variety. You can also apply the same transition effect to multiple slides, or to all slides in the presentation.

Applying a transition from the Random category tells PowerPoint to apply a different transition to each slide in the presentation.

Apply a Transition

1. Select slide(s) in Normal or Slide Sorter view.

Note: *To select multiple slides, click the first slide, and then press Ctrl while clicking additional slides.*

2. Click the **Transitions** tab.
3. Click ▾ on the **Transitions** group.

   The gallery of transitions appears.
4. Click a transition in the gallery.

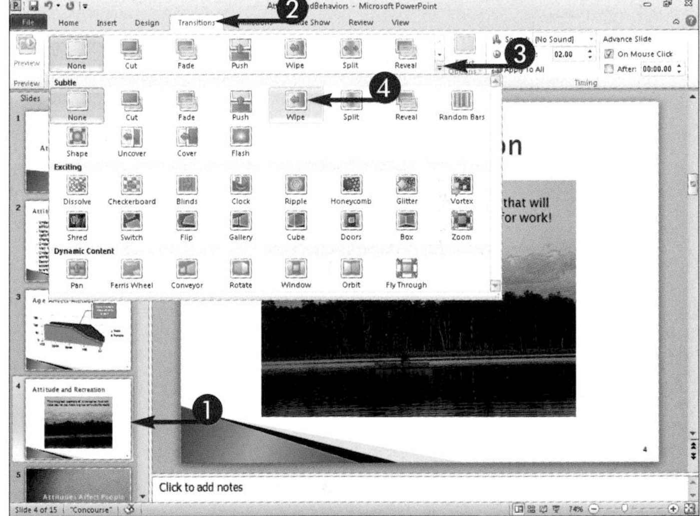

PowerPoint applies the transition to the slide(s).

- A star appears beside the slide's thumbnail, denoting that a transition has been applied.
- You can click **Apply to All** to apply to all slides in the presentation.

5. Click **Preview** to see the transition.

- The transition runs.

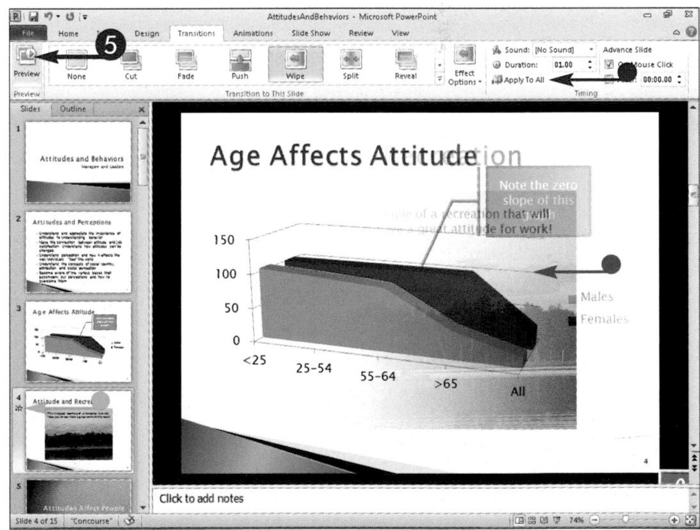

Remove a Transition

Sometimes while designing a presentation, you may apply a transition and then decide that it just does not work. PowerPoint enables you to remove any transition in your presentation if you change your mind.

Remove a Transition

1. Select slide(s) with a transition in Normal or Slide Sorter view.

***Note:** To select multiple slides, click the first slide, and then press Ctrl while clicking additional slides.*

2. Click the **Transitions** tab.
3. Click ▾ on the **Transitions** group.

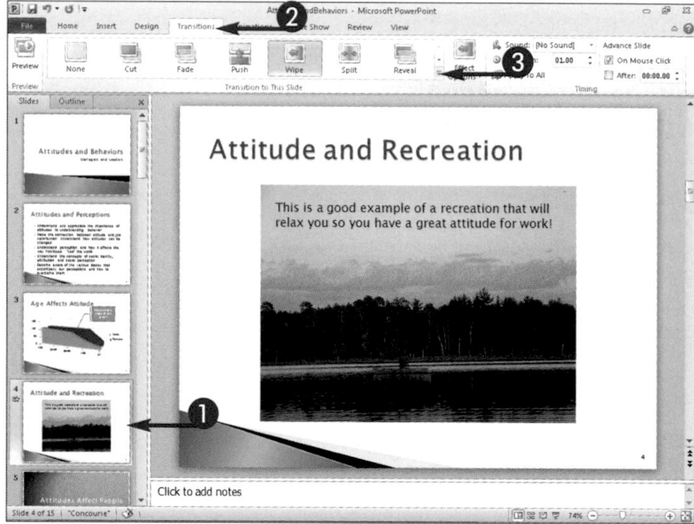

The gallery of transitions appears.

4. Click **None**.

PowerPoint removes the transition.

- You can click **Apply to All** to remove transitions from all slides in the presentation.

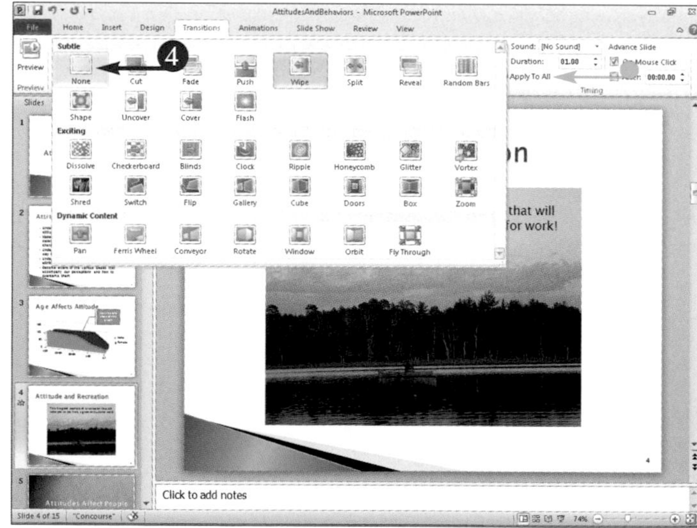

Advance a Slide after a Set Time Interval

When you run a slide show, you can use one of two methods to advance from slide to slide. You can advance slides manually by clicking the slide or you can set a timer that automatically advances the slide show to the next slide after a set amount of time. You can change these settings in either Normal or Slide Sorter view.

Advance a Slide after a Set Time Interval

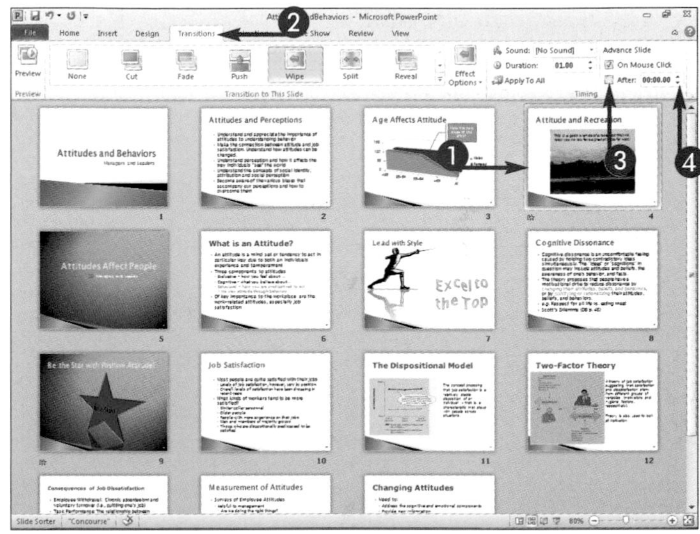

1. Select slide(s) with a transition in Slide Sorter view.

***Note:** To select multiple slides, click the first slide, and then press Ctrl while clicking additional slides.*

2. Click the **Transitions** tab.
3. Click **After** (☐ changes to ☑) — this makes the slide automatically advance.
4. Click ⬍ to set a time interval.

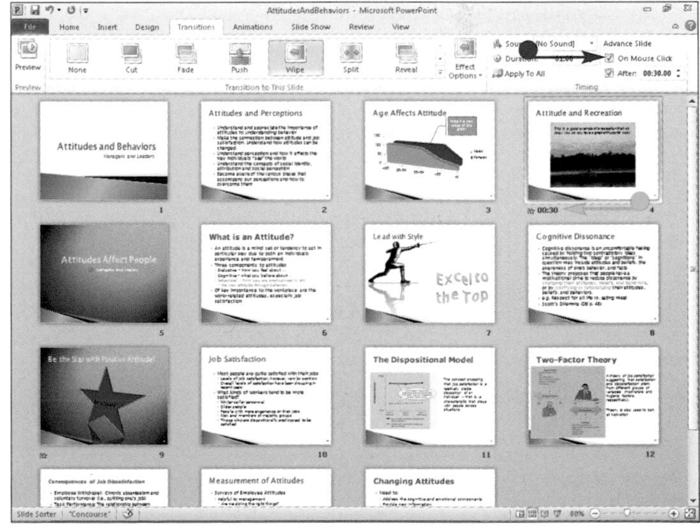

The automatic advance is set with a delay of 30 seconds.

- The time interval is denoted under the slide.
- If you leave the On Mouse Click check box selected, you can also advance the slide by clicking your mouse.

Add a Transition Sound

You can apply a sound to one or more slides in a presentation to accent important points. When used appropriately, transition sounds highlight important information during a slide show. Generally, using transition sounds sparingly means the sounds will have greater impact, drawing attention to the most important information. Having the same sound for every slide has less impact.

Add a Transition Sound

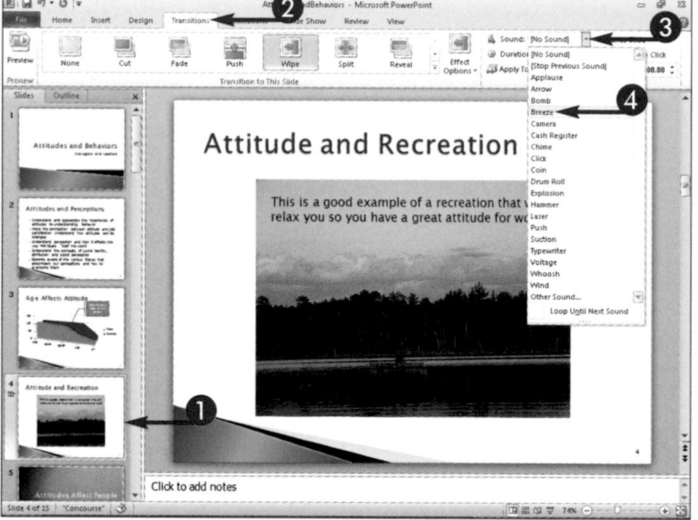

1. Select slide(s) with a transition in Normal or Slide Sorter view.

***Note:** To select multiple slides, click the first slide, and then press Ctrl while clicking additional slides.*

2. Click the **Transitions** tab.
3. Click ▾ on the **Sound** drop-down list.
4. Click a sound.

   In this example, Breeze was clicked.

***Note:** Select **[No Sound]** from the menu to remove a sound from a transition.*

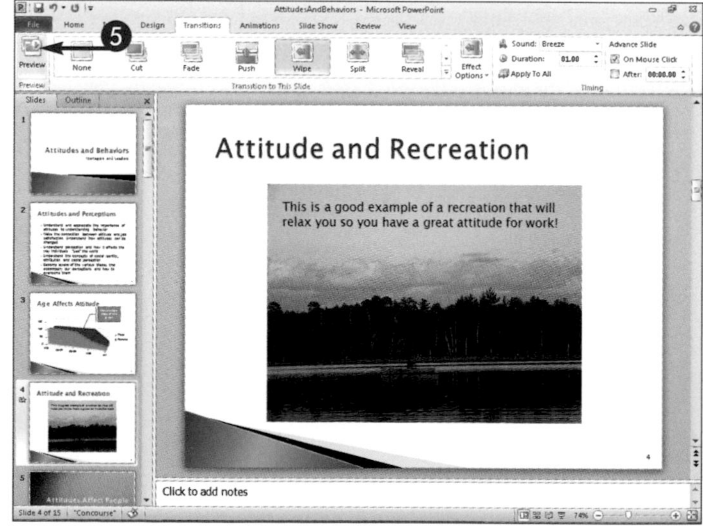

The sound is applied to the transition.

5. Click **Preview** to hear the sound.

   The transition sound plays.

***Note:** Preview is available only if you apply a transition to the slide.*

Set a Transition Speed

You can further customize a transition by setting a transition speed. The transition speed controls the rate at which the transition effect plays. For fade-and-dissolve transitions, you might prefer a slow transition speed so the audience gets the full effect. For transitions such as wipes, you might prefer a faster speed that keeps the slide show moving.

Set a Transition Speed

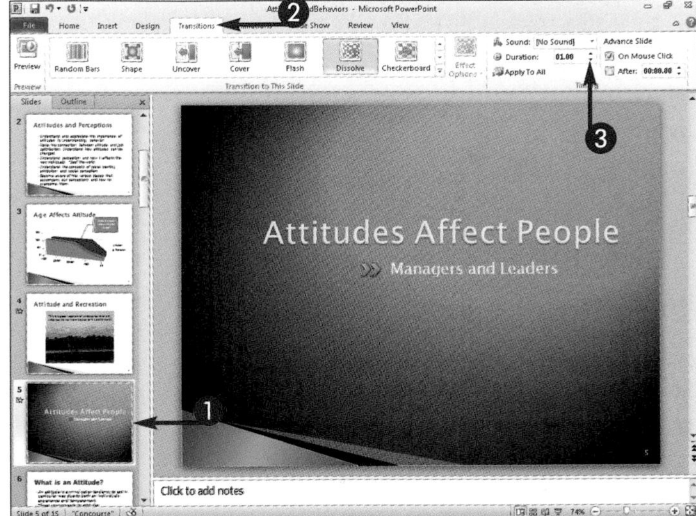

1. Select slide(s) with a transition in Normal or Slide Sorter view.

***Note:** To select multiple slides, click the first slide, and then press Ctrl while clicking additional slides.*

2. Click the **Transitions** tab.
3. Click ⬍ on **Duration** to change the transition speed.

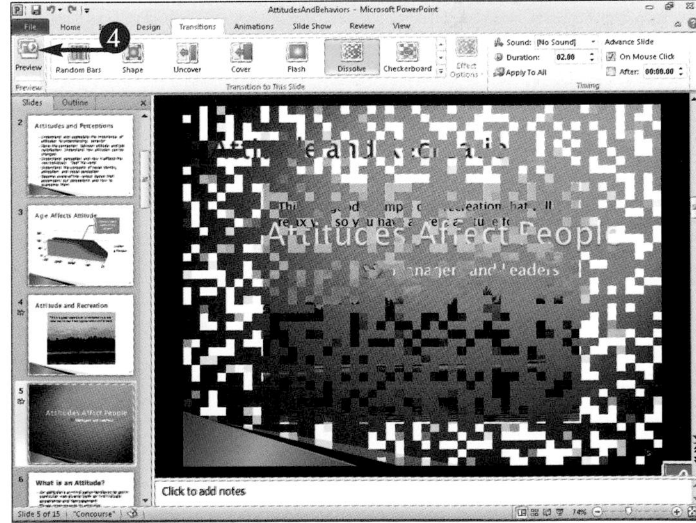

4. Click **Preview** to view the transition at the speed you specified.

The transition plays.

CHAPTER

12

Including Media Enhancements

PowerPoint 2010 enables you to build exciting visual and sound effects into your presentations. You can place photographs, videos, and audio clips anywhere on your slides to enhance your presentation. You can also add dramatic artistic effects to your photographs or remove the background from them. Finally, you can edit your photos and videos directly in PowerPoint to make them impeccable.

Insert a Picture

If you have an image file stored on your computer, for example your company logo or a picture of your product, you can insert the image onto a PowerPoint slide.

After you insert an image file, it becomes an object on your slide. To learn how to move, resize, and format objects, see Chapter 9.

Insert a Picture

1. Select a slide in Normal view.
2. Click the **Insert** tab.
3. Click **Picture**.

   The Insert Picture dialog box appears.
4. Select the folder containing the file.
5. Click the file.
6. Click **Insert**.

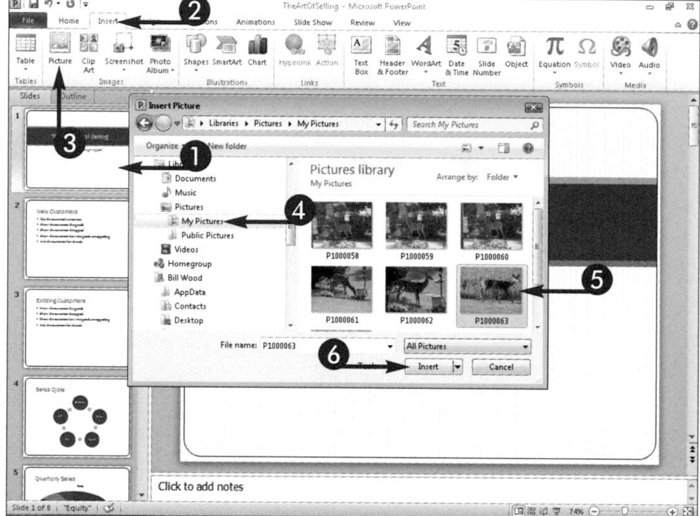

- The image appears on your slide.

  Size and position the image as needed.

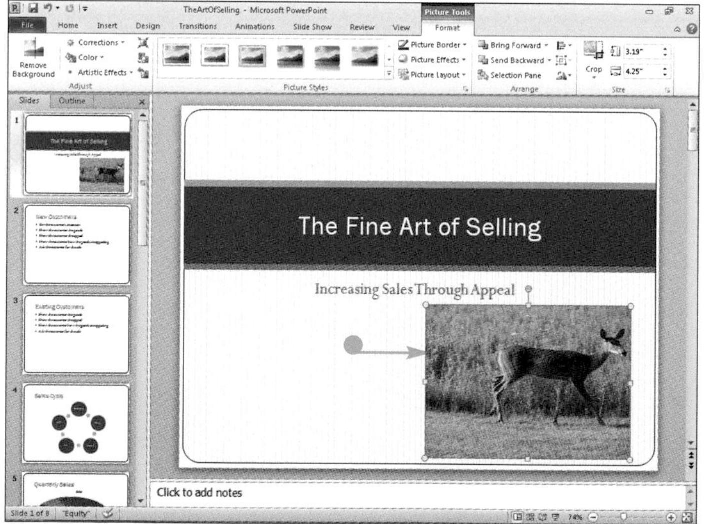

Add a Border

After you insert a picture, you may want to set it apart from the rest of the slide by adding a border to it. A border makes the picture crisp and helps it stand out from other items on the slide.

Add a Border

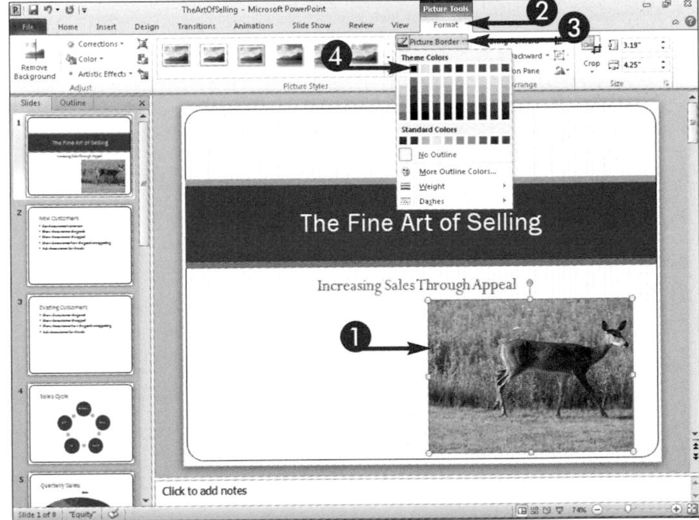

1. Click a picture.
2. Click the **Picture Tools Format** tab.
3. Click **Picture Border**.

   The gallery of borders appears.
4. Click a border color.

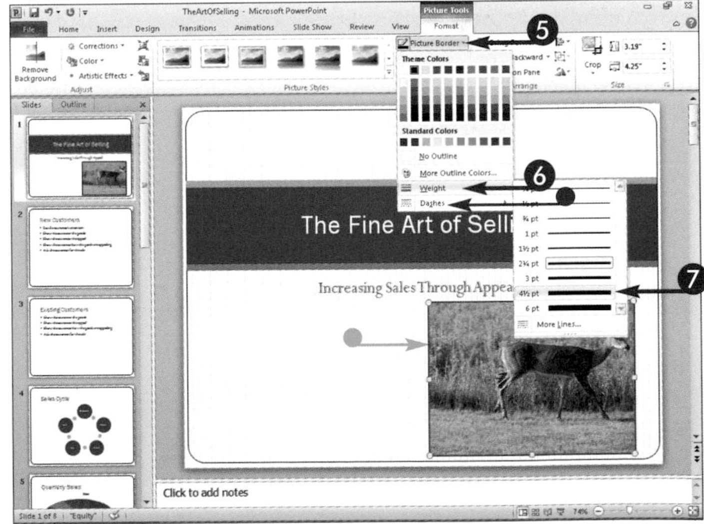

- The border appears around your picture.

5. Click **Picture Border**.
6. Click **Weight**.
7. Click a border thickness.

   The border thickness changes.

- You can click **Dashes** to change the border to something other than solid.

Adjust Brightness and Contrast

You can adjust the brightness and contrast of a picture in PowerPoint to maximize its visual impact. Many times, a picture is not perfect when taken, or it does not show well on a screen. Adjusting the brightness and contrast may be all the picture needs to look good.

Adjust Brightness and Contrast

1. Click a picture.
2. Click the **Picture Tools Format** tab.
3. Click **Corrections**.

   The gallery of corrections appears.

4. Click a choice of **Brightness and Contrast** from the gallery.

- You can also apply a Sharpen and Soften effect.

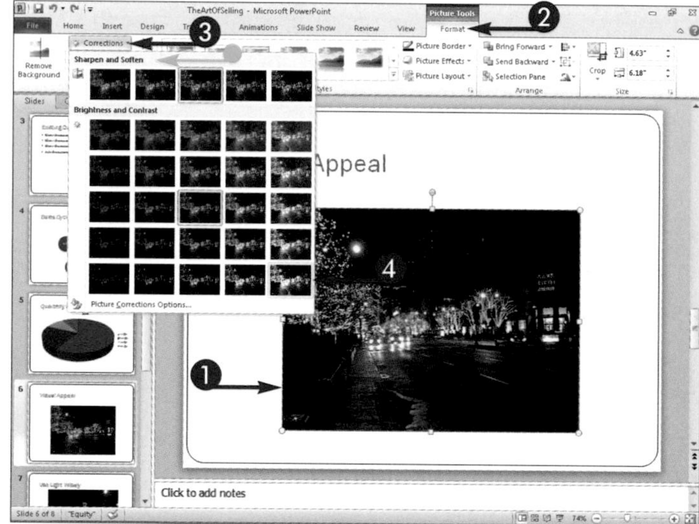

- The Brightness and Contrast is adjusted.

Adjust Color

You can adjust the color of your pictures to make them pleasing to the eye, or recolor them for interesting effects. Standard color variations are determined by the theme of the presentation, but many other variations are available also.

Adjust Color

1. Click a picture.
2. Click the **Picture Tools Format** tab.
3. Click **Color**.

   The gallery of colors appears.

4. Click your choice of **Color Saturation**, **Color Tone**, or **Recolor** options.

   In this example, a recolor option was selected.

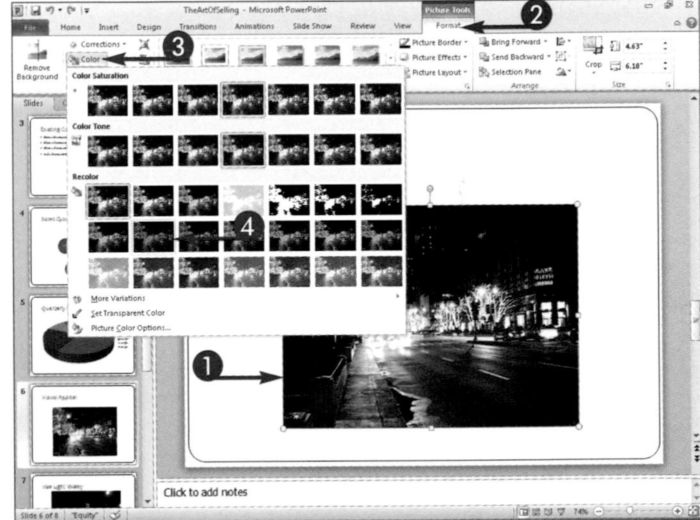

- The color is adjusted.

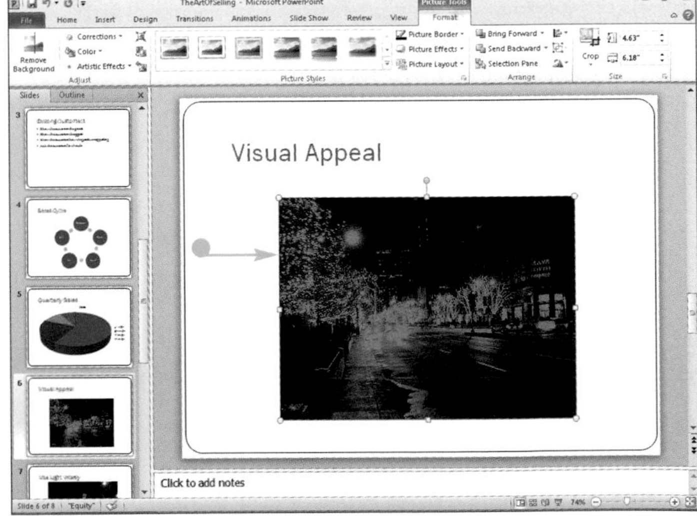

Crop a Picture

You can crop a picture so that the main object of the picture fills the entire picture. When you reduce the size of a picture, the objects in the picture shrink accordingly. Cropping simply trims the edges from pictures like cutting them with a scissors would.

Crop a Picture

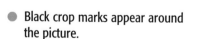

1. Select a picture.
2. Click the **Picture Tools Format** tab.
3. Click **Crop**.

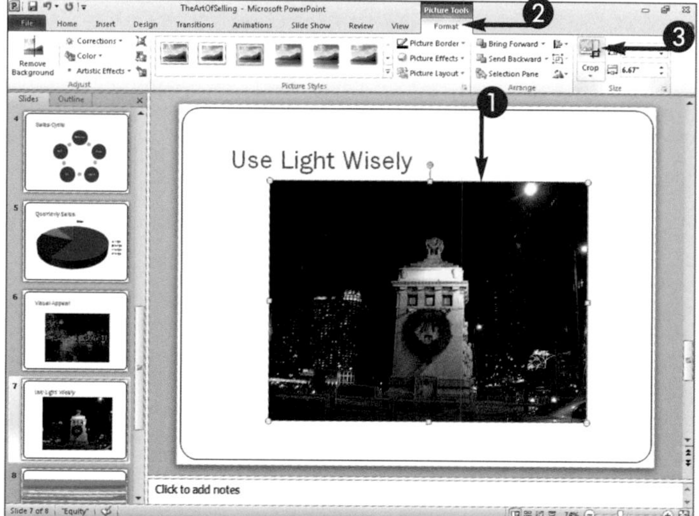

- Black crop marks appear around the picture.

4. Click and drag a crop mark inward to remove a portion of the picture.

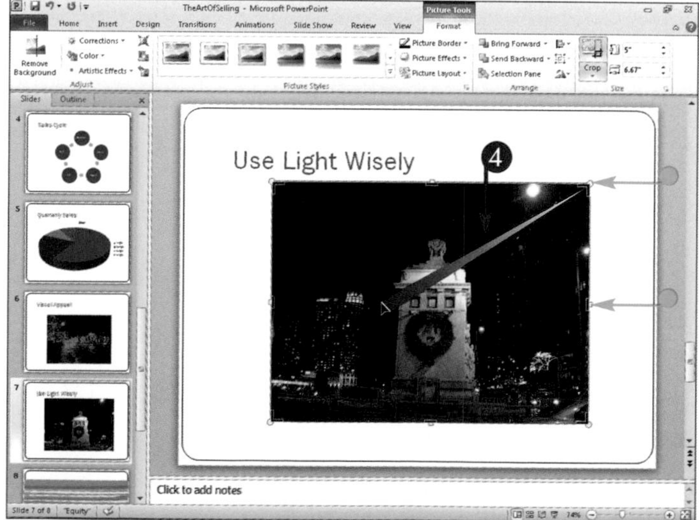

- When you release the mouse button, you can see both the original picture and the cropped picture.

5. Click **Crop** again.

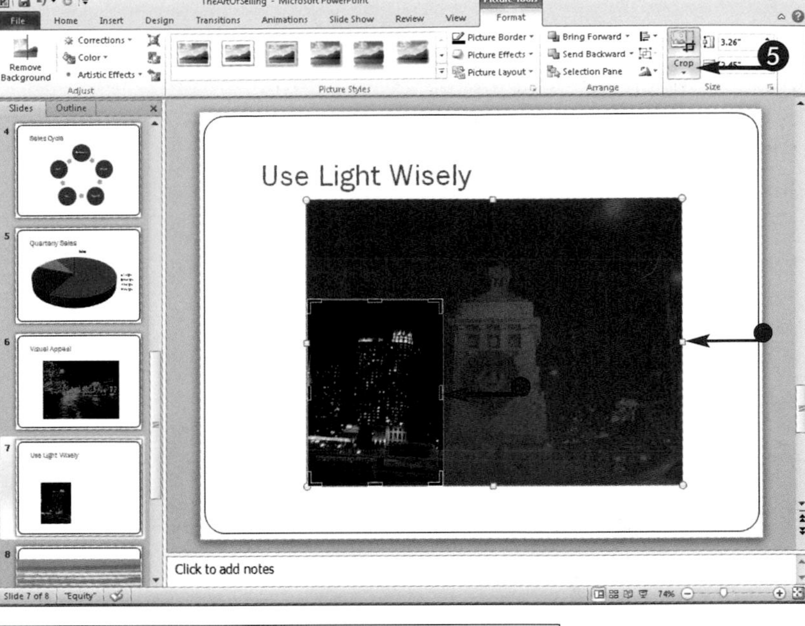

- The picture is cropped.

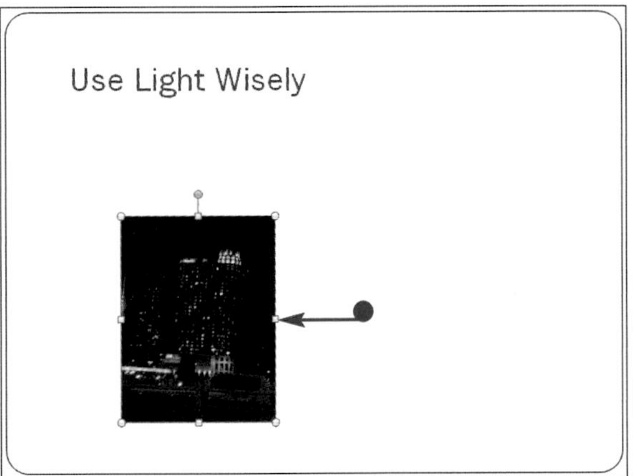

TIP

Can I crop a picture to an interesting shape?

Yes. Follow these steps:

1. Select a picture.
2. Click the **Picture Tools Format** tab.
3. Click the **Crop** ▾.
4. Click **Crop to Shape**.
5. Click a shape from the gallery.

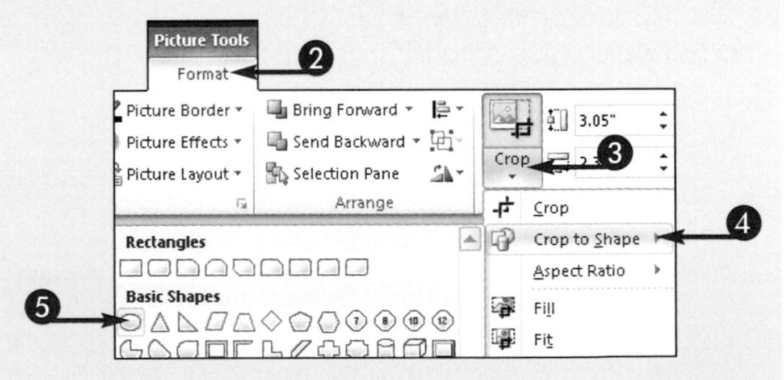

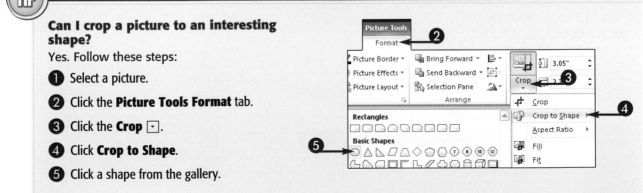

Remove the Background from a Picture

There may be times when you want to remove the background of a picture so you can work with just the main object of the picture. You can remove a background from a picture easily and simply with this exciting automated PowerPoint feature.

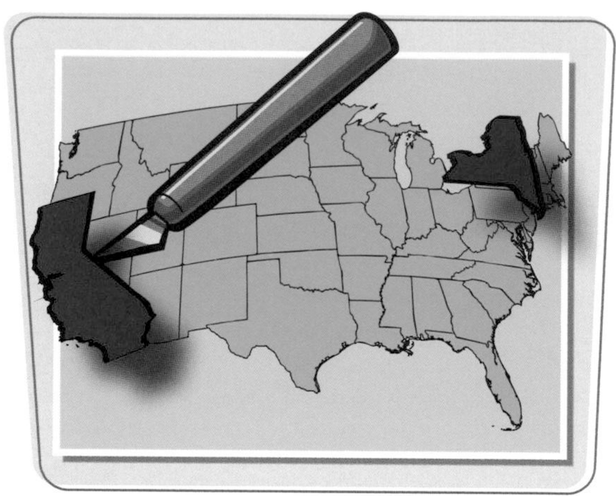

Remove the Background from a Picture

1. Select a picture.
2. Click the **Picture Tools Format** tab.
3. Click **Remove Background**.

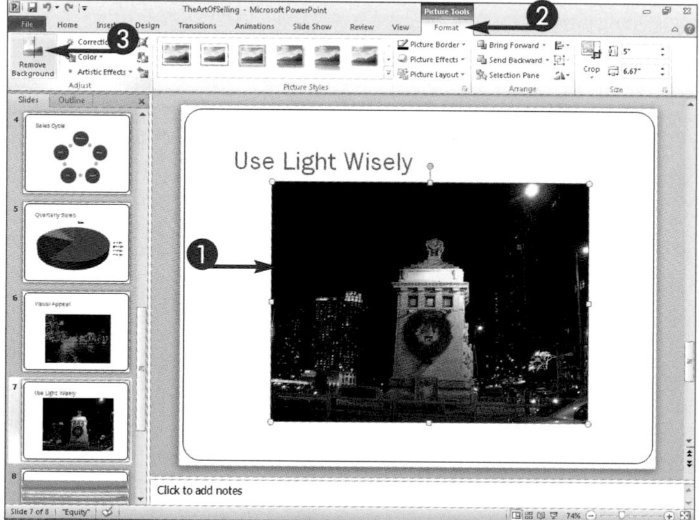

- PowerPoint displays a marquee with handles.
- The background becomes magenta.
- PowerPoint automatically detects the object in the foreground.

4. Adjust the marquee until PowerPoint detects the foreground object that you want. To adjust the marquee, click and drag the handles on the marquee.

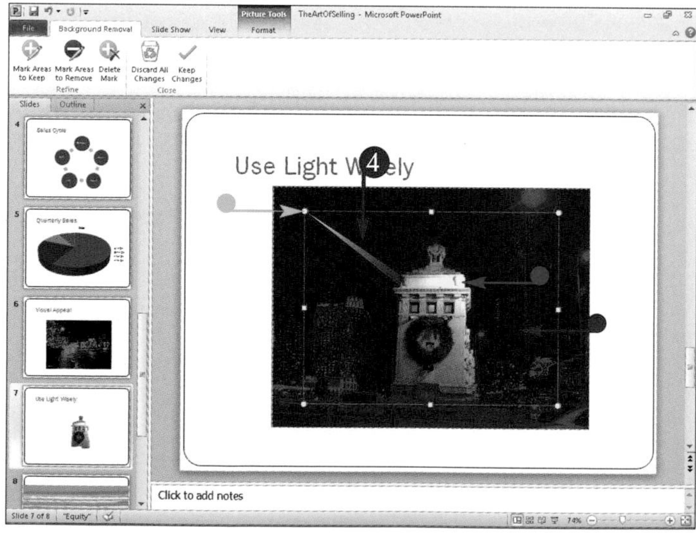

- PowerPoint detects the foreground object based upon your adjustment of the marquee.

***Note:** Very small adjustments to the marquee help PowerPoint determine the object that you want in the foreground.*

5 Click **Keep Changes**.

- To escape without saving changes, click **Discard All Changes**.

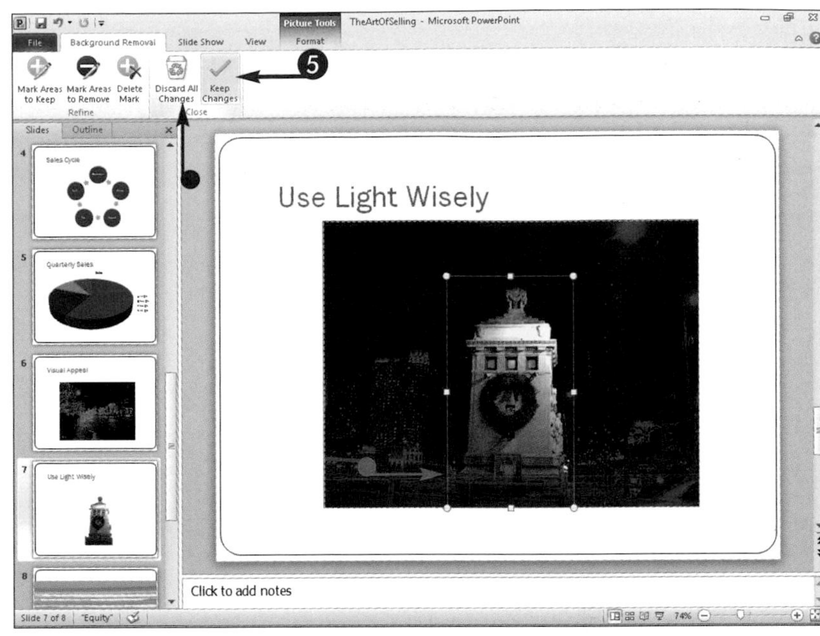

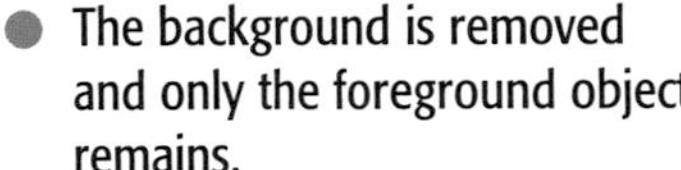

- The background is removed and only the foreground object remains.

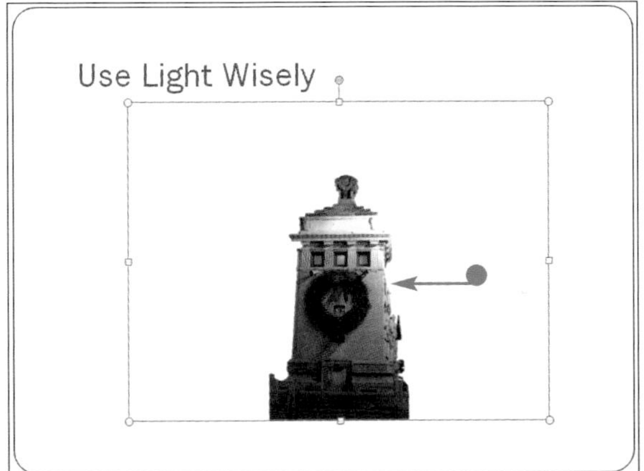

TIP

How can I include or exclude an image detail?

You can fine-tune the foreground object that PowerPoint automatically detects.

1 Follow Steps **1** to **3** to access the **Background Removal** selections.

2 Click **Mark Areas to Keep** or **Mark Areas to Remove**.

3 Click and drag across the detail to include or exclude it.

- PowerPoint marks the detail with a circled plus or minus.

To reverse your selection, click Delete Mark, and then click the mark.

Using Artistic Effects

You may want to add an interesting effect to a photo to add spice to your slide show. Many common special effects are available at the click of a button in graphics programs. Several artistic effects are available in PowerPoint itself. You can apply effects such as pixilation, blurring, and pencil sketch without leaving PowerPoint.

Using Artistic Effects

1. Select a picture.
2. Click the **Picture Tools Format** tab.
3. Click **Artistic Effects**.

   The gallery of artistic effects appears.
4. Click an artistic effect.

   In this example, **Pencil Sketch** was clicked.

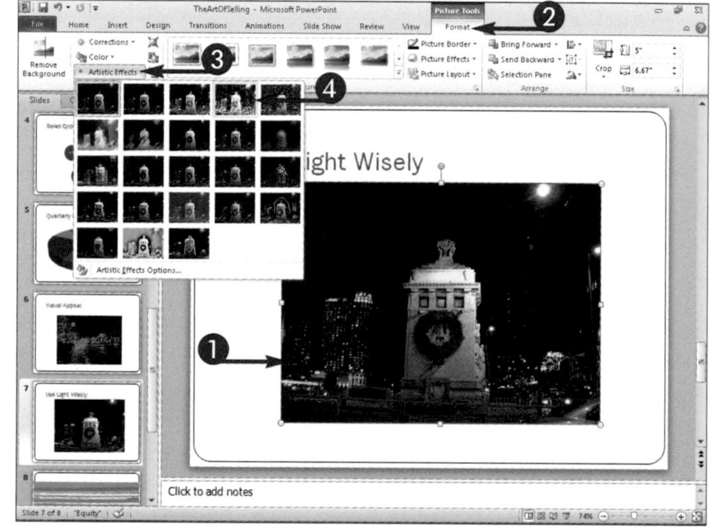

- PowerPoint applies the artistic effect.

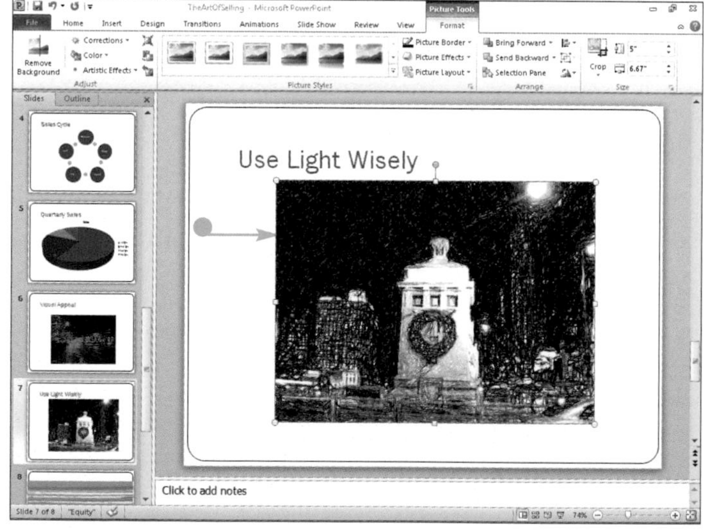

Compress Pictures

Image files can be very large. When you insert them into your presentation, your PowerPoint file also becomes large. This can slow PowerPoint's performance during your presentation. You can improve performance by compressing image files, which has little impact on their quality. Compressing pictures makes any changes to images permanent — you cannot reverse those changes.

Compress Pictures

1. Select a picture.
2. Click the **Picture Tools Format** tab.
3. Click **Compress Pictures** ( ).

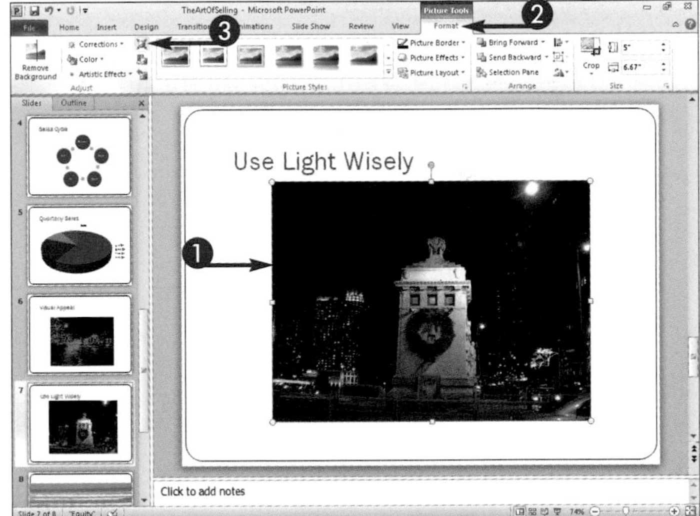

The Compress Pictures dialog box appears.

- You can click **Apply only to this picture** (changes to) to compress all pictures in your presentation.

4. Click an appropriate resolution under **Target output** (changes to), depending on how you intend to use your presentation.
5. Click **OK**.

PowerPoint compresses the picture(s).

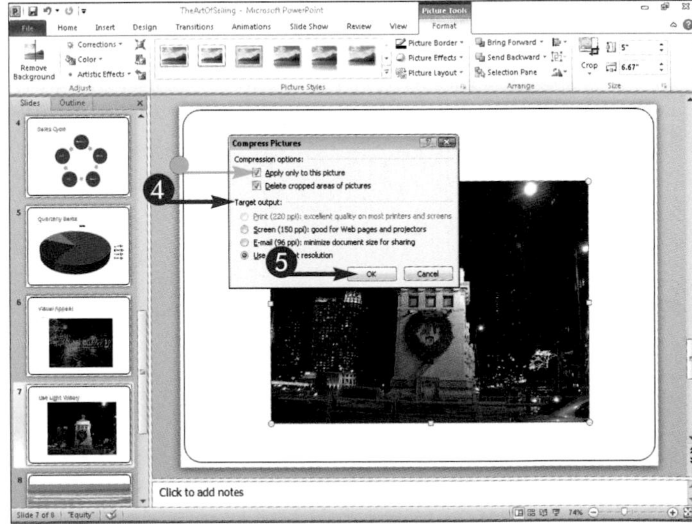

Using Layout Effects

There are times when you may have several pictures on one slide and you want to organize or compare them. You can make pictures look sharp by combining them with SmartArt Graphics. SmartArt Graphics enables you to combine pictures in many interesting groupings, and then apply text to the individual pictures or the entire group.

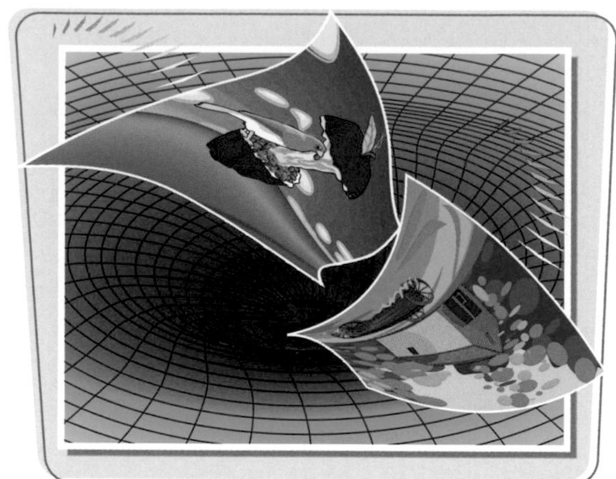

Using Layout Effects

Apply a Layout

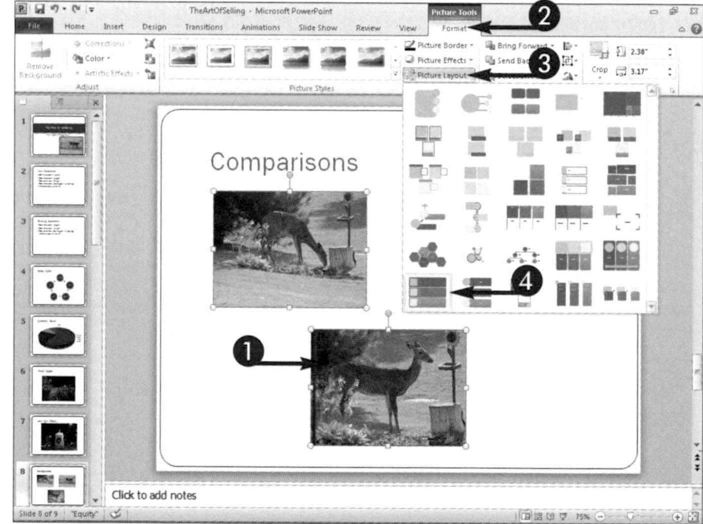

1. Select pictures in Normal view.

Note: To select multiple pictures, click the first picture, and then press Ctrl *while clicking additional pictures.*

2. Click the **Picture Tools Format** tab.
3. Click **Picture Layout**.

   The gallery of picture layouts appears.

4. Click a picture layout.

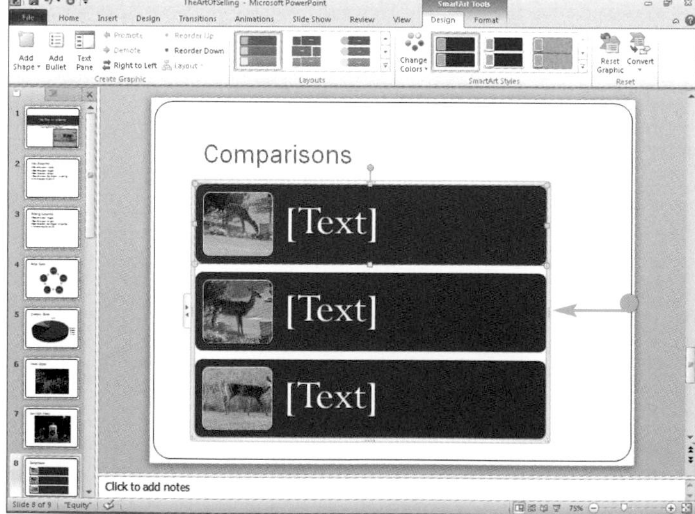

- PowerPoint applies the SmartArt Graphics picture layout to the pictures.

Note: See Chapter 6 to learn how to edit SmartArt Graphics and how to enter text into the SmartArt Graphics.

Change a Picture

1. Click a picture.
2. Click the **Picture Tools Format** tab.
3. Click **Change Pictures** (🖼).

   The Insert Picture dialog box appears.

4. Click the folder containing the picture file.
5. Click the picture.
6. Click **Insert**.

- The picture is changed to the image you selected.

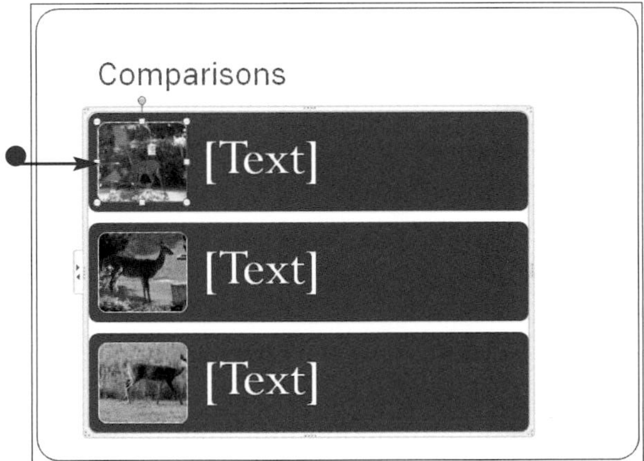

TIP

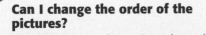

Can I change the order of the pictures?

Yes. PowerPoint determines the order of the pictures when you apply a Picture Layout. To change the order of the pictures

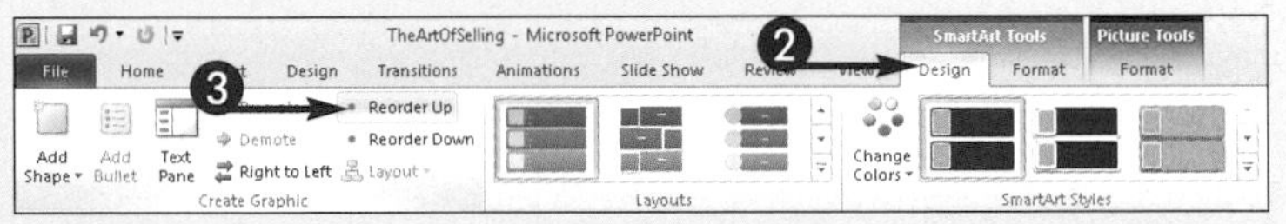

1. Click a picture in the SmartArt layout.
2. Click the **SmartArt Tools Design** tab.
3. Click either **Reorder Up** or **Reorder Down**.

   The picture moves in the direction you specified.

Insert Video Clips

Bring experts or a recorded instructional into your presentation with videos. You can make your slide show livelier by inserting a video on a slide, and then playing it during the show.

For more on inserting video clips, see Chapter 6.

Insert Video Clips

1. Select a slide in Normal view.
2. Click the **Insert** tab.
3. Click **Video**.

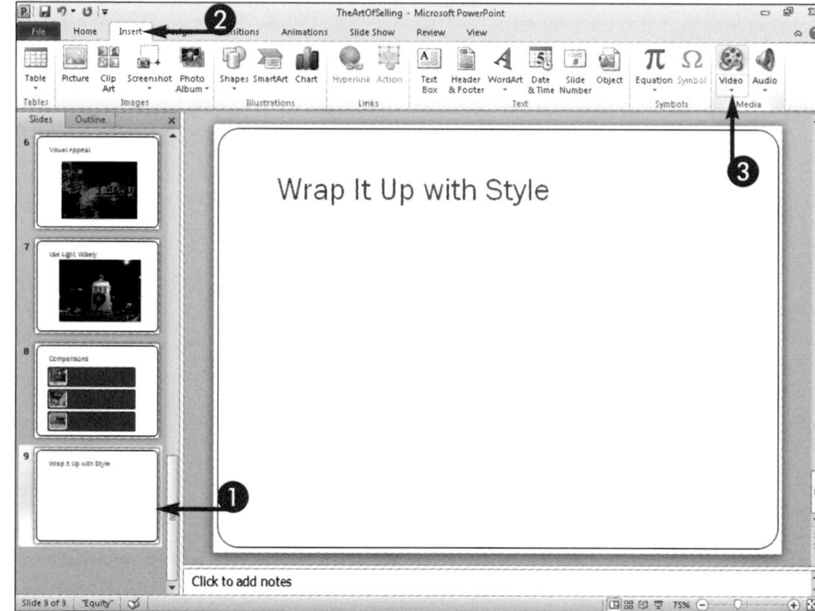

The Insert Video dialog box appears.

4. Select the folder containing the file.
5. Click the file.

   In this example Wildlife was clicked.
6. Click **Insert**.

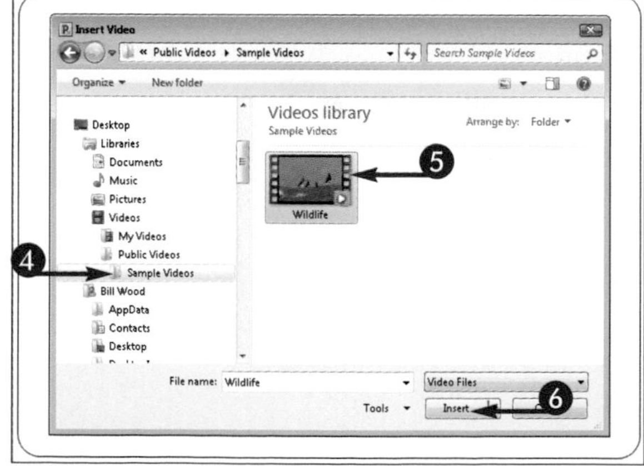

- The video appears on your slide.

  Size and position the video as needed.

Note: *To learn how to position and resize objects, see Chapter 9.*

- Note the Control Bar at the bottom of the inserted clip. Whether you are in Normal view or Slide Show view, this appears when you position the mouse over the video.

7. Click the **Video Tools Playback** or **Video Tools Format** tab.
8. Click **Play** (▶ changes to ⏸).

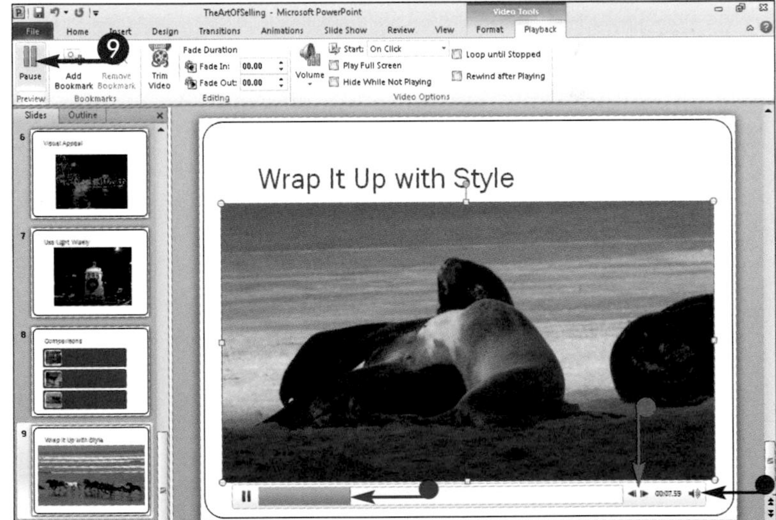

- The slide shows the progress of the video playing. Click anywhere on the slide to jump to any part of the video.
- You can click the **Move Forward** (⏩) and **Move Back** buttons (⏪) to jump back or forth 0.25 seconds.
- You can use the **Volume** button (🔊) to adjust the sound.

9. Click **Pause** (⏸ changes to ▶).

   The video stops playing.

TIP

Can I play the video in full screen during the slide show?

Yes, and then PowerPoint automatically shows the slide show again when the video is done. To make the video play full screen

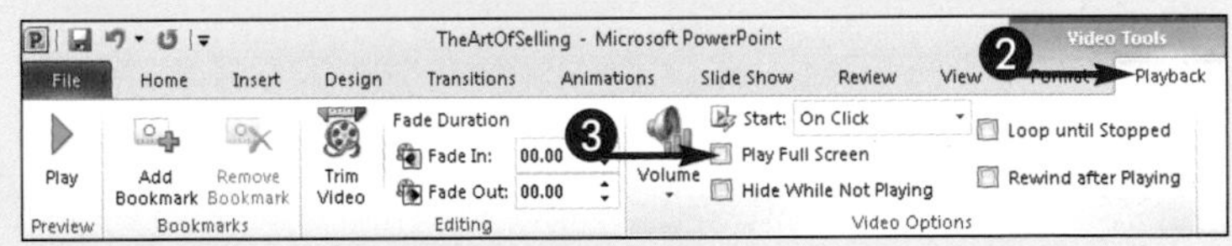

1. Click the video clip.
2. Click the **Video Tools Playback** tab.
3. Click **Play Full Screen** (☐ changes to ☑).

   The video now plays in the entire screen when you play it during the slide show.

Insert Audio Clips

Bring interesting sound effects into your presentation with audio clips. You can draw your audience into your slide show by playing audio at just the right time during the show. You can play audio clips automatically or at the click of a button.

For more on inserting audio clips, see Chapter 6.

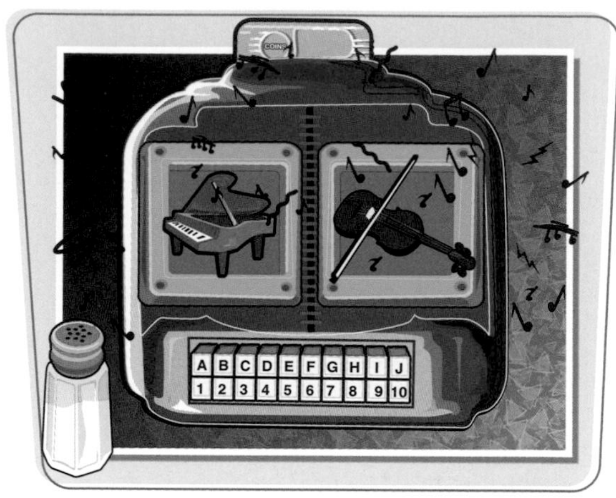

Insert Audio Clips

1. Select a slide in Normal view.
2. Click the **Insert** tab.
3. Click **Audio**.

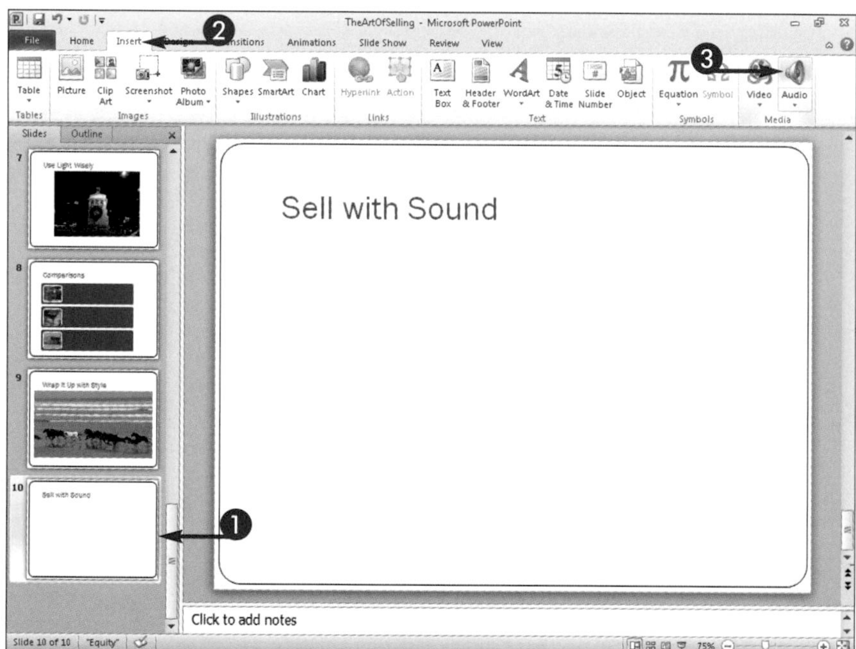

The Insert Audio dialog box appears.

4. Select the folder containing the file.
5. Click the file.

   In this example, Kalimba was clicked.
6. Click **Insert**.

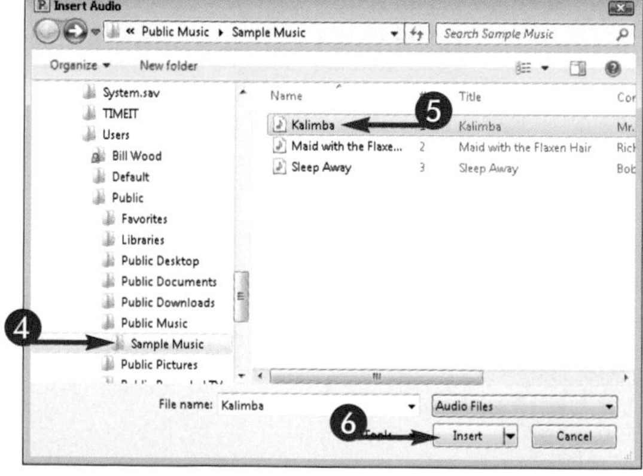

- An icon representing the audio appears on your slide.
- Note the Control Bar at the bottom of the icon. Whether you are in Normal view or Slide Show view, this appears when you position ⇖ over the Audio Megaphone.

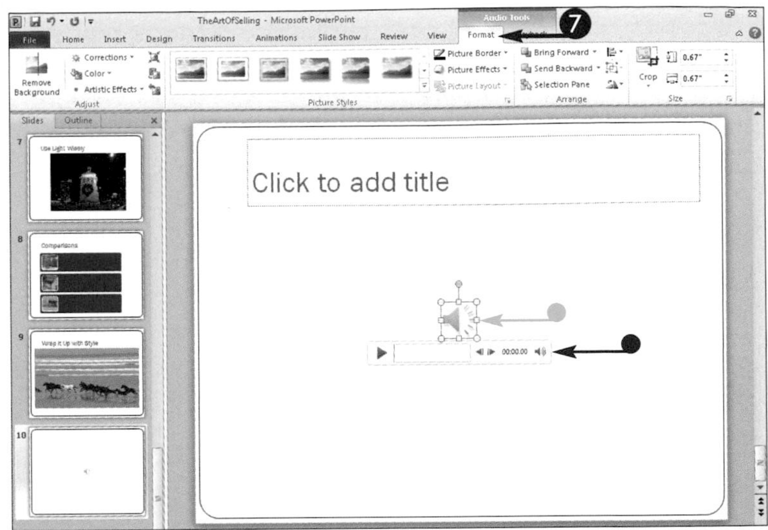

7. Click the **Audio Tools Format** tab.

   You can change the icon image with the tools on the Audio Tools Format tab.

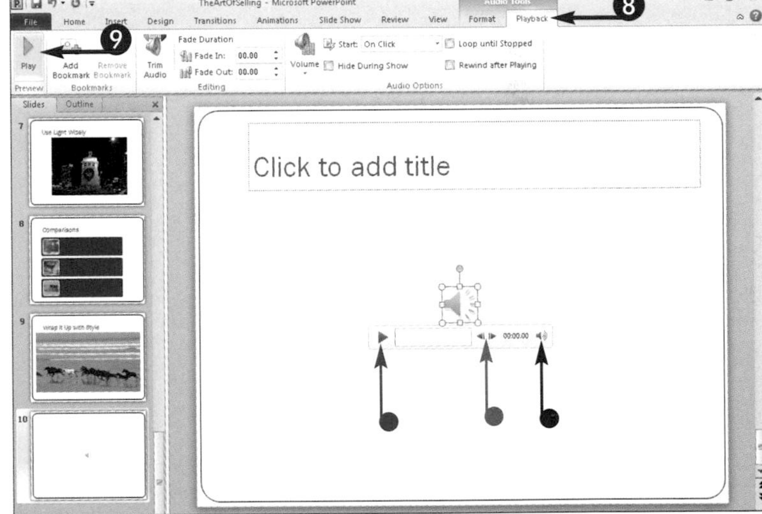

8. Click the **Audio Tools Playback** tab.
9. Click **Play** (▶ changes to ⏸).

   The audio plays.

- The slide shows the progress of the audio playing. Click anywhere on the slide to jump to any part of the video.
- You can click the **Move Forward** (▶) and **Move Back** buttons (◀) to jump back or forth 0.25 seconds.
- You can use the **Volume** button (🔊) to adjust the sound.

Can I set up the audio clip so it starts automatically when I go to that slide?

Yes. Working in Normal view, follow these steps:

1. Click the audio icon.
2. Click the **Audio Tools Playback** tab.
3. Click the **Start** ▾.
4. Click **Automatically**.

- Click **Play across slides** if you want the audio to play after the slide show advances to another slide.

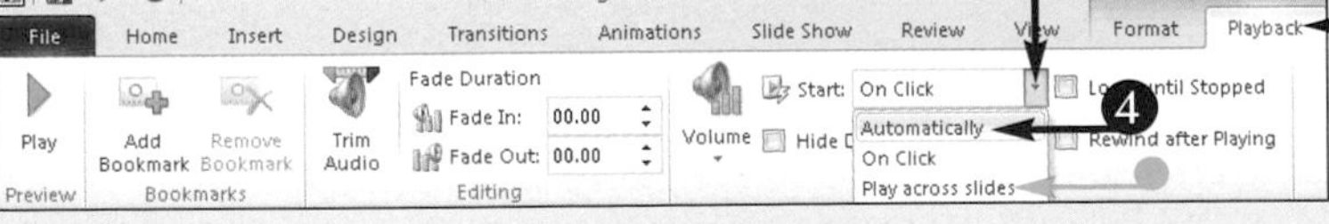

Your audio will now play when the slide show advances to this slide.

Trim Video Clips

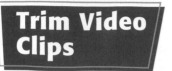

Many times you will not want to play an entire video in a PowerPoint presentation. You may want to only play a snippet of a video during a slide show to show a little information about something. You can trim the video in PowerPoint without special software.

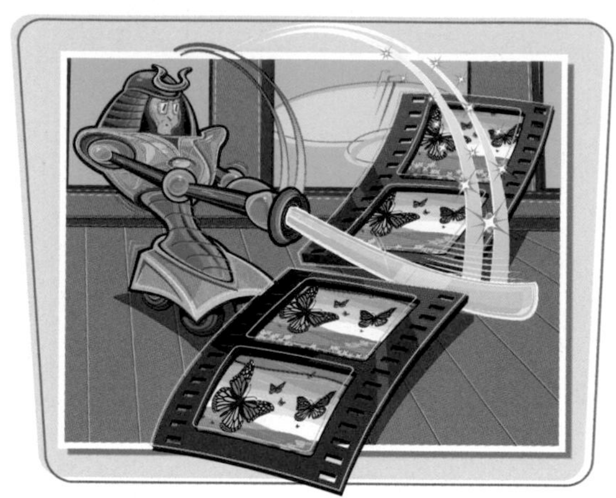

Trim Video Clips

1. Click a video clip.
2. Click the **Video Tools Playback** tab.
3. Click **Trim Video**.

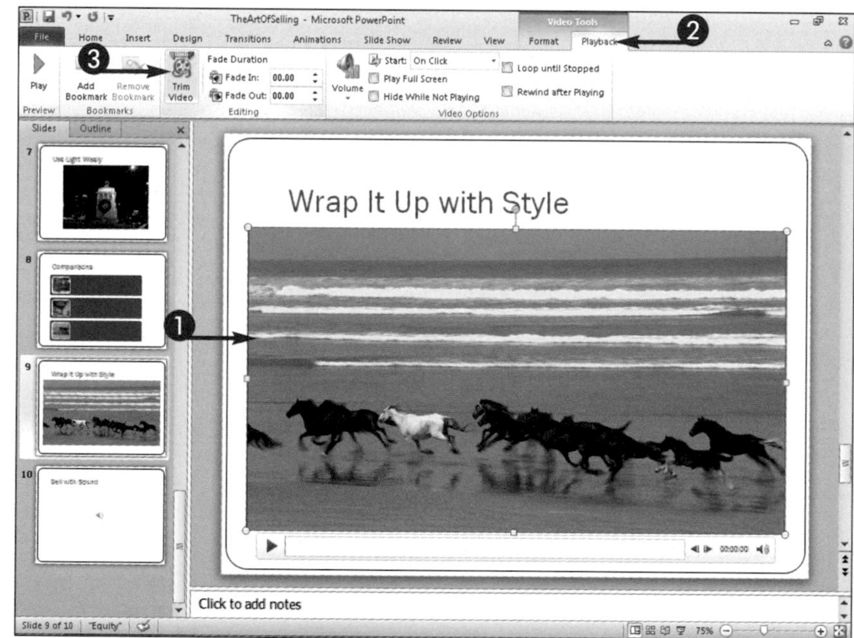

The Trim Video dialog box appears.

4. Click anywhere on the play slide.

- The video frame that plays at that particular time shows in the window.
- The time is shown for that particular point in the video.

5. Click the **Play** button (▶) to play the video from that point.

- Click the **Previous Frame** (◀) or **Next Frame** button (▶)to move one frame backward or forward.

6 Click the **Pause** button (⏸) to stop the video.

7 Click and drag the green marker where you want the video to begin.

8 Click and drag the red marker where you want to video to end.

- When you release the click, the frame at that particular point is shown in the window.

9 Click **OK**.

The dialog box closes and the video is trimmed to the shortened time that you specified.

10 Click the **Video Tools Playback** tab.

11 Click **Play** (▶ changes to ⏸) to view the trimmed video.

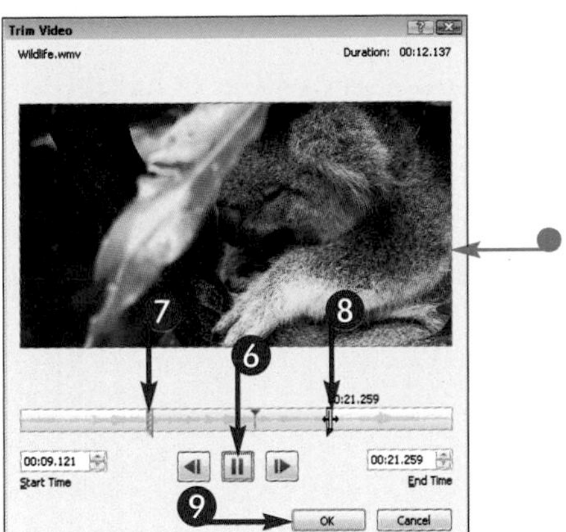

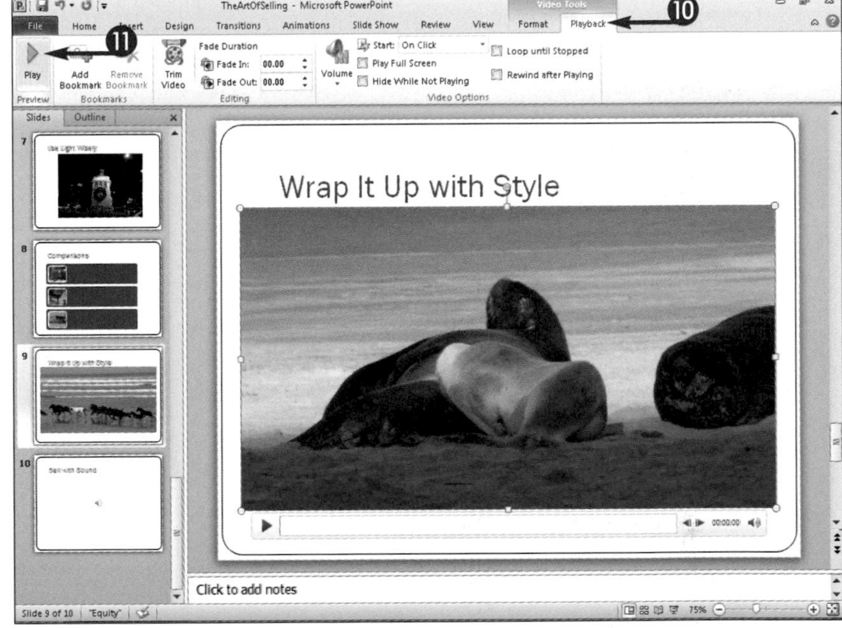

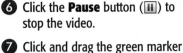

TIPS

What is the Fade Duration?

The Fade Duration is an effect that fades the beginning and/or end of the video for the amount of time set in the Fade In and Fade Out fields. It is an interesting effect that gives the video a soft feel.

What is the Hide While Not Playing feature?

The Hide While Not Playing feature hides the video if it is not playing. You need to start the video automatically though, because you cannot start the video when it is hidden. This feature is convenient because the video clip hides after it is done playing.

Trim Audio Clips

You may have an interesting part of a song to play for your audience, or a clip from an interview to share with them. Typically, you will not want to play an entire audio clip for them. You can trim an audio clip in PowerPoint to make the audio clip the perfect length for your purpose.

Trim Audio Clips

1. Click an audio clip.
2. Click the **Audio Tools Playback** tab.
3. Click **Trim Audio**.

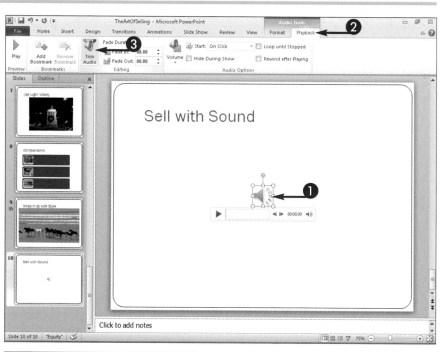

The Trim Audio dialog box appears.

4. Click anywhere on the play slide.

- The time is shown for that particular point in the audio clip.

5. Click the **Play** button (▶) to play the audio from that point.

- Click the **Previous Frame** (◀|) or **Next Frame** button (|▶) to move 0.1 second backward or forward.

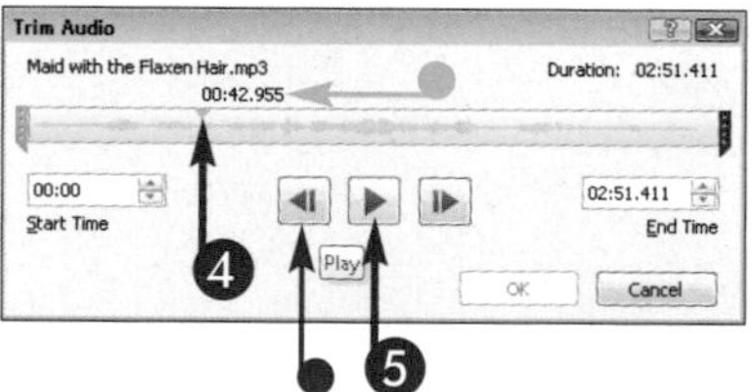

❻ Click the **Pause** button (⏸) to stop the video.

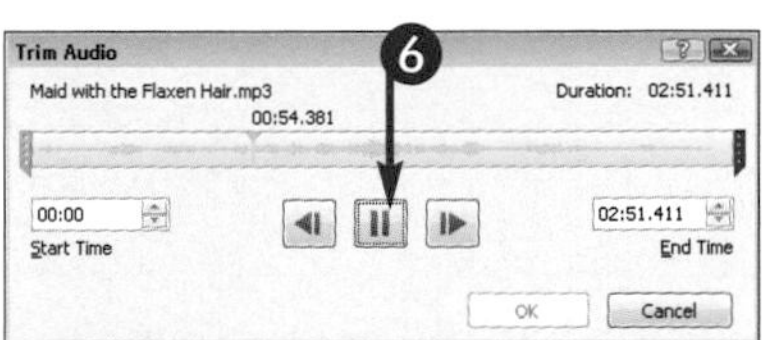

❼ Click and drag the green marker where you want the audio to begin.

❽ Click and drag the red marker where you want to audio to end.

❾ Click **OK**.

The dialog box closes and the audio is trimmed to the shortened time that you specified.

❿ Click **Play** (▶ changes to ⏸) to listen to the trimmed audio.

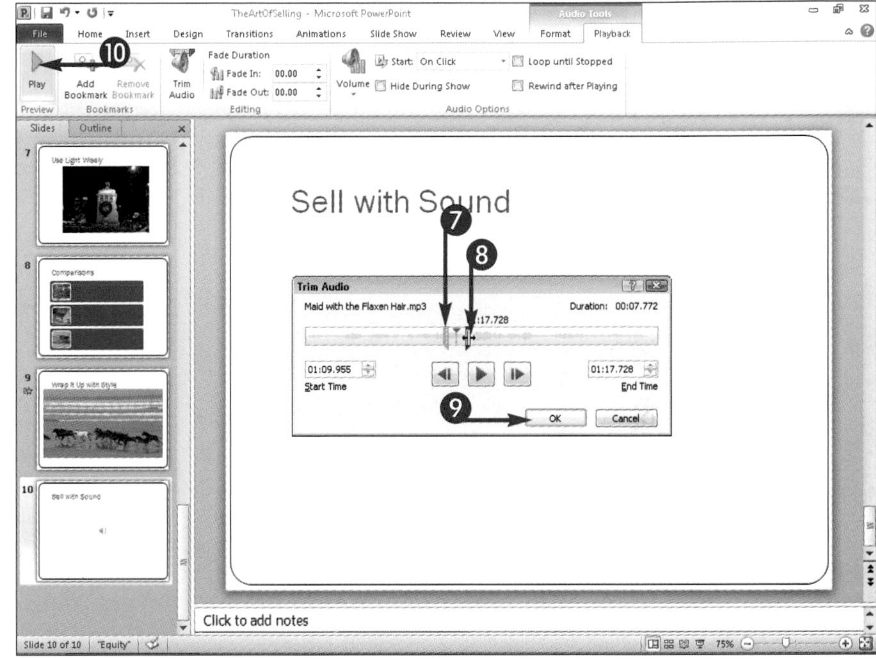

TIPS

What is Loop until Stopped?

A video or audio clip may end before you are ready to advance the slide. Loop until stopped makes the video or audio continuously loop until you stop it or until you advance to the next slide.

What is Rewind after Playing?

When an audio or video clip finishes playing, it stays at the end of the clip. If you click the **Play** button (▶), it does nothing. If you select Rewind after Playing, the clip will play again when you click ▶.

Insert a Screenshot

You may want to show something from your computer in a slide show. You can take a screenshot of an open window or a section of the computer display and insert it onto a slide without leaving PowerPoint. The screenshot feature is a fast and convenient way to take a snapshot of something on your computer and put it into a presentation.

Insert a Screenshot

Open Window

1. Select a slide in Normal view.
2. Click the **Insert** tab.
3. Click **Screenshot**.

   The gallery of Available Windows appears.

4. Click a window on the gallery.

- PowerPoint inserts the window screenshot onto the slide.

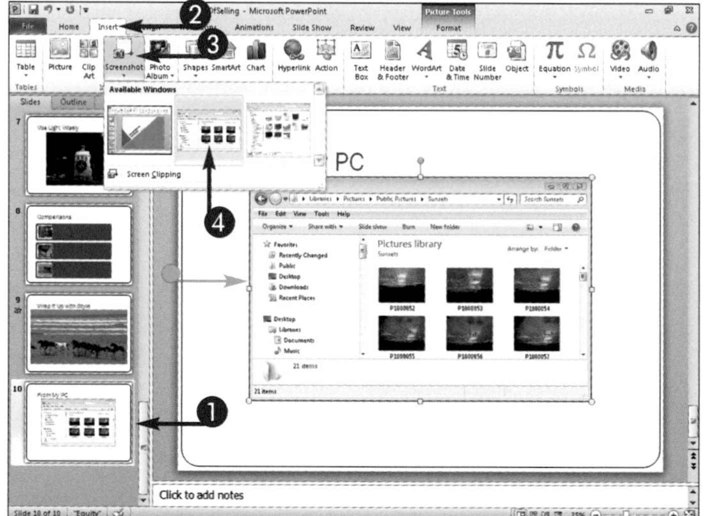

Section of Screen

1. Select a slide in Normal view.
2. Click the **Insert** tab.
3. Click **Screenshot**.

   The gallery of Available Windows appears.

4. Click **Screen Clipping**.

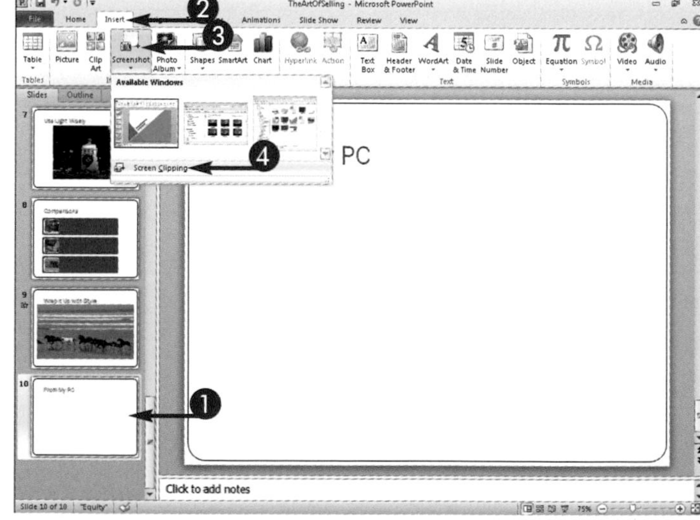

The PowerPoint window disappears, showing the computer screen (↖ changes to +).

5 Click and drag across the section of screen that you want in your screenshot.

The PowerPoint window reappears and the screenshot is inserted onto the slide.

Size and position the screenshot as needed.

Note: *To learn how to position and resize objects, see Chapter 9.*

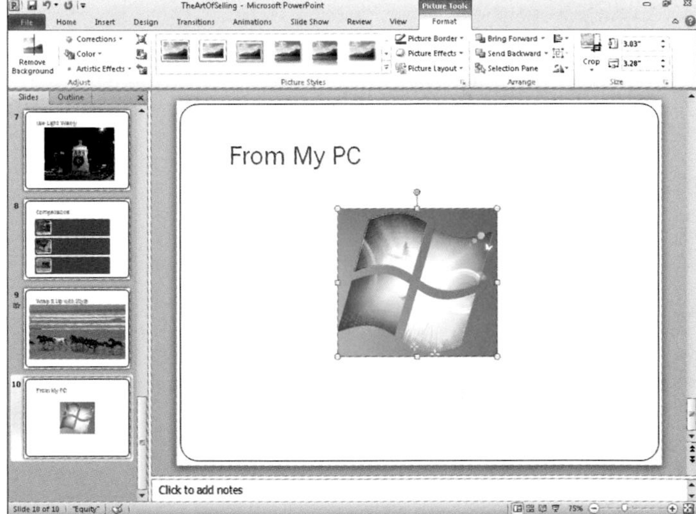

TIPS

Why can I not see all my open windows?

The Available Windows gallery shows only open windows that are not minimized. If an open window is not shown in the gallery, go to the Windows taskbar and restore the window, and then take the screenshot.

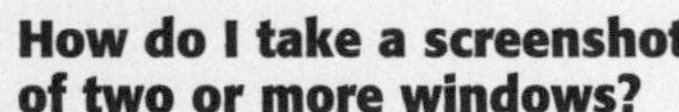

How do I take a screenshot of two or more windows?

Minimize the PowerPoint window. Restore the windows and arrange them the way you want them in the screenshot. Restore the PowerPoint window and click the **Insert** tab. Click **Screenshot,** and then click **Screen Clipping.** Click and drag across the windows with the crosshair pointer (+).

CHAPTER 13

Finishing, Setting Up, and Running a Slide Show

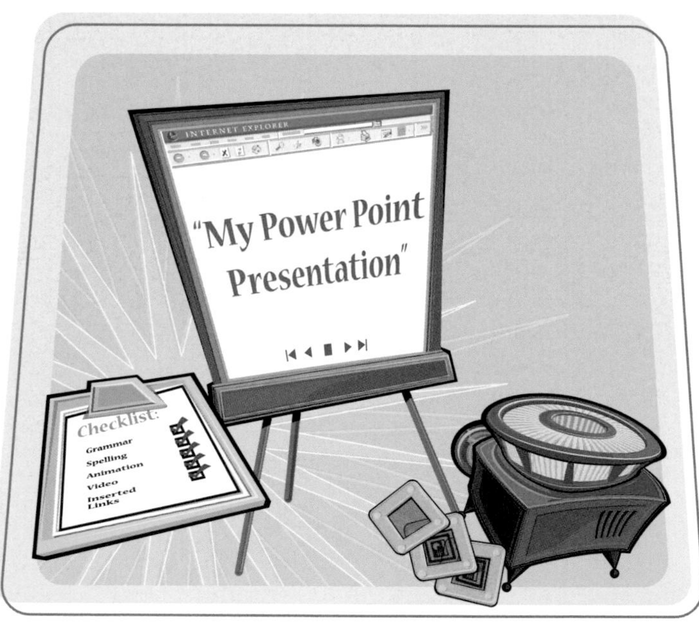

After you add all your slide content, tweak your slide design, and add graphics, animations, and transitions, you are almost done. Now, you perform the final tasks to complete your presentation and finally run your slide show!

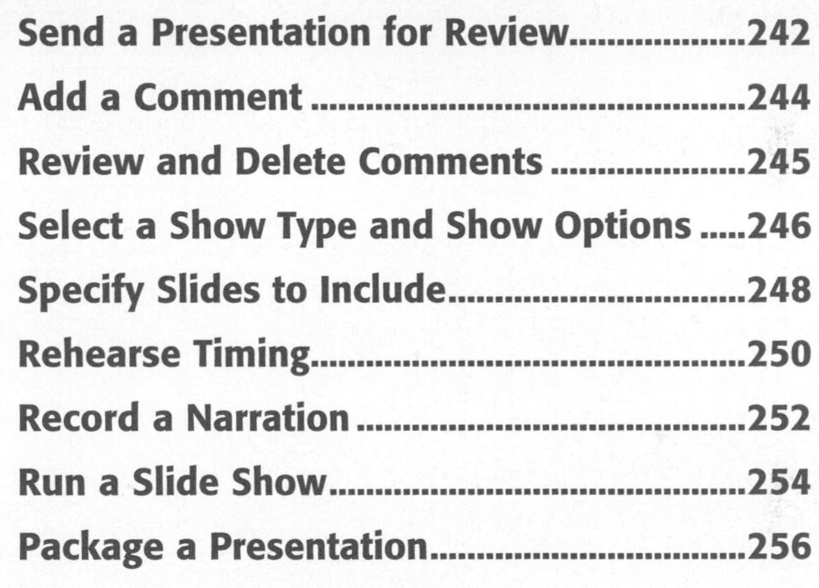

Send a Presentation for Review

You may want to seek feedback on your presentation before you give a slide show. A second opinion helps because another viewer can spot errors you missed or suggest improvements. You can e-mail your presentation to someone for review. That person can add comments to the file, and then e-mail it back to you. You can then implement suggestions as needed.

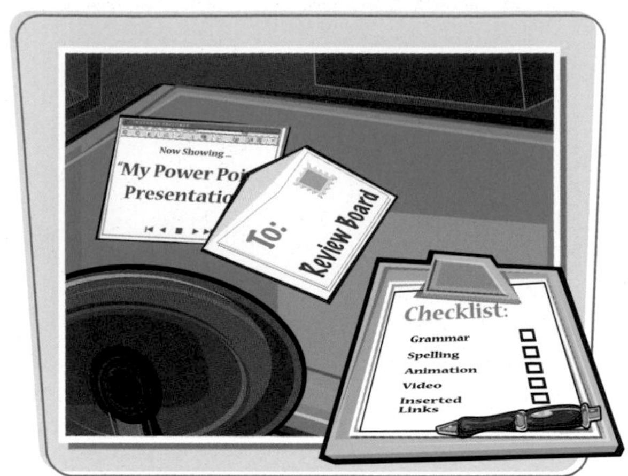

Send a Presentation for Review

Note: *These steps assume your e-mail program is properly configured to work with other applications.*

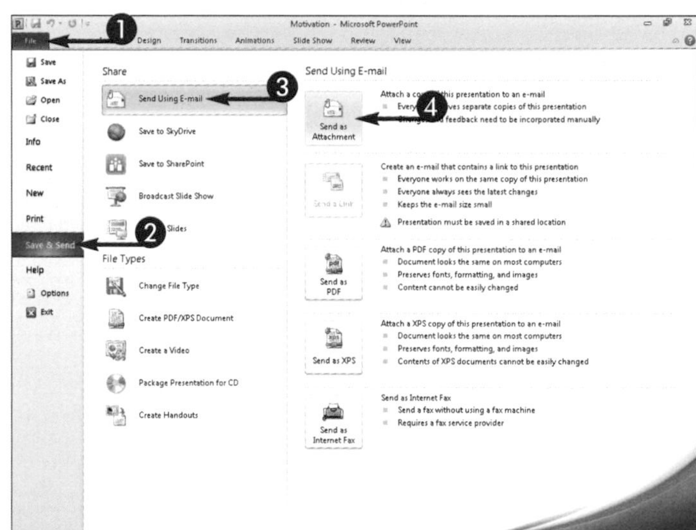

1. Click the **File** tab.
2. Click **Save & Send**.
3. Click **Send Using E-mail**.
4. Click **Send as Attachment**.

An e-mail message window appears.

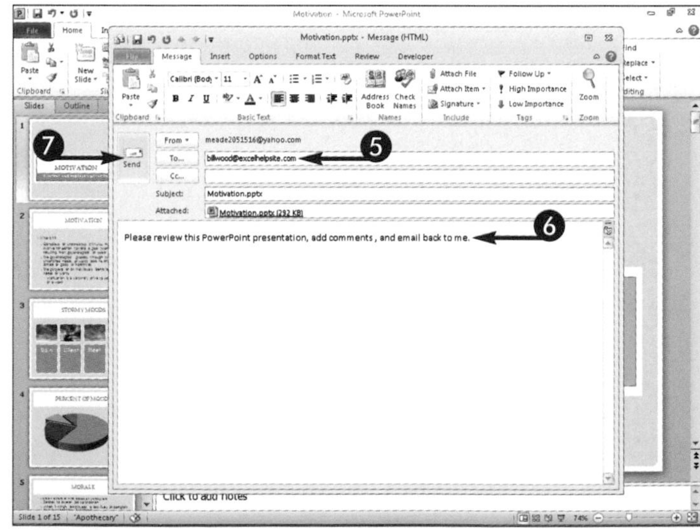

5. Click the **To** text box and type the recipient's e-mail address.
6. Click the message pane and type text for the message.
7. Click **Send**.

PowerPoint and your e-mail program send the message with the presentation attached.

1. After you receive a file back from a reviewer, open the e-mail.
2. Right-click the PowerPoint attachment.
3. Click **Open**.

- You can also save the PowerPoint file to your computer.

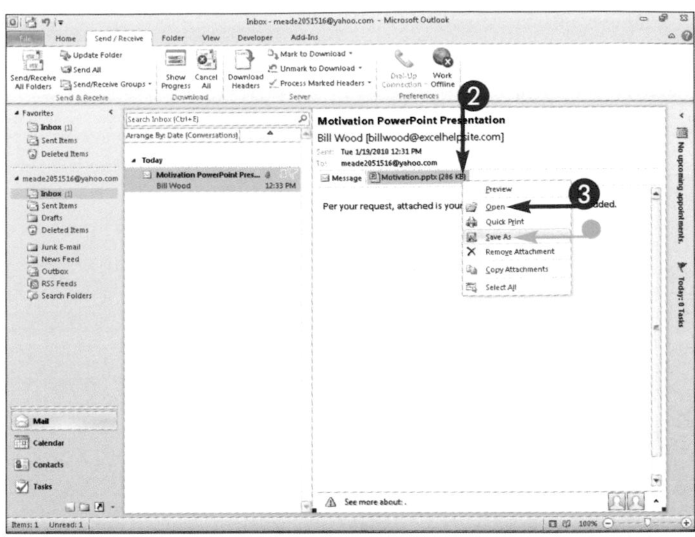

The PowerPoint presentation opens.

4. Click a comment to review it.

Note: *See the section "Review and Delete Comments" in this chapter to learn more.*

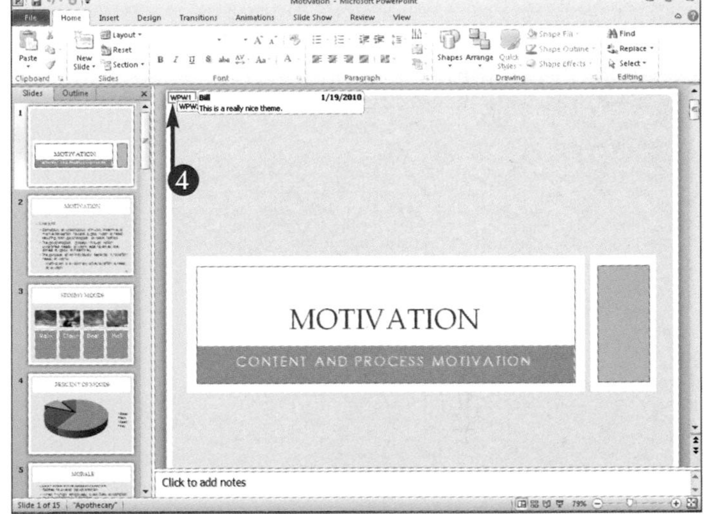

When I e-mail a presentation for review, what does the recipient need to do?

The recipient needs to open the presentation in PowerPoint and review it. That person must select a slide, click the **Review** tab, and then click the **New Comment** command to add comments. PowerPoint adds the reviewer's initials and a number to each comment. See "Add a Comment" in this chapter to learn more.

My recipient cannot open my PowerPoint 2007 file. What do I do?

PowerPoint 2007 enables you to save files in a format compatible with older PowerPoint versions. To save in a compatible format before sending, click the **File** tab, and then click **Save & Send**. Click **Change File Type**, and then click **PowerPoint 97-2003 Presentation** in the Presentation File Types list. The Save As dialog box opens with the proper file type specified. Continue like any other save.

Add a Comment

If you have been asked to review a presentation, use the comments feature to communicate your thoughts to the presentation's author. PowerPoint identifies each comment with a sticky note icon, making it easy for the author to find and consider each comment.

After you add your comments, save the file and send it to the author.

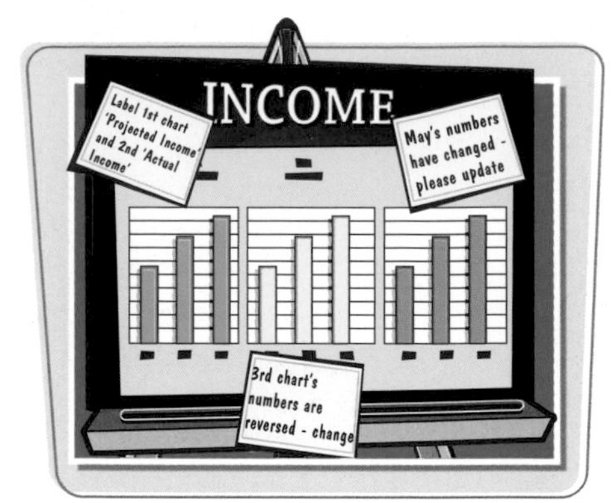

Add a Comment

1. Select a slide in Normal view.

- If you want the comment to appear next to a particular object on the slide, select that object.

2. Click the **Review** tab.
3. Click **New Comment**.

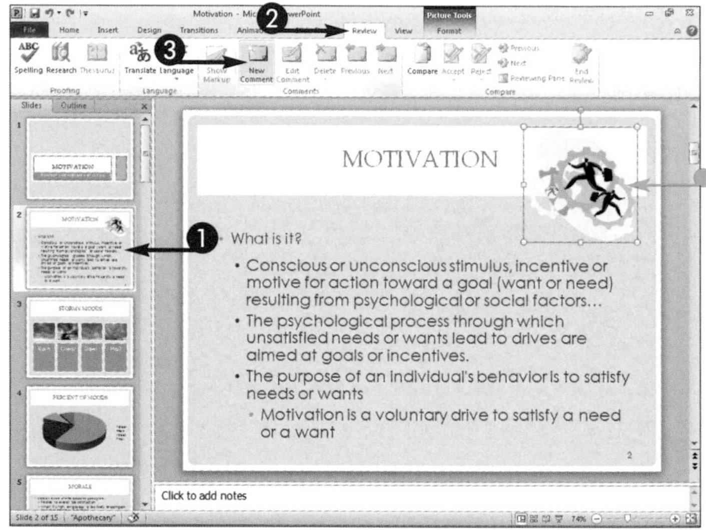

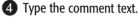

The comment marker and box appear.

4. Type the comment text.
5. Click outside the comment box when finished.

The comment box closes, leaving only the comment marker visible on-screen.

Note: *You can click and drag the comments marker to move it.*

- If you did not select an object on the slide, the comment marker appears in the upper-left corner of the slide.
- If you selected an object on the slide, the comment marker appears next to that object.

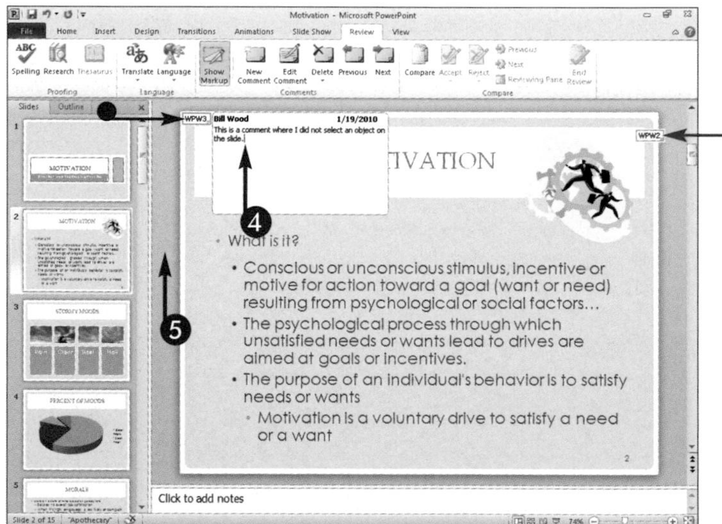

Review and Delete Comments

A presentation with comments in it is like a presentation printout with sticky notes from other people on it. You can page through the presentation file, read the individual notes, and decide whether to make any changes based on them. You can then delete (throw away) individual comments or hide all comments.

Review and Delete Comments

1. Select a slide with a comment in Normal view.
2. Click the **Review** tab.

Note: *Show Markup is a toggle for hiding comments — when highlighted, the comment marks are visible; if not highlighted, they are hidden. Click it to toggle between the two choices. Comments never appear during a slide show.*

3. Click **Show Markup** if it is not highlighted.

   Comment markers appear.

4. Click the comment marker.

   The comment box opens, so you can review the comment text.

5. Click the **Delete** ▾ to delete the current comment.
6. Click **Delete**.

- Click **Previous** and **Next** to move between comments.

Note: *Comments print by default when you print slides. However, there is a print option to hide them during printing.*

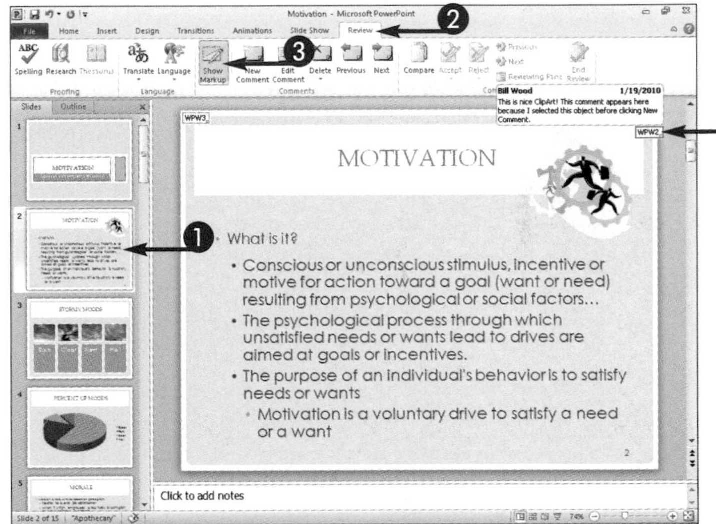

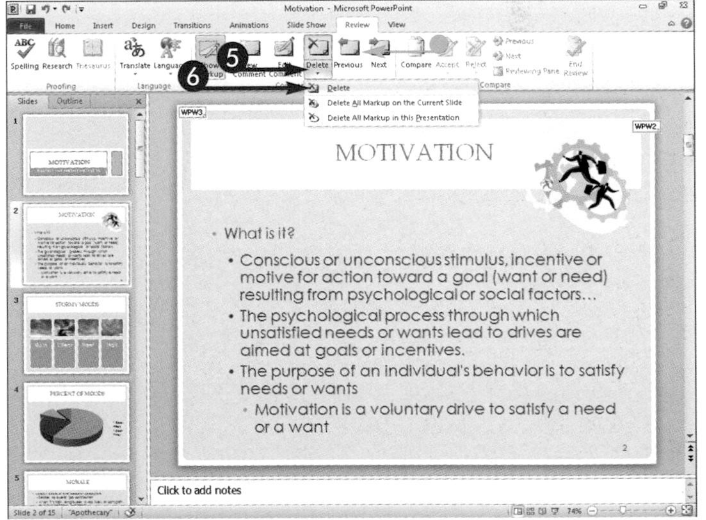

Select a Show Type and Show Options

Before you run your slide show for the first time, you should check the settings for the type of slide show, and some of the options for running the slide show. These options include whether the slide show should repeat continuously, whether you want to use narration and animations, and the pen color for annotations made on the screen during the slide show.

Select a Show Type and Show Options

1. In Normal view, click the **Slide Show** tab.
2. Click **Set Up Slide Show**.

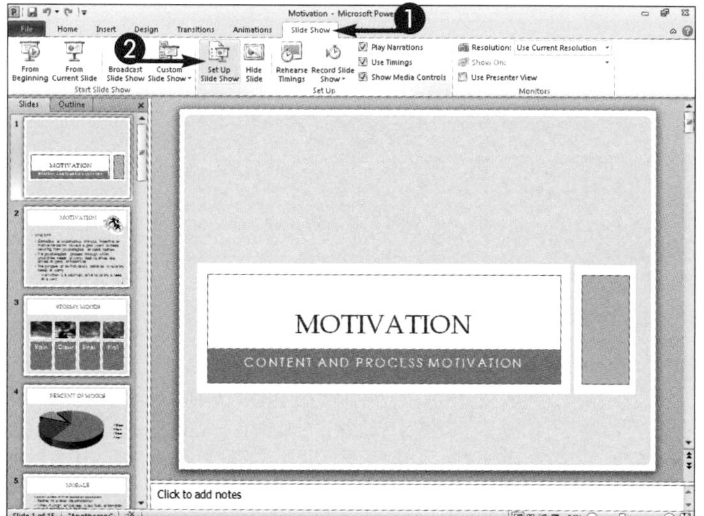

The Set Up Show dialog box appears.

3. Click an option to select whether you want your slide show presented by a speaker, viewed by a person on a computer, or viewed at a kiosk (◎ changes to ◉).
4. Click either the **Manually** option (slides advance with a mouse click) or the **Using timings, if present** option (slides advance automatically if timings were set) (◎ changes to ◉).

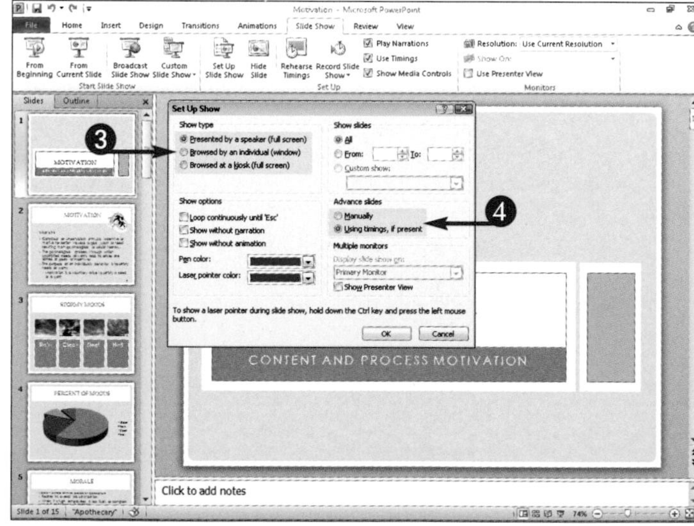

5 Click one or more options to select whether you want your show to loop continuously, be shown without narration, or be shown without animation (☐ changes to ☑).

6 Click the **Pen color** ▾ and select a color from the palette.

Note: *Pen is available only when a speaker presents a show. See Chapter 16 for more information.*

7 Click the **Laser pointer color** ▾ and select a color from the palette.

Note: *Press* Ctrl *+the left mouse button to show the laser pointer during a show.*

8 Click the **Show Presenter View** option to use that feature (☐ changes to ☑).

Note: *Presenter View is discussed in Chapter 16.*

9 Click **OK**.

PowerPoint applies your new settings and closes the dialog box.

10 Click the **Save** icon (💾) to save the settings.

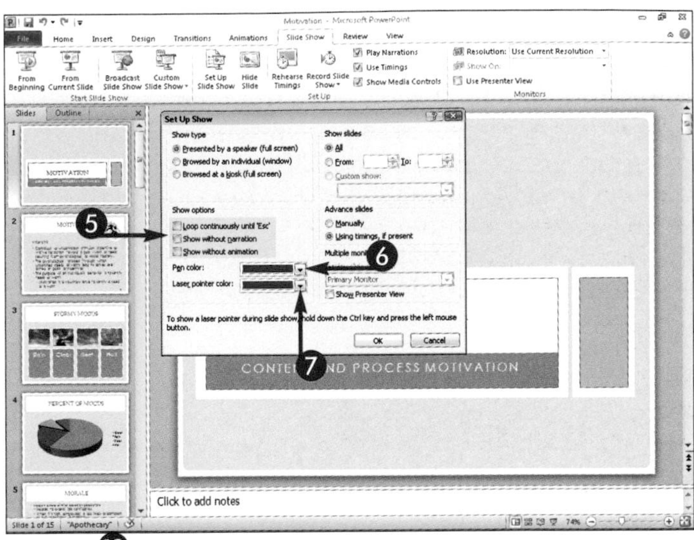

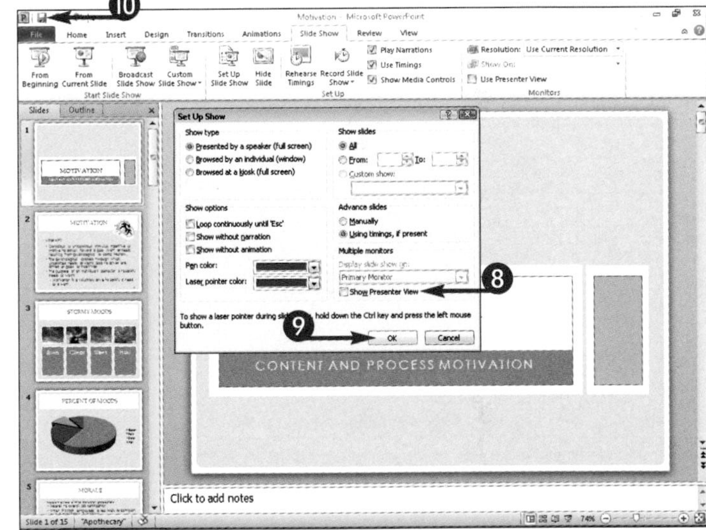

Why would I want to show my presentation without animation?

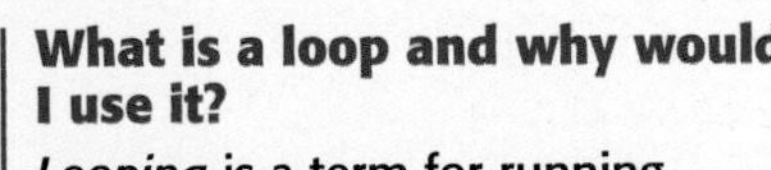

Animations are fun, but on computers lacking adequate resources, they may run slowly and delay your show. If you are using an older computer to present your show, preview it to be sure that animations run smoothly. If they do not, change this setting to avoid any problems.

What is a loop and why would I use it?

Looping is a term for running media, such as songs or videos, over and over again from beginning to end. If you plan to show your presentation at an informational booth or kiosk, where passersby may stop, watch a bit, and then move on, you probably want the presentation to loop. To do this, click **Loop continuously until 'Esc'** (☐ changes to ☑).

Specify Slides to Include

Sometimes you create a larger presentation, but decide that you want to show only some of the slides to a particular audience. To limit the slides displayed, you can save a custom slide show or you can specify a range of slides to play back in the Set Up Show dialog box.

Specify Slides to Include

Create a Custom Show

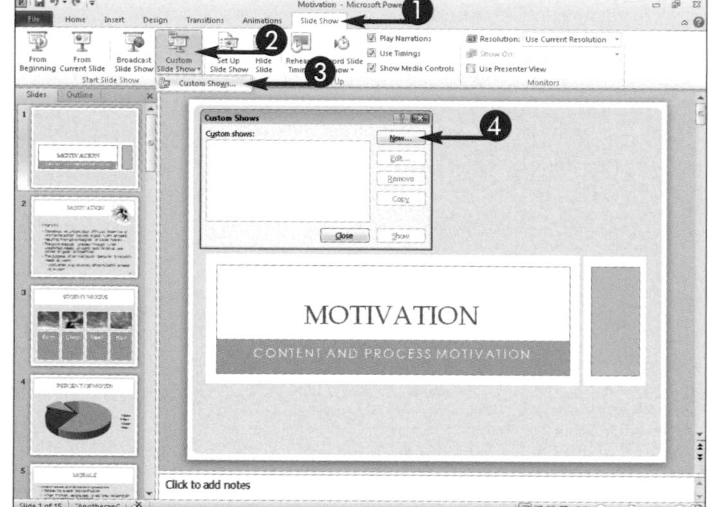

1. In Normal view, click the **Slide Show** tab.
2. Click **Custom Slide Show**.
3. Click **Custom Shows**.

   The Custom Shows dialog box appears.

4. Click **New**.

   The Define Custom Show dialog box appears.

5. Type a name in the **Slide show name** text box.

   Mini Show was typed.

6. Click a slide in the **Slides in presentation** box.
7. Click **Add**.

   The slide is added to the Slides in custom show list.

   Repeat Steps **6** and **7** to add other slides to the custom show.

8. Click **OK**.
9. Click **Close** in the Custom Shows dialog box.

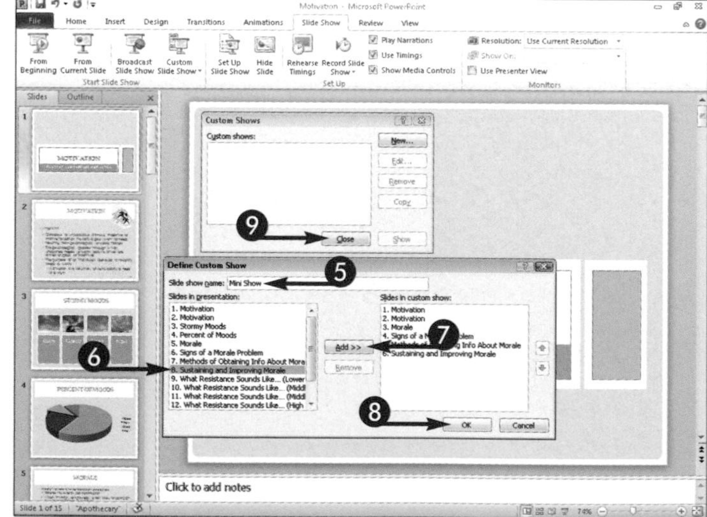

Specify which Slides to Show

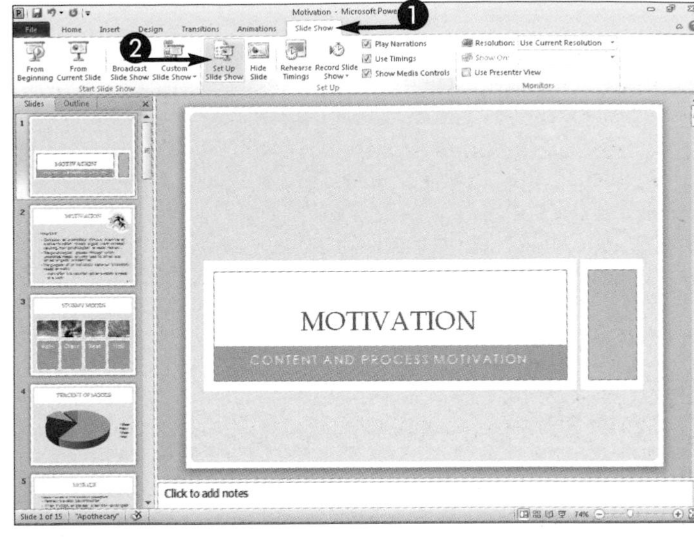

❶ In Normal view, click the **Slide Show** tab.

❷ Click **Set Up Slide Show**.

The Set Up Show dialog box appears.

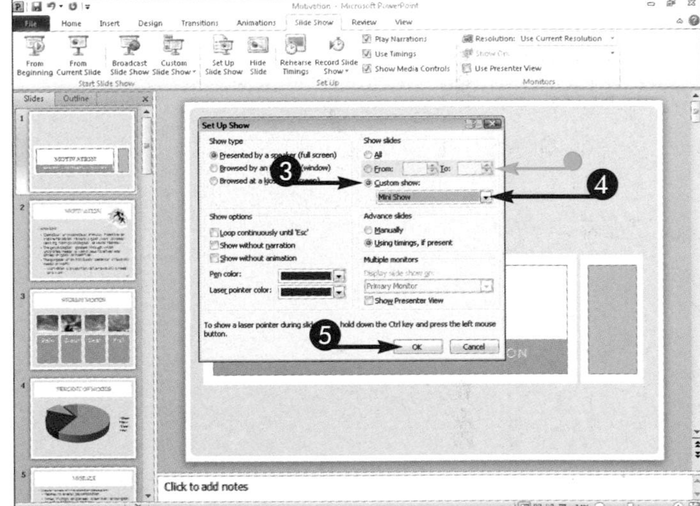

❸ If you saved a custom show and want to show it, click the **Custom show** option (◎ changes to ◉).

❹ Click the drop-down list ▾ and click a show from the list.

● To specify a range of slides to show, click **From** (◎ changes to ◉) and then enter the first and last slide numbers of the range in **From** and **To**.

❺ Click **OK**.

PowerPoint saves the show settings. Only the specified slides will appear when you run the slide show.

Is there a quick way to show my custom slide show?

Yes. Open the presentation in which you created the custom slide show. Click the **Slide Show** tab, and then click the **Custom Slide Show** button. A menu appears with the names of all custom shows you saved in the file. Click the name of the custom slide show to begin the custom slide show.

What if I do not want to show a slide right in the middle of my presentation?

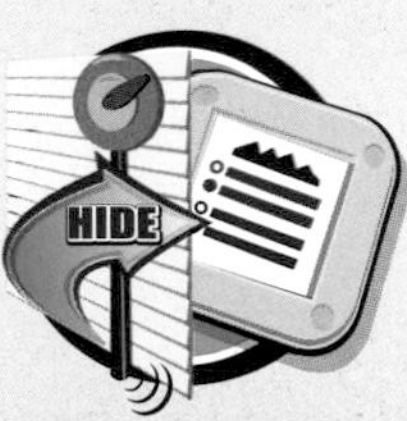

With a large presentation it may be inconvenient to build a custom show that excludes only one slide. In this case, just hide the slide. Click **Slide Sorter** (▦) to change to Slide Sorter view, right-click the slide, and then click **Hide Slide** on the shortcut menu.

Rehearse Timing

You can use the Rehearse Timings command to time a practice run of your presentation to ensure that it takes the proper amount of time to deliver. You can also use it to set a display time for each slide before the presentation advances automatically to the next slide. The Rehearse Timings feature helps you arrange your presentation so it fits into the time allotted for it.

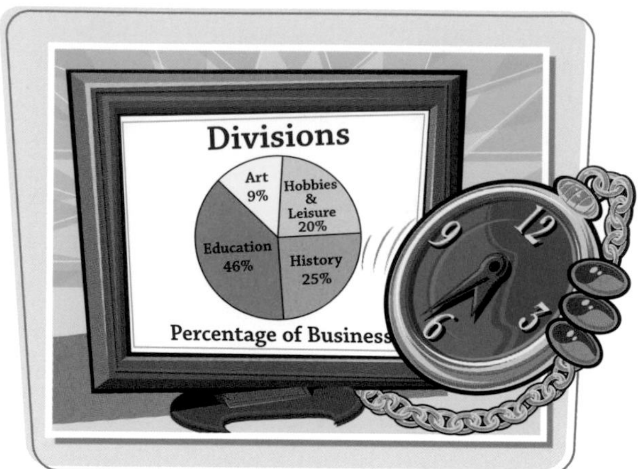

Rehearse Timing

1. Click the **Slide Show** tab.
2. Click **Rehearse Timings**.

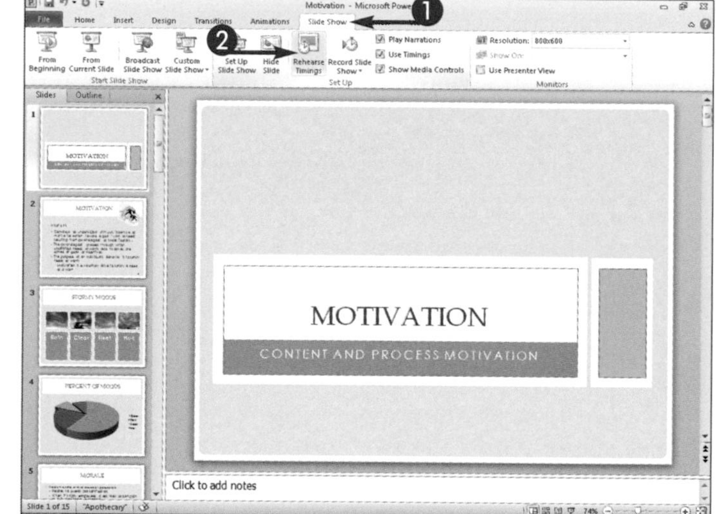

The slide show begins with the Recording toolbar open.

3. Rehearse the slide materials, clicking **Next** (➡) to advance the slide show to the next slide.

- Click **Pause** (⏸) to stop the timing.
- The elapsed time of the current slide.
- The elapsed time of the entire slide show.
- Click ☒ to exit the slide show before the end of the show.

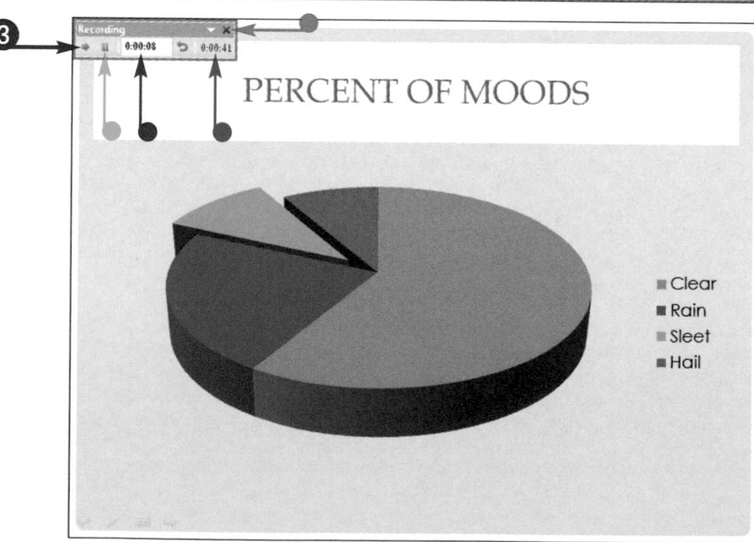

After the last slide, a message box informs you of the total elapsed time and asks if you want to save the timings.

4. Click **Yes** to save timings, or **No** to exit the rehearsal without saving timings.

- The presentation reappears in Slide Sorter view, where you can see the timing applied to each slide below its thumbnail.

5. Click 💾 to save the timings.

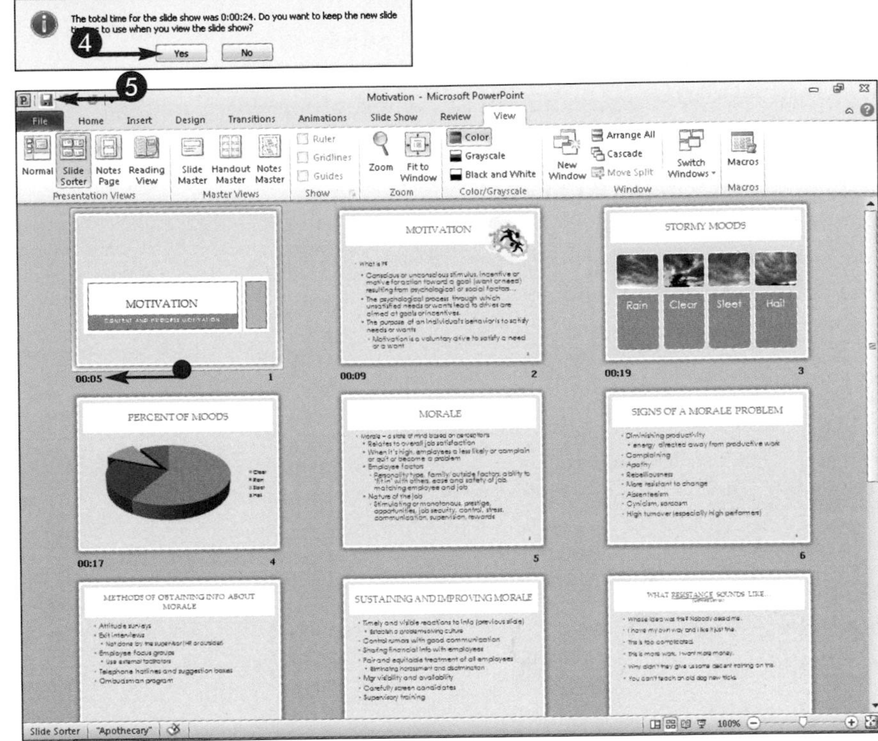

How do I clear the timings from a presentation?

To clear the timings from the presentation

1. Click the **Slide Show** tab.
2. Click ▾ on **Record Slide Show**.
3. Click **Clear**.
4. Click **Clear Timings on All Slides** to remove the timings from the slides.

- Click **Use Timings** (☑ changes to ☐) to prevent the slide show from advancing without clearing the timings.

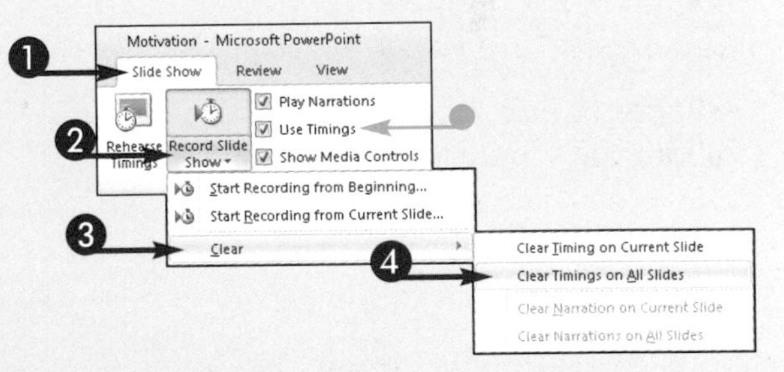

Record a Narration

If you do not intend to present your PowerPoint show live, or if you are presenting it on the Web, you can record a narration that talks the viewer through your key points. Recording a narration also sets up your presentation to advance automatically at the end of each slide's narration.

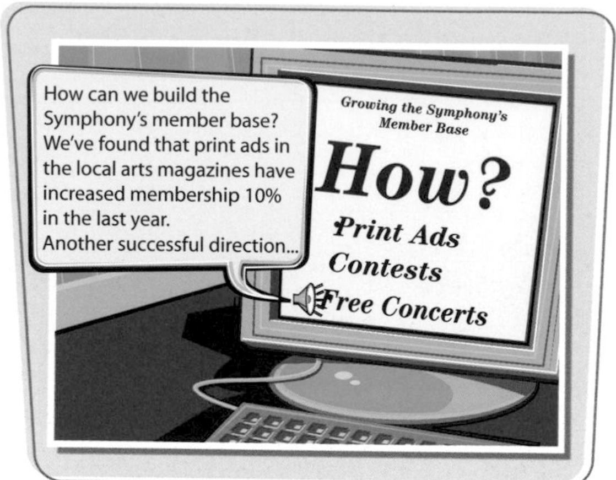

Record a Narration

1. Plug a microphone into your computer.
2. Click the **Slide Show** tab.
3. Click ▾ on **Record Slide Show**.
4. Click **Start Recording from Beginning**.

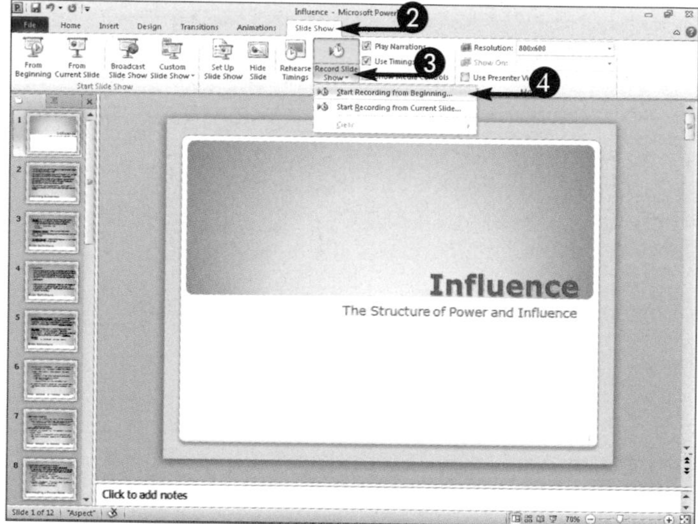

The Record Slide Show dialog box appears.

5. Click **Start Recording**.

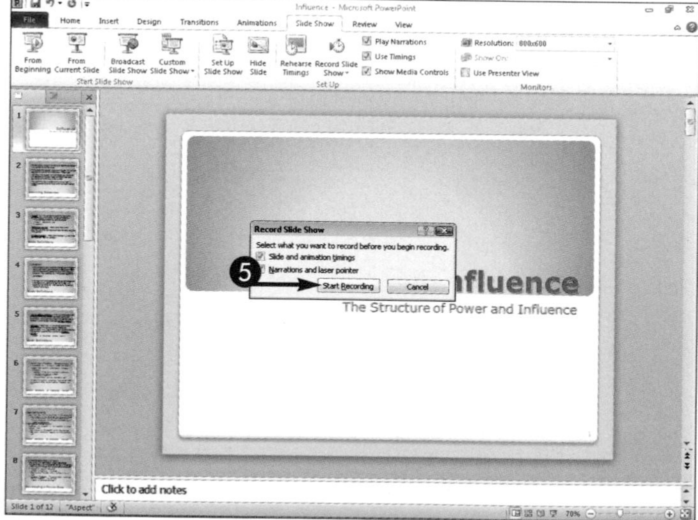

The slide show begins and with the Recording toolbar open.

6 Narrate the slide, speaking clearly into the microphone.

7 Click ➡ to advance the slides.

- Click ⏸ to pause the timing and narration.
- Click ☒ to exit the slide show before the end of the show.

When the slide show ends, Slide Sorter view reappears.

- The timings are shown below the slide thumbnails.
- Slides with narration display a speaker icon.
- To run the show with the slides automatically advancing, make sure both **Play Narrations** and **Use Timings** are selected (☐ changes to ☑).

8 Click 💾 to save the narration.

Note: *To ensure proper setup, see the section "Select a Show Type and Show Options" in this chapter.*

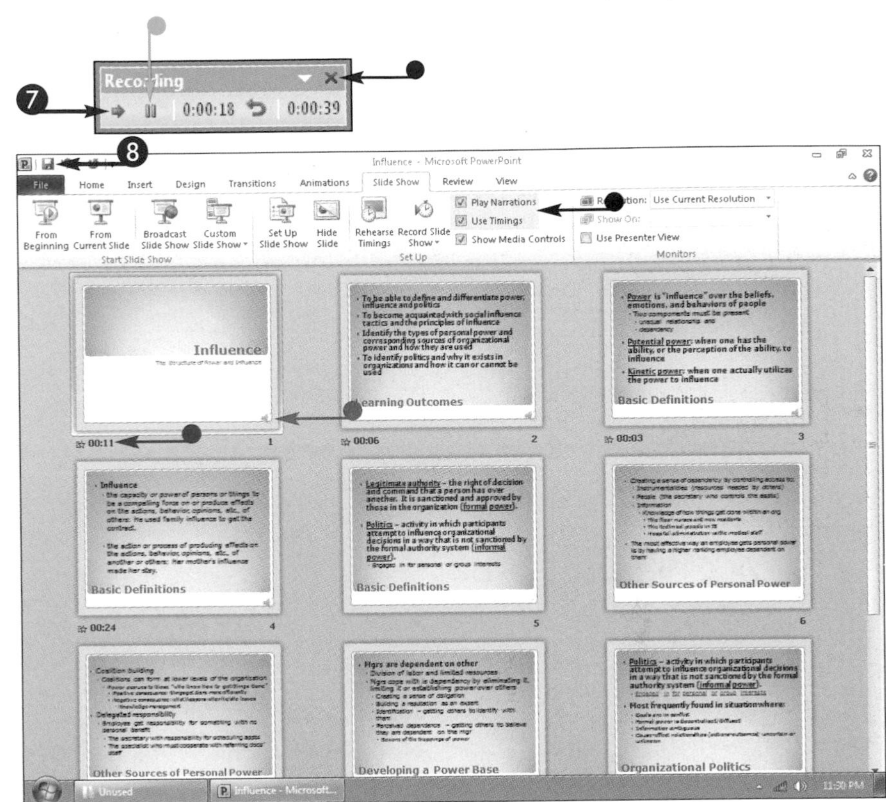

TIP

Do I need to rerecord the narration to remove it from a few slides?

No. You can remove the narration by following these steps:

1. Select a slide whose narration you want to remove.
2. Click the **Slide Show** tab.
3. Click ▾ on **Record Slide Show**.
4. Click **Clear**.
5. Click **Clear Narration on Current Slide**.

The Narration is removed and the speaker icon disappears from the slide.

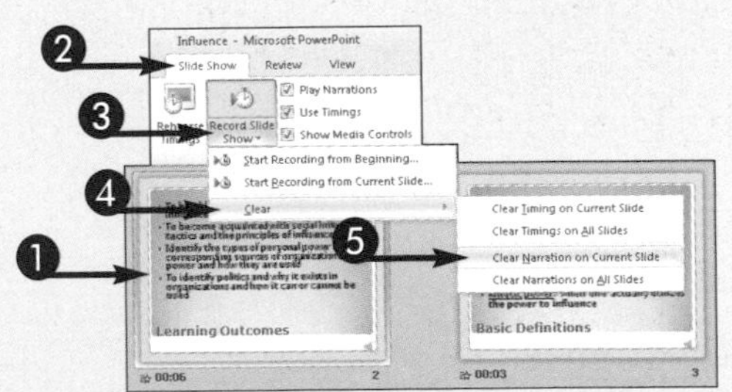

Run a Slide Show

You typed a lot of text, inserted graphics and animations, and worked with design settings. Depending on how you set up your slide show, it either runs itself of you will control it. Either way, it all starts with a click of a button, and then the use of some navigation tools. See Chapter 16 for more about running a slide show.

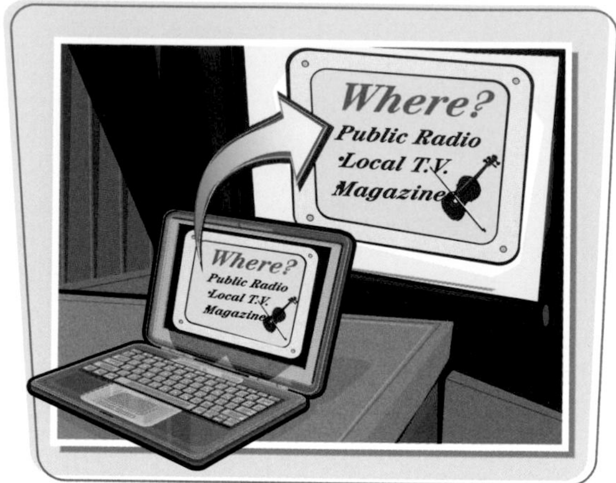

Run a Slide Show

❶ Click the **Slide Show** tab.

❷ Click **From Beginning**.

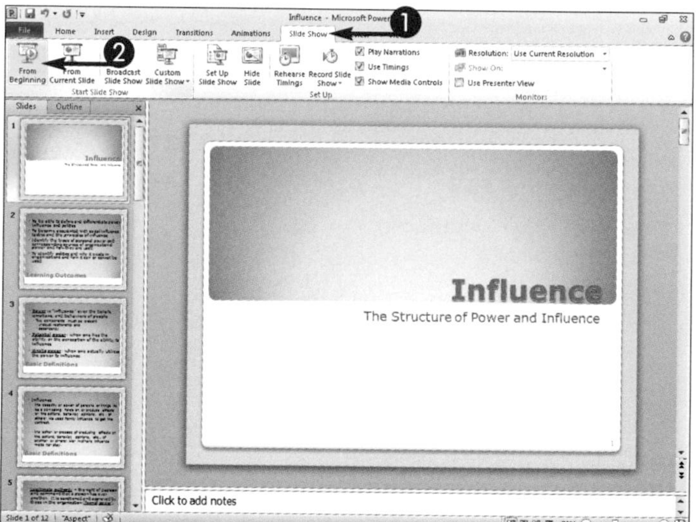

The slide show begins.

- When you move the mouse, the on-screen toolbar shows faintly in the lower-left corner.

❸ Click the slide to advance to the next slide, or you can press Enter or click the **Next** button on the on-screen toolbar.

***Note:** A mouse click may advance the slide or possibly activate an animation. Some animation may be configured to run when an object on the slide is clicked.*

***Note:** The slide may be configured to advance automatically, but you can still advance it manually.*

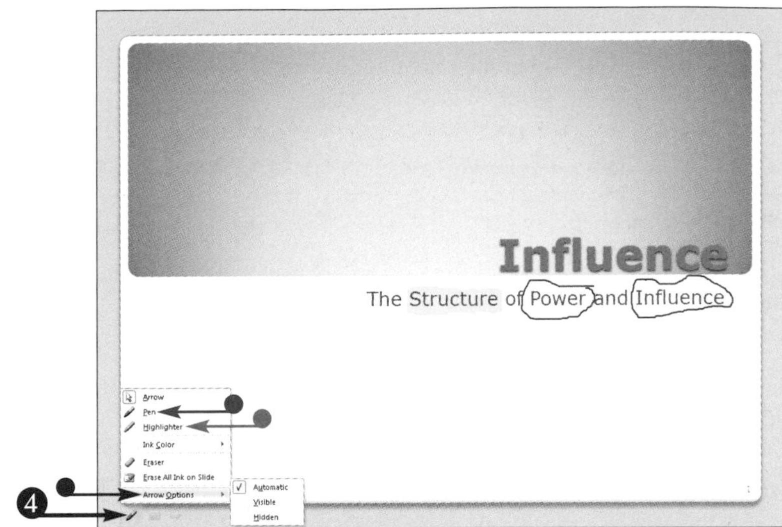

4 Click the **Pen** button (🖉) to display the menu for making annotations.

- Click **Arrow Options** to set how you see the pointer during the show.

***Note:** The default setting is Arrow, which is used to perform Slide Show navigations. The Automatic setting hides the arrow if there is no activity.*

- Click **Pen** to make annotations.
- Click **Highlighter** to highlight items.

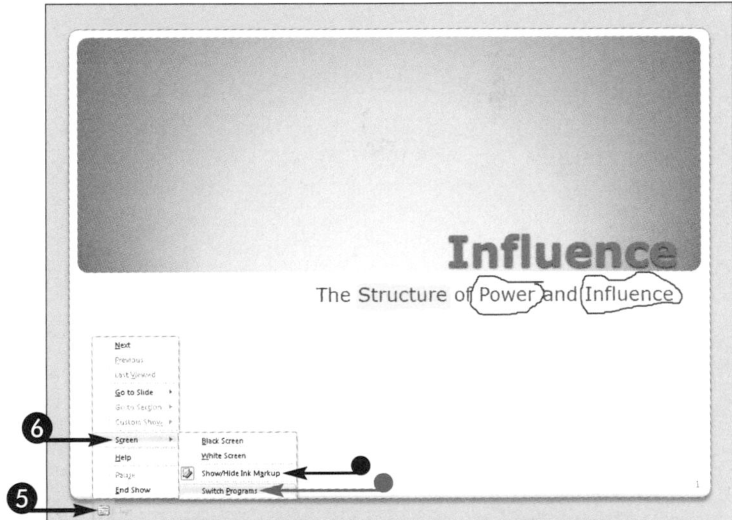

5 Click the **Menu** button (▤).

6 Click **Screen**.

- Click **Show/Hide Ink Markup** to hide all annotations.
- Click **Switch Programs** to switch to another program during the show.

PowerPoint returns to its previous view when the slide show ends.

***Note:** You may end the slide show at any time by pressing Esc.*

Can I save the annotations I made during the slide show?

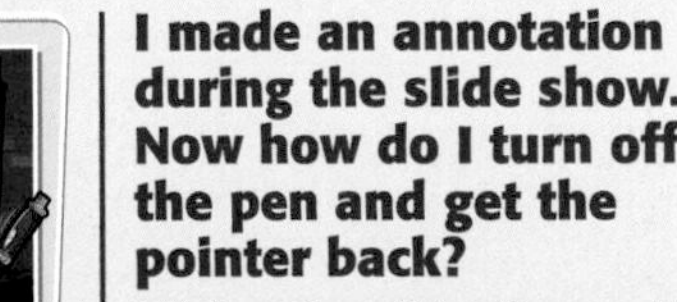

Yes, but the **Prompt to keep ink annotations when exiting** option must be selected in the Advanced tab of the PowerPoint Options dialog box (see Chapter 2). If it is, PowerPoint asks if you want to save your annotations when you exit the slide show — this is your only chance to save them.

I made an annotation during the slide show. Now how do I turn off the pen and get the pointer back?

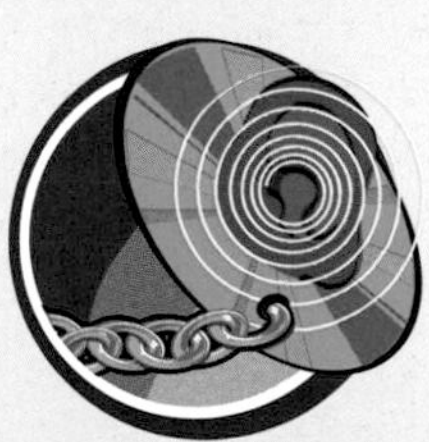

During the slide show, click 🖉 on the Navigation Tools and then click **Arrow** (it is above the Pen command that you used to turn on the pen). This is the setting that you usually want to use to navigate during a slide show.

Package a Presentation

You can save a presentation in a format that includes a PowerPoint viewer, plus any files needed to view your presentation. This viewer enables the presentation to be viewed on a computer that does not have PowerPoint installed on it.

If any media were linked to the presentation instead of embedded in it, the package includes those files, plus the package embeds fonts into the presentation.

Package a Presentation

1. Click the **File** tab
2. Click **Save & Send**.
3. Click **Package Presentation for CD**.
4. Click **Package for CD**.

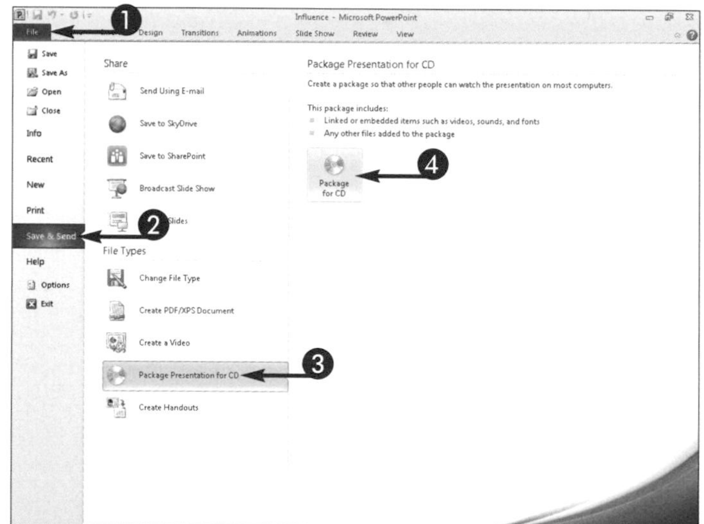

The Package for CD dialog box appears.

5. Click **Copy to Folder**.

- You can also insert a CD in your CD drive and then click **Copy to CD** — PowerPoint will burn the presentation files directly to the CD.

The Copy to Folder dialog box appears.

6. Click in the **Folder name** text box, and then type a name.

In this example, PresentationCD was typed.

- Note the folder location where the presentation package will be saved.

7. Click **OK**.

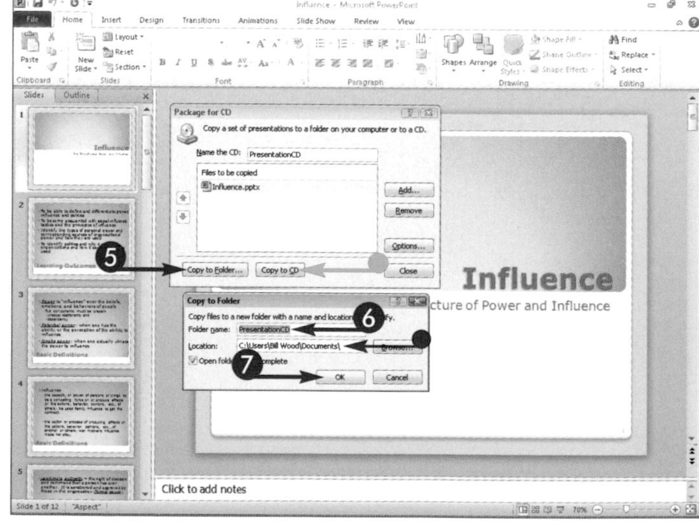

8 Click **Yes** in reply to the message that asks, "Do you want to include linked files in your package?"

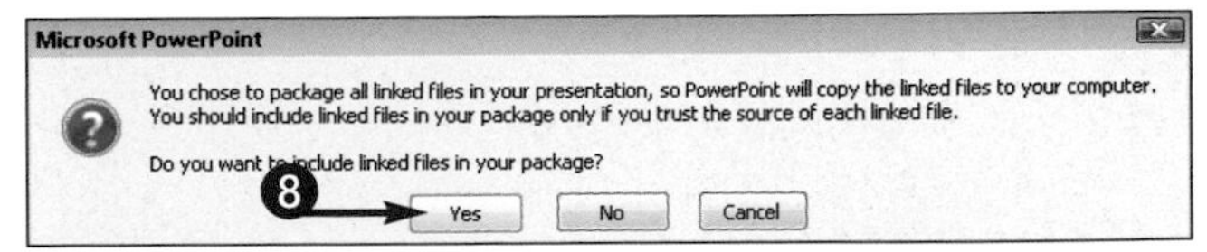

- PowerPoint creates a presentation package, including all necessary files, and saves it in the folder location specified.

***Note:** Send the entire folder (in this example, PresentationCD) to anyone who wants to view the Influence presentation.*

- To view the slide show, double-click the **Influence** presentation.

  If the computer does not have PowerPoint, this action opens a Web page to download the PowerPoint viewer; if the computer has PowerPoint, the presentation simply opens.

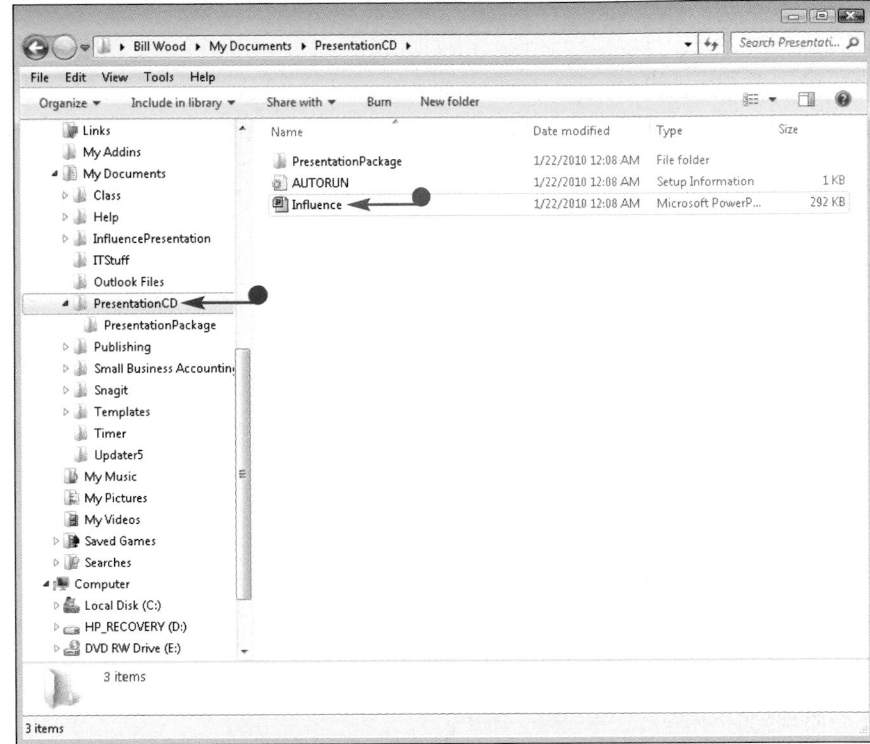

What is the purpose of the Options button?

Click the **Options** button to open the Options dialog box. You will find the options **Linked files** and **Embedded TrueType Fonts** — always keep these selected. This ensures that your presentation will look the way you intended. See Chapter 2 for more on embedded fonts. You can also set a password to open the presentation and check for personal data that may be in the presentation.

What is the laser tool?

PowerPoint 2010 has a new feature that looks like someone is pointing a laser at the screen. You can activate and use this feature during a slide show. To use it, simply press and hold Ctrl while you click and drag the mouse. Use it to point out important points during the slide show.

CHAPTER

14

Printing Presentations

There are several reasons to print a presentation. You may want a hard copy of your slides to review away from your computer, or you might want to print handouts for your audience to follow during your live presentation. Finally, you might print your presentation outline to preserve a hard copy of the presentation text.

Using Print Preview

It is a good practice to see what your slides look like on-screen before you use resources printing. Slides with colorful or dark backgrounds can use a lot of printer ink. You can use the Print Preview feature to see what your printout looks like before printing so you do not waste these resources.

Using Print Preview

1. Click the **File** tab.
2. Click **Print**.

   The slide show is displayed in the Print Preview view.

- You can use the navigation arrows or enter a page number in the text box to navigate through the pages.
- You can drag the Zoom slider or click the **Zoom In** (⊕) or **Zoom Out** (⊖) buttons at the ends of the slider to zoom.

3. Click **Edit Header & Footer**.

   The Header and Footer dialog box appears.

4. Select settings for Date and time, Slide number, and Footer (☐ changes to ☑).

   In this example, Date and time was selected.

Note: *See Chapter 8 to learn more about Header and Footer.*

5. Click **Apply to All**.

- Alternatively, you can click **Apply** to apply the setting to only the currently visible page.

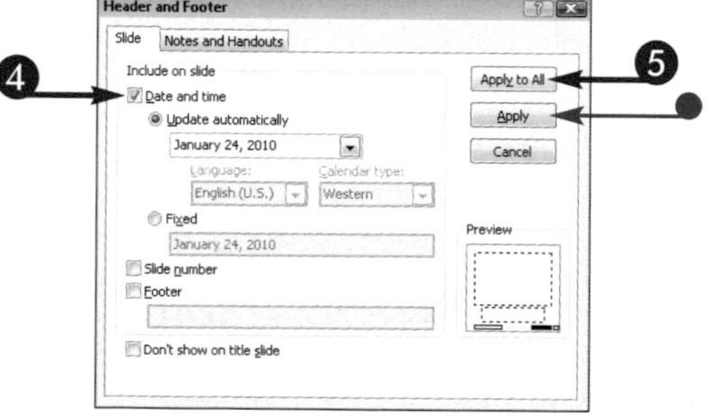

PowerPoint applies your new settings and closes the Header and Footer dialog box.

- The date and time appear in the Print Preview.

6. To change printers, click the **Printer** ▾.
7. Click a printer.

   The printer is changed.

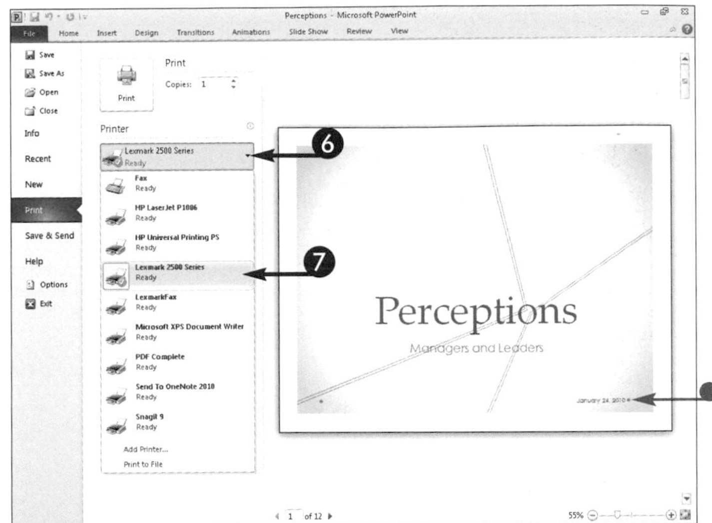

8. Click the spinner (⬍) on **Copies** or type a number in the text box to change the number of copies to print.
9. Click **Print**.

   PowerPoint prints the presentation.

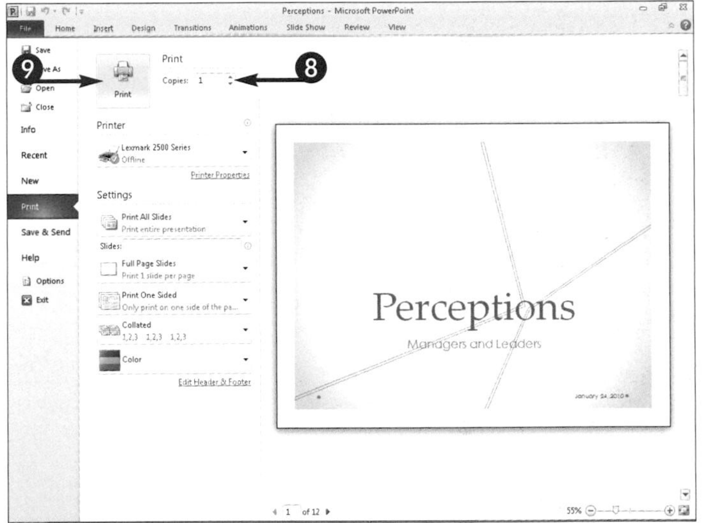

TIPS

Why is my Print Preview black and white when I have it set up for color?

Make sure that a color printer is selected for printing. PowerPoint knows if a black-and-white printer is selected for printing, so it automatically shows the Print Preview in black and white. If you have a color printer available, select it from the Printer list, and then the Print Preview becomes color.

How can I tell quickly how many pages will print if I choose to print multiple slides per page?

Look at the lower-left corner of the Print Preview screen. The status area will say how many total pages will print and which page you currently have displayed in Print Preview. So, for example, if you have 11 slides and want to print 2 slides per page, it will say 2 of 6, with 6 being the total number of pages and 2 being the current page number.

Print Slides

You can print a single slide, your entire presentation, or selected slides. You can print slides in black and white, or you can print slides in color if you have a color printer available. Slides will print with the orientation specified on the Design tab.

Print Slides

1. Click the **File** tab.
2. Click **Print**.

   The slide show is displayed in Print Preview view.
3. Click the **Settings** ▾.
4. Click **Custom Range**.

- You can click **Print Current Slide** to print the slide that is currently visible in Print Preview.
- You can click **Print Selection** to print the slide that is currently selected in Normal view.

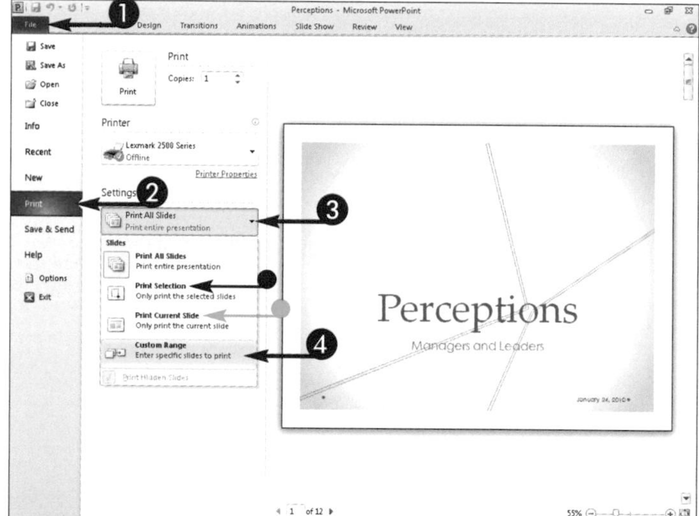

5. Type the slide numbers you want to print in the **Slides** text box, separated by commas.

- Click the **Information** icon (ⓘ) for more information.

   In this example, 1, 3, 7–9 was typed, which will print slide numbers 1, 3, 7, 8, and 9.
6. Click **Print**.

   PowerPoint prints your selection of slides.

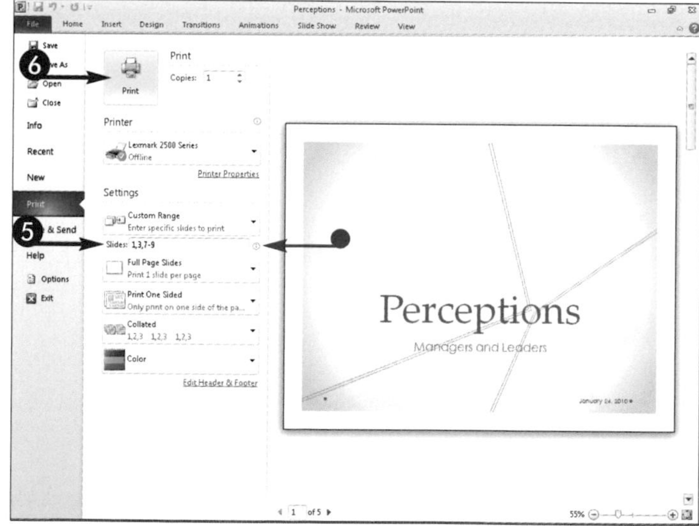

Print Hidden Slides

You may decide not to show every slide in a presentation, but you want to print the entire presentation for someone to review it. For example, you may decide to hide information concerning managers while showing a presentation to workers, but you want Human Resources to review it.

By default, hidden slides are printed, but you can easily adjust print settings to exclude hidden slides from printing.

Print Hidden Slides

❶ Click the **File** tab.

❷ Click **Print**.

The slide show is displayed in Print Preview view.

- Note that 12 pages are scheduled to print.

❸ Click the **Settings** ▾.

❹ Click **Print Hidden Slides** (☑ disappears).

Note: *This choice is disabled if there are no hidden slides in the presentation.*

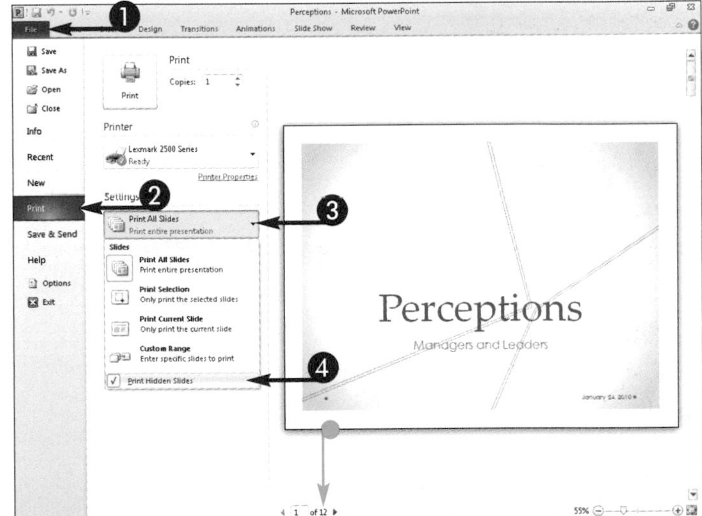

- Note that only 10 pages are now scheduled to print.

❺ Click **Print**.

PowerPoint prints the presentation without the two hidden slides.

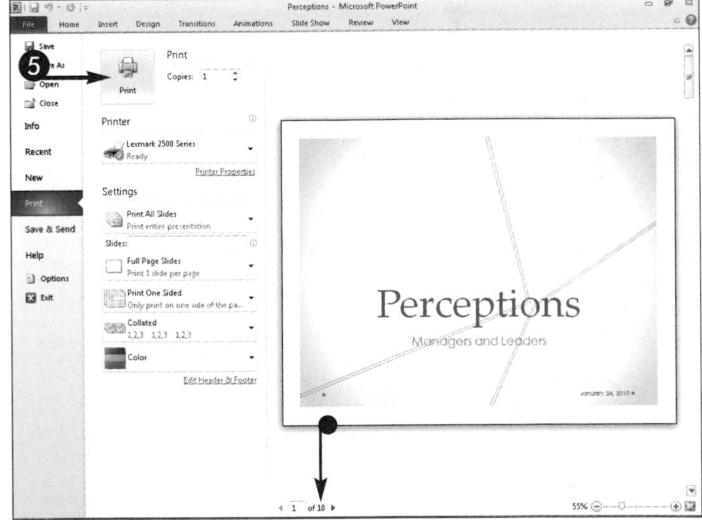

Print Handouts

Presentation handouts help audience members follow along and give them a place where they can write notes for future reference. You can print from one to nine slides on a handout page.

Printing several slides per page can save paper when you want to print handouts for a lengthy presentation, but make sure your audience can read the slides when there are several per page.

Print Handouts

1. Click the **File** tab.
2. Click **Print**.

   The slide show is displayed in Print Preview view.
3. Click the **Settings** ▾.

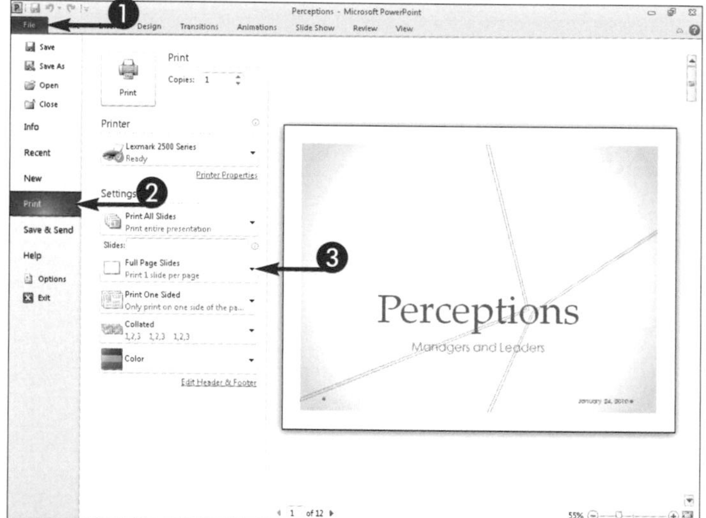

The gallery of print layouts appears.

4. Click a layout under the **Handouts** heading.

   In this example, 2 Slides was clicked.

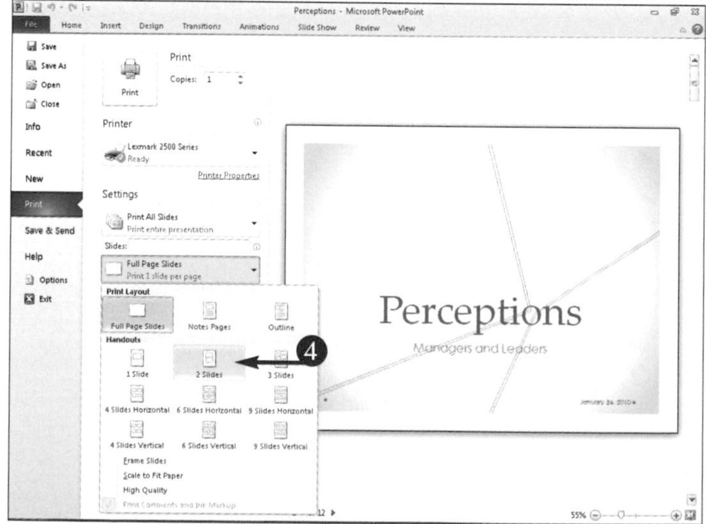

The slide layout changes on Print Preview, and the orientation drop-down list appears under the Settings heading.

5. Click the **Settings** ▾.
6. Click an orientation.

   In this example, Landscape Orientation was clicked.

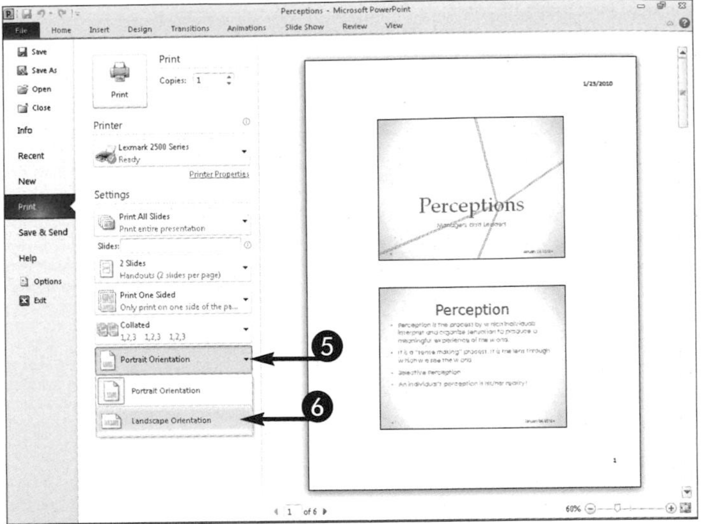

The page orientation of Print Preview changes.

7. Click **Print**.

   PowerPoint prints the presentation in the layout you specified.

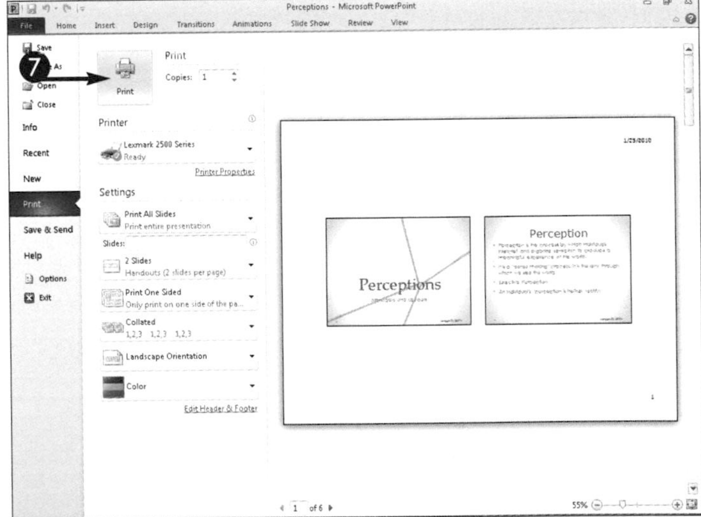

TIP

Can I add a background color to the handout page itself, or hide information like the page number?

Yes. Go to Handout Master view (see Chapter 8). Once there, you can make the changes:

- Enable (☑) or disable (☐) page information by clicking the check boxes in the Placeholders group.
- In this example, Page Number is disabled (☑).
- Click **Background Styles** and select a background from the gallery.
- Click **Close Master View** when you finish.

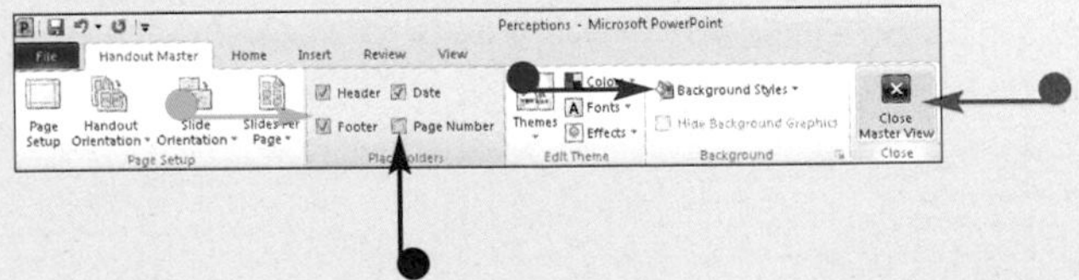

Print the Outline Only

Sometimes you want to focus only on the presentation text and not the graphic details. You may want to give a copy of the outline to audience members as a reference. You can print the presentation outline to do just that.

The printed outline includes titles, subtitles, and bullet points, but does not include any text entered in footers or inserted text boxes.

Print the Outline Only

1. Click the **File** tab.
2. Click **Print**.

   The slide show is displayed in Print Preview view.

3. Click the **Settings** ▾.

   The gallery of print layouts appears.

4. Click **Outline**.

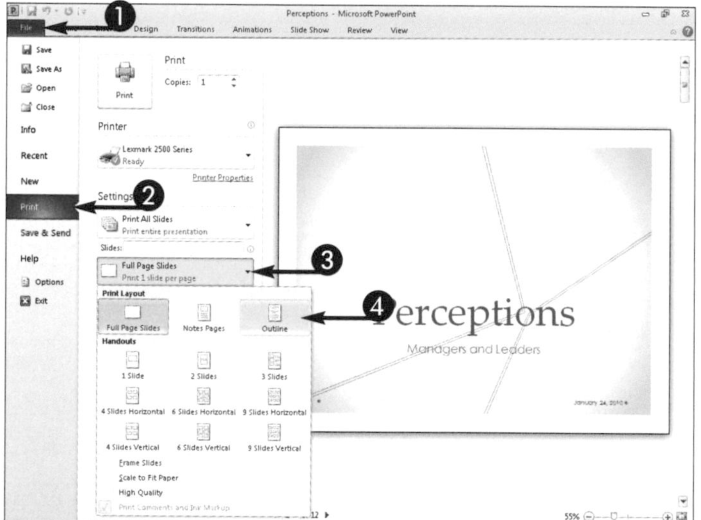

Print Preview becomes Outline view, and the orientation drop-down list appears under the Settings heading.

- You can change the orientation of the page.

5. Click **Print**.

   PowerPoint prints the outline.

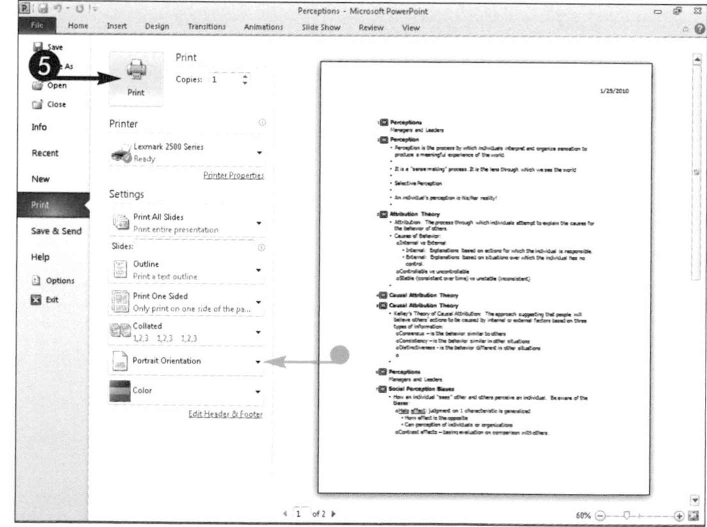

Print Notes

The slide show presenter may want a cheat sheet with additional facts or answers to likely audience questions. You can print each slide with associated notes that were typed in the Notes pane of Normal view. The speaker can then refer to the notes pages during the presentation, or possibly give it to audience members as a reference.

Print Notes

1. Click the **File** tab.
2. Click **Print**.

   The slide show is displayed in Print Preview view.

3. Click the **Settings** ▾.

   The gallery of print layouts appears.

4. Click **Notes Pages**.

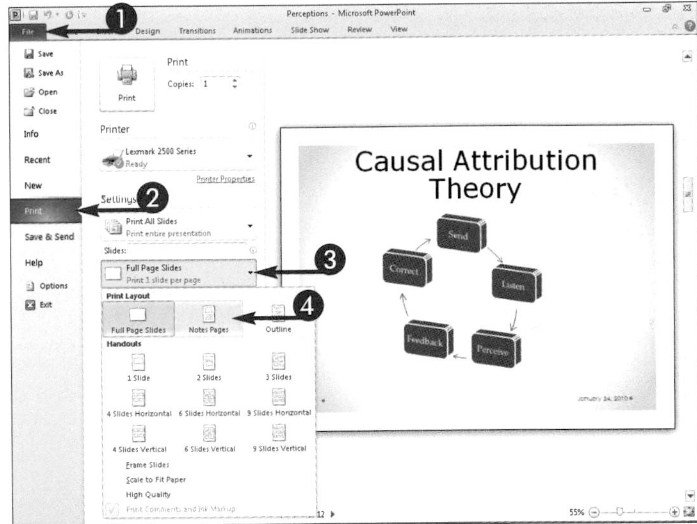

Print Preview becomes Notes Pages view, and the orientation drop-down list appears under the Settings heading.

- You can change the orientation of the page.

5. Click **Print**.

   PowerPoint prints the Notes Pages.

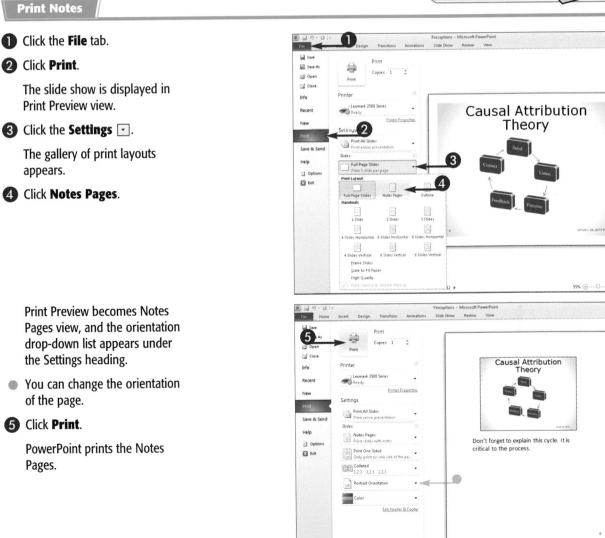

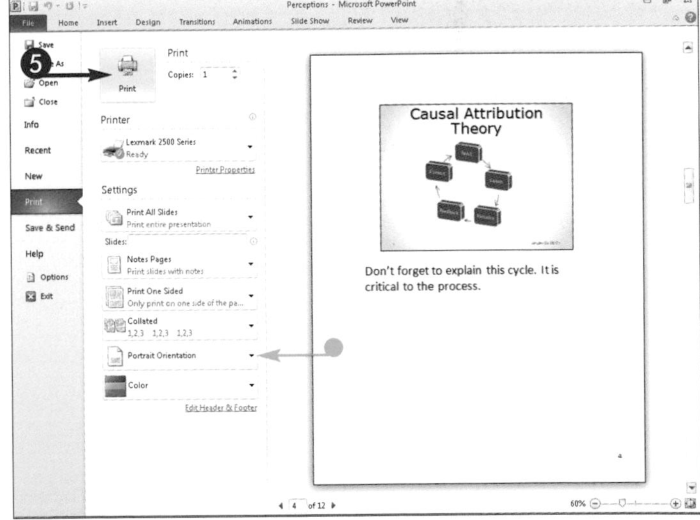

Print in Black and White or Grayscale

You can print a presentation in color (if you have a color printer), black and white, or grayscale. Grayscale provides some shading to help you see graphic and background elements. Black and white shows no shading and will show no background color or pattern.

For draft printouts, using grayscale or black and white reduces the use of expensive color ink.

Print in Black and White or Grayscale

1. Click the **File** tab.
2. Click **Print**.

   The slide show is displayed in Print Preview view.
3. Click the **Settings** ▾.
4. Click **Grayscale**.

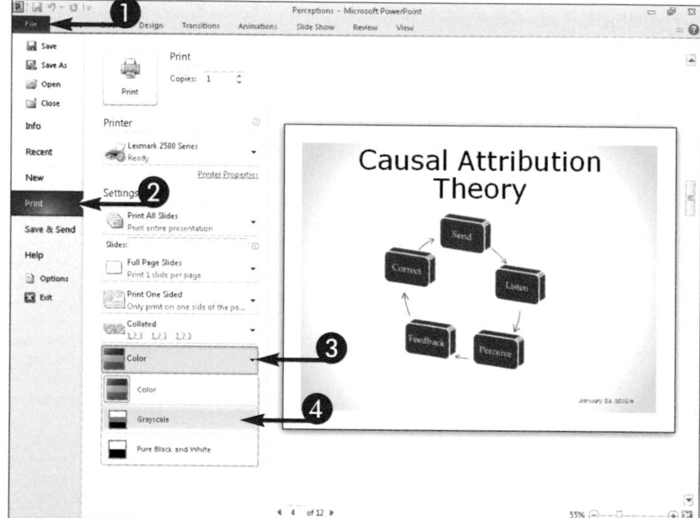

Print Preview appears in grayscale.

5. Click **Print**.

   PowerPoint prints the presentation in grayscale.

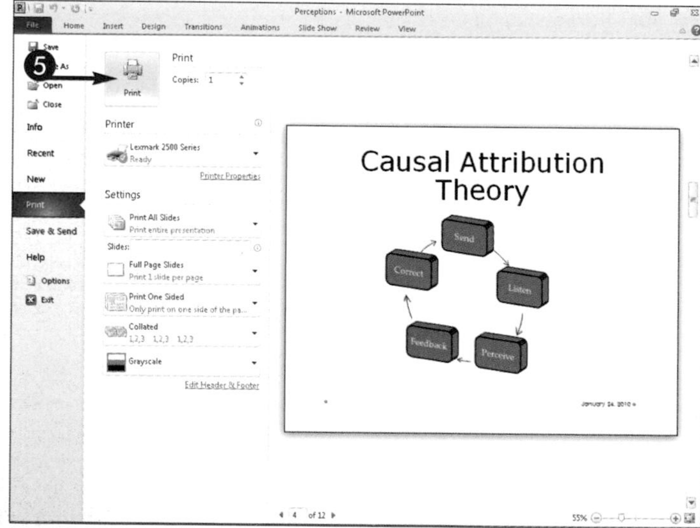

Frame Slides

You can print slides with a frame, which places a neat borderline around the edge of the slides and defines them on a printed page.

By default, slides print without any kind of border around them. Sometimes adding a frame improves the appearance of the printout by defining the edge of the slides, especially if the slide background is white or very light.

Frame Slides

1. Click the **File** tab.
2. Click **Print**.

   The slide show is displayed in Print Preview view.
3. Click the Settings ▾.

   The gallery of print layouts appears.
4. Click **Frame Slides** (☑ appears next to it to show it is selected).

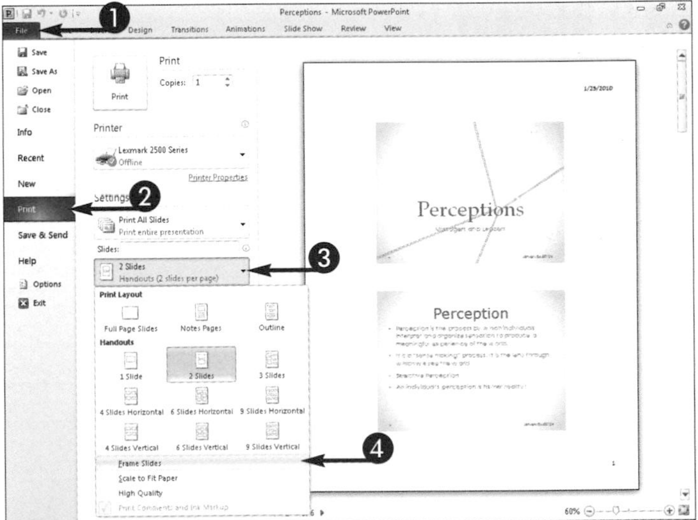

- Print Preview appears with borders around the slides.

5. Click **Print**.

   PowerPoint prints the presentation.

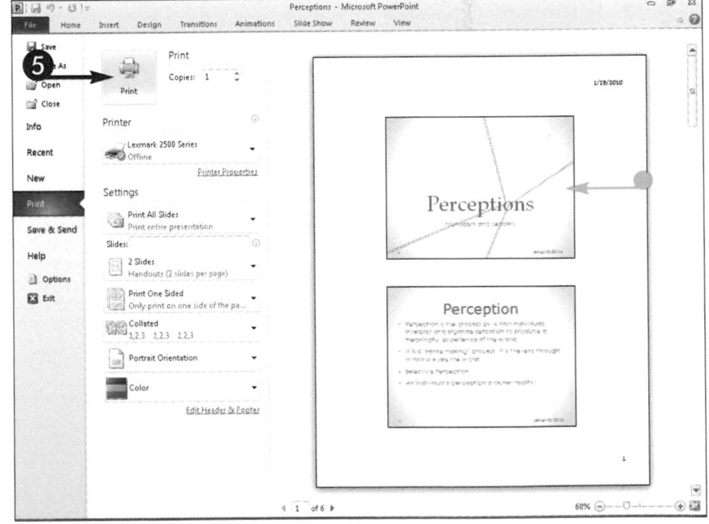

CHAPTER 15

Publishing Presentations

PowerPoint enables you to share your presentation in many different ways. You can save your slide show as different file types such as a PDF, Word, or video file. You can publish slides as JPEG or TIFF graphics.

Share Presentations

PowerPoint presentations have become so portable and versatile that posting them as Web pages is no longer needed and is no longer available in 2010. There now are easier, more efficient, and more effective ways to show your slide show to others. You can share your presentation with e-mail, network drives, SharePoint, or Internet sites.

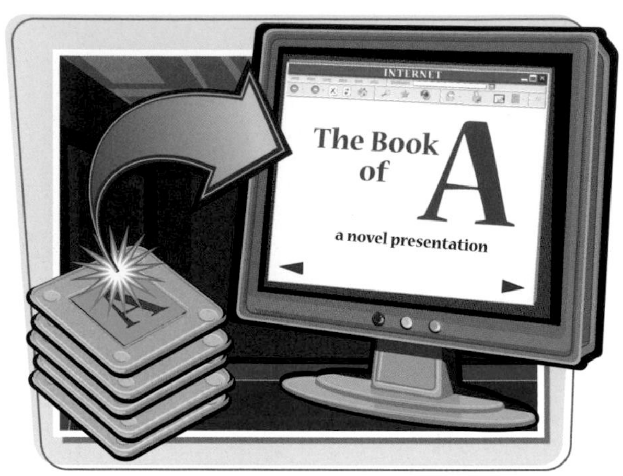

E-mail a Presentation

E-mail is an excellent way to send your presentation to others because most people today are proficient with e-mail. You may simply want others to view a slide show, or have someone review the presentation to get his or her opinion on it. Save the presentation as the appropriate file type for your purpose, and then e-mail it as an attachment, or save it to a shared location and e-mail a link.

Presenting in Alternative Ways

You cannot necessarily always be somewhere to present a slide show, or your audience may not be together at the same location. Your viewers may be traffic passing a shop or an exhibit at a convention. Regardless of these factors, PowerPoint gives you the ability to present your slide show. You can present your slide show remotely over the Web or on a monitor in an exhibit or kiosk.

Compare PowerPoint Presentations

PowerPoint enables you to compare a presentation that others have edited with the original. E-mail a copy to a peer for review and changes, or place a copy on a network drive and allow peers to review and edit it from there. After everyone has made changes, you can open the original and compare the two.

Create a Video of a Presentation

Creating a video of your presentation gives you complete control over how it is shown and how it is distributed. It enables you to distribute the presentation by any means, and allows almost anybody to view it because it is saved as a Windows Media Video (WMV) file, which can be view on most computers.

Broadcast a Slide Show

You can broadcast a slide show, which allows you to present your slide show live from a remote location to anyone who has access to the Internet. PowerPoint creates a link that you can share with other people. All your audience needs is a Web browser and a link to the broadcast!

Share Your Presentation with SkyDrive or SharePoint

You can post a presentation to SkyDrive or SharePoint, but the process involves knowledge of those services, and therefore is outside the scope of this book. SharePoint is a service used by some companies to share documents. SkyDrive is a storage location that is available to anybody that has a Microsoft Live account, and can be accessed by most computers that have access to the Internet.

Compare Presentations

If you have someone review your presentation and make changes, usually you want to compare the changes to the original. You can easily compare the edited presentation with the original by using PowerPoint's automation. You can accept or reject changes that others have made to a presentation while comparing the edited version with the original.

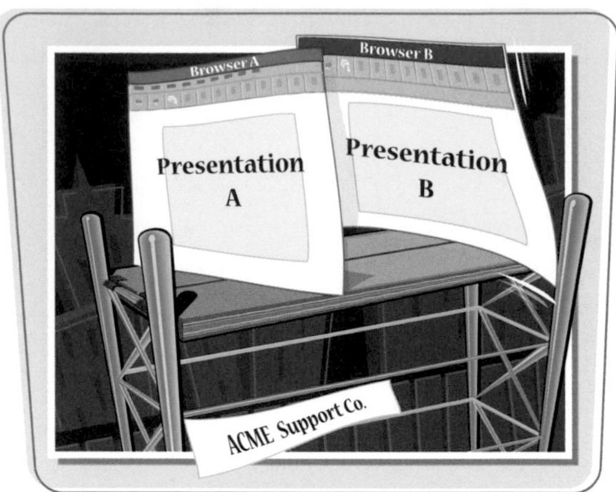

Compare Presentations

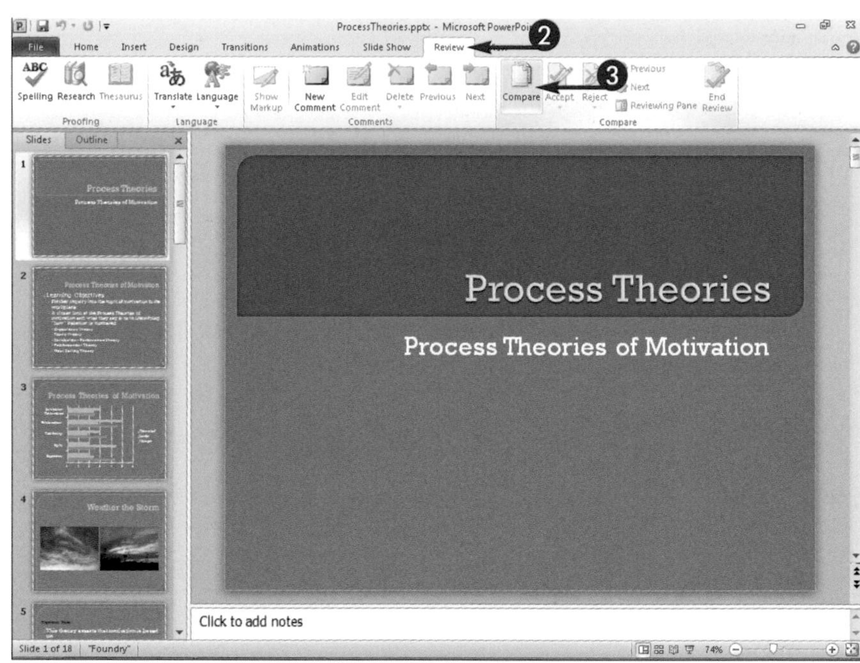

1. Open the original presentation that you sent to others for review and changes.

***Note:** To learn how to open a presentation, see Chapter 3.*

2. Click the **Review** tab while in Normal view.

3. Click **Compare**.

The Choose File to Merge with Current Presentation dialog box appears.

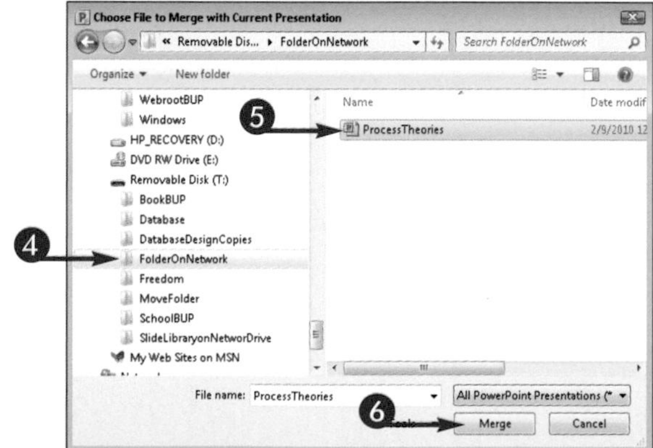

4. Click the folder that contains the edited presentation.

In this example, FolderOnNetwork was clicked.

5. Click the presentation that was edited by others.

***Note:** The name of the edited presentation does not need to be the same as the original.*

6. Click **Merge**.

- PowerPoint compares the presentation and the Reviewing Pane (aka Revisions Pane) appears.

7 Click a slide you think has changes from the original.

- All changes appear with a ▢ next to them.
- All changes are listed in the Details tab of the Reviewing Pane.

8 Click a ▢.

A box showing details of the changes for this object appears.

9 Click a detail to accept a change (☐ changes to ☑).

Note: *Changes that remain unselected (☐) are rejected.*

- The change is applied immediately.
- Icons with check marks (☑) contain accepted changes.

10 Repeat Steps **7** to **9** for other slides that have changes.

11 Click **End Review**.

A dialog box appears and asks if you want to end the review.

12 Click **Yes**.

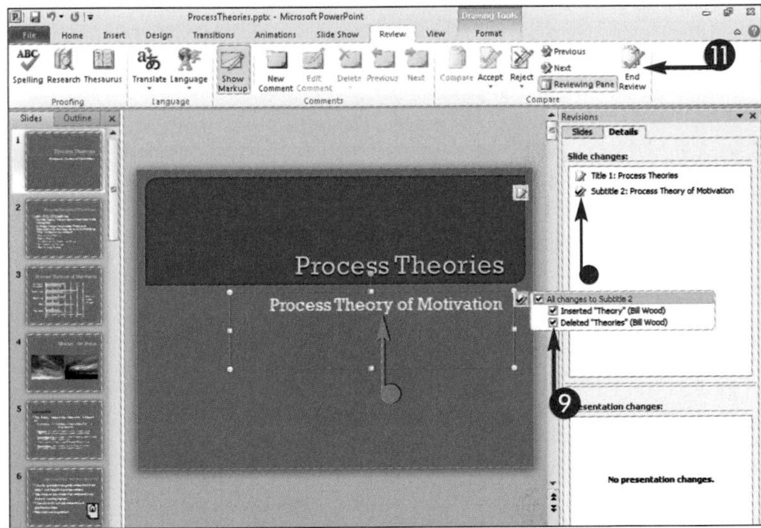

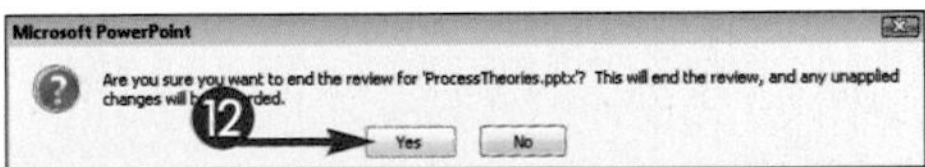

Can I see the slides from the edited presentation?

Yes. The Reviewing Pane automatically appears with the Details tab displayed. Click the **Slides** tab. PowerPoint shows you the slide from the edited presentation that correlates to the slide that is selected in your presentation.

Is there a way to accept all changes on a slide?

Yes. Click the **Review** tab and then click ▾ on the **Accept** button. On the menu that appears, click **Accept All Changes to the Current Slide**. Note that you can also accept changes to the entire presentation.

Make a PDF Document from a Presentation

You can make a PDF (portable document format) file from your presentation so that anyone with a PDF reader can view your presentation — all without buying a PDF writer! A PDF file can be viewed on computer monitors or it can be printed on paper. Saving a presentation as a PDF file preserves your presentation's fonts, formatting, and images.

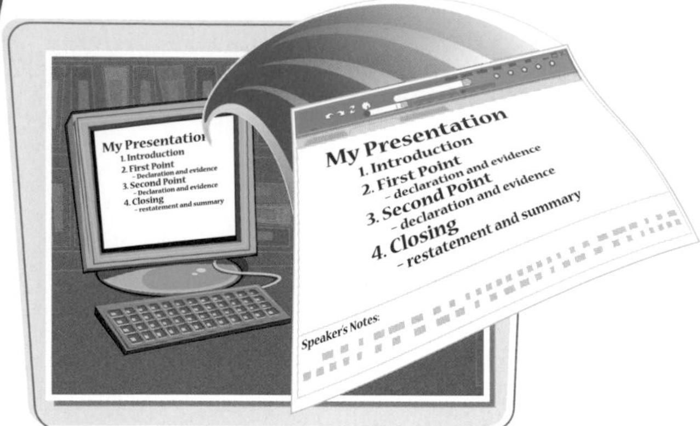

Make a PDF Document from a Presentation

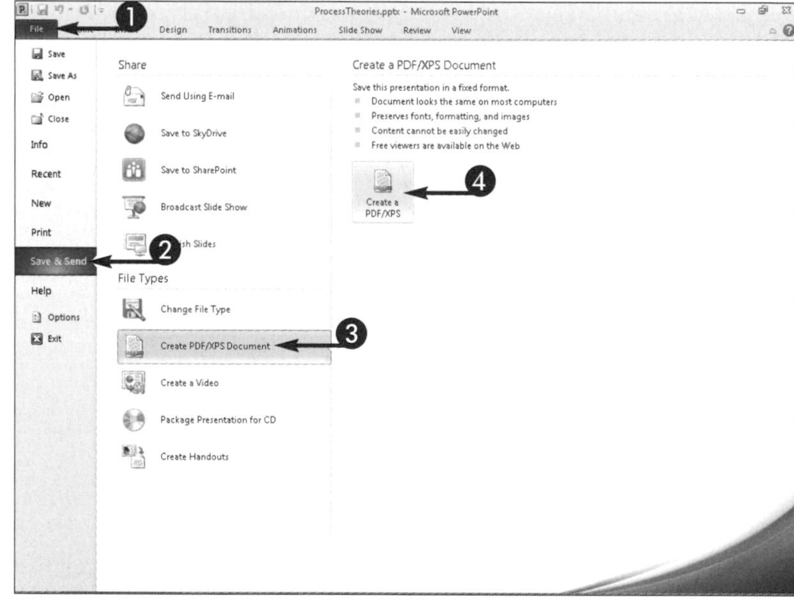

1. In Normal view, click the **File** tab.
2. Click **Save & Send**.
3. Click **Create PDF/XPS Document**.
4. Click **Create a PDF/XPS**.

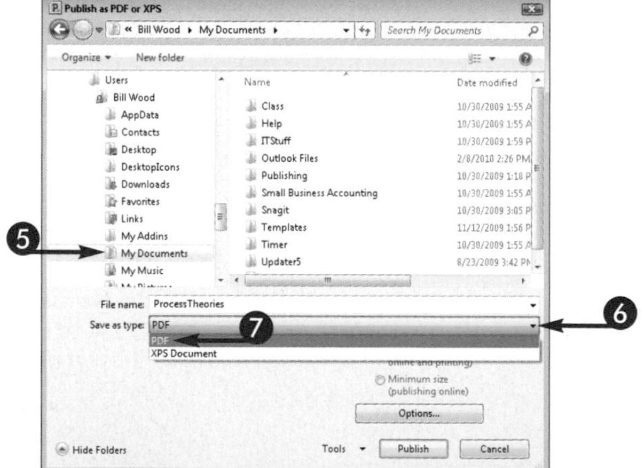

The Publish as PDF or XPS dialog box appears.

5. Click the folder where you want to save your file.
6. Click the **Save as type** ▾.
7. Click **PDF**.

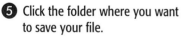

8. Click in the **File name** text box to select it, and then type a file name.

   In this example, MotivationTheory was typed.

- Make sure **Open file after publishing** is selected (☑).

9. Click **Publish**.

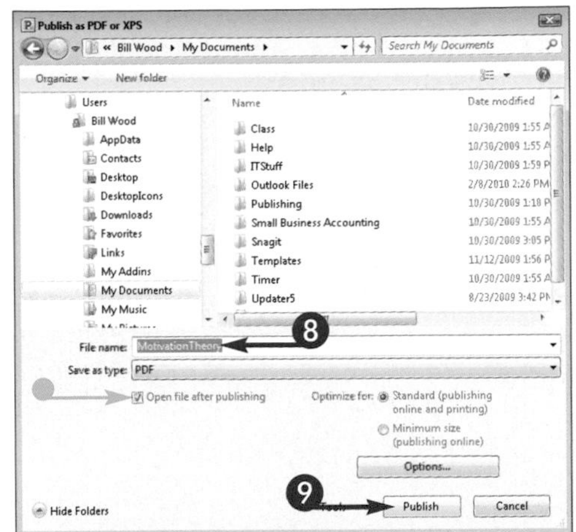

The dialog box closes and PowerPoint creates the PDF file in the specified folder, and then opens the file with your PDF reader.

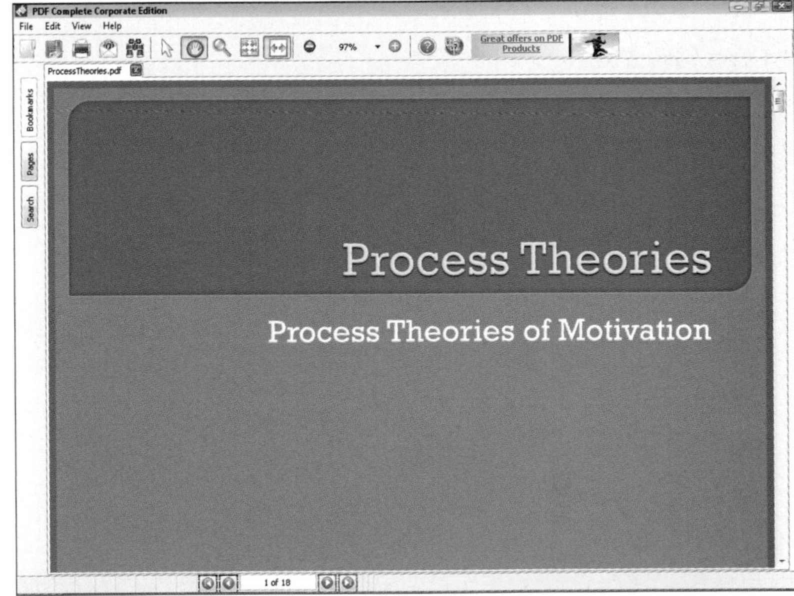

TIPS

Can I get a PDF reader if I do not have one?

Yes. PDF viewers are free, so almost any computer can open a PDF file. Most computers already have a PDF reader installed at the time of purchase, but if you don't have one, you can go to the Adobe Web site, `www.adobe.com`, and download its Acrobat Reader.

What is the advantage to preserving the fonts, formatting, and images of my presentation?

Computers can have different sets of fonts loaded with their software. It is possible that a computer viewing your presentation does not have the font you used. Preserving the fonts, formatting, and images carries that information along with the presentation so it looks the same on any computer.

Create a Video of a Presentation

You can create a video of your presentation that you can take or send anywhere. Almost anybody can view it because it is saved as a Windows Media Video (WMV) format, which can be viewed on most computers. You can use timings and narrations that you saved in the presentation or you set a time to advance slides while you create the video.

Create a Video of a Presentation

❶ Click the **File** tab.

❷ Click **Save & Send**.

❸ Click **Create a Video**.

❹ Click the Use Recorded Timing and Narrations ▾ under Create a Video.

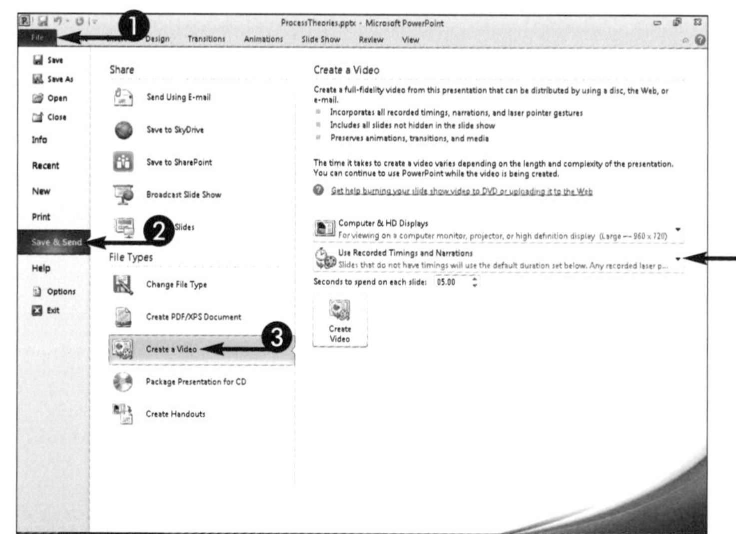

The drop-down list appears.

❺ If you have no recorded timings, click **Don't Use Recorded Timings and Narrations**.

● Click **Use Recorded Timings and Narrations** if you recorded them in your presentation and want to use them.

Note: *If you have narrations and timings in your presentation, you probably want to use them.*

● Click **Record Timings and Narrations** if you want to record them at this time.

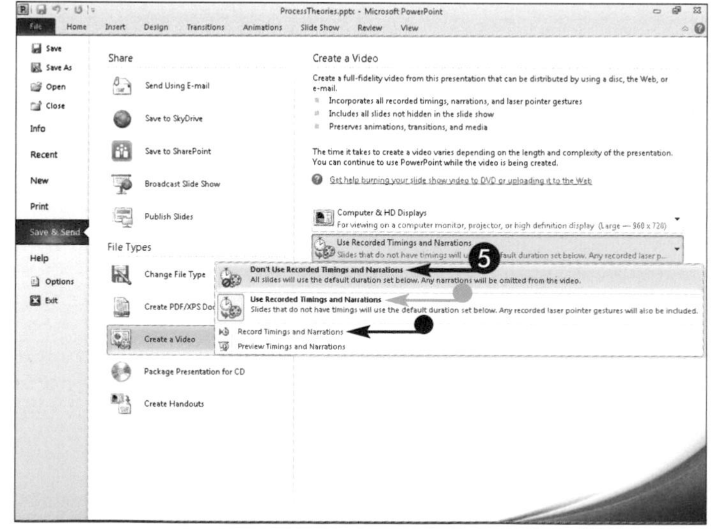

6. If you clicked **Don't Use Recorded Timings and Narrations** in the previous step, click ⬍ to change the time in the **Seconds to spend on each slide** text box, or click the text box and type the time directly into the text box.

- Notice you can change the resolution of the video.

7. Click **Create Video**.

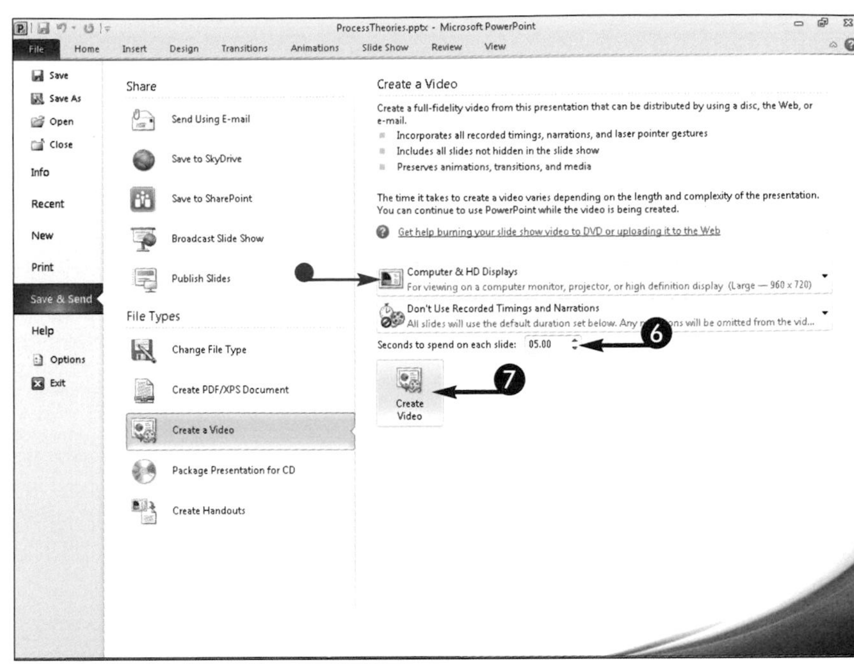

The Save As dialog box appears.

8. Click the folder where you want to save the video.
9. Click the **File name** text box to select it, and then type a filename.

   In this example, Motivation was typed.

10. Click **Save**.

    The dialog box closes and PowerPoint creates the video file in the specified folder.

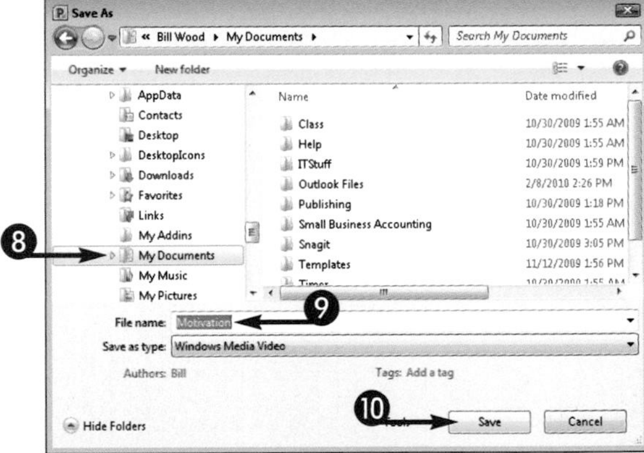

When I click Save, nothing seems to happen – why?

It takes a long time for PowerPoint to make the video. Curiously enough, it does not notify you when it is done. However, while it's working, you will see a status meter at the bottom in the status bar. When it disappears the video is done.

Why would I want to change the resolution?

The higher the resolution of your video, the bigger the file and the more memory it takes to run it. This affects load times and sometimes the quality of playback if computer resources are limited. The drop-down list has settings for the Internet and for portable devices. You may choose to change the resolution if that is your target audience.

Create Handouts with Microsoft Word

Sometimes you may want more versatility than the PowerPoint handouts give you. You can automatically create handouts with Microsoft Word to get all the versatility and control you need. After PowerPoint creates the Word document, you can edit it just like any other Word document. You can even edit the slides by double-clicking them.

The Word document is not automatically saved. Remember to save it.

Create Handouts with Microsoft Word

1. Click the **File** tab.
2. Click **Save & Send**.
3. Click **Create Handouts**.
4. Click **Create Handouts**.

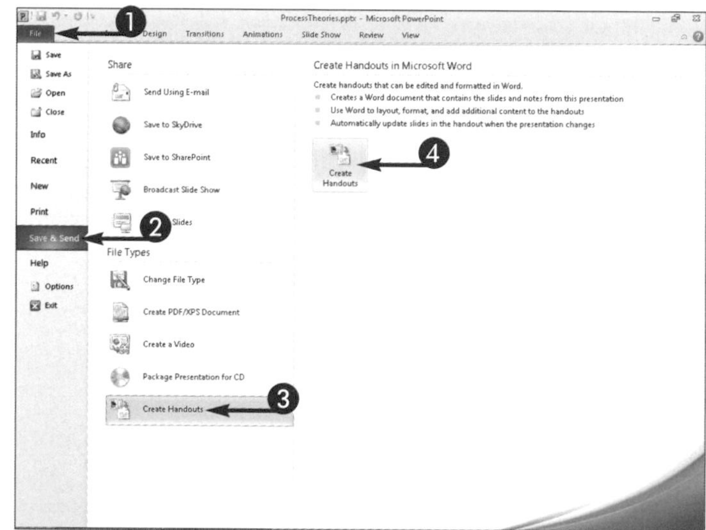

5. Click an option under **Page layout in Microsoft Word** (◎ changes to ◉).
6. Click an option under **Add slides to Microsoft Word document** (◎ changes to ◉).
7. Click **OK**.

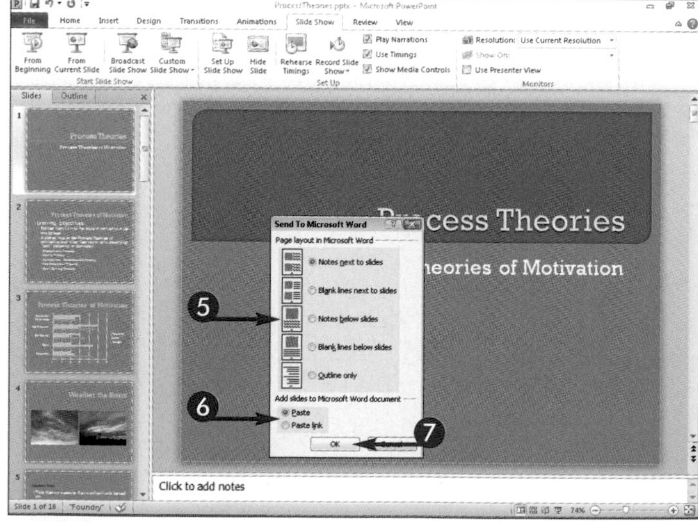

PowerPoint creates a Word document that appears with the layout you chose.

Note: *The Word document may appear only as a blinking icon on the Windows taskbar. Click the icon to see the Word document.*

Note: *The Word document is not saved automatically. If you are keeping it, save it now.*

8. Edit the Word document just like any other Word document.

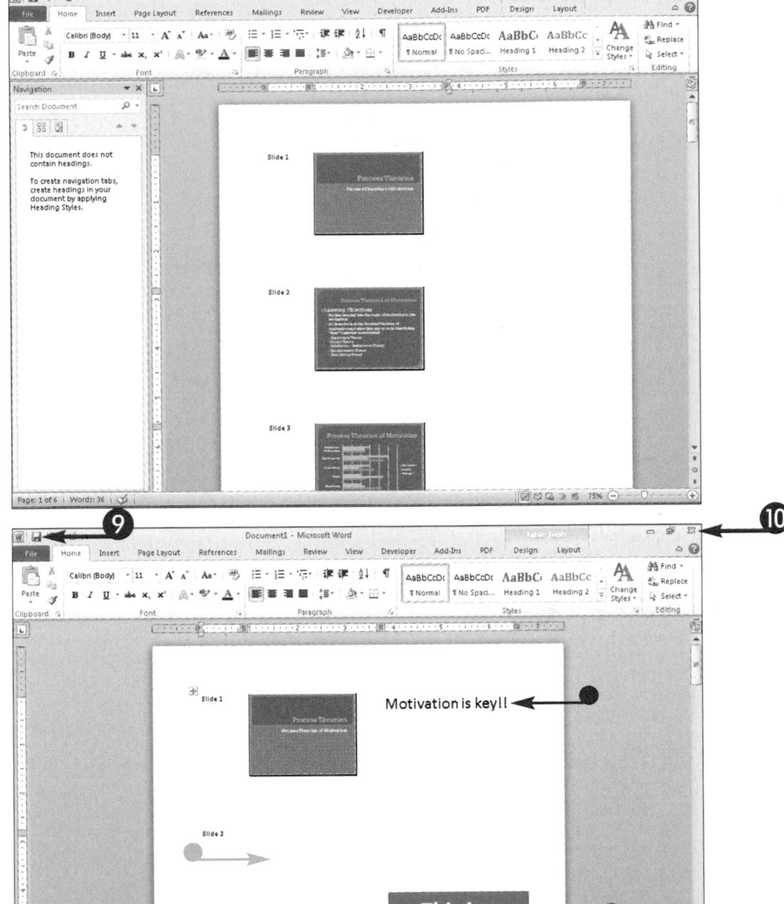

- You can delete slides or double-click slides to edit them.
- You can type text or change the slide names.
- You can add graphics.

9. Click the **Save** icon (💾) to save the Word document.
10. Click the **Close** button (☒) to close the Word document.

TIPS

Why does my computer lock up when I try to create handouts with Microsoft Word?

First, the process takes a while, so please be patient. Second, the Word document may open minimized, which means it only appears on the Windows taskbar. Go to the Windows taskbar and click the Word document (it should be blinking). The document that PowerPoint created will appear.

In Step 6, what is the difference between Paste and Paste link?

If you choose **Paste,** PowerPoint pastes slide objects into the Word document. If you select **Paste link**, the slides in Word are linked to the presentation. When you edit the slides, they change in both the PowerPoint presentation and the Word document. Choosing **Paste link** creates a smaller Word document.

Save a Presentation as a Slide Show

You can save a presentation in such a way that it opens automatically as a slide show. Make it easy on others and yourself while viewing your presentation with a PowerPoint Show.

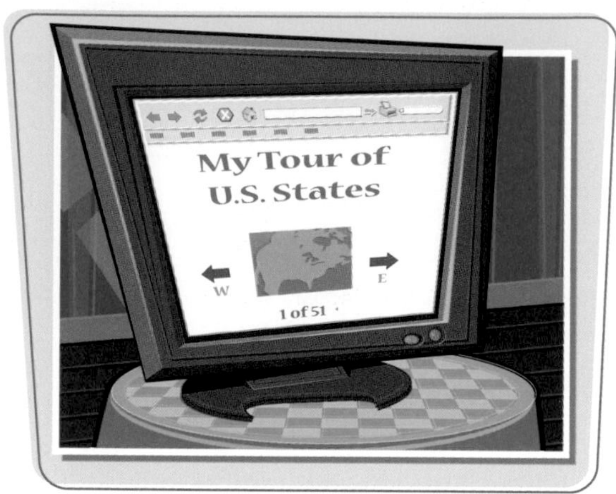

Save a Presentation as a Slide Show

1. Click the **File** tab.
2. Click **Save & Send**.
3. Click **Change File Type**.

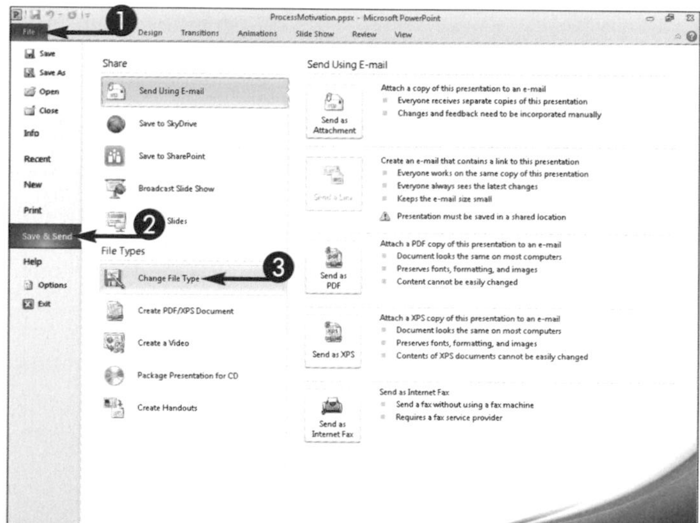

- The Change File Type menu appears.

4. Click **PowerPoint Show**.

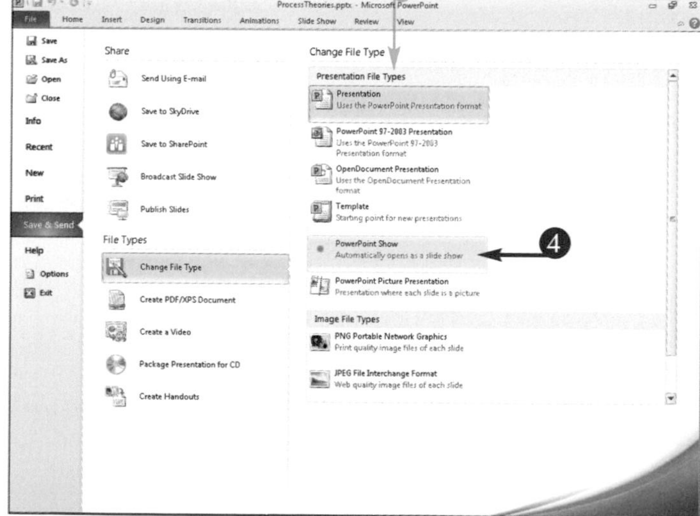

The Save As dialog box appears.

5. Click the folder where you want to save your file.
6. Click the **File name** text box to select it, and then type a filename.

   In this example, ProcessMotivation was typed.

- Make sure PowerPoint Show appears in the Save as type box. If not, click the **Save as type** ▾ and select it from the drop-down list.

7. Click **Save**.

   The dialog box closes and PowerPoint creates the PowerPoint Show file in the specified folder.

   Find the file in the specified folder and open it. It opens as a slide show.

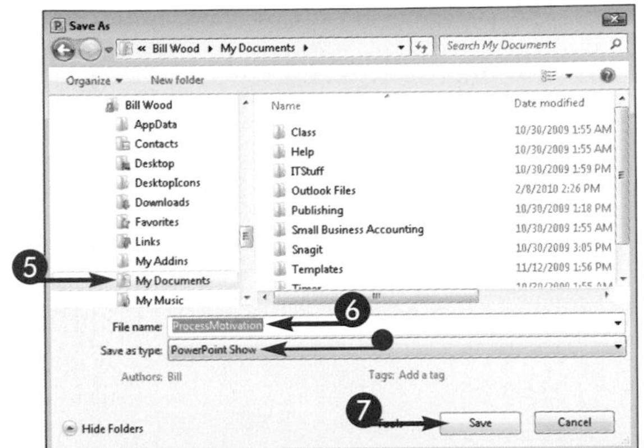

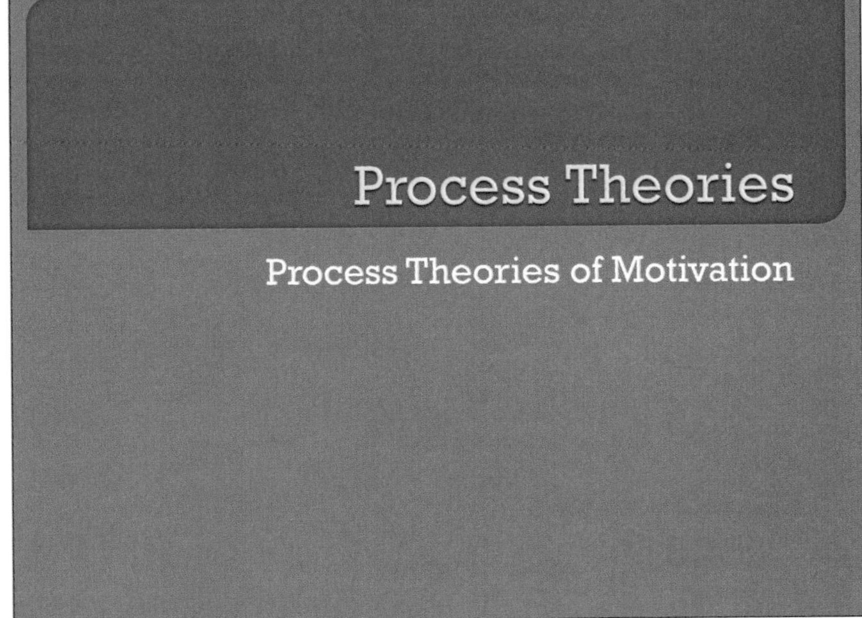

TIPS

What does the PPSX mean?

PPSX is the particular extension of a PowerPoint Show file. PPTX is the extension for a PowerPoint presentation; PPTM is the extension for a presentation that has macros in it; and POTX is the extension for a PowerPoint Template. PPT is a presentation in the 97-2003 format and ODP is the OpenDocument presentation format.

Are there other advantages to sending a PowerPoint Show (PPSX) to someone instead of a standard presentation (PPTX)?

Yes. If you send this format to others instead of the standard presentation format, they will not be able to see or change the details of your design. They also will not be able to copy any part of your presentation.

Publish Slides as Graphics

You can create a graphic of each slide in your presentation so that you can use them for unusual applications. You may want to post them on a Web site, make high-quality prints, or make them part of a database.

There is no need to create a new folder to hold the graphic files – a new folder is created during this process.

Publish Slides as Graphics

1. Click the **File** tab.
2. Click **Save & Send**.
3. Click **Change File Type**.

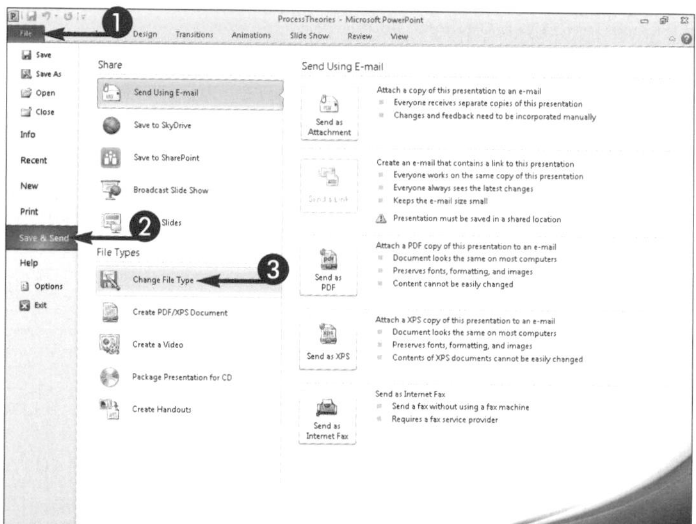

- The Change File Type menu appears.

4. Click **JPEG File Interchange Format**.

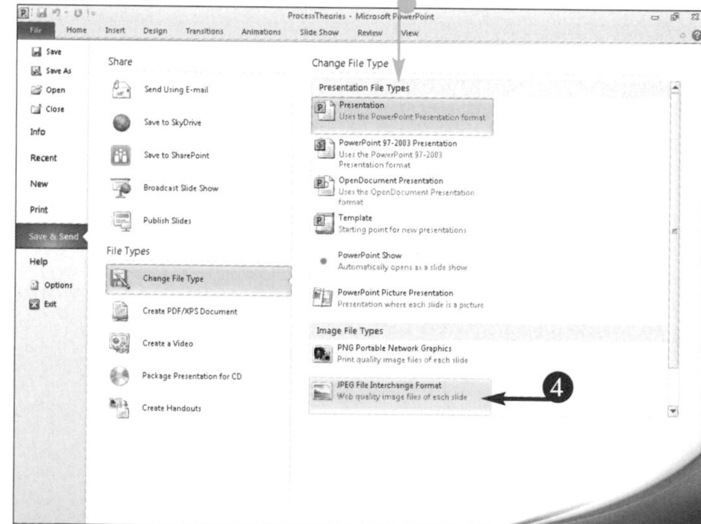

The Save As dialog box appears.

5. Click the folder where you want to save your file.
6. Click the **File name** text box to select it, and then type a filename.

   In this example, Motivation was typed.

- Make sure JPEG File Interchange Format appears in the Save as type box. If not, click the **Save as type** ▾ and select it from the drop-down list.

7. Click **Save**.

   A dialog box appears asking if you want to save all slides or the current slide.

8. Click **Every Slide**.

- You can click **Current Slide Only** if you want to save only the current slide.

   A dialog box appears.

9. Click **OK**.

   PowerPoint creates a JPEG picture graphic for each slide in the folder you specified.

   In this example, PowerPoint created a folder called Motivation in the specified folder — the Motivation folder contains the picture graphics.

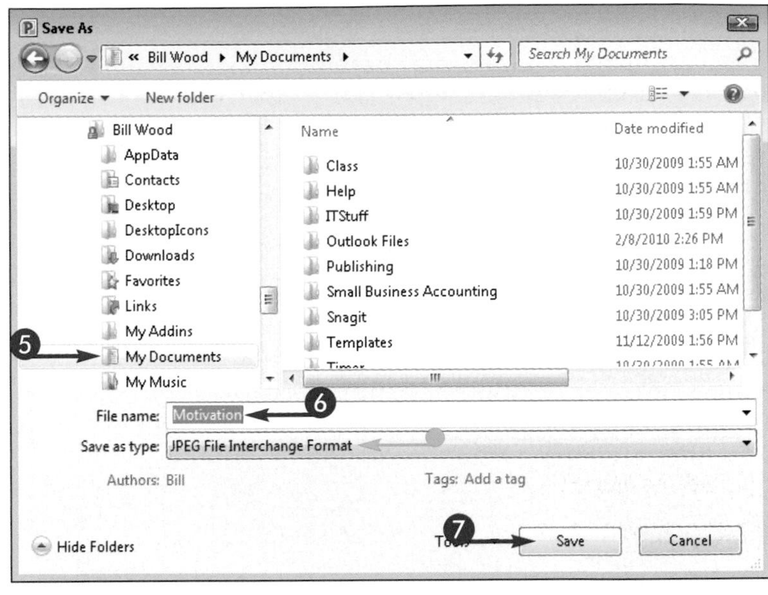

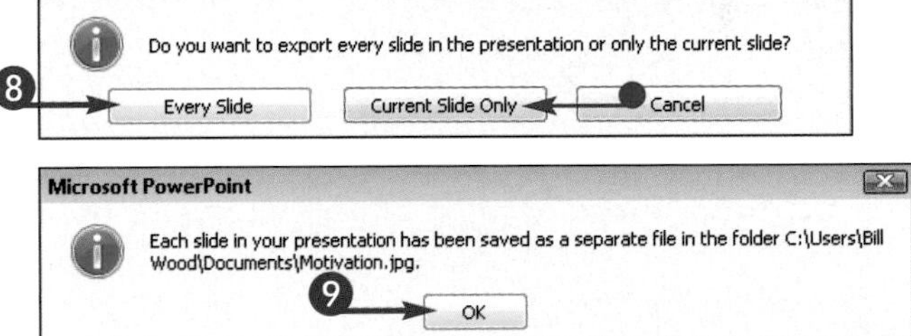

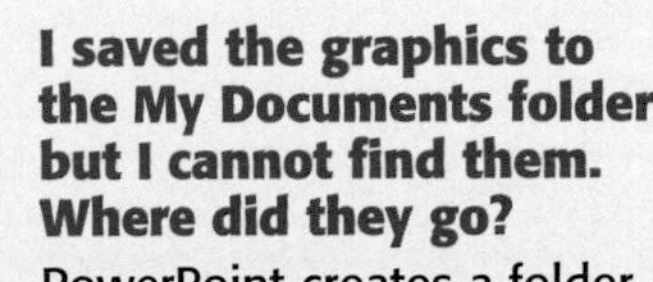

How does the Image File Type PNG differ from JPEG?

A JPEG is a picture type that is compressed and trades image quality for smaller file size. The PNG format uses a compression format that does not trade image quality for file size, so the image quality is better than JPEG. PNG produces better results for certain applications like printing. PNG files are larger than the comparable JPEG files.

I saved the graphics to the My Documents folder, but I cannot find them. Where did they go?

PowerPoint creates a folder for you and places all the graphics in it. You will find this folder in the folder you specified (My Documents in this case) and it will be named whatever you entered into the File name text box.

Broadcast a Presentation

You can present a slide show without a physical meeting room. PowerPoint 2010 includes a new feature that enables you to remotely present a slide show to anyone with an Internet connection. Make the connection, send a link to your audience, and enjoy the show.

You must have a Microsoft Windows Live ID to use the Broadcast Slide Show feature — see the Tip section for details.

Broadcast a Presentation

1. Click the **File** tab.
2. Click **Save & Send**.
3. Click **Broadcast Slide Show**.
4. Click **Broadcast Slide Show**.

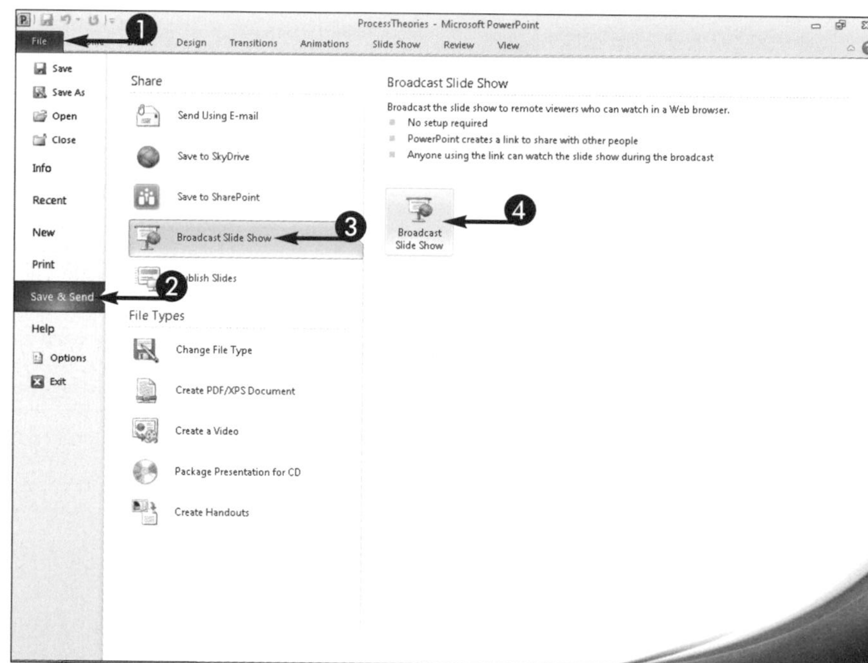

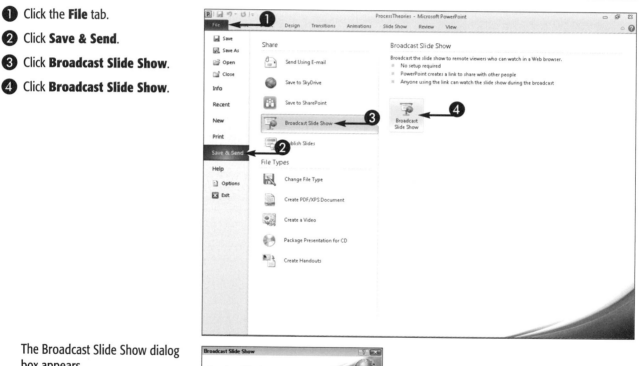

The Broadcast Slide Show dialog box appears.

5. Click **Start Broadcast**.

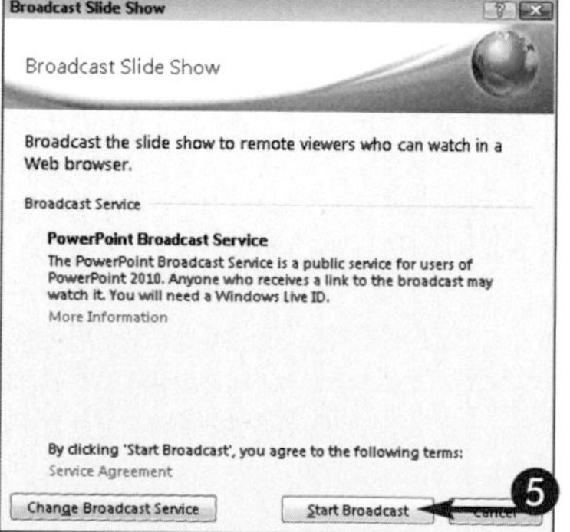

The Windows Security dialog box appears.

6. Click **User name** and type your Windows Live ID user name.
7. Click **Password** and type your Windows Live ID password.
8. Click **OK**.

   The Broadcast Slide Show dialog box appears.

9. Click **Send in Email**.

   Microsoft Outlook opens a new e-mail with this link pasted in it. Send this link to your audience members. When they receive it, they simply click the link to join the broadcast.

10. After audience members have received the e-mail and verified the connection, click **Start Slide Show**.

    The slide show begins.

    When the slide show ends, PowerPoint displays the Broadcast view.

11. Click **End Broadcast** to exit the Broadcast view.

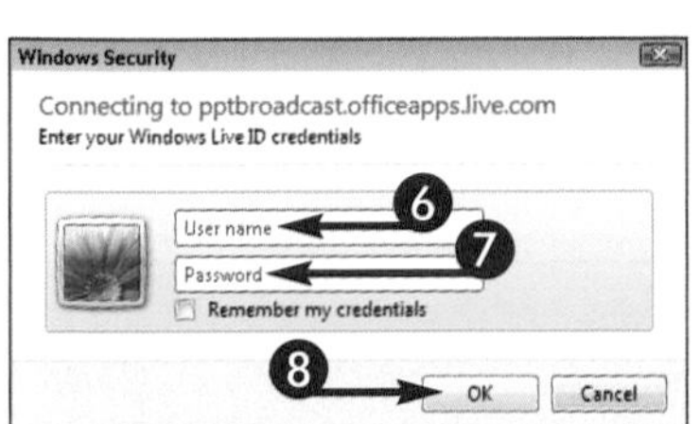

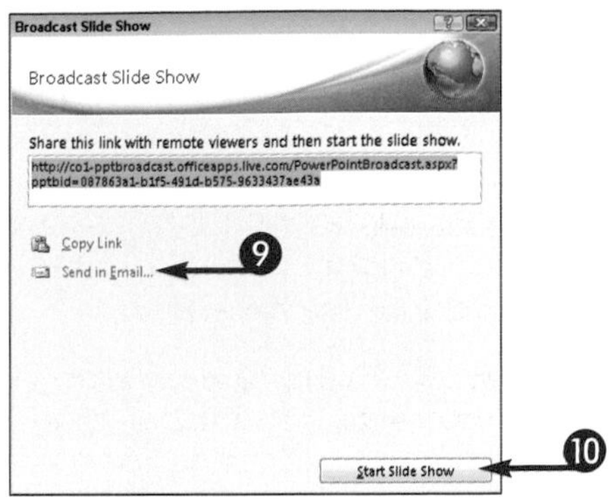

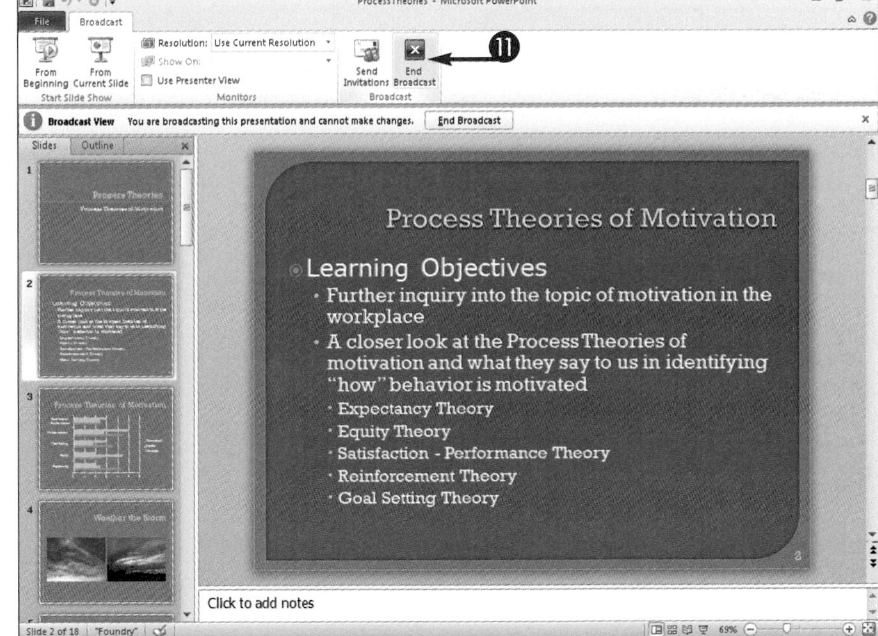

TIPS

Can I send the link to audience members if I do not use Outlook?

Yes. Before you begin the broadcast, open your e-mail program and start a new e-mail. When the dialog box showing the link appears, click **Copy Link**, and then paste it in the body of the e-mail and send it. You can press Ctrl + P to paste the link.

How do I get a Windows Live ID?

Windows Live is a free service provided by Microsoft. Go to `www.microsoft.live.com` and click the **Sign up** button. Type the required information into the text fields on the **Create your Windows Live ID** Web page, and then click **I accept**.

CHAPTER 16

Finalizing and Making a Presentation

Before you present your PowerPoint slide show, you should be sure you understand the tools available to you during the show. Familiarity with the tools will enable things to flow smoothly during your presentation.

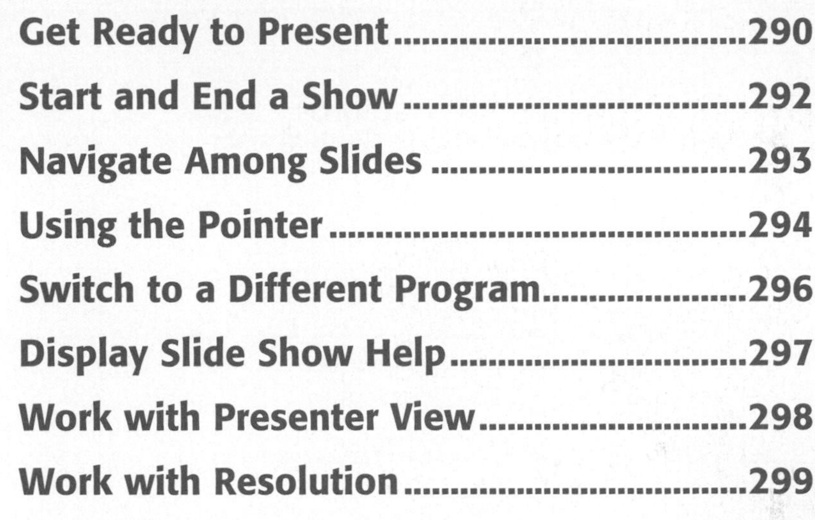

Get Ready to Present

A successful live presentation requires solid content, good design, and a prepared presenter. Preparing to make a presentation involves double-checking your presentation for problems and getting comfortable with your material and presentation environment.

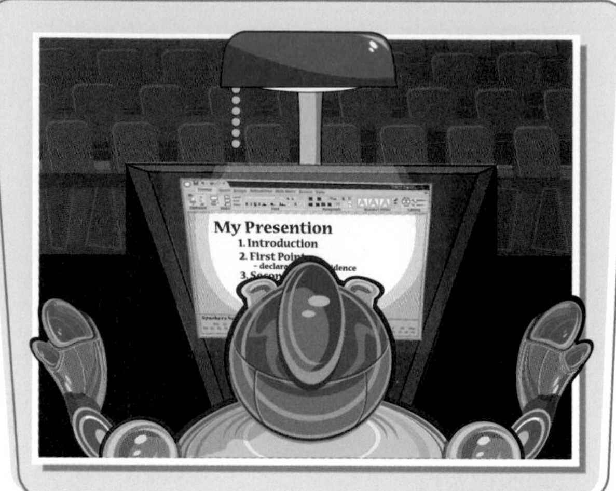

Check Your Presentation for Errors

Checking your slides for details such as spelling, grammar, and typos can save you a lot of embarrassment at showtime. Use the presentation outline to review the text so you are not distracted by design elements. A person should not proofread his or her own work. Have a third party review the presentation. That person may catch errors that you miss.

Rehearse the Slide Show

Practicing your presentation several times before you present it to an audience makes you feel comfortable with the material and your presentation style. Rehearse in front of a mirror or a friend, or even record yourself with a video camera and play the recording back. You can spot undesirable mannerisms or expressions that you want to try to avoid.

Verify Your Timing

Use the Rehearse Timings feature in PowerPoint to check your timing, and then edit your presentation or change the pacing to fit the time allotted to you. Review how long you take to present each slide, and use the information to make necessary changes to the presentation. See Chapter 11 for more about rehearsing your show.

Record a Narration

If you do not intend to deliver a live presentation, consider recording a narration. Even if your slide content is well prepared and explains your points nicely, a human voice can add a dimension to any presentation and help keep viewers focused. See Chapter 13 for information about recording a narration.

Know Your Presentation Space

To avoid problems during your presentation, visit the site before the presentation if you can. Knowing the size of the room, the acoustics, and the layout of the stage and audience seating can help you prepare. If the space is large, you may need a microphone. Close the blinds if the space is too bright to easily see the slide show.

Set Up Your Show

Be sure to check those all-important slide show settings. See Chapter 13 to review these. Before the slide show, you should set up the format for the presentation, such as live presentation versus one shown at a kiosk, which slides to include, monitors and resolution, and how you will control the advancement of the slides.

Save Your Presentation for the Road

Your presentation does you no good if it is sitting on your desktop while you are presenting on the road. You need a copy of the presentation. Even if you are using your laptop, bring a backup. You should package the presentation with the PowerPoint viewer in case you find yourself on a computer without PowerPoint — package any files that are linked to the presentation as well.

Start and End a Show

You are done creating your presentation and packaging it. All you need is to start the Slide Show view to run the show. You can end the show at any time or view all the slides.

You have the option to end the show with the last slide or with a black screen that instructs you to click to close the show.

Start and End a Show

Start a Show

1. Click the **Slide Show** tab.
2. Click **From Beginning**.

- You can click **From Current Slide** to start at the current slide.

Note: *You can also press* F5 *to begin the show.*

The slide show begins.

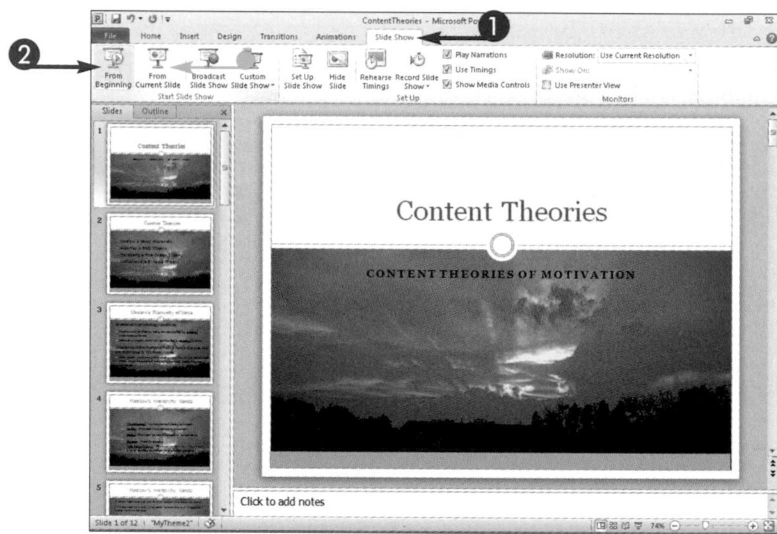

End a Show

1. To end the show before you reach the last slide, click the on-screen **Menu** icon (▤) or right-click the screen.
2. Click **End Show**.

The slide show closes. You can also press Esc to end the show.

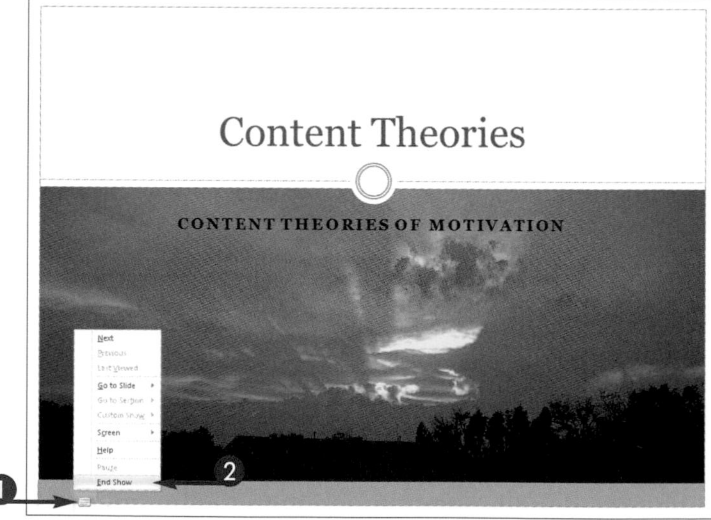

Navigate Among Slides

You can use the shortcut menu, the Slide Show on-screen toolbar, or click the screen to move through a slide show. You can also press ⬆ and ⬇ to move forward and backward through the slide show.

Navigate Among Slides

1. With your presentation in Slide Show view, press ⬇ or click the screen to display the next slide.

   In this example, the screen was clicked.

2. Move the mouse to the lower-left corner of the screen.

   The on-screen toolbar appears faintly.

3. Click the **Previous** icon (⬅), or press ⬆ to display the previous slide.

4. Click ▤.
5. Click **Go to Slide**.
6. Click a slide title.

   The selected slide appears.

***Note:** See Chapter 13 for more information.*

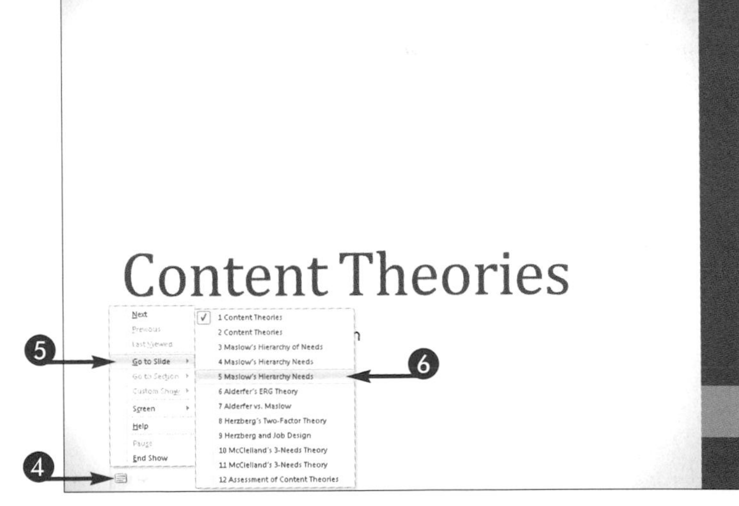

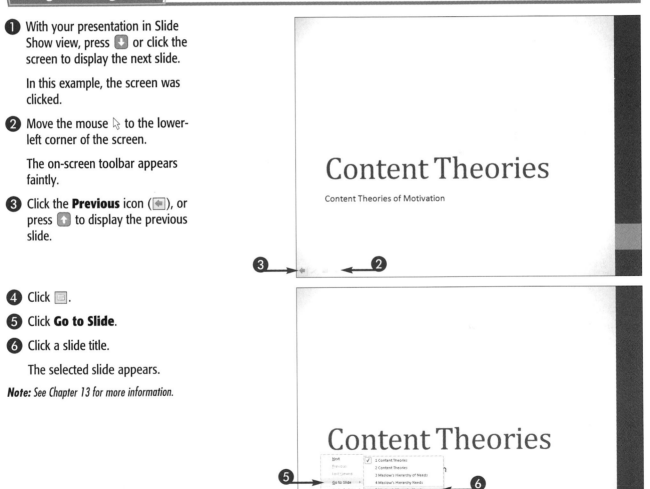

Using the Pointer

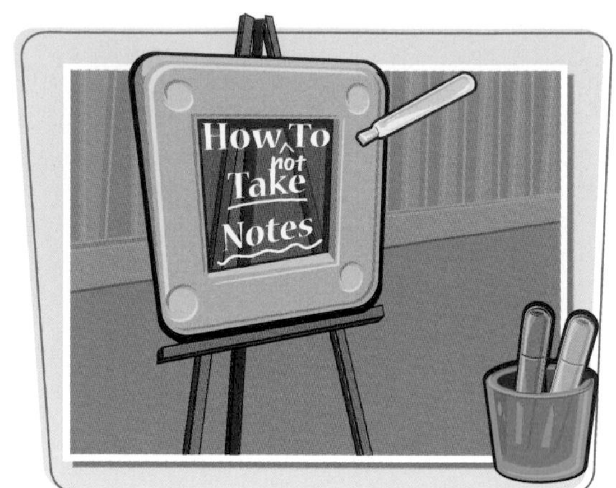

PowerPoint enables you to draw freehand on your screen during a presentation with a pointer tool. You can use it to highlight or annotate important points in the slide show. You can choose the style of pen pointer and the color of the line.

When you exit your slide show, PowerPoint asks if you want to save annotations, but only if that option is enabled in the PowerPoint Options dialog box (see Chapter 2).

Using the Pointer

Choose a Pointer Style

1. With your presentation in Slide Show view, move the pointer to the lower-left corner of the screen.

   The on-screen toolbar appears faintly.

2. Click the **Pen** icon on the toolbar.
3. Click a pointer style.

   Pen draws a thin solid line.

   Highlighter draws a thick, translucent line.

   Arrow displays the pointer.

   In this example, **Pen** was clicked.

4. Click and drag on the screen with the mouse.

   A line appears where you dragged the mouse.

Change Ink Color

1. Click ✎ on the toolbar.
2. Click **Ink Color**.

   A color palette appears.

3. Click a color.

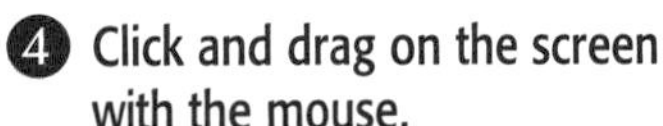

4. Click and drag on the screen with the mouse.

   A line in the selected color appears where you dragged the mouse.

5. When you are finished, click **Arrow** on the menu or press Esc to turn off the Pen or Highlighter.

TIP

Can I delete some of the annotations I drew during the presentation?

Yes. You can use the Erase feature:

1. Click ✎.
   - Click **Erase All Ink on Slide** to clear all annotations on the current slide.
2. Click **Eraser** (pointer changes to eraser).
3. Click the annotations you want to erase.
4. Click **Arrow** on the menu or press Esc to turn off the Eraser.

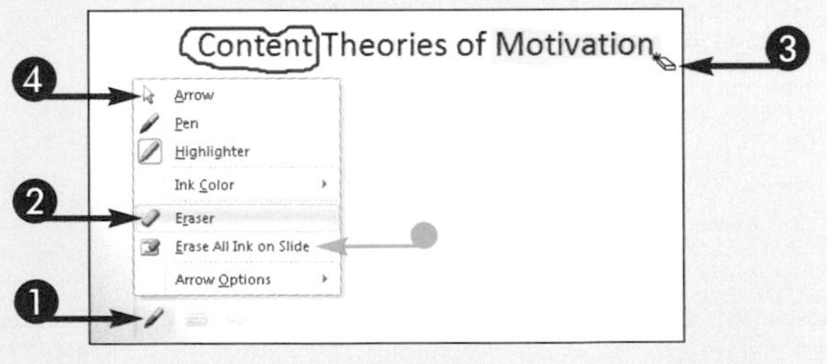

Switch to a Different Program

If you have the need, you can switch to another program during a slide show. For example, if you are giving a presentation on Microsoft Word, you may need to go to Word to demonstrate a feature that you are showing in your slide show.

To return to your slide show, simply minimize or close the other program.

Switch to a Different Program

1. With your presentation in Slide Show view, move the to the lower-left corner of the screen.

   The on-screen toolbar faintly appears.

Note: You can also right-click the screen to display the menu.

2. Click on the toolbar.
3. Click **Screen**.
4. Click **Switch Programs**.

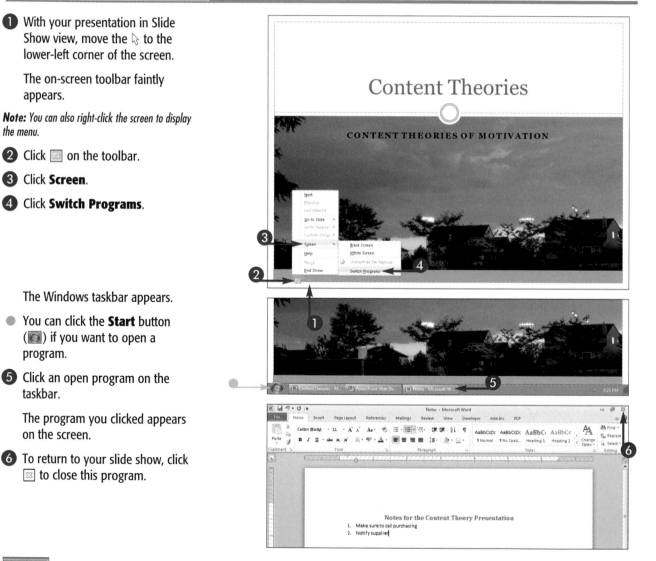

   The Windows taskbar appears.

- You can click the **Start** button ( ) if you want to open a program.

5. Click an open program on the taskbar.

   The program you clicked appears on the screen.

6. To return to your slide show, click to close this program.

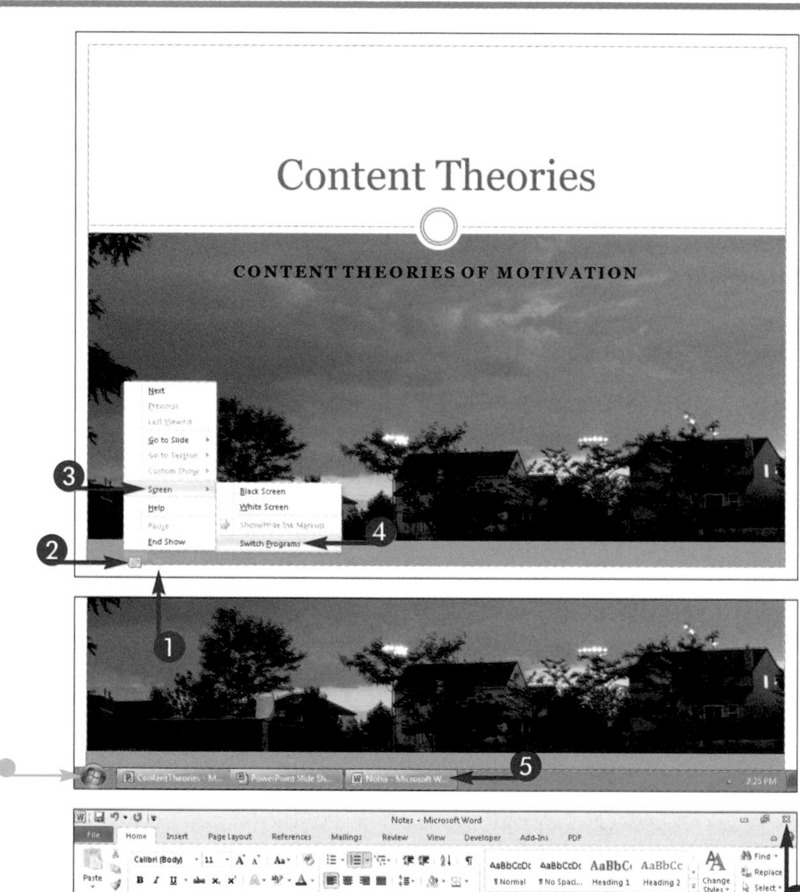

Display Slide Show Help

If you need help running your show after starting it, you need not stop the show and open PowerPoint Help. Slide Show view includes a help screen that shows the shortcuts for running the show and managing presentation features such as pointer options.

Display Slide Show Help

1. With your presentation in Slide Show view, move the pointer to the lower-left corner of the screen.

   The on-screen toolbar appears faintly.

2. Click the menu button on the toolbar.

***Note:** You can also right-click the screen to display the menu.*

3. Click **Help**.

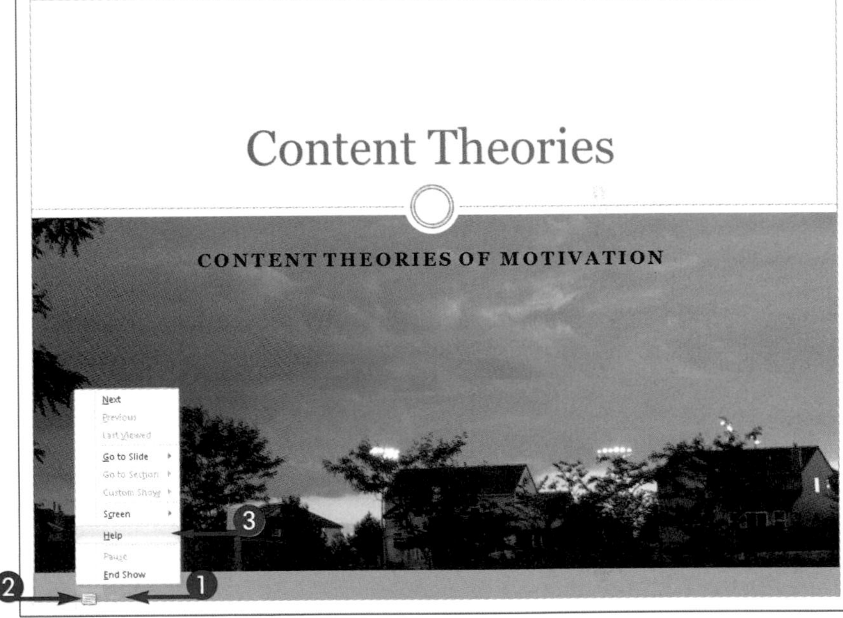

The Help window appears.

- The shortcuts are categorized with a tab for each category.

4. Look up the shortcut to perform the procedure you want.
5. When you finish, click **OK**.

   The Help window closes.

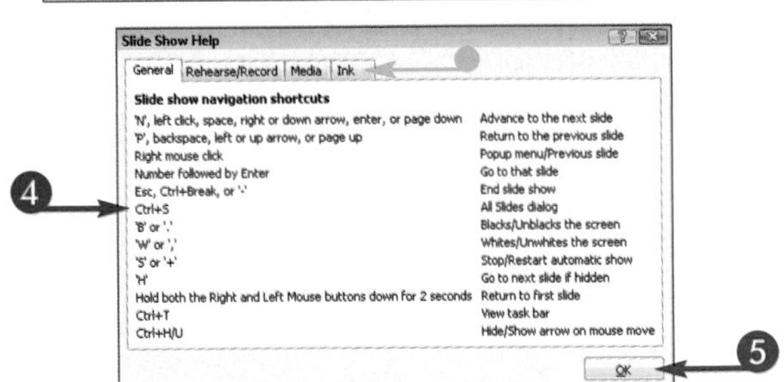

Work with Presenter View

You can view your presentation complete with speaker notes on your computer, while the audience views only the slide show on the main screen. With Presenter View, you can see your notes, the slide show controls are handy, and PowerPoint Help shows only on your monitor.

Before enabling Presenter View, connect the device that the audience views and place it in Extended Desktop mode. See the book *Teach Yourself VISUALLY Windows 7* (Wiley, 2009) to learn how.

Work with Presenter View

1. Click the **Slide Show** tab.
2. Click **Use Presenter View** (☐ changes to ☑).
3. Click the **Show on** ▾.
4. Click the device that the audience will view.

***Note:** Primary Monitor is your laptop.*

5. Begin the slide show.

***Note:** See the section "Start and End a Show" in this chapter.*

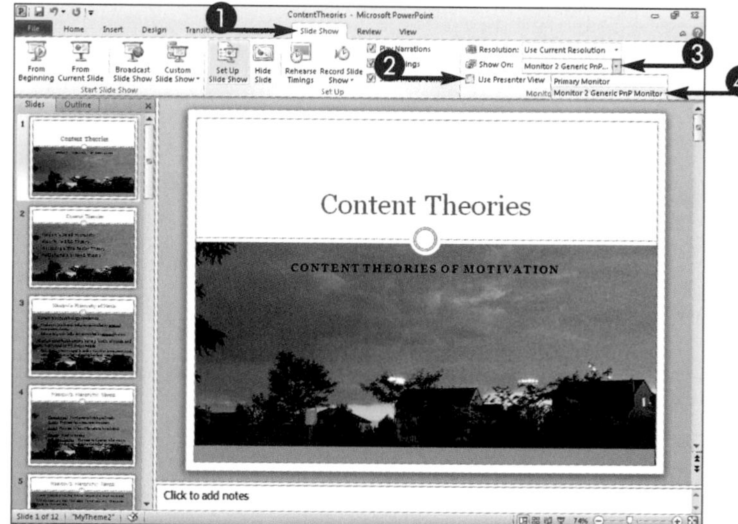

Your laptop shows the Presenter View.

- The toolbar is identical to the on-screen toolbar and is used the same way.

6. Click **Zoom** to change the Notes font size.

- The elapsed time of the slide shows.
- You can click the **Help** icon (?) for help.

7. Click a slide thumbnail to go to that slide.

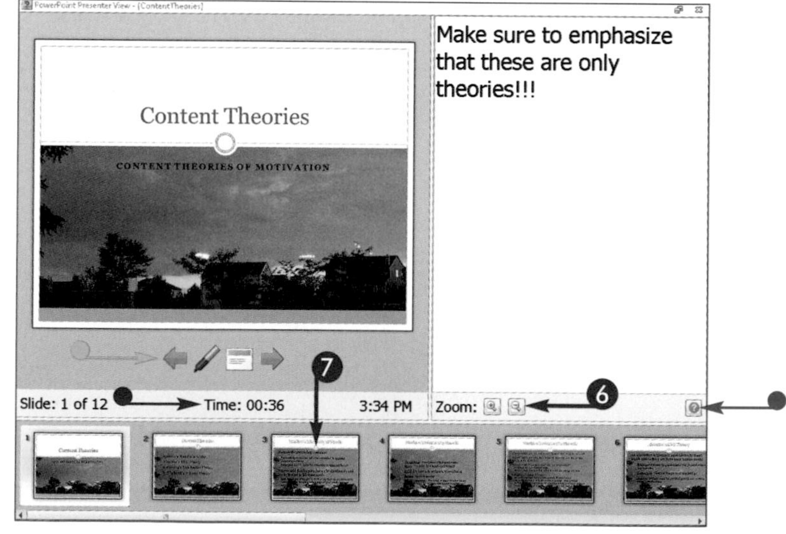

Work with Resolution

You can change resolution to match the resolution of the display. If your slide show is being shown on a kiosk with a resolution of 800 × 600, you should choose that resolution for your presentation. If the speed of play is lethargic, you can reduce the resolution to 640 × 480, though it may affect the image quality of your slides.

The Use Current Resolution setting usually works fine — experiment to see which resolution works best.

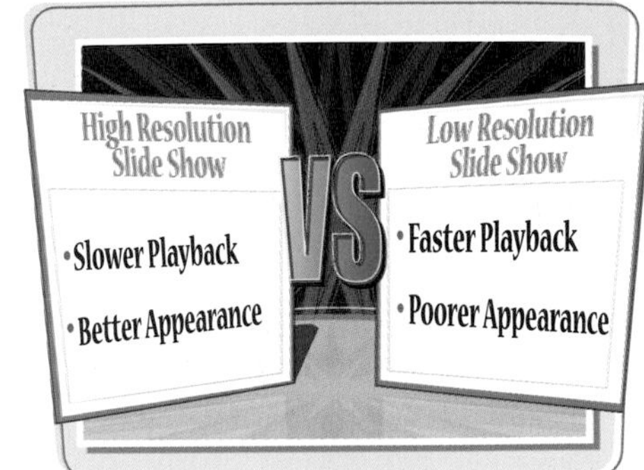

Work with Resolution

1. Click the **Slide Show** tab.
2. Click the **Resolution** ▾.
3. Click a resolution on the list.

   In this example, 800 × 600 was clicked.

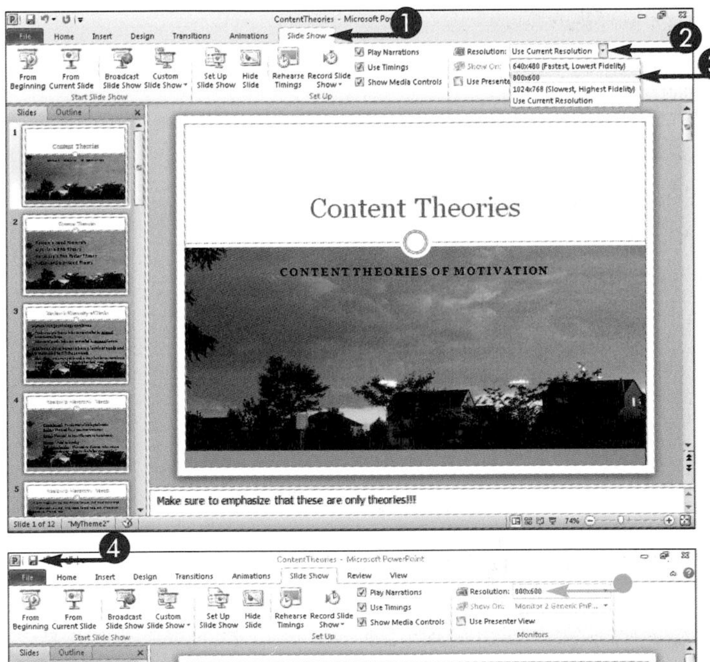

- PowerPoint saves the resolution setting and uses it when you run this slide show.

***Note:** Changing this setting only affects the current presentation — it does not affect any other PowerPoint presentation.*

4. Click the Save icon to save the changes.

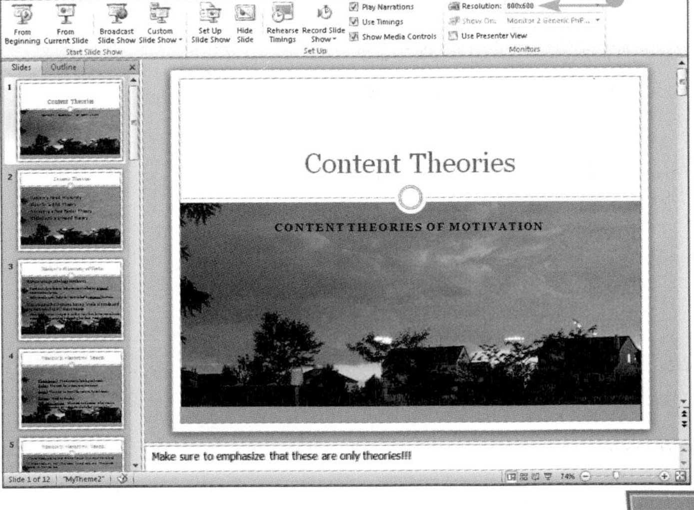

Index

Index

Q

R

S

Index

T